Codename GREENKIL

Elizabeth Wheaton

Codename GREENKIL

The 1979 Greensboro Killings

With a new afterword

The University of Georgia Press
Athens and London

Published in 2009 by the University of Georgia Press
Athens, Georgia 30602
www.ugapress.org
© 1987, 2009 by Elizabeth Wheaton
All rights reserved
Set in 10 on 12 Linotron 202 Times Roman

Printed digitally in the United States of America

The Library of Congress has cataloged the hardcover edition of this book as follows:

Wheaton, Elizabeth.
　Codename GREENKIL : the 1979 Greensboro killings / Elizabeth Wheaton.
　　x, 328 p. : ill. ; 24 cm.
　　Includes bibliographical references (p. 294–314) and index.
　　ISBN 0-8203-0935-4 (alk. paper)
　　1. Greensboro (N.C.)—History. 2. Riots—North Carolina—Greensboro. 3. Communist Workers Party (U.S.) 4. National Socialist Party of America. I. Title. II. Title: Code name GREENKIL.
F264.G8W48 1987　　　975.6'62—dc19　　　86-25081

Paperback ISBN-13: 978-0-8203-3148-5
　　　　　　ISBN-10: 0-8203-3148-1

British Library Cataloging-in-Publication Data available

In memory of my mother
Alice Margaret Hunter Ege
a gentle woman.

And in loving gratitude to my father
Stanford O. Ege
a generous man.

Contents

Acknowledgments   ix
Prologue   3
Part 1   Metamorphosis   7
Part 2   Escalation   73
Part 3   Aftermath   149
Part 4   Answers   239
Epilogue   288
GREENKIL Revisited, 2009   294
Notes   310
Index   331

Acknowledgments

The research for and writing of this book spanned nearly three years; it had its inception in 1981, when I researched and coauthored "The Third of November," a special thirty-two-page report on the killings for the Institute for Southern Studies in Durham, North Carolina. To all the institute staff members who encouraged, supported, prodded, and put up with me during that exhilarating, exasperating project, I owe my first debt of gratitude.

That report served as my introduction, via Paul Bermanzohn, to the Viking Press, which, although we parted ways in 1985, provided the advance that enabled me to launch into a book-length project.

The J. Roderick MacArthur Foundation and two anonymous supporters made crucial financial supplements to the Viking advance. Their generosity gave me the freedom to devote full time to the book.

To the people who read the manuscript and helped me over tremendous writing and psychological hurdles, I can only say, again and again, thank you: Jim Clark, my long-time friend and mentor, now with the Creative Writing Program at the University of North Carolina at Greensboro; Bob Hall, the backbone of the Institute for Southern Studies; Katherine Fulton, the superbly skilled editor of the *North Carolina Independent*; and David Garrow, political scientist at the City College of New York and pre-eminent biographer of Martin Luther King.

My daughter, Kelley, and our housemate, Libby Flynt, have endured everything from the wails of writers' block–induced frustration to the grim discovery of autopsy reports on the kitchen table with understanding and grace.

Gayle Korotkin, of the Greensboro Civil Rights Fund, gave me access to every legal or investigative document that was not sealed by court order. Her assistance was invaluable.

There are a number of people who gave countless hours of their time and who trusted me when they had every reason to be skeptical, yet gave me access to information that would not otherwise have been available. For reasons that will become obvious to the reader, these people cannot be publicly acknowledged. But they know who they are, and I trust that I have conveyed the depth of my gratitude to each of them privately.

Finally, my thanks and apologies to all the people who granted interviews whose names I was compelled to edit out for the sake of clarity and continuity in this still-too-complex manuscript.

Each of these people and institutions played a crucial role in producing *GREENKIL*; each of them has helped me to achieve a balance when I felt overwhelmed by the controversy and contradictions of the story, as well as by my own biases.

This book is a tribute to each of you.

Elizabeth Wheaton

July 1986

Codename GREENKIL

Prologue

GREENKIL is the haunting codename given one of the Federal Bureau of Investigation's most extensive criminal civil rights investigations in the agency's history: The *GREEN*sboro *KIL*lings.

On November 3, 1979, in a Greensboro, North Carolina, housing project known as Morningside Homes, a group of Klan and Nazis opened fire on a Communist-sponsored anti-Klan demonstration. Five of the demonstrators were killed; nine others were wounded.

Although a Greensboro police detective followed the racists to the rally site, he was unable to stop the carnage. Scores of other officers assigned to cover the march did not arrive until after the shooting stopped. There were, however, numerous reporters and photographers on the scene; two television photographers recorded much of the bloody melee on videotape.

With the videotaped evidence, there seemed little doubt that the shooters, captured by police as they attempted to drive out of the area, would be convicted of first-degree murder. Slightly more than a year later, an all-white jury announced its verdict: not guilty. Self-defense, the jurors said.

Conspiracy and cover-up, said the surviving demonstrators—members and supporters of the Communist Workers Party. The CWP had made the conspiracy allegation moments after the shooting stopped on November 3: the killings were political assassinations, planned at the highest levels of government and executed by the Klan and Nazis, "hired guns for the bourgeoisie."

For many observers, the acquittals could not be reconciled with the evidence. As farfetched as the CWP's assassination theory sounded, a conspiracy of some sort seemed to be the most plausible explanation for the lack of convictions.

The GREENKIL investigation, which began shortly after the shootings and provided much of the evidence for the murder trial, was reopened immediately following the acquittals. In 1983, based on additional evidence provided through GREENKIL, a federal grand jury indicted nine of the Klan and Nazis for conspiracy to violate the demonstrators' civil rights. A year later, on Palm Sunday, 1984, another all-white jury reached its verdict: not guilty.

Was this trial, too, part of an elaborate cover-up, as the Communists maintained? Was the million-dollar GREENKIL investigation designed to fail in the prosecution of the Klan and Nazi shooters and conspirators? Was it orchestrated to shield a massive local, state, and federal conspiracy to assassinate the CWP leadership?

The widows and survivors of the Greensboro killings sought to prove their allegations through a $48 million civil suit filed against sixty-five defendants, including members of the Klan and Nazis, the Greensboro Police Department, and agents of the FBI and the Treasury Department's Bureau of Alcohol, Tobacco and Firearms. The verdict: No conspiracy. The jury did, however, award token damages—less than $400,000 for the death of one of the five slain demonstrators and the injuries of two of the ten wounded plaintiffs. They found five Klan-Nazis, a police informant, and two police officers liable.

Like the trials before it, the civil suit brought out a wealth of information about the people, the institutions, and the events that led to the bloodbath in Greensboro. But like the trials before it, the civil suit failed to provide a clearcut explanation for the astonishing series of events and movements of key players, without which the tragedy could not have occurred.

The full story of the Greensboro killings may never be revealed, not because there is a lack of information but because there are a multiplicity of perspectives from which we can view the available facts. It is as though we were looking through a kaleidoscope and the events fell into one pattern when viewed through the CWP's perspective, another through that of the Klan and Nazis, and yet another through that of the police and federal agents. Each pattern has its own logic, but when they are superimposed, the image becomes a jumble of contradictions and conflict. One can only see that there are no heroes in this story; there are many, many fools.

In 1963, Southern author Lillian Smith asked, "Why are we so blind to each disaster as it begins slowly, slowly, and then rushes toward us!"[1] The Greensboro tragedy did not occur in a vacuum. The groundwork was laid in the age-old conflict between leftist revolutionaries, fascists, and civil authority. It was nurtured in a state which prides itself as "progressive," yet is home to a flourishing and powerful reactionary element. North Carolina's schizophrenic social and political atmosphere simultaneously fed and frustrated the left- and right-wing extremists, giving them the impetus to act out their hostilities in ever-narrowing theaters of conflict.

Into this political whirlwind came local and federal law enforcement authorities. Hampered by their own myopia regarding the antagonists, fettered by a militaristic chain of command and separation of powers, the officers who could have intervened were instead swept into the center of the event and its aftermath.

Still, we want to know: How could the killings have happened? Who is responsible? The answers to those questions are as complex as the society that spawned the people, the organizations, and the agencies that clashed in those terror-filled moments in Greensboro.

To understand we must look back nearly a generation—to the 1960s—when the historical foundation for the tragedy began to form. It was a period of intense social upheaval, a period in which reactionaries, revolutionaries, and authorities alike were visible, vocal, and often violent. If, by the mid-1970s, it appeared that those forces had moderated, the decade was only relatively—and deceptively—quiet.

> We live in terror because persuasion is no longer possible. . . . This silence is the end of the world.
>
> —Albert Camus, *Neither Victims nor Executioners*

Part 1

Metamorphosis

Chapter 1

> The main content of the anti-Klan campaign should be militant, direct action—a confrontation with the Klan would be best if we can get it.
> —Communist Workers Party "Directive," Re: "Death to the Klan" march, November 3, 1979

November Third

Eddie Dawson spat the words out: "You Communist bastard. You asked for the Klan and you got 'em."[1]

Paul Bermanzohn was stunned. The man glaring down at him from the passenger side of the tan pickup truck was the same man with whom he had talked amiably just two days earlier, following a Communist Workers Party news conference on the steps of the Greensboro Police Department. Bermanzohn had spoken about the rise of the Klan, the need for militant counteraction, and the upcoming "Death to the Klan" march his group was sponsoring. The man had seemed interested, although he expressed some surprise that there was still such a thing as the Klan in 1979.

Bermanzohn did not have time to remember much else about the man. Looking back down Everitt Street to his left, he saw a long line of cars and trucks rolling slowly behind the pickup. His mind registered: Klan, lots of them.

It happened so quickly. Shouts: *"Death* to the Klan." "Niggers, kikes, remember China Grove." *"Death, death, death to the Klan."*

A fight broke out, then gunfire. Bermanzohn ran. Everybody ran. More shooting, more shouting. He glanced over his shoulder toward the noise. They were beating on his friends. He turned to help, grabbed the handle of a picket stick with both hands, like a Louisville Slugger, and headed back toward the fight. The sign on his picket said "DEATH TO THE KLAN."

As Bermanzohn moved to help his friends, Dawson and his driver sped away. Seconds later, Bermanzohn felt a tremendous force that swept him off his feet and left him lying in a crumpled heap on the ground, blood oozing from his skull, double-aught buckshot pellets lodged in his brain. An emergency room physician himself, Bermanzohn could hear the cries: "Doctors! We need a doctor! Please, where are the doctors?"

He couldn't move. Someone else would help. He felt peaceful. The earth seemed to cradle him. One of the other doctors would help, Bermanzohn thought. Jim or Mike—they were two of the finest doctors Bermanzohn knew. They could handle anything.

But Jim was dead. Dr. James Michael Waller, thirty-six, was sprawled on his stomach not twenty feet from where Bermanzohn lay. His back was riddled with buckshot.[2]

Mike was dying. Dr. Michael Ronald Nathan, thirty-two, lay moaning on his back in the middle of Carver Drive, the right side of his face and skull nearly blown away by a shotgun blast.

On the other side of Carver, directly across from Bermanzohn and Waller, were two other demonstrators. A single buckshot pellet had struck Sandra Neely Smith, twenty-eight, in the head, killing her instantly. Just a few feet from her body, a friend was frantically trying to resuscitate William Evan Sampson, thirty-one.[3] It was hopeless. Two buckshot pellets had pierced his heart; he would bleed to death in a matter of minutes.

Cesar Vincent Cauce, too, was dead. The twenty-five-year-old Cuban exile had struggled for life for perhaps thirty seconds after a .38 caliber bullet tore through his neck and into his chest cavity, hitting almost every vital organ before exiting through his back.[4]

As Paul Bermanzohn drifted in and out of consciousness, Eddie Dawson and his driver, Jim Buck, drove to a nearby bar, an old Klan hangout. They had heard gunfire as they pulled away from the rally site, and they knew that the Klan's plans to harass the demonstrators had turned into something more. Buck ordered a beer, Dawson a Coke, and they watched the bar's television screen for the news bulletin they knew would interrupt the football game any moment. It did: An unknown number of anti-Klan demonstrators had been shot, several were dead; fourteen men, believed to be Klan members, had been captured with an arsenal of weapons.

Dawson's words reverberated: "You asked for the Klan and you got 'em."

The Catalyst

A decade earlier, no one would have predicted that Dawson's and Bermanzohn's lives would be permanently linked in one of the most controversial tragedies in Southern history.

Metamorphosis

The summer of 1969 marked the opening of a new world for Paul Bermanzohn. His parents, Nazi concentration camp survivors, had settled in the Bronx and eked out a living on his father's earnings as a tailor. Young Paul was brilliant, hardworking, and popular. His lush black hair and piercing eyes made a dramatic impression; his frequent laughter, his fondness for the absurd, and his boundless energy made a lasting one.

When he graduated from City College of New York in 1969, Bermanzohn held the student body presidency, a fistful of honors, a scholarship, and tuition loans for the Duke University School of Medicine. Although he had been elected president of the student body on an antiwar platform, Bermanzohn had not considered himself an activist at City College. "I felt like I should have done more," he recalled. "There were times when it was important to do something but I sort of backed down. I remember thinking about that a lot, and the example of [Martin Luther] King really had an effect on me. Facing all those people down—he was serious business." Durham-bound, Bermanzohn knew that his medical studies would take up most of his waking hours, but he resolved to make time to put his idealism into practice. Serious business: liberal political activism and medicine.

On Independence Day, 1969, Eddie Dawson was in some serious business of his own in Swan Quarter, North Carolina. Swan Quarter is a small coastal village, which was once a favorite hideout of the notorious eighteenth-century pirate Blackbeard, a name that would come to haunt Dawson in 1979 and for many years afterward.[5]

For the time being, Dawson and his fellow Klan members could count themselves as Swan Quarter's second most notorious gang of interlopers. They had managed to turn the tiny, isolated town's quiet July Fourth celebration into a riot between the Klan and local blacks.

Dawson's criminal record is almost as long as Bermanzohn's list of academic honors: in addition to a history of gambling and alcohol-related problems, Dawson was convicted of participating in the Swan Quarter riot, twice convicted of going AWOL during World War II, and in 1967 set legal precedent as the first North Carolinian in two hundred years to be convicted and sentenced under an obscure common law against being "armed to the terror of the public."[6] Dawson, Jim Buck, and two other Klan members were captured at a roadblock following a shooting spree during which they fired into several unoccupied black-owned stores in Alamance County, thirty miles east of Greensboro.

In 1969, the chance that Eddie Dawson and Paul Bermanzohn would meet anywhere other than an emergency room seemed remote. But the catalyst for their meeting was already in place: the FBI's Counter-Intelligence Program—COINTELPRO.

From its inception in 1956 to 1976, when Congress imposed restraints on the FBI's domestic political surveillance,[7] COINTELPRO used informants, undercover agents, and provocateurs to disrupt organizations ranging from the nonviolent American Friends Service Committee and Southern Christian Leadership Conference to militant extremists of the Black Panthers, Weatherman, the Klans, and American Nazis. In its milder forms, COINTELPRO used anonymous letter campaigns to foster internal mistrust among the organization's members or to falsely accuse organizations of misappropriating donations. The Black Panthers' free breakfast program for underprivileged children was one such target.

The pattern especially prevalent in the agency's dealings with Klan and Nazi groups was to use an informant or undercover agent to create a split to draw members away from an existing group and form a new faction. Dawson was involved in just such a split in the North Carolina chapter of the United Klans of America following the Swan Quarter trial. He became an FBI informant in November 1969, at about the same time that he and several other Swan Quarter defendants formed the North Carolina Knights of the Ku Klux Klan.[8]

The Nazi group that was involved in the Greensboro killings, the National Socialist Party of America, was yet another product of COINTELPRO, formed by Frank Collin after he was ousted from the National Socialist White People's Party. The FBI had discovered that Collin was part Jewish and dutifully passed the information to the Nazis.[9]

On the left, COINTELPRO proved far more dangerous. In at least two instances, FBI informants were involved in murder. Informant Gary Thomas Rowe rode with the Klan when they killed civil rights worker Viola Liuzzo. Another FBI informant, Black Panther leader Fred Hampton's bodyguard, gave the Chicago police information that enabled them to storm the Panther house and fatally shoot Hampton, under the pretext that the Panthers had fired first.

Although the full extent of the FBI's infiltration and provocation of radical groups was not revealed until the mid-1970s, leftists in particular were acutely aware of the tactics federal and local law enforcement agencies were using to disrupt their organizing efforts. Many who witnessed this government interference in lawful organizing efforts concluded that that social change could no longer be accomplished through traditional political means.[10] Revolution, they felt, was the only solution. Some, like the Weatherman and the Symbionese Liberation Army, went underground and turned to terrorism. Others took a less dramatic, more intellectual course: they studied, independently and in groups, the writings of the world's foremost revolutionary theorists—

Marx, Lenin, Fanon, Guevara, Mao. They read and talked and found like-minded people with whom they intensified their study and focused discussions on ways in which revolutionary theory could be adapted to advanced capitalist America. Scores of what were called "New Communist" groups were thus spawned in the late 1960s and early 1970s.

This was the political atmosphere in which Paul Bermanzohn chose between two medical schools in 1969. His choice might have been decided by the flip of a coin, but he heard that after Martin Luther King's assassination, Duke students had taken over the university administration building to protest both the murder and the university's refusal to recognize a union for black campus workers. Not bad, Bermanzohn thought, not bad at all. The choice was made: Bermanzohn wanted to combine social activism with medicine, and the takeover proved to him that Duke was the place to do it.

Duke University is an unlikely breeding ground for revolutionaries. Built in the 1920s by tobacco baron James B. Duke, it was, according to a pervasive but unsubstantiated rumor, a monument to his ego. The story is that he offered one of the Ivy League universities a million or two to change its name to Duke. Rebuffed, Duke returned to Durham, where he made a similar offer to Trinity College. It was accepted, and Duke began hiring European artisan-builders to create his namesake, which has been dubbed the "Harvard of the South."

Coming from the Bronx to Duke was like landing on another planet for Bermanzohn. The entrance to the west campus, where the medical school is located, is marked by massive stone columns. Narrow roads and pathways wind through pastoral woods and gardens to a courtyard surrounded by buildings of the most exquisite stone- and masonry-work imaginable. As one stands in the campus courtyard that faces the cathedral-sized Duke Chapel, the city of Durham seems as far removed as the Bronx. Only when the wind shifts, blowing from the east, does the heavy odor from the downtown tobacco factories remind Dukies of their neighbors and the source of the university's wealth.

Steady work in the tobacco factories lured many poor sharecroppers and tenant farmers—black and white—to the city in the early 1900s.[11] Today, Durham remains a working-class town with a large black population. A few of Durham's blacks have made fortunes in insurance, banking, and the law, but most still struggle to make ends meet, the legacy of racism in education and employment locking them out of their white counterparts' trek toward the middle class.

For black workers who wanted to escape the dirt and noise of factory work, employment at Duke seemed an alluring option. But by the time of Martin

Michael Nathan

Luther King's assassination—four years after the Civil Rights Act became law—Duke's black work force remained locked in the menial jobs that had been opened to them decades earlier: food service and maintenance. Their pay averaged eighty cents an hour, less than half the minimum wage.[12]

The contrast between Duke's service workers and its students could hardly have been more vivid. The workers: black, uneducated, impoverished, trapped in dead-end jobs. The students: white and rich, with high intellects, born of privileged primary and secondary school educations, and on the fast track toward lucrative professional careers.

Mike Nathan was one of the few students who did not fit the Duke mold.

Michael Ronald Nathan, M.D. Chief of Pediatrics, Lincoln Community Health Center, Durham. Beloved husband of Martha (Marty) Arthur Nathan; father of Leah, three months of age. Inducted into the Communist Workers Party on his deathbed. Died Monday, November 5, 1979.

Nathan was a gentle man, a quiet man who rarely talked about himself. His concern had always been directed toward others—people in need.[13]

Poverty and Nathan were no strangers. He was only fourteen when his father, a Washington, D.C., printer, died. With no financial or family reserves, his mother did her best to support Mike on her salary as a department store clerk. Esther Nathan was justifiably proud of her only child; he drove himself to excel in high school in order to qualify for college scholarships. He wanted to be a doctor. He chose Duke University.

In 1967, Nathan entered a Duke-sponsored work-study program in order to supplement his tuition grants and scholarships. He took the assignment gladly: to live and work in a low-income area of Durham known as Edgemont, helping the tenants to organize for better housing conditions and services. Nathan loved the work; he identified with the people of Edgemont and understood their needs and frustrations.

It was there that Nathan met the woman who became his first wife, Sally Avery. Avery was a prelaw student at Duke. She, too, was on scholarship, but her background was strictly middle class. When Duke assigned her to the work-study project, she was apprehensive that the tenants might not accept her because she had no firsthand experience with poverty. Her fears were short-lived. Nathan took her door-to-door, introducing her to the folks with whom she would live and work. Their trust and respect for Mike were so great that they accepted Avery without question. She and Nathan quickly became a team, on campus as well as in Edgemont. They were liberal idealists who were not afraid to work for what they believed was right.

What was right for Nathan and Avery in the spring of 1968 was to picket on campus in support of a union organizing drive for the black food service workers.

Anti-unionism is as much a way of life in North Carolina as textiles and tobacco. The state has historically ranked at or near the bottom of the national scales for average wages and for percentage of unionized workers.[14] The correlation is obvious. For workers and managers alike, there is a decades-old pattern of massive resistance to union organizing. North Carolina's most infamous unionization battle, the Gastonia strike of 1929, pitted the same forces that collided fifty years later in Greensboro: militant labor organizers, the police, and anti-Communist vigilantes.[15]

Nineteen sixty-eight saw a core of idealistic and somewhat naive Duke students pick up the union organizing banner, focusing their efforts on behalf of the campus workers who served them. That is what Avery and Nathan were doing when word hit campus that King had been assassinated in Memphis where he had gone to help organize sanitation workers. Angry and inspired, Duke students surrounded the university administration building and began working on a list of demands on behalf of the campus workers.

The students felt it was logical and appropriate for a delegation to go directly to the most powerful person on campus: Duke president Douglas Knight. They would ask him to recognize the union, to bring black workers' pay up to minimum wage, and to resign from his "racist" country club. Sally Avery felt, at first, that "it wasn't any big deal. We marched to Knight's house. Some of us went inside the house thinking we would talk to him, he would see the truth of our demands and agree with us. Then we would all go home."

"But once we were in there, two hundred students, it became very heavy because he refused to even deal with the demands. After that there were rumors that the Klan had surrounded the house and were going to attack. It was very, very heavy. For me it was actually risking something for what I thought was right."

The Klan did not attack. They didn't even show up. Back on campus, however, Durham police launched an assault on the students who remained at the administration building. It was, on a small scale, Gastonia revisited. Despite repeated beatings and arrests, the protesting students camped on the quad for a week. When the vigil ended, campus workers still had no union recognition.

Avery and Nathan were disillusioned and frustrated. Having a just cause and trying to reason with people in power did not seem to change anything. Nevertheless, they increased their support work for the union organizing drive; they passed out literature, went to meetings and demonstrations, talked to workers, students, faculty, and their contacts in Durham. It was hard work, slow going, but on the whole productive. Organizing was getting into their blood.

The young activists married in the spring of 1969. That fall he brought home a first-year med student who was, like him, Jewish and poor: Paul Bermanzohn. "We just fell into each other," Bermanzohn remembers. "We hit it off real fast. We'd be at a meeting and I'd be the only one saying something and he'd jump in. I'd do the same for him. We agreed on just about everything."

Medicine and social activism. Neither Bermanzohn nor Nathan knew it then, but that combination of interests would one day lead them to a kindred spirit, a person who would steer them on the path toward revolution—and disaster. His name was Jim Waller.

James Michael Waller, M.D. Former Fellow in Pediatric Infectious Diseases, Duke University. Beloved husband of Signe Burke Goldstein Waller; friend and stepfather to her two children, Antonia and Alex. Member of the

Metamorphosis

Jim Waller (Courtesy of Jim Waters, WFMY-TV, Greensboro)

Central Committee, Communist Workers Party. Died Saturday, November 3, 1979.

As a pediatric resident in New York's Lincoln Hospital, Waller kept an emergency medical kit with him at all times, as he had done since the 1968 Democratic convention in his native Chicago.[16] The police attacks on antiwar demonstrators gave Waller his first taste of political repression: he walked through the sea of protesters, patching up gashes, splinting fractures, calming those who thought they might die from the violent retching induced by tear gas. They did not have guns. They did not have any kind of weapons, most of them, except their voices and their numbers. They did not deserve this. But Waller understood that police violence was now part of the territory: if you were going to demonstrate, you had better be prepared to get hurt. So he kept his medical kit stocked and ready, not comprehending—yet—that the violence was seldom as spontaneous as it seemed.

Unlike Bermanzohn and Nathan, Waller grew up in a moderately affluent family. But he shared their Jewish heritage, their intellect and determination, and their refusal to accept the existence of poverty in the richest nation in the world. As a student at the University of Chicago Medical School, Waller worked in a clinic in one of Chicago's poorest neighborhoods, Woodlawn. On Saturdays he would bring black children from the clinic to his father's nearby shop to teach them about hygiene and nutrition, hoping that knowledge of fundamental health care would help stave off the incidence of poverty-related disease in at least a few of the kids.

To the children of Woodlawn, Waller was not just some medico who poked here, probed there, and walked away muttering and scribbling on his charts. Not only was he genuinely concerned about his patients as people, but he knew how to fight the big guys—and win. Waller tackled the University of Chicago Medical School in a humorous and totally characteristic battle to keep the school officials from forcing him to shave his beard. He formed a group called SWAB—"Save Waller's Beard"—and circulated petitions and got coverage in the *Chicago Tribune*. He made the school officials look petty and ridiculous, and they finally relented. He knew how to fight, Jim Waller did, and he did it with great humor. He was a big Jewish guy with the blackest beard you ever saw. "Blackbeard," they called him.

Between the completion of his studies in Chicago and his residency in New York, Waller got a chance to go to Cuba with a group of Americans who were invited to see the changes brought by the revolution. There he saw a system that provided free medical care, quality medical care. Waller saw that Cuban children did not suffer from the illnesses of the poor. There was no great wealth in Cuba, but the needs of all its people were met. Not at all like Woodlawn. Something was very, very wrong in the United States of America, Waller concluded. When he got to New York, he began reading everything he could find on revolution and communism, and he wrote long, soul-searching letters to his father, whom he adored.

Political transformation did not come on so suddenly for the Durham activists, but the process was well under way as Paul Bermanzohn and Mike Nathan completed their second year of medical school. Steadfast in their support for the Duke union drive, they had earned a reputation among Durham blacks as progressive medical students. "A number of people in the community wanted to get Duke to open a night clinic," said Bermanzohn, "because a lot of people work and can't go to the doctor during the day. They were steered toward us. We were bright-eyed medical students, so we agreed to help them make their way through the administration. All we wanted was for them to open the facilities at night so people could get better health care. It seemed a simple thing to do. We got the runaround from the administration. It was an education for everybody."

Again for Nathan, and now for Bermanzohn, the lesson was driven home: it is not enough to reason with people in power on reasonable requests. And again, they turned to organizing as a way to force the administration to listen to reason. With a small core of progressives, they started a chapter of the Medical Committee for Human Rights (MCHR), a national organization of health-care activists whose slogan was "No profits in health care." Bermanzohn characterized MCHR as "not terribly radical. It seemed the sensible thing to do. Money ought to go to help people out. Isn't that what medical school was for? Or was it? That's what we were there for."

Jewish, poor, socially concerned—those were not traits typical of either students or faculty at Duke Medical School. "Jesus," Bermanzohn said, shaking his head, "Duke was filled with these upper-class kids. Some of them were kind of caricatures of themselves. I would always ask things like, 'What do you want to do when you get out of medical school—when you grow up?' And this one guy said, 'I want to earn six figures.' I thought, where are these people coming from?"

Nathan and Bermanzohn shared growing doubts about their futures in medicine. They loved the study and the clinical work, but the elite Duke atmosphere bordered on the insufferable. Nathan had almost decided to drop out when he got a chance to work in a Guatemalan clinic for the summer. Away from Duke, he realized that he wanted more than anything to practice medicine, that it was possible to be a good doctor without suppressing compassion, and that his skill and sensitivity were desperately needed. If becoming a doctor meant three more years in a school he hated, so be it. Sacrifice for what is right, he felt, was really no sacrifice at all.

Bermanzohn went in a different direction. Duke granted him a year's leave of absence to work as a health specialist for Operation Breakthrough, a federal antipoverty program. Sally Avery had been at Breakthrough for almost a year, organizing white welfare recipients, when Bermanzohn arrived. Almost immediately the two joined forces in a campaign that would have a profound effect on their political development.

Like most Southern towns, Durham had two hospitals: Watts, on the west side of town, served white people; Lincoln, on the east side, served the blacks. A new hospital was needed; no one argued the fact. But the plans for the new Durham County General were being developed in a state of near secrecy. Health activists, including the local chapter of MCHR, formed a coalition with local citizens and began to raise questions about the new hospital.

Appalled at what they saw of the proposals for the hospital, some staff members in the Durham County Health Department secretly passed the plans to the coalition. Small clinics were to be closed. The hospital would be built several miles north of town, beyond the reach of existing public transportation. No outpatient facilities were planned; instead, there would be a huge complex for doctors' offices. Coalition members realized the implications: Durham County General was being built for the profit of realtors, bankers, and doctors; the community's needs were secondary.

"We started raising some sand," said Bermanzohn. "What's going on here? Who's going to pay for it? Tax money. So people ought to have a say in it." And have a say they did. The coalition forced the hospital planning board to hold public meetings, and the activists attended en masse. They took photographs of board members, the proposed hospital site, the clinics that were to close, the realtors and bankers who pushed the boondoggle. They prepared a slide show and took it to community centers, churches, civic groups, anyone who would watch and listen and do something.

Bermanzohn and Avery spent night after night mimeographing fact sheets and announcements for meetings. The coalition's literature reached low-income, middle-income, students, professionals, and blue-collar workers, black and white.

Still optimistic about working within the system, Bermanzohn arranged a secret meeting with an official of the state Department of Public Health. The official promised to help, to conduct a state investigation. Bermanzohn thought it was all buddy-buddy: "We thought he was there to help us. He's a public servant, right? So he screwed us, just didn't do any of the things he said he was going to do."

The coalition won on a few issues, but without the state investigation, they lost on the big ones: the location of the hospital and the construction of the office complex. Bermanzohn viewed the state official's betrayal philosophically. "I thank him for the education."

For the young activists in Durham, the lesson hit home: none of it had worked, or so it seemed. Not the demonstrations, not the unions, not the community-campus coalitions, not even the hallowed electoral process. Richard Nixon had been overwhelmingly elected to his second term in the White House, despite Watergate, despite the illegal bombings of Cambodia and Hanoi, despite using the FBI and CIA to carry out dirty tricks against his political opponents, despite corruption, conspiracies, and deceit. And in North Carolina, riding Nixon's coattails into the U.S. Senate was a reactionary right-winger named Jesse Helms.

"That's what really opened me up to studying communism," said Sally Avery. "I kept fighting for those values of what's right for the people and coming up against brick walls. It's like, are you serious about this thing or aren't you? It took quite a bit of experience for me to realize that there is a need for revolution and there is a science for making revolution, and that I ought to start looking into it."

Marxist revolution. A number of ultra-left sects studied the science intensely, convinced that the old Communist Party-U.S.A. had sold out to the capitalist system. The CP-USA had been around since the 1920s, and what had it accomplished? It had made some headway in union organizing in its early years, but had been steadily backsliding into oblivion since then. It was time to launch a new communist party, a party that went beyond Marxism to incorporate the more recent teachings of Lenin and Mao. A party that would draw from the working class—the proletariat—a cadre of militant organizers—the vanguard—to lead the struggle against capitalist rule.

By 1974, a host of preparty communist groups was active.[17] The October League, which grew out of the Georgia Communist League, was predominantly white and based in the South. The Revolutionary Workers League was all black, with strongholds in the South, the Northeast, and the West Coast. In New York, the Puerto Rican Revolutionary Organization and the Asian Study Group drew from their ethnic constituencies. The Asian Study Group became the Workers Viewpoint Organization, and in October of 1979, less than a month before the Greensboro killings, it changed its name again to the Communist Workers Party.

Paul Bermanzohn, Sally Avery, and a small core of Durham radicals, many drawn from the coalition that worked on the Durham County General campaign, began to study the journals of the New Communist groups in addition to the revolutionary classics. From their readings, they learned that the party can only evolve from study, discussion, action based on the study and discussion, criticism and self-criticism of the action, repeating the process again and again to develop "the correct line." Because each independent study group goes through a slightly different process, different "correct lines" emerge. Debates between groups, called polemics, supposedly result in the ultimate correct line, which then becomes the platform for the vanguard party—the way forward.

For some of the Durham radicals, the process was exciting, exhilarating. But others were not so enthralled. Gradually, ever so gradually, the political divisions deepened, and as they did, friendships dissolved. As Tim McGloin, a cofounder of the Durham Medical Committee for Human Rights, described it, "The political work was the bottom line. Friendships developed out of intense work together, and when the political differences emerged, the friendships shattered."

Shattered. Jim Waller was on the verge of a first-class burnout.[18] The Lincoln Health Collective in New York's South Bronx had been his personal as well as professional life for the past several years. Unlike the Durham radicals, the Lincoln group not only shared political and social ideals but also lived together, worked together, and pooled their salaries. Conceived primarily as a mutual support system, the collective gradually sapped more strength than it generated. Typically, Waller stuck with the collective until it disintegrated.

Why hadn't it worked? The collective had been formed around the classic Marxist principle, from each according to ability, to each according to need. But it flopped. Waller badgered himself with questions, hypotheses, analyses. He talked with people in all factions of New York's New Communist movement, and he studied—Waller never merely "read"—everything he could find on communism and revolution.

Duke Medical School offered Waller a fellowship in pediatric infectious disease, a field which fascinated him. It seemed to be an ideal way of breaking with the frustrations and disappointments of New York. But Waller was not quite ready to make the transition. He needed to think, to be alone, to get away. Most of his life had been spent in two of the biggest cities in the world, but Waller's father had gone to great lengths to insure that Jim and his sister knew how to handle themselves in the woods, on the lakes and rivers. As always, Waller had learned his lessons well. So when the time came to be alone, away, Waller stuffed a few essentials in his backpack and headed for the backwoods, somewhere in Canada.

Jim Waller walked and he thought. He fished and he thought. He searched for berries and mushrooms and for the answer. His father worried, he knew, and so he sent reassuring notes whenever he could. He swatted horseflies and watched in awe as eagles rode the currents above the earth. In beauty and quiet and solitude, Dr. James Michael Waller thought about dirt and poverty and disease, about a society rich enough to conquer it all and sick enough not to.

Chapter 2

> In these rising times of both revolution and
> fascism, anything that holds our struggles back
> HELPS FASCISM.
> —*Workers Viewpoint Journal*, May 1975

The Education

As Jim Waller left the Canadian woods for the sterile corridors of Duke University Hospital, Congress was about to impeach Richard M. Nixon. To Waller, the presidency was just one part of the corrupt capitalist system. Nixon had been caught, that was all; he would be replaced by someone who was a little more subtle and the system would go on as it always had, using the poor and working classes to line the pockets of the rich capitalists. Waller came to North Carolina intent on finding a core of radicals who would study with him and work with him to topple the system.

"I never will forget," said Paul Bermanzohn of the first time he met Waller. "He was wearing a blue fishnet shirt, real trim, real tan from six months in Canada. He looked terrific, very healthy, his white, white teeth against his black beard.

"He was a very deep-thinking guy, the kind of guy who really ponders stuff. He wanted to know what we were studying and was a little, well, not too crazy about us at first because we weren't terribly politically heavy."

Waller was not the only advocate for intensified communist study among the Durham radicals. Owusu Sadaukai, a member of the Revolutionary Workers League (RWL), had come to Durham to work as business agent for the American Federation of State, County and Municipal Employees (AFSCME) at Duke. The food service workers' Local 77, voted in two years after the 1968 demonstrations, had withered to almost nothing. Sadaukai's task was to rekindle enough interest in the union to petition for—and win—a new election. He sought support from any circles on campus or in the community that he could penetrate. One was the Durham Health Collective, which included among its members Bermanzohn, Avery, and Waller.

Sadaukai was not interested in recruiting the white radicals into the RWL. There was extreme resistance among the black revolutionaries to any suggestion of a merger with whites. It was fear, really. Fear that the whites would take over, as they usually did in any multiracial organization.

Sadaukai was in a slightly different position at Duke, however. The black cafeteria workers were fragmented and defeated; white workers, some of whom were organized under Local 465 of the Operating Engineers, were distrustful; and student and community support for the union drive had waned. There were financial problems and organizational problems. Most important, said Sadaukai, was "to get people believing in the union. At one point I was almost working by myself, during the early stages, trying to hand out leaflets at two, three shifts."

Gradually, Sadaukai revived union interest, and the renewed activity drew the attention of the Durham Health Collective. Sadaukai found in them both active union recruiters and an audience for Marxist-Leninist philosophy. His priority was to organize enough workers to vote the union in; if in the process the white Durham radicals were won to communism, so much the better. But if they wanted to belong to a party, they could find their own.

Owusu Sadaukai: "One who clears the way for others." His birth name, he called it his "slave name," was Howard Fuller. An all-star basketball player turned community organizer from Milwaukee, Fuller came to North Carolina—"1965," he recalls, "May third, two o'clock in the afternoon"—to work with Operation Breakthrough in Durham. Eleven years later, he would return to Milwaukee, emotionally devastated by the revolutionary world he helped to create.

Charismatic. That is the near-universal description of Howard Fuller.[1] He was also characterized as articulate, keenly intelligent, and perceptive. It did not take long for a guy with Fuller's talent to realize that Operation Breakthrough was not the solution for poverty.

Fuller entered antipoverty work with the notion that the key to solving the problem was a two-pronged educational effort. Those who controlled jobs and schools and housing and medicine and food must be made aware of what poverty and discrimination do to people. If they could only see it firsthand, talk to poor people, listen to poor people, surely they would do something. Poor people, on the other hand, needed to know how to work within the system. Simple things like petitioning for water and sewer service, lodging complaints against slumlords, filing for government benefits—just learn the rules and use them.

Metamorphosis 25

It didn't work. Poor people still got the shaft. Powerful people continued to blame the poor for their failures. And race seemed to be the dominant factor. Fuller began talking about Black Power. It was time to leave Operation Breakthrough.

The Foundation for Community Development (FCD), funded by the Ford Foundation and run by the state, was established in 1963 by Governor Terry Sanford, ostensibly to help blacks organize a political base from which to gain access to the system. Political power. Fuller was chosen the FCD's director in 1967.[2] Black Power. It was through the FCD that Fuller met the person who in 1976 would assume his role as the leading black revolutionary in North Carolina and would become one of the key figures in the Greensboro killings: Nelson Johnson.

A native of Halifax County in eastern North Carolina, Johnson seemed a more likely candidate for a COINTELPRO spy than for a revolutionary when he enrolled in North Carolina Agricultural and Technical State University, one of Greensboro's two historically black colleges, in 1966. He had spent the previous three years in the air force, guarding nuclear weapons at Strategic Air Command bases in the United States and at a NATO-commanded Canadian air base in Baden-Baden, Germany. Prior to coming to A&T, Johnson says, he was always "on the wrong side" of political issues: he supported Nixon in the 1960 elections, volunteered for duty in Vietnam, and thought Malcolm X was "an evil person."

Johnson's political education began in a Great Society program called YES—Youth Educational Services—which paid black and white college students to tutor black kids in the community. There was just one hitch: the youngsters preferred the white tutors. Johnson began to question the concept of integration. "I was really bothered by the degree to which the black kids wanted a white tutor," he said. "What the oppression of black people does to how you think was becoming apparent to me—what they saw as valuable, what they saw as beautiful, how they wanted to spend their time." Johnson was uncomfortable with militants who agitated under the banner of Black Power. But his experience in YES convinced him that if blacks were ever to achieve equity in American society, they were going to have to take a more aggressive, more unified stance to challenge the white power structure.

Six years after the historic 1960 sit-ins at Woolworth's, however, many of Greensboro's lunch counters and restaurants were still closed to blacks. A group of black and white college students staged yet another sit-in at the Apple Cellar near the University of North Carolina at Greensboro. Johnson was among the protesters.

Police arrested the white students for "violating dress codes" and took them from the restaurant. When the blacks went outside to protest the arrests, they were charged with interfering with a police officer and hauled off to jail. A judge later dismissed the charges against the white students. Johnson and the other black students were convicted.

Integrated groups, including Johnson, again invaded the Apple Cellar. This time a police officer told them that if they did not leave immediately there would be "trouble." The students took the hint. When they emerged from the Cellar, however, the trouble was already there and waiting: a line of about thirty men in blue uniforms and silver helmets shouting racial epithets. It was the Klan, led by George Dorsett, Eddie Dawson's mentor who, like Dawson, was later revealed to be an FBI informant.[3]

The students were forced to walk—slowly and quietly—past their tormentors to get to their cars. Humiliated, frustrated, angry, Johnson began to recognize the futility of working within a system of which blacks were not, and maybe never could be, a part—the futility of playing by the rules when the rules themselves were different for blacks and whites. Johnson began to think that maybe the Black Power advocates were right.

When Johnson and Fuller met, they hit it off immediately. They saw eye-to-eye on just about everything: the white power structure, black poverty, and the strategy and tactics for changing the system. Both men were quickly gaining reputations among North Carolina blacks for their analytical abilities and their organizing skills. White North Carolina was not so receptive. While mouthing platitudes about the state's progress in race relations, white leaders felt threatened.[4] They were losing control. It was one thing to give a token here, a token there. It was quite another for black radicals to demand concessions, worse yet for them to know where and how to apply pressure to get them.

There was little the Greensboro city powers could do about Nelson Johnson, though. Not only was he a campus leader, but he had the respect and support of many influential blacks in the community. He was not a moderate by anyone's definition, but he was bringing the campus and the community together. And he did not talk violence.

In February 1968, a massacre took place in Orangeburg, South Carolina. Police shot several students taking part in a demonstration to desegregate a bowling alley. At A&T, Johnson organized a spontaneous and dramatic protest. Pushing a casket and carrying an effigy of the governor of South Carolina, hundreds of students marched with Johnson from the campus to city hall. The effigy went up in flames.

A phone rang in the police department. It was Ed Dawson. "I asked them [the police] why they weren't arrested for burning an effigy in front of city hall, starting a fire and all that. They just watched out the window, watched 'em burn the thing, then they went out and put the fire out. They said, 'You want someone arrested, you come down and swear out a warrant for them.'"

There were no arrests. The students walked back to A&T without incident. In the weeks that followed, however, the police refusal to arrest the demonstrators was a hot topic among Greensboro Klan members.

Two months later was the assassination in Memphis. King and the Dream were dead. It was beginning to look like open season on black activists. The campus at A&T, like much of the rest of black America, erupted into a shouting, brick-throwing, roving melee. A station wagon drove up to the crowd; two white men inside started shooting, and then the car sped off. None of the students was injured, but neither were the would-be assailants captured. City officials called in the National Guard, a city-wide curfew was imposed, and order was briefly restored. Until someone—no one knows who—opened fire on campus. This time three police officers were wounded.

It was Johnson's first involvement with violent conflict. Although he was not a party to the shootings, he saw the city's takeover of A&T, which had always before been able to resolve campus disturbances quietly and nonviolently, as further evidence of the futility of working within the white-dominated system. To make matters worse, he and Fuller, with whom Johnson was working in the FCD, were being accused of stockpiling rifles and ammunition. The charges were based on an informant-supplied tip which the FBI passed to the Greensboro police, who then gave the information to the local news media in an attempt to discredit the black activists. The charges were false.[5]

Both men started cutting their ties with whites. Johnson formed the Greensboro Association of Poor People (GAPP), an organization which advocated for the poor within the system but which drew more and more heavily on confrontational tactics to achieve its goals. In Durham, Fuller began working on a dream of his own: *Malcolm X Liberation University*, an independent school for young blacks that would help them rediscover their heritage, put them in touch with the African homeland, and cultivate political and practical skills along with the intellectual. Fuller traveled to college campuses throughout the country, raising money and recruiting students for the 1969 school year.

Johnson's work with GAPP was also drawing students together, from Dudley High School as well as from the two black colleges in the city, A&T and Bennett College. His dream of a campus-community coalition was becoming a reality—and a threat, or so the city powers thought, based on reports funnelled through the FBI to city police from a GAPP informant.

Apparently no one in law enforcement bothered to double-check when the informant said that GAPP was a Black Panther front. It was not. No one bothered to double-check when the informant said that the group advocated violence and was arming itself. It was not.[6]

So, in the spring of 1969, when GAPP member Claude Barnes was elected student body president at Dudley on a write-in ballot, city officials pressed the school to void his election. The school capitulated, installing Barnes's runner-up. Over the next few weeks, the tension at Dudley and A&T rose in direct proportion to the heavy-handedness of school and city authorities. Some students were expelled; others walked out in protest. More students were expelled; more walked out. They sought help from their friends at A&T, and the campus seethed.

Again, the city called for the National Guard and imposed a curfew. And again, gunfire erupted. This time an A&T student, Willie Grimes, was killed. It was Johnson's second brush with violent conflict.

In 1970, Fuller adopted the name Owusu Sadaukai and moved the fledgling Malcolm X Liberation University from Durham to Greensboro in order to take advantage of the core of black activists Johnson and others had cultivated on the campuses and in the community. They were Pan-Africanists now, convinced that liberation for black Americans would be accomplished only after African blacks overthrew white colonial rule. All contact, all cooperation with whites was terminated.

The Greensboro Association of Poor People's ties to the system—the white-dominated system—were too close. Johnson withdrew and brought together students from A&T, Bennett, and Malcolm X to form the Student Organization for Black Unity (SOBU). One of their early recruits was a dynamic young woman from South Carolina, Sandra Neely.

Sandra Neely Smith. Textile Worker, Cannon Mills, Kannapolis, North Carolina. Beloved only child of Mr. and Mrs. Smith Neely, Piedmont, South Carolina. Died Saturday, November 3, 1979.

Everyone who met Sandi Neely was captivated by her. She combined strength with sensitivity, intense political dedication with exuberance for everything and everyone around her. She lifted people's spirits with her songs and her laughter; she challenged anything she did not believe was right or just.[7]

Neely chose to attend Bennett College for its strong activist tradition during the sit-ins and later desegregation efforts. She wanted to become a nurse, to help people. As a student, Neely was involved with GAPP as well as SOBU at

Metamorphosis

Sandi Smith (Courtesy of Jim Waters, WFMY-TV, Greensboro)

first. But as her relationship with Nelson Johnson and his wife Joyce deepened, she too moved from moderate integrationist to Pan-African militance.

Surveillance

The FBI was watching. The Bureau had informants in SOBU, as it had in the Foundation for Community Development and GAPP.[8] The files for SOBU, as well as those for Malcolm X Liberation University, contain similar erroneous information: they were stockpiling weapons, their leaders were addicted to drugs and alcohol, they were planning to take over black colleges.

Neither Johnson nor Sadaukai was that stupid. Both were opposed to the use of drugs, and they considered alcohol a drug. They knew they were being watched and they were not about to take any unnecessary chances. The discovery of a cache of arms might be all the excuse police or federal agents needed to conduct a murderous raid like the one that had resulted in the death of Fred Hampton in Chicago. What Johnson and Sadaukai did want to do was to recruit black students to SOBU and to develop a network of independent, black-controlled colleges like Malcolm X. If that was a threat to black institutions like A&T or Howard or Fisk or Spelman, it was a very small one, indeed.

Still, the FBI persisted, compiling thousands of pages of reports on Johnson, Sadaukai, and their organizations in a file captioned "Planned Takeover of Black Colleges," reams of paper representing who-knows-how-many tax dollars or how many hours of agent-informant work. The only outcome of these so-called investigations was the eventual demise of Malcolm X Liberation University, not because the FBI ever found evidence of criminal wrongdoing but because they planted false information which led one of the school's major funding sources to withdraw its support.[9]

The FBI's sabotage was not the sole reason for Sadaukai's decision to close Malcolm X. In 1972, he had organized the African Liberation Support Committee (ALSC), an outgrowth of a massive African Liberation Day demonstration in Washington. The ALSC developed a strong chapter network throughout the United States, many of which raised thousands of dollars to send to revolutionary groups in Mozambique, Tanzania, Angola, and Rhodesia. Sadaukai made numerous trips to Africa to witness the liberation effort firsthand and to offer the financial and personal support of black radicals in America. The message he got from the African revolutionaries was not what he anticipated: we need your support for African liberation, he was told, but we do not need your bodies; our enemy is U.S. capitalism and imperialism, so go home and make revolution there.

The post-Watergate revelations of the political abuses of U.S. intelligence agencies profoundly reinforced the Africans' message. From the FBI to the CIA to the IRS, from military intelligence to the National Security Agency, it seemed that just about every information-gathering and security agency of the federal government was involved in criminal activities against law-abiding citizens here and abroad. If room for doubt ever existed, these proofs of illegal standard operating procedures at the highest levels of government sealed the verdict for Sadaukai: the only solution was revolution.

The shift in Sadaukai's political philosophy did not produce an immediate or unified response from those in the ALSC, SOBU, and Malcolm X, whose work was firmly rooted in Pan-Africanism, however. Nelson Johnson was one who made the transition early on, and he and Sadaukai led their groups into a series of highly charged debates on the merits of Marxism versus Pan-Africanism.[10] Cleve Sellers, former program secretary for the Student Nonviolent Coordinating Committee who became deeply involved in SOBU, the ALSC, and Malcolm X, was torn by the debates—personally and politically.

"Owusu got to the point where he decided that MXLU's emphasis was too much on Africa, that there was an error made in the philosophical basis of Malcolm X, and he decided to no longer pursue the independent educational institution. That's when the crumbling began. A lot of people were frustrated and angered. Many people who were associated with Malcolm X got split and split again.

"The concern was that the African liberation struggle was a multinational struggle, a socialist-communist struggle, and people who were talking about Pan-Africanism were narrowing the struggle and not giving the movement the proper perspective. Many of us [in the ALSC] who considered ourselves Pan-Africanist were purged, and ALSC took on another character."

By 1974, Malcolm X Liberation University was gone, SOBU had changed its name to YOBU—Youth Organized for Black Unity—to reflect the fact that it was no longer a student-led group, Nelson Johnson and Sandi Neely got jobs at Greensboro's Cone Mills, and Owusu Sadaukai returned to Durham to organize Duke workers for Local 77. The ALSC was still in existence, but the splits and purges had left the organization much smaller and less vibrant. Sadaukai, Nelson and Joyce Johnson, and Neely and her new husband, Mark Smith, found political sanctuary in the Revolutionary Workers League.

White activists in Durham had experienced a similar organizational devastation. They saw working relationships and friendships disintegrate as the New Communists attempted to sway their organizations to revolution. The Durham group was settling on a trinity of revolutionary theorists—Marx, Lenin, and Mao—who would show them "the road forward" to communist revolution in the United States. But for the people who were left by the wayside, who were purged or dropped out from frustration or exhaustion, that road looked more like a road to oblivion, to isolation.

Like the black Greensboro revolutionaries, the Durham group adopted the classic Marxist strategy of infusing communism in the working class through labor unions. From Lenin, though, the Marxist identification of the enemy as bourgeois capitalism was expanded to include reformists.

"Reformists are more sinister enemies than outright reactionaries, for they will leech off the working class movement and blood suck its political independence," proclaimed the *Workers Viewpoint Journal* in 1974. According to Lenininst analysis, the civil rights movement, the women's movement, even the labor movement are reformist because they work through the bourgeois capitalist system to achieve social gains rather than work to topple the system itself. Reformism, the Leninists maintain, gives the working class the illusion of a free society. It breeds complacency and thus blinds the proletariat to the need for revolution.[11]

Another fundamental Leninist principle is that the truth comes out as a product of "struggle." Differences of opinion are resolved through polemics, and the point of consensus becomes the party principle: the correct line.

In the writings of Chairman Mao they found a few maxims which made for an impenetrable shield against outside criticism. "There is no construction without destruction," Mao counseled. "Destruction means criticism and repudiation, it means revolution. It involves reasoning things out, which is construction. Put destruction first and in the process you have construction."[12]

If the correct line is later discovered to be inaccurate, if a destructive act results in nothing positive but destroys something essential and irreplaceable, Mao had an answer for that, too. Being correct is only relative, he said; making mistakes is absolute. Just fight, fail, fight again, fail again, then hoist yourself up by your breeches and fight again. The essence of what the *Workers Viewpoint Journal* called M-L-M-T-T-T (for Marxist-Leninist-Mao-Tse-Tung-Thought) is that its practitioners could do no wrong.

The *Journal*'s interpretation of M-L-M-T-T-T settled on a political precipice: "In these times of both rising revolution and fascism, anything that holds our struggles back HELPS FASCISM. And that is just what reformism does."[13]

Although Bermanzohn, Waller, Avery, and the Durham Communists had not yet affiliated with the Workers Viewpoint Organization, they studied its journal intensely. "We were trying to figure out how to chart a political course," said Bermanzohn. "It was very exciting. We'd have these discussions. We believed in the Marxist-Leninist principles that the truth comes out as the product of struggle.

"The central task was to reconstitute a genuine communist party in this country. We studied an enormous amount of stuff. Very, very detailed. It took time to develop a sort of group dynamic, fighting out differences. We'd fight over commas for days—not nitpicking but really trying to understand how to fight for socialism in America."

After graduation from Duke Medical School, Bermanzohn was accepted for a psychiatric residency at the University of North Carolina's Memorial Hospital in Chapel Hill. He gave up the residency when it became clear that he could not devote as much time as he felt necessary to political work. Instead, he got two part-time jobs, one at the Alamance County Hospital emergency room, the other at the student health center at the University of North Carolina at Greensboro. His spare time and much of his salary went for travel, literature, and purchasing supplies for what was now called the Durham Organizing Committee. The name change reflected the former health collective members' recognition that the revolution could succeed only if it were broadly based.

Jim Waller and Bermanzohn spent countless hours on the road together—to Atlanta, Philadelphia, Chicago, New York. They met with every national New Communist group and a few local organizations they felt had national potential. Their energy and determination were astonishing. They worked, studied, debated, criticized, traveled, wrote, leafleted, picketed, met, and met again. It was exhausting just to witness, and those who could not—or did not want to—maintain the pace fell by the wayside.

"I never met anybody with such intense political energy," said Durham health activist Tim McGloin of Bermanzohn. "His dedication and commitment were really inspiring." For McGloin, however, inspiration soon degenerated into bewilderment. "I was constantly at meetings—and I have a family—getting exposed to the fine points of Marxism-Leninism and not quite being able to decipher all that. Some of us wanted to continue organizing around health issues, but the political foundations for Marxist-Leninist organizing were being laid. In 1975 the tensions got heavy enough for me personally that I left my teaching position at N.C. Central. I left Durham."

McGloin saw an obsession in Bermanzohn and the others: "Constantly questioning, looking for the solution. The Line. Ironically, I feel that that is a very bourgeois approach to political revolution. 'I want the answer. There has to be an answer.' We've been trained this way; we've been through school, found answers. But it is very bourgeois to want the answer, to want the solution, and zip, here's how to do it. It just isn't that simple. You know, if you substitute the political rhetoric with religious rhetoric, you'd have a born-again. To be saved; to accept the line."

Chapter 3

> Around this theme of "proof" we have piled confusions which have intensified anxiety until some of us are unable to relate to anything. Instead, we try to find a system to fuse ourselves with, or we spin our ideologies and chain ourselves to them.
> —Lillian Smith, *Killers of the Dream*

The Socialist Road

"The line" by 1975 was to be openly communist; the name "Durham Organizing Committee" would no longer do. They called themselves the Communist Workers Committee (CWC)—Jim Waller, Paul Bermanzohn, and Sally Avery were its lifeblood. Through Sadaukai and the Revolutionary Workers League, they would soon join forces with the black revolutionaries in Greensboro, Nelson Johnson and Sandi and Mark Smith, to organize textile workers at Cone Mills.

"There was increasingly a sense of urgency about doing the political work that needed to be done," said Bermanzohn. Their studies led them to the conclusion, he said, "that if you are serious about trying to organize people, you have to share your life with them in a pretty deep way." For Waller, that concept would lead him to quit his Duke fellowship to get a job cutting grooves in corduroy at Cone Mills' Haw River plant, twenty-five miles east of Greensboro. Many factors led to that decision, but one was pure Jim Waller.

"He had a kid he was treating in the hospital," Bermanzohn remembers. "Pediatric infectious disease is a heartbreaker, little kids sick as dogs. It's hard work, emotionally draining. But Jim was a devoted guy, so he was visiting this kid on his own time. Then at the end of the month, he finds out that all this extra time he'd been spending with the kid, they were billing the family. Every visit, an extra thirty-five dollars the family had to pay. So he raised some sand down there: 'What the hell's going on? You trying to bankrupt the family because I'm trying to take care of the kid?' He was so pissed. So he resigned and got a job that was consistent with the overall thrust of our work."

Cesar Cauce (Courtesy of Jim Waters, WFMY-TV, Greensboro)

Mike Nathan took another direction. After graduation from medical school in 1973, he left Durham—and revolutionary politics—for a pediatric residency at Parkland Hospital in Dallas. He separated from Sally Avery, later divorcing her. Avery had decided to forego law school in order to continue her political work, to maintain the roots she had so painstakingly laid down in Durham—the friends, the contacts, the knowledge of the community and the issues that affected it.

Besides, the CWC was winning new recruits. Not "workers" in the Marxist sense of the word. Not yet. But the elite Duke atmosphere had spawned another mini-cadre of activists, students from working-class or impoverished backgrounds whose entrance to the university was through scholarships. Among them were Cesar Cauce and Martha Arthur.

Cesar Vincente Cauce. Data Terminal Operator, Duke University. Beloved husband of Floris Caton Cauce. Delegate, Founding Congress, Communist Workers Party. Died November 3, 1979.

Cesar Cauce was a bear of a man, six feet tall, weighing 220 pounds. His face was surrounded by a bush of reddish-brown hair and a beard. A chance encounter with Cauce in a dark alley would be terrifying, until he smiled. He smiled a lot, laughed a lot; he enjoyed people and life and himself.[1]

Cauce was born into the elite of Cuban society. His father had been a member of Batista's cabinet before Fidel Castro seized control. At the age of five, young Cauce fled to Miami with his family. Raised in the Cuban ghetto, Cauce learned a lot about discrimination and oppression. Much more than his parents, still longing for the prestige and power of prerevolutionary Cuba, were willing to recognize.

As a student at Miami-Dade Junior College, Cauce took part in organizing the antiwar demonstrations at the 1972 Democratic Convention. There he became involved with a religious-based nonviolent peace group from Durham whose members convinced Cauce that Duke was the place to finish his undergraduate work. Scholarship in hand, Cauce entered the Harvard of the South with plans to one day become a professor of Latin American history.

During his first year at Duke, Cauce was peripherally involved with the Durham Communists through union support work. But by the time he graduated—magna cum laude—he had joined Avery, Bermanzohn, and Waller as one of the key figures in the CWC. So committed was he to revolutionary work that he gave up a full scholarship to graduate school at Berkeley. Instead, he got a job as a data terminal operator at Duke in order to work from within to help organize for Local 77.

Marty Arthur; no one called her Martha. Like Bermanzohn and Nathan, whom she would later marry, Arthur went to Duke as a medical student. The daughter of a bus driver from Westerville, Ohio, she learned early of working-class and civil rights struggles. As president of his union, Arthur's father spent whatever spare time he had advocating for decent wages and working conditions for the drivers and the admission of the black baggage handlers into the union. "He was a real model for me," Arthur said. "Those two issues—the working person as a force in society and antiracism—I can't remember when they were not a significant portion of my life."

For a while, Arthur sublimated the lessons of her father. Because of severe high blood pressure, he was given a desk job at the union office in Homewood, Illinois. There Marty attended one of the Chicago area's most affluent high schools. Money was the predominant issue at Homewood-Flossmore High, and the bus driver's kid tried her best to adopt the priorities of her schoolmates.

One of those priorities was to go to an Ivy League college. Arthur chose Pembroke. She got full scholarships all the way through, but gradually the question of class began to seep back into her thinking. "My roommate was the granddaughter of the governor of Colorado, the cousin of Morris Udall." Arthur tried desperately to mold herself into the upper class, "but then there came a point at which, yeah, I could make it. But—what the fuck—did I want to?"

The question was not, and never is, an easy one to resolve. Arthur decided to become a doctor; she could help people, poor people and working-class people like her father, and still earn good money. Again with full scholarships, she joined the largest class of women to enter any of the nation's medical schools. For her, as for Bermanzohn and Nathan before her, Duke University School of Medicine offered a rude awakening. The women's movement was at its height, and yet, according to Arthur, Duke's physiology professors continued to illustrate their lectures with *Playboy* centerfolds.

But it was the clinical experience that shook Arthur back to her roots. "They put the medical students in the public clinic," she said. "Private patients never saw a medical student unless their doctor *allowed* it. They have something called the 'green test.' You either have insurance or cash up front, or you're public.

"I remember one thing that particularly disturbed me. The private physicians were shoving public patients off the Coronary Care Unit in order to have their la-de-dah rich patients there. Shoving patients off CCU who hadn't recovered from their heart attacks so they could take up the beds with their rich patients and make more money! And I remember the thought flashing into my mind that my father, who had severe heart disease, he would have been shoved. He never passed anybody's green test."

At Duke, Arthur said, she saw "class conflict in terms of life and death." She was therefore keenly receptive to Paul Bermanzohn and the other Duke radicals whose backgrounds and experiences were so similar to hers. She did not become politically active until close to the end of her medical studies, when Mike Nathan returned to the Durham area and to his revolutionary world. Mike talked with her about his experience in Guatemala, about his anger and frustration with big city medicine and big hospitals, about the need for revolution. They fell in love, moved in together, and began working with the CWC.

The Crossroad

In late 1975, there were serious negotiations to merge various ethnic factions of the New Communist movement into one multiracial, working-class revolutionary vanguard. The predominantly Asian Workers Viewpoint Organization, the Puerto Rican Revolutionary Organization, the Hispanic August 29th Group, and the black Revolutionary Workers League engaged in intense and sometimes fierce polemics to convince each other's memberships that they alone had the correct line.

The CWC was open to merger with either the WVO or the RWL. They were impressed with the political line of the WVO, and they often used it as a standard by which to measure the "correctness" of the other groups' stances.[2] But their direct contact with the WVO was limited and infrequent. On the other hand, they had worked for nearly two years with Owusu Sadaukai and the RWL. They considered Sadaukai a folk hero, as they did his comrade in Greensboro, Nelson Johnson. The predominantly white CWC was eager to merge with the black revolutionaries, to make a visible demonstration of their ideal of black-white unity. Since the national RWL leadership seemed inclined towards uniting with the WVO, however, the Durham Communists decided to hang back until the national organization made a move one way or the other.

The RWL was split over the merger question. The separatist forces had the upper hand, focusing their argument on the need to build their organization into a party. As the struggle over the correct line intensified, they took the position that party building took precedence over all other organizing activities—including union organizing. Sadaukai was torn. Local 77 had been his life for two years. He did not want to give it up. His close friends and comrades, Nelson and Joyce Johnson, were not receptive to the new RWL line. He did not want to give them up, either. He agonized over the decision. He started stuttering and was unable to concentrate. So much of his life was invested in the revolution.

"Because you believe so deeply in humanity and what's happening to people," Sadaukai said, "that's what sustains you. The more you get into it, the more you see how people are suffering, the more you then start dealing with other people who see things the same way. You develop a view of the world and of people in the world, and you find that group of people who share your view and then you talk together a lot. And pretty soon that *is* the world." Sadaukai chose to ignore the symptoms of burnout, to ignore his gut feelings about the importance of his union work and his friends. He chose to stay in his political world, the Revolutionary Workers League.

As Nelson and Joyce Johnson became more involved with the Durham Communists, they broke with the RWL, leaving Sandi and Mark Smith, as well. They formed yet another organization, the Bolshevik Organizing Committee, through which they would intensify their organizing at Cone. The CWC sent a team from Durham to join the effort.

It was classic communist strategy, the fusion of the communist and workers' movements, said Bermanzohn. "They are born out of the same thing—capitalism. One is the movement to improve the conditions of work, that is the trade union movement. The other is a movement to change the conditions of life, that's the communist movement."

There is also the fact that workers hold the power to stop the very functioning of society, to stop the factories, the trains, the post office. Workers—not doctors, not the Duke Class of '74, but factory workers, blue-collar workers, laborers—are in the unique position to take a society into revolution. The plan was to recruit workers by reviving interest in the withering-to-nonexistent Textile Workers Union locals in the Cone mills. It then would be relatively easy to get the enthusiastic and knowledgeable Communist organizers elected to leadership positions as shop stewards, newsletter committees, and officers of the locals, from which they could gain control of the union itself.[3] Ultimately, the goal was to engineer a strike. This, the Communist organizers felt, would force Cone to its corporate knees and knock a hole in the armor of the capitalist world.

But the realities of North Carolina's sociopolitical atmosphere were almost hopelessly skewed against the militant organizers. Racism and anti-communism are as deeply ingrained in the state as antiunionism. The fusion of Greensboro's black Communists with Durham's white Communists in order to unionize black and white workers at one of the South's textile giants was a threat to that reactionary element. The fact that they were openly Communist made the organizers easy targets for antiunion forces. And as their attempts to organize intensified, the Communists' tactics drove many potential allies in the labor and leftist movements further and further away.

June 1976. Everyone was talking revolution. It was the bicentennial. The CWC and the Bolshevik Organizing Committee had another reason to celebrate. Jerry Tung, general secretary of the Workers Viewpoint Organization's Central Committee, was coming to Durham to engage in polemics with the Revolutionary Workers League. "The WVO had written an enormously powerful journal analyzing the political positions of the RWL, very heavy," said Bermanzohn. "They followed it with a tour by Jerry Tung. One of his bold forays was going into what was then called 'Owusu Country,' to North Carolina where Owusu had held sway for a good ten years. The undisputed revolutionary leader in the area, no doubt about it."

At the outset, the polemics seemed to be a pathetic mismatch: Sadaukai, the striking black man whose gift for words was legendary in North Carolina, versus Tung, a small, stern-looking Chinese-American from New York who delivered unremarkable phrases like "the chickens have come home to roost" in a heavy Asian dialect.[4]

"We thought that this Jerry Tung guy was just going to get eaten up," said Bermanzohn. "That would be the end of Jerry Tung, because Owusu was such a charismatic figure. What happened was very, very interesting. Jerry gave a presentation for about two hours, connected stuff real clearly. Owusu was called on to respond and it was like nothing. He couldn't deal with the stuff. He looked real bad. They had another RWL person speak. The upshot of the forum was a real rout. Jerry annihilated them."

Sadaukai remembers it differently: "The polemics, to the extent you could call it that, actually took place between Jerry Tung and a woman named Abla Thomas who at the time represented the leadership of RWL. RWL had been engaging in these so-called polemics with WVO in different places, so she came down to run what was in essence the national line of RWL. Had I engaged in polemics with Jerry Tung and been whipped or otherwise, I certainly would admit it."

The fact was that Sadaukai himself found the WVO position more persuasive than the RWL's. When he tried to convince his organization's leadership and local members to reconsider a merger, however, he was purged. "It really flipped me out," said Sadaukai. "But I could think well enough to know I didn't want to be involved in that any longer." He returned to his hometown of Milwaukee, took back the name Howard Fuller, took part in a number of community organizing efforts, and eventually became a high level official in the Wisconsin Department of Labor.

The disintegration of the Revolutionary Workers League was complete within a few months after the Durham polemics. COINTELPRO? The pattern was there: disrupt and neutralize. Bermanzohn, Avery, and Johnson firmly believe that the RWL's demise was the result of manipulation by federal agent-saboteurs. Howard Fuller is not convinced, though he is suspicious. "Some very strange things happened to a group of people who had been working together for a long time. Other people who we did not know came in and in a very short time busted apart what had been a fairly stable group of people."

Dragons, Spies, and Swastikas

COINTELPRO was terminated as a distinct FBI program in 1971. But it was not until 1976, following congressional hearings that exposed the rampant and continuing abuses of the intelligence agencies, that Attorney General Edward Levi imposed guidelines restricting the Bureau's infiltration and disruption of domestic political groups. Eddie Dawson's last payoff from the FBI came on August 31, 1976. Over the course of seven years, Dawson earned a total of $6,329.19,[5] a rather paltry amount when compared to that of Panther informant William O'Neal: $30,000 over three years.[6]

The difference, of course, is that Dawson's work never resulted in any criminal charges against the Klan or in the "elimination" of a national leader like Fred Hampton. The level of pay is a good indication of which type of informant the FBI considered more valuable. O'Neal was a provocateur; Dawson was a watchdog. "Never, never did I do anything to get our people in trouble," Dawson said. "I did more to keep them out of trouble."

Eddie Dawson is an intriguing man. He is a rebel in the purest sense of the word: he quit school after the seventh grade; in 1942 he was convicted of going AWOL from the army after being charged twice with insubordination; a year later he escaped from the army stockade, only to be captured and convicted of a second AWOL and desertion; in five trials prior to 1985, Dawson never took the witness stand in his defense. Antiauthoritarian to the core, Dawson refuses to call anyone "boss"; at sixty-six years of age, he continues to work as a self-employed carpenter.

Yet Dawson capitulated to the FBI, snitching on his friends and fellow Klan members. For a man like Dawson to become the FBI's lackey, a stool pigeon, seems a contradiction, but in fact it is totally in character. He was in control. He alone decided what information to pass to the FBI; he alone was in a position to stop Klan members from taking actions that would result in their arrest. He could, to some extent, manipulate both organizations, and that gave him a sense of power. The 007 Complex. It was Eddie Dawson's secret world—his and his alone.

As much as he sounds like the ultimate villain, it is hard not to like Dawson. He is gregarious, humorous, and surprisingly candid. He loves to talk, especially about his days with the Klan and the FBI.

Dawson joined the Klan in the early 1960s, shortly after he moved to Greensboro. Called "Yankee" because of his thick New Jersey accent, Dawson was initially suspected by the Klan members of being an FBI plant. The real FBI informant was the Greensboro Klan's own leader, George Dorsett, who liked Dawson's spunk and quickly moved him into the Klan hierarchy.

During Dawson's nine-month stint in prison for the 1967 Alamance County terrorizing incident, the state's grand dragon for the United Klans of America, Bob Jones, was jailed for refusing to comply with a congressional subpoena for Klan membership records. Dorsett took advantage of the void in state leadership to further weaken the group by accusing Jones of embezzlement. He broke off and formed a rival faction, the Confederate Knights of the Ku Klux Klan. Although Dawson and Dorsett had been a tight pair, Dawson chose to stay with the UKA when he returned from prison. It was then that the FBI made its first overtures, threatening to prosecute him on other charges if he refused to cooperate.

Then came the Swan Quarter riot. Dawson insists that his association with the FBI began after he left the United Klans, but his behavior in the months that followed Swan Quarter—just three months after his release from prison—smacks of classic COINTELPRO. Charged with felony riot and facing ten years in jail and a ten-thousand-dollar fine, Dawson and his thirteen co-defendants were represented by Arthur Hanes, the one-time attorney for Klan hero James Earl Ray. The UKA paid Hanes fifteen thousand dollars to negotiate a plea bargain: the Klan members pleaded guilty to participating in a riot, a misdemeanor, and got five years' probation and a one-thousand-dollar fine each.

With his criminal record, Dawson should have kissed the ground Hanes walked on for getting him off so lightly. Instead, he was furious. He could, he said, have gotten one of North Carolina's best criminal attorneys, Robert Cahoon (who later served as lead defense counsel in the 1980 Klan-Nazi trial) for a mere three thousand dollars. Cahoon, Dawson felt, would not have copped a plea; he would have gotten acquittals. The FBI continued to pressure Dawson, feeding his suspicions about the guilty pleas and the amount of money the Klan paid Hanes. Then, to add to Dawson's sense of betrayal, the UKA refused to pay the defendants' thousand-dollar fines.

His complaints may have been valid, but his method of resolving them left the UKA once again leaderless, with many of its members deserting to form another rival faction. Dawson accused the UKA of pocketing part of Hanes's fifteen-thousand-dollar fee and demanded to see a canceled check. The charges were suspiciously similar to those made earlier by Dorsett against Bob Jones. And as Dorsett did when the Klan did not respond to his satisfaction, Dawson took the floor of a statewide meeting and made his accusations before the entire membership. He and the man who led the UKA during Jones's absence and a host of their followers were, in Klan parlance, banished that day. Soon there was another Klan in the state, the North Carolina Knights of the Ku Klux Klan, with Dawson as chief of security.

Dawson claims that it was only after his perceived mistreatment and subsequent banishment from the UKA that he agreed to cooperate with the FBI in exchange for getting him off probation. "I hated that probation with a passion," said Dawson, and it sounds very logical. But FBI records show that Dawson's first payoff was on November 7, 1969.[7] He says he left the UKA at the fourth monthly meeting following the Swan Quarter riot. The fourth month after July is November.

One of the dissident members who followed Dawson to the North Carolina Knights was a young hothead named Virgil Griffin. Then twenty-five, Griffin was much more the stereotypical Klan member than Dawson was. Sullen and inarticulate, Griffin projects an aura of violence just waiting to erupt. He became NCKKKK's grand dragon in 1971 and refused to hold another election until 1976 when Dawson, in his last act as an FBI informant, demanded to run against him. Since the organization had no more than a handful of members in the entire state, Dawson won the vote easily. He never called another meeting. That was the end of the North Carolina Knights of the Ku Klux Klan.[8]

The phenomenon of Klan leaders turning informant is odd and apparently contradictory. But it may be symbolic of the needs of many, if not most, Klan members for power, prestige, and respect. Their day-to-day lives are characterized by poverty, ignorance, and violence. The Klan offers an outlet for their frustrations and targets—black, Jews, Communists, homosexuals—for their hostilities, all under the banner of patriotism. But it is an illusion. The power a Klan member feels when marching, robed and hooded, through the streets is quickly lost when he or she returns home. Without educations, they are locked in menial jobs; without decent incomes, they are imprisoned in the world into which they were born.

Hopeless and resentful, they grab whatever measure of gratification they can find. It may be burning a cross or shouting racial epithets or assaulting someone. Or it may be becoming an informant, for the informant has not only a dual source of power but a dual illusion of patriotism. Questions of allegiance apparently do not arise for people like George Dorsett or Eddie Dawson.

Griffin never was too choosy about the company he kept, however. In 1974, much to Eddie Dawson's and the FBI's chagrin, Griffin joined forces with the National Socialist White People's Party to picket a demonstration in Raleigh. It was the Fourth of July. Angela Davis was to speak at a rally sponsored by the National Alliance Against Racist and Political Repression protesting the incarceration of two groups of black activists and their supporters who had been arrested and convicted in highly questionable investigations and proscecutions, the Wilmington Ten and the Charlotte Three. Griffin and the Nazis could not resist the temptation to confront a card-carrying black Communist. But when the dozen or so Klansmen and Nazis saw that they would be facing five thousand demonstrators, the showdown was called off.[9]

Griffin maintained his liaison with the Nazis despite protests from Dawson and others. "We'll not march with those people no more," Dawson scolded. "You mention Klan and that's bad enough, but you mention *Nazi* and Klan, well, there's just no word for it." Griffin could not have cared less. The grand dragon, he knew, could do whatever he damn-well pleased. And it pleased Griffin to join forces—if a dozen or so could be called a force—with the

Nazis. Especially when they got the chance to confront Communists. Especially black Communists.

Dawson was playing a little game with the Communists himself. At least, he thought they were Communists. The U.S. Labor Party, which presented itself as an ultra-left sect advocating workers' rule, had a small band of members in Greensboro in 1974.[10] Dawson began attending their meetings, and he passed information about the group to the Greensboro police as well as the FBI. He insists that he was never paid for this information, that he just did it for the hell of it. Dawson is curious, and he loves nothing more than a good political debate. He did not hide his Klan membership from the Labor Party; neither did he hide his "communist" affiliation from the Klan. He was just getting to know the enemy, he told the Klan.

Dawson got a kick out of party members who tried to convince him to join their revolution. He argued with them for hours, later joking with his Klan buddies about the discussions. Some of them did not understand what Dawson was up to. They accused him of being a communist and threatened to kick him out of the Klan. Virgil Griffin finally stepped in, telling them that he knew Dawson was Klan through and through, that they should just let him spy on the Communists if that was what he wanted.

The Labor Party announced that it would hold a picket at a Greensboro shopping center, and Dawson knew this was his chance to regain the confidence of the Klan. He phoned his pals and told them to meet at his trailer on Saturday morning to demonstrate against the Communists. Then he called the Greensboro police and the FBI to let them know what was going to happen.

It went off just as Dawson had hoped it would. He and the Klan, in uniforms and robes, arrived at the shopping center shortly before the Labor Party did. Police were everywhere. Dawson and his men stood in line with their arms folded across their chests, waiting for the Labor Party to arrive. He saw the cars pull in. "The gang arrived there in the parking lot and got out and put their sandwich signs on," Dawson said. "Then they looked down there (at the Klan) and took their sandwich signs off and went about their business." It was great fun, Dawson's little game. He had humiliated the so-called Communists and reestablished his credibility with the Klan, all under the watchful eye of the police and FBI. The Yankee rebel had them in the palm of his hand.

By the mid-1970s, the North Carolina Klans were disintegrating from the same kind of splits that had fractured the African Liberation Support Committee and other leftist groups. With only a handful of members, Griffin's group was hard-pressed to maintain the image of a fearsome and powerful band of vigilantes. As loathsome as the Nazis were, even to most Klan members, they were the only group in the region that was willing and able to march publicly with the North Carolina Knights. Still, the showings of Griffin's Klan and the

Metamorphosis

National Socialist White People's Party (NSWPP) could hardly be called massive: a dozen in Raleigh, twenty in Charlotte, ten or so in Wilmington.[11]

One man who was a member of the NSWPP at the time would be instrumental in bringing the Klan and Nazis together prior to the deadly confrontation in Greensboro. He would also be responsible for destroying the National Socialist Party of America in 1979 and 1980, after which he would mysteriously disappear. His name was Harold Covington.

An articulate, perceptive, and pathologically racist Chapel Hill High School graduate, Covington became a virtuoso in the art of deception. He created a mythology about himself and his Nazis which raised sinister questions, questions that were left unchallenged for many years.

One myth, a minor but easily disproved one, is Covington's portrayal of himself as a former reporter for the *Chapel Hill Newspaper*.[12] The truth is that as a high school student, Covington volunteered to write a column on school activities for the local paper. A few columns later, the publisher told Covington to take a hike.[13] The young racist was attempting to use the column as a forum for airing his grievances about the school. His main grievance, which never made the pages of the *Chapel Hill Newspaper*, was that the school's blacks were teasing and harassing him unmercifully. Not that he should expect benevolence from a people he openly despised, but the black students' behavior reinforced Covington's opinion that the race was inherently violent and inferior.

Covington joined the NSWPP and the U.S. Army at about the time he was handed his high school diploma in 1971. Two years later, he boasts, he was "eased out of the Army with an honorable discharge" in response to his racist agitation at Schofield Barracks, Hawaii.[14] Given his history in Chapel Hill, that may well be true, but there is nothing in his record to either confirm or disprove it.

Within a month after his discharge from the army, Covington landed in Johannesburg, South Africa. It was nothing short of racist heaven. White supremacy. Apartheid. Covington worked as a payroll clerk by day, studied Hitler at night, and dreamed of leading the revolution—the national socialist revolution.

In 1974, Covington left Johannesburg for Bulawayo, Zimbabwe, then called Rhodesia, where he fabricated his most dramatic story, one that in 1979 raised the possibility of a CIA connection to the Greensboro killings. Covington claims that he was a mercenary in the Rhodesian Army, that he organized a Rhodesian White People's Party, and that he was kicked out of the country because his brand of racism was too vile for even the white supremacist Rhodesians.[15]

In 1983, the FBI attempted to find Covington in order to bring him before a federal grand jury and disprove allegations made by both the CWP and the Nazis that he was a CIA operative who had been put under federal protection as part of the coverup of the Greensboro killings. The FBI tracked Covington to South Africa and then lost him, adding yet another piece to the mystery of Harold Covington. The Zimbabwe government, however, was able to dispel at least part of the myth: there was no evidence that Covington had served in the Rhodesian Army, as a mercenary or otherwise; the record showed that he was employed by an engineering and construction firm, probably as a low-level clerk.

Covington had, indeed, formed a Rhodesian White People's Party, as well as a group called South African Friends of the Movement. His deportation was the result of sending threatening letters to the Bulawayo Hebrew Congregation, which, the FBI was told, "angered and shocked the Jewish community" and "caused them to be apprehensive as to what might happen to them." He was handed prohibited immigration papers and deported in early 1976.[16]

Returning to North Carolina, Covington settled in Raleigh. There he switched his allegiance to the National Socialist Party of America (NSPA), which was then overtaking the NSWPP as *the* American Nazi party. Like the North Carolina Knights, NSPA was a product of COINTELPRO. Its leader, Frank Collin, was ousted from the NSWPP in 1970 as the result of an FBI-instigated smear campaign. For a Nazi, it was the ultimate smear: Frank Collin's real name was Frank Cohn—and he was half-Jewish.[17] To Collin—or Cohn—it really did not matter. His Nazi leanings far outweighed his racial heritage; and he could take comfort that the same allegations had been made against his idol, Adolph Hitler.

Harold Covington may or may not have known about Collin's Jewish heritage. What he surely knew was that Collin was in the news, and Covington wanted a piece of that action. He knew that frequent media exposure, the more controversial the better, was the most effective way of recruiting a core of followers, the power base he needed one day to take control of the NSPA.

As Covington set out to organize a Nazi base in North Carolina, Virgil Griffin's NCKKKK was gasping its last breaths. Eddie Dawson estimated that as 1975 rolled into 1976, Griffin had no more than fifteen members statewide.

Saturday in downtown Greensboro. A short-sighted urban renewal program in the late sixties and early seventies had left the city's center an off-hours wasteland. Businesspeople and shopkeepers fled to Greensboro's bedroom communities at the close of office hours each day. Only the black businesses stayed open on Saturdays, but they did a brisk trade with black college students and working people.

Virgil Griffin at 1975 Klan rally in Greensboro (Photograph by Ken Hinson)

Ed Dawson (left) at 1975 Klan rally in Greensboro (Photograph by Ken Hinson)

A winter Saturday at the close of 1975, then, was not the ideal choice for a Klan rally on the plaza of the city's governmental center. Dawson and Griffin held one anyway. Even if no crowds came, the media would be there, which meant they would get a couple of minutes on the Saturday night news and a column or two in the Sunday paper.

A couple of men hauled loudspeakers onto the plaza; then they brought out two hastily made wooden crosses which had little stickers that said, "White Power." Dawson came out in his tan security uniform, followed by Griffin and a few others in Klan robes.

The plaza was almost deserted—almost, but not quite. As Dawson picked up the microphone, a couple of young blacks made a dash to the business district down the street. Within moments they were running back toward the plaza with twenty or thirty others close on their heels. They stood in a circle at the bottom of the plaza steps, listening quietly as Dawson and then Griffin rattled on about white supremacy, about blacks taking away white jobs, white schools, and white women.

The young blacks began to snicker at the absurdity of the racist rantings. From the middle of the crowd someone started singing, "M-I-C-K-E-Y M-O-U-S-E." Soon all the young people, including a few white onlookers, were singing in unison, drowning out the loudspeakers. A few formed a line, snake-dancing to the strains of the Mickey Mouse song, and everyone latched on—black and white. Dawson and Griffin were furious, but the crowd just laughed and sang and danced until they got tired of it and wandered away. It was Greensboro's last public Klan rally.[18]

Chapter 4

> The fundamental reason for the superiority of totalitarian propaganda over the propaganda of other parties and movements is that its content, for the members of the movement at any rate, is no longer an objective issue about which people may have opinions, but has become as real and untouchable an element in their lives as the rules of arithmetic.
> —Hannah Arendt, *The Origins of Totalitarianism*

Destruction = Construction

From almost the moment the shooting stopped on November 3, the Communist Workers Party—the widows and survivors—proclaimed that the government attacked their North Carolina leadership in order to thwart their highly successful labor organizing. They point to the Carolina Brown Lung Association, the Amalgamated Clothing and Textile Workers locals at Cone Mills, and AFSCME Local 77 at Duke Hospital as examples of the importance of the organizing work they were involved in from 1974 to 1979. That they put enormous, almost superhuman, amounts of time, energy, and thought into those organizing drives is not in question. To this day, however, the impact of the Communists' efforts on the organizations they profess to support is a matter of heated controversy. The story of these organizing campaigns is a crucial link in understanding how a group of highly intelligent idealists became a band of revolutionaries so isolated from reality that they were blind to the folly of challenging the Ku Klux Klan in 1979.

The Carolina Brown Lung Association

As members of the Revolutionary Workers League, Sandi Neely and Nelson Johnson got jobs at Cone Mills, Johnson at the Printworks and Neely—ironically—at the plant called Revolution. The Printworks, where patterns were dyed into fabrics, was unionized. Revolution, which manufactured flannel, was not.

Spinning and weaving the soft, fuzzy flannel released clouds of cotton dust into the air, dust so thick it clogged the workers' breathing masks in a matter of minutes. The ventilation ducts on Revolution's exterior walls looked like over-soaped washing machines perpetually burping globs of white froth. Even the grass outside the plant wore a year-round snowy haze.

The workers learned to tolerate the dust, or so they thought. Until they had worked in the stuff for fifteen or twenty years and realized they could not sleep for all the coughing and wheezing. Until they looked a generation older than they really were because their bodies were not getting enough oxygen. Thousands upon thousands were forced to leave the textile mills because they could no longer work—there or anyplace else.

Although known in medical literature for centuries and compensated for in England since the 1940s, it was not until 1971 that Burlington Industries' newly appointed chief physician, Dr. Harold "Bud" Imbus, publicly connected exposure to cotton dust with breathing impairment in the United States.[1] Imbus did not go so far as to label the syndrome an identifiable occupational disease. But it was: byssinosis—brown lung.

The textile industry was horrified. For decades, company doctors had been telling dust-asphyxiated workers that they could not breathe because they smoked too much or they had emphysema or tuberculosis or they just had bad lungs. But they never, never told the truth—that cotton dust kills.

Sandi Neely knew the truth. So did Paul Bermanzohn. When he returned to Duke for his third year of medical school, he had the opportunity to take an elective. He chose to work with the Department of Environmental Medicine on a study of brown lung. With a team of students from Duke and the University of North Carolina medical schools, they examined and interviewed textile workers and conducted experiments on lab animals, testing different elements of cotton under varied exposures. Finally they documented what Dr. Imbus could not or would not: long-term exposure to cotton dust causes byssinosis, a reduced capacity of the lungs to expel air.

If caught early enough, brown lung deterioration can be stopped, even reversed, if the worker is transferred to a low-dust area of the plant.[2] As with most health problems, however, the best solution is prevention. Clean up the mills by installing special exhaust and filtration devices. Short of that, regular testing of workers can catch brown lung before any permanent damage is done.

It wasn't to be quite that easy, though. The textile manufacturers stonewalled in exactly the same way the tobacco industry has done since the first surgeon general's report. There was no conclusive identification of what substance in, or associated with, cotton dust caused the disease, they said. A few in the textile industry insisted—as some do to this day—that there was no such disease as byssinosis.

The textile barons could almost be excused for clinging to their illusions. They were, after all, taking their cue from no one less that the president of the United States. Among the lesser-known abuses of Nixon's Watergate era was the refusal of his secretary of labor to issue maximum exposure standards in five industries targeted by the Labor Department in 1972. The cotton dust standard was one of the five.

By the spring of 1974, however, brown lung drew the attention of North Carolina–based activists and researchers (leftists but not communists) who had become involved in occupational health issues through work with the United Mine Workers and the Textile Workers Union's J. P. Stevens campaign. Organizers from the Institute for Southern Studies and the North Carolina Public Interest Research Group (NC-PIRG) met that spring to lay the groundwork for a brown lung movement modeled after the coal miners' Black Lung Association. Their first step would be to investigate occupational safety and health regulations and workers' compensation laws. The organizers realized that there was little point in helping brown lung victims to organize if they could not be shown how to use the laws to get compensation and medical treatment.[3]

That summer, PIRG received a small grant to begin the research phase of the brown lung project. Staff member Thad Moore pored over medical studies and law books and went through old newspaper morgues. Then he got on the phone. He called lawyers, officials of the Textile Workers Union of America (TWUA), and one of the Duke brown lung researchers, Paul Bermanzohn, for technical assistance and support. According to Moore, Bermanzohn "told me that brown lung was not an issue for him at that time." Moore persevered, laying the groundwork for a joint PIRG-TWUA lawsuit challenging the Nixon administration's failure to issue cotton dust standards. He also worked on a PIRG exposé of the state Occupational Safety and Health Administration which was later released under the title "Caution: NC-OSHA Is Dangerous to Your Health." And he found a way—maybe a long shot, but worth a try—to use workers' compensation laws to obtain benefits for brown lung victims. It was time to move from research to organizing.

In Greensboro, Moore found a godsend for the brown lung movement: a retired textile worker and union activist who had testified before a 1968 congressional subcommittee on the establishment of a cotton dust standard. "It's the greatest gift in the world to get a Lacy Wright," said Moore. "First thing he said to me was, 'What we need is an organization.'" And together the inexperienced organizer and the indomitable brown lung victim set out to build one.

Lacy Wright had worked for Cone Mills for forty-four years, until 1966. By then, his lungs functioned at 34 percent of normal capacity. Nobody called it brown lung then. Nobody called it byssinosis. But Wright knew that whatever it was, it was caused by cotton dust. For ten years before his retirement he had tried to persuade Cone to do something about the dust. "They brushed it aside," he said. The cotton dust hearings were no more encouraging.

When he left Cone, Wright told himself, "I'm gonna get me a rocking chair and just rock." He planned to wait with his wife for the angels to find them, caring for each other in their handbuilt log house just north of Greensboro. "There was no compensation at that time," he said. "We didn't know we had any rights until Thad came down and started talking about it."

Wright knew scores of brown lung victims; he took Moore from door to door, the veteran and the novice, Wright talking as only a mill worker can about the dust and the sickness, Moore talking about rights and organizing.

The Wrights' house soon became the unofficial center for brown lung organizing in North Carolina. Moore, with support from other young activists, did the legwork that many of the disabled workers could not. When they were not bedridden or in the hospital, however, the brown lung victims did plenty. They spread the word to their former co-workers. They formed an advisory board that included prominent local lawyers, clergy, and public health officials. They did the arduous, unglamorous, unrecognized work that would one day lead to one of the most effective forces in the labor history of the Carolinas: the Carolina Brown Lung Association (CBLA).

But even before the CBLA took its name, it was a source of tension between the Durham Communists and more moderate activists. Bermanzohn phoned Moore. "He told me that they had made a decision—I didn't know who 'they' were at the time—that brown lung was an important issue to be dealing with. I remember some of us joking, 'Is this a blessing or a curse?' We were conscious of there being liabilities in working with them. The cost was that they would run their political agenda—move people to talking about revolution."

"It's not as though most of us [organizers] wouldn't agree that there's some rotten stuff going on. The whole story of brown lung is a shameful history for corporate America. But for us, the [revolutionary] agenda they ran undermined the focus for organizing. We were painfully aware of how difficult it was to get people together in the first place."

Bermanzohn concedes, "A big part of my interest in the thing was that brown lung is really a disease of capitalism. It's a very preventable disease that's not prevented because it's very unprofitable to prevent." He and Jim Waller had been conducting diabetes screening clinics in Durham, but brown lung offered a unique opportunity to show workers a direct physical connection, and a devastating one at that, between disease and the evils of the capitalist system.

It is not clear who first proposed organizing brown lung screening clinics, but the concept was essential to the success of the movement. "This was in the days when people weren't quite sure the thing was real," said Len Stanley, one of the original brown lung activists. "Certainly studies do not convince workers. And everything they heard from doctors, mostly company doctors, was against this. But it was clear that people were not going to believe that they had brown lung unless a doctor told them so."

Southern textile workers are keenly aware that they are a stereotype in radical circles because of their low wages and the conditions in which they work, that over the years the mills have been perceived as fertile territory for organizing radical movements. They may not be highly educated, but they hate to be manipulated by anybody. This is one of the reasons that Moore, who was from a rural North Carolina working-class background, and Wright did much of the face-to-face organizing. The disabled workers trusted their motives, and if Wright and Moore said that the other occupational health activists were okay, the workers would give them a chance to earn their trust. But it had to be earned.

There was a difference, though, with doctors. Moore described it as "the cult of the doctor," a near-universal attitude that the bearer of a medical degree is somehow above mere humans. Waller and Bermanzohn were eager to help with the screening clinics, and although Moore was leery of the doctors' motivations, he had no choice. No other doctors would donate their services to the clinics.

The first brown lung screening clinic was held on June 10, 1975, at the Hope View Presbyterian Church in Greensboro. Moore remembers Waller, but not Bermanzohn, helping to recruit people for the clinic—volunteers and victims alike. "Jim's work was invaluable," said Stanley. Waller developed a flow plan which efficiently moved scores of people through an initial interview, a breathing test, and a final consultation with a doctor who would interpret the tests. Stanley describes Waller's work as "a model for future brown lung clinics."

But there were problems. After the first clinic, one of the retired workers angrily told Moore that Waller had tried to talk with him about communism. "I remember being very upset about that," said Moore, "because we'd had some talks about that kind of thing with them."

It was a potentially divisive issue for the fledgling organization. The screening clinics were a fundamental part of the brown lung organizing strategy, but if the workers heard that the clinic doctors were going to lecture them on communism, they would stay away in droves. The choice was either to drop the clinic idea altogether or to accept the generosity of the Communist doctors and try to convince them to keep their rhetoric to a minimum. In reality, there was no choice, not if brown lung organizing was to move forward.

Bermanzohn now points proudly to a photograph of himself and Waller with several older people, brown lung victims, under a banner that reads "Carolina Brown Lung Association." "That was the beginning of the Brown Lung Association," says Bermanzohn. That meeting, though, held in Columbia, South Carolina, in the late summer of 1975, was long after Moore and Wright began knocking on doors in Greensboro, and months after the Hope View screening clinic. By the time Bermanzohn and Waller became involved, Moore and other brown lung activists had already raised money to open an office and to pay for legal services, printing, travel, and other essential costs of running an organization.

While quick to praise the doctors' skillful technical assistance and clinical work, brown lung activists remain impassioned about what they perceived as an attempt to take over the movement. "They were more interested in organizing the Communist Party than in helping the Brown Lung Association," said Wright. "They asked me one time if the textile workers would accept communism. I said, 'No, and if I have anything to say about it, they never will.' You couldn't be nice to them. They'd just rag you to death. If I can't sell textile workers on brown lung, how on earth are they gonna sell them on something like communism?"

A leftist herself, Stanley is even more critical. "I feel they're divorced from the reality of other people's lives. Do you raise the cry for revolution the first time people have ever thought about those questions that are part of the whole process in their understanding?"

The brown lung victims knew only that they were sick, that their illness *might* have been caused by cotton dust. For most of them, there was, at most, a vague connection between the disease and a capitalist system that placed profits ahead of people's health. Stanley continued, "Then you skip over the whole process for them because you've 'arrived' and you think if they could only see what you see, ideologically, then they'll be won over. It's a contradiction in Marxist terms: people's understanding comes out of their condition, not out of somebody else's analysis of their condition."

Bermanzohn was invited to the Columbia brown lung meeting as the featured speaker. According to Moore, Bermanzohn abided by their request to keep revolutionary politics out of his speech. The meeting proved to be an intensely moving experience for everyone involved. For Waller, who accompanied Bermanzohn, it was a turning point in his life.

"I never will forget that meeting," said Bermanzohn. "It was like a sea of gray heads. There wasn't a silent breather in the room—a cacophony of noise, coughing and wheezing. But when I started talking about byssinosis all these people started telling stories about their lungs and what happened to their brother and their father. It was like a Bible thing, people getting up and testifying.

"It had a profound effect on Jim. We drove back and the whole way he just kept talking about it."

The brown lung meeting was one of the experiences that eventually led Waller to resign his fellowship in order to get work in the textile mills, in order to organize from within. Although based on an intensely moving personal experience, his decision was purely political.

The brown lung victims saw it differently. Getting compensation for the disabled and forcing the industry to clean up the mills were the only issues for Wright and the Brown Lung Association. They had no room, no time, in their lives for things like socialism or communism or revolution. And they made their feelings known, without qualification, to Bermanzohn and Waller.

"There was a lot of reluctance to allow people to talk about the political origins of the disease, the profit incentive being placed over people's needs," Bermanzohn admitted. "There was a great deal of trepidation. The word *capitalism* always engenders the word *rhetoric*. There was that very heavy concern that we were taking the thing someplace it shouldn't be. The growing political repression was one of the reasons Jim and I left."

For the Communists, the issue was not that the brown lung victims had a tremendous amount of work to do in a very short time; it was not that the disease had consumed them and was now the only thing they had the breath left to fight. The resolve of the victims and organizers to hold fast to their movement and their issues was seen as "political repression."

Another reason that Bermanzohn and Waller left the Brown Lung Association was to focus on the workers who held the power to bring a revolution into being: "active" workers. Not sickly, retired brown lung victims, but young, healthy factory workers. Waller would work from within, getting a job at Cone Mills' Haw River plant. Bermanzohn stuck with his medical work but convinced Marty Arthur to take up the clinic work with the Brown Lung Association and another occupational health effort that Stanley had organized with rubber workers in Fayetteville, North Carolina. Arthur worked reasonably well in the clinics, and although Stanley knew that she was involved with the Communists, she did not reject her assistance out of hand—not until it was too late.

April 1977 was a landmark for the Carolina Brown Lung Association. A delegation from each of the association's six chapters was to go to Washington to testify at hearings to establish cotton dust exposure standards. All of them were in poor health, but their spirit and their faith, they knew, would sustain them. Stanley accompanied the group on the three-day round-trip, as keyed up about the hearings as she was about the campaign she had helped to organize at the Kelly-Springfield tire plant in Fayetteville.

Working closely with Robert Lee, president of the Rubber Workers local at Kelly-Springfield, Stanley found that the rubber workers suffered a respiratory syndrome not unlike brown lung. But the rubber workers had no access to university-sponsored studies to document the cause of their breathing problems, and the company refused to release any information on the chemicals involved in the manufacturing process.

Stanley was cautious and selective about the doctors she approached to work with them on a brown lung–type screening clinic. Marty Arthur was one. They prepared fact sheets on the health effects of working in rubber processing and began to plan the clinics. With volunteers from a spinoff of the brown lung group, the North Carolina Occupational Safety and Health Project (NCOSH), Stanley and Lee set up a planning committee and coordinated the publicity and outreach to bring workers to the first clinic.

Stanley remembers that shortly before the clinic, Arthur told her that the Workers Viewpoint Organization wanted to do a clinic follow-up, to start working with the Rubber Workers on in-plant organizing. "I was very shocked," said Stanley. "That's what we were doing, working with the union on that. You just can't be a doctor at a screening clinic and then take over the organizing effort. Her response was, 'You're empire-building. You can't own every occupational health organizing effort that exists.'"

Stanley thought she had been able to stall Arthur and that the Communists could not move in on the rubber plant organizing without a good fight from the organizers as well as Lee and the union. The clinic went as planned. The union gave the results to the media: fifty out of seventy-five people screened had some level of breathing impairment; it could have something to do with conditions in the plant, with the unknown chemicals used by the workers.

"The company went ape-shit," said Stanley, "trying to discredit the clinic results." In negotiations with Lee and the union, though, Kelly-Springfield began to make overtures, indicating they might give the union the names of the chemicals.

The week after the rubber workers' clinic, Stanley went to Washington with the Brown Lung Association. Sometime during the week, Arthur contacted Lee to set up a follow-up meeting. Lee had no reason to be suspicious; Arthur was, after all, one of the doctors whose work had forced Kelly-Springfield into negotiations. He brought together the plant's shop stewards, workers from a new bargaining unit in the plant, and an international representative of the Rubber Workers Union, all eager to hear what the young doctor had to say. They did not expect to hear Arthur talk about communism, about uniting the working class to overthrow the capitalists and eventually the United States government. But that's what they heard.

Stanley was euphoric when she returned from Washington. "We took over one hundred people to those cotton dust hearings, people who'd never been out of North Carolina. They could feel their strength and their legitimacy for the first time in their lives."

The phone rang. It was Robert Lee. Stanley could barely contain her excitement. "I said, 'Oh, Robert! Did you see it on TV? Are you calling about brown lung …?'

"He said, 'No.'

"'Well, what's up?'

"'Are y'all communists?'

"'What? *What*?' I felt myself draining. He proceeded to tell me the whole story, about Marty calling him and setting up the meeting and him getting everything together.

"He said, 'I can't believe you did this to me. Treat me like I'm stupid and dupe me.'

"It was funny in retrospect because one of the things he said to me was, 'I want to tell you how stupid *she* is. She said that the Russians weren't true communists, only the Chinese were true communists. Anybody with any sense knows the Russians are communist.'

"She even went on about their internal line struggle! I just couldn't believe it. We were in this untenable situation where we had to say, 'We're different. We're the people who've been working with y'all all along. We're in one organization and these other people are in another. But because they're mostly doctors, we had to get them to work at the screening clinic. And then they took over.'

"What he said to me at the end of that conversation was, 'Everything is ruined. We had such a good thing going. We had the company over a barrel;

they were going to give us the names of all the chemicals we were exposed to. The clinic just had them running. And now they've got *me* by the balls. The company called me in and said to drop the suit to find out what chemicals we were working with and they wouldn't let it out that we had communist doctors at the clinic.'

"But of course, it got around. The whole credibility of occupational health was destroyed. A year's worth of work was completely down the drain. Robert was burned incredibly. I felt ridiculous trying to explain the difference between the groups.

"What he said at the very end before he hung up on me was, 'Look, I think I sort of believe you. But it's not going to make any difference to anybody else. The way I've been taught all my life is, you wallow with a dog that's got fleas and you get fleas.'

"And there was nothing else I could say. He was right."

Local 77

When Owusu Sadaukai returned to Durham in 1974 to start a new organizing drive for AFSCME Local 77 at Duke, Sally Avery, Paul Bermanzohn, and Cesar Cauce had just started publishing a newsletter for the Duke workers, *Tell It Like It Is*. To show the necessity for union representation, each issue contained the story of at least one worker who had been unfairly treated by management—fired, demoted, or censured. *Tell It* would win no prizes for design or writing style, but it was, for a time, an effective tool in the organizing campaign.

In 1974, only Duke's campus service workers were represented by Local 77. In addition to reactivating that group, AFSCME sought to bring the maids and cafeteria workers in Duke Hospital into the bargaining unit. Avery and Cauce got jobs in the hospital, Avery as a clerical worker and Cauce as a data terminal operator, in order to organize from within. The task was not easy. To get the National Labor Relations Board (NLRB) to certify an election, the organizers had to get a majority of the hospital's eight hundred service workers to sign cards asking for the election.

By 1975, Local 77 had more than enough cards signed to petition the NLRB for an election. "Our plan was to unionize the eight hundred service workers and then go after clericals and technicians," said Avery. "It was a matter of organizing what we knew we could get and expanding on that."

Duke threw a monkey-wrench into the organizing effort, however. "Duke challenged the union," Avery said. "Their proposal [to NLRB] was to have three thousand in the bargaining unit, including secretaries and administrators. That was more than triple the bargaining unit we had asked for."

The election was delayed for more than a year while the NLRB considered how it should rule in the dispute. In the meantime, Avery and Cauce began using Duke's employee grievance procedures to advocate for nonunionized workers who felt they had been discriminated against or treated unfairly on the job. "That was our contribution to the union," said Avery. "We mastered the Duke grievance procedure and used it. We took them [workers] through the channels and were winning."

During the year it took the NLRB to make a decision on the Duke elections, though, *Tell It* became more of a communist propaganda tool than a forum for workers' grievances. It expounded on issues such as the Carter and Ford presidential race, capitalism in the Soviet Union, imperialism in Angola, and the rise of fascism in the U.S.[4] These were no doubt important issues, but hardly relevant to a Duke hospital cafeteria worker who wanted to know whether a union would make a real difference in the workplace.

Then came the polemics between the Revolutionary Workers League and the Workers Viewpoint Organization. Owusu Sadaukai left, and with him went the determination to work cooperatively with the white Communists on the union effort. RWL members who sat with Avery and Cauce on the union organizing committee put out leaflets accusing the whites of racism, of working in league with Duke management. They accused Bermanzohn of being an undercover agent. Finally, they purged Avery and Cauce from the organizing committee.[5]

The NLRB made its decision in September 1976: the bargaining unit was to include two thousand workers—clerical and laboratory workers in addition to the service workers.[6] The election was scheduled for November.

What happened next stunned Durham's noncommunist union leaders and supporters. The warring Communist groups began to leaflet Duke workers with single-spaced, legal-sized diatribes criticizing each other's political line and accusing each other of working in Duke's interest. This was within weeks of the union election, the culmination of two years of difficult, frustrating, and exhausting work to win union representation and bargaining rights for the hospital workers. When the vote was taken, Local 77 lost by thirty votes.[7]

Union elections are rarely won by wide margins. Five percent one way or the other is all it takes to make or break a union drive. C. P. Ellis, business agent for Duke's unionized maintenance workers, had worked very closely with Sadaukai, Avery, and Cauce on the Local 77 drive. He praises their union support work, their energy and determination. But Ellis, like everyone but the Communists themselves, blames the election defeat on the eleventh-hour injection of a struggle over the Communist line into the debate. Duke management was just waiting to spring its union-busting trap, and the Communists walked right into it.

Communists on the organizing committee; black Communists fighting white Communists. It did not take much to derail the unionization drive. "The old business of divide and conquer was used," said Ellis. "And they were successful. Most of the people who work at Duke are middle-of-the-roaders—a little bit to the right, maybe some liberals. They [the Communists] were divisive. And in my opinion, they helped defeat that election."

The Textile Workers Union

Throughout the hectic summer and fall of 1976, personal and political relationships among the Durham and Greensboro Communists took dramatic turns. Paul Bermanzohn and Sally Avery got married. "We had worked together for a long time, grew up politically together and wanted the same things," Bermanzohn said. "And then we realized, what are we looking for? This was a good shot, at least. We had a very compatible kind of deal here."

Mike Nathan and Marty Arthur were living together and would soon move to Charlottesville, Virginia, where Arthur completed her medical training at the University of Virginia. Both became active in procuring medical supplies to send to revolutionary forces in southern Africa, an effort that they continued after they got married and returned to Durham in 1978.

Things did not go so well for Sandi and Mark Smith. They chose to stay with the Revolutionary Workers League rather than join the Workers Viewpoint Organization with Nelson and Joyce Johnson. But then Mark Smith was purged from the RWL; Sandi quit soon after, and both of them dropped out of political work. Their marriage was suffering, and for a while they separated. A friendship suffered, too. Joyce Johnson, who considered Sandi Smith her best friend, said later, "My friendship with Sandi ended when RWL disintegrated. I gave up on her when she pulled back on things."[8]

The friendship was not lost, however. When the Greensboro and Durham Communists merged with the Workers Viewpoint Organization in December 1976, Jerry Tung instructed the new comrades that they were not to desert those who temporarily left the road forward. They were to be pursued for recruitment.[9]

"Sandi was always a reasonable person," said Nelson Johnson, "but her early political involvement was more activist than it was political training.

She would tend to get swayed to this side or that. Anchoring—how to look at a situation and size it up so you're not tossed from one discussion to another—involves some serious and substantial study which we undertook with her and her husband Mark. They came to agree with our point of view and joined the WVO."

By the end of 1976, Nelson Johnson had quit his job at Cone to work as a full-time organizer for the WVO. Jim Waller, on the other hand, got a job at Cone's Haw River plant, as did several other WVO members and supporters. Their mission was to organize, to agitate against the bourgeois capitalists, to recruit workers to the revolutionary struggle. The springboard for their drive was the union; then known as the Textile Workers Union of America, it merged with another union to become the Amalgamated Clothing and Textile Workers Union (ACTWU) in 1976.

Cone Mills and the Textile Workers Union were an especially easy target for the Communist organizers. Although workers in the larger plants were unionized on paper, the union was virtually impotent.[10] For more than twenty years, Cone had held the union to a near-paralyzing contract clause—the waiver of the right to a dues check-off—that was the by-product of a union schism in 1952.

Without a check-off, in which union dues are automatically deducted from workers' paychecks, the rival union had no way to ensure collection of the funds to run the organization and provide benefits for the workers. It soon floundered, and two years after the split its members voted to rejoin the Textile Workers. But the damage had been done. Cone refused to renegotiate the contract to include dues check-off.

U.S. labor law mandates that unions grant full protection and benefits to every worker in a collective bargaining unit, whether or not all the workers pay their dues or are even members of the union. Failure to enforce contract rights for just one worker in one plant can result in federal prosecution, not only of the local union officers but of the national or international union itself. Thus, union officials are very cautious about launching organizing campaigns in plants where worker support is too thin to fulfill the federal legal requirement of contract enforcement.

Even in plants in which union locals existed, the union had to monitor the situation closely. The Textile Workers allowed several locals to become defunct rather than jeopardize the entire union for a handful of inactive members in what were essentially nonunion shops. Revolution was one such plant. Sandi Smith and several other WVO members formed an organizing committee in an attempt to get enough worker support to petition for a new union election.

There were Textile Workers Union locals at Haw River, where Waller went, and at Greensboro's White Oak plant, where a majority of WVO's organizers got jobs, but the union leadership had no illusions about what the Communists were up to. Throughout the period from late 1975 to early 1977, as their numbers grew, the Communists at Cone increased their militant rhetoric against the union "misleaders." Julius Fry, then manager of the union's Central North Carolina Joint Board, was frustrated by the Communist strategy. "I oughtn't give a damn about who organizes Cone—whether they're Maoists or whatever—if people could get a good union going. But I became convinced that the goal was not to have a union; it was to have their own organization.

"I told one of them one time over at White Oak, I said, 'I don't give a damn about your philosophy. But when you come in and act as if the union is the enemy, the union may have its place but only as a stepping stone for some other group, hell, I can't sit idly by with all that going on."

With no dues check-off at Cone, it was fairly simple for the Communists to take over union locals. Said Fry, "They would pay their dues religiously so they would be qualified to meet and vote. A lot of people got disgusted with what was going on and they'd just move on. That left only them in the voting group."

It was a no-win situation for the old-line union leadership. If they criticized the WVO's tactics, the Communists used the criticisms as examples of the "misleaders'" corruption. The old guard, the militants charged, had allowed the union to wither to nothing.[11] The new militant members, on the other hand, were the ones who filed grievances and got scores of workers to sign union cards. The criticism of the militants by the union leaders was only proof that the "misleaders" did not really want strong locals, that they were in league with Cone management.

By far the majority of union members and workers were opposed to the revolutionary direction the Cone locals were taking. Some dropped out of the union in disgust; others stayed to fight. A minority were drawn to the militants.

One of the most alluring WVO organizers at White Oak was a strikingly handsome former Harvard divinity student who later left medical school to work at Cone. His name was Bill Sampson.

William Evan Sampson. Textile Worker, Cone Mills, Greensboro, North Carolina. Beloved husband of Dale Deering Sampson. Member, Communist Workers Party. Died Saturday, November 3, 1979.

At the time he went to Cone in 1977, Bill Sampson had seen more, studied more, done more than most people accomplish in a lifetime.[12] In college,

Metamorphosis

Bill Sampson (Courtesy of Jim Waters, WFMY-TV, Greensboro)

Sampson spent a year at the Sorbonne and on his return was elected Phi Beta Kappa. As a Harvard divinity student, Sampson began an intensive study of communism. He joined the October League, a New Communist rival of the WVO's, and entered medical school at the University of Virginia in Charlottesville. In the fall of 1976, Jerry Tung engaged in polemics with the October League. Sampson was in the audience. He renounced the league shortly thereafter.

By the summer of 1977, Sampson had dropped out of medical school, joined the WVO, and married Dale Deering, a Winston-Salem social worker he had introduced to communism. They both got jobs at Cone's White Oak plant to assist the WVO's organizing effort. Like a magnet, Sampson's work at Cone drew some people to him and repelled others. Those who were drawn to him are passionate in their praise for his work and for his kindness and dedication.

Rand Manzella considered Sampson his best friend. They met on Manzella's first day at work in White Oak's dye house. Sampson saw that the new worker was having difficulty maneuvering the two-hundred-pound bags of thread, or warp, and he took it upon himself to show Manzella how to move and break the huge bags. "He was the kindest person I have ever met," said Manzella. "He would work very hard helping people. He did this every day and never got tired of it."

Sampson recruited Manzella to the union and began talking to him about communism. "I always try to keep an open mind," Manzella explained. "I grew up in the projects and learned things aren't always what they seem to be. At first I was a little shocked, but I wasn't sure what a communist was. So I asked him. He said a communist thought the system should be run by the common person—that's what he was doing, that's what he was all about."

Bill Johnson is another Cone worker, then a fifteen-year veteran, who was attracted to Sampson and the WVO by their loyalty to their friends, their eagerness to take up workplace issues, and their labor philosophy. Simply and emphatically, Johnson says, "The workers should share the harvest." Johnson found that as a shop steward, Sampson "would come to the rescue in a minute." And not only in the plant. "If there was some work you needed to do on your house," he said, "just call them and you'd have a half dozen of them there in half an hour. They were the most humanitarian people I ever met in my life."

For Johnson, Manzella, and other Cone workers associated with the WVO, the Communists' generosity had no limits. If there was a need—whether to harvest a tobacco crop, serve as pall-bearers at a funeral, or treat a sick child—they would find the volunteers necessary to accomplish the task.

There seemed to be an almost schizophrenic aspect to the way the Communists dealt with other people and organizations, however. They immediately grasped the needs of those they considered allies and went all out to fulfill them, but they would not give an inch to those they considered adversaries. They would not listen to their concerns or compromise in any way. They were, in Nelson Johnson's words, "anchored"—firmly wedged in an intractable ideology that simultaneously fed their illusions about their strength and impact and closed them off from outside criticism.

To Lacy Wright, a lifetime member of the Textile Workers Union, the WVO "like to destroyed the union here. I went over to the Sunday meetings. You couldn't conduct a meeting to save your life. One would get up and talk and talk, then another and another. I told them one Sunday all they were doing was using the democratic process to destroy an organization and make dictators out of those at the head."

The WVO was also not above manipulating those they privately scorned in order to gain credibility for themselves. Wright recalls one such incident with great bitterness. After months of low-profile organizing, Sandi Smith was ready to announce the formation of the Revolution Organizing Committee at Cone Mills. But she needed a drawing card, something that would attract workers who might otherwise not be interested in a meeting of the plant militants. Smith approached Wright, asking that he tape record a statement about brown lung which could be played for the workers at the organizing committee meeting.

"I was very skeptical," said Wright. He did not want any link between the Brown Lung Association and the Communist organizing group, but he was determined to get the word about brown lung to any textile worker who would listen. "I told her I'd make a tape telling what brown lung is, how it affects you. Then they took the tape to the conference and said the Brown Lung Association was backing the conference."

Such tactics did not go unnoticed among North Carolina's left-wing activists. Although they shared many of the same ideals—racial equality, workers' rights, and the need for radical social change in America—they were appalled and angered at the damage the WVO did to the organizations it exploited. Many of the noncommunist leftists refused to have anything more to do with anyone associated with the WVO.

The Communists refused to see their political isolation for what it was. Just as they viewed their destructiveness, in Maoist terms, as construction, they saw the leftists' refusal to work with them as proof that the "reformists" were as politically and morally bankrupt as the bourgeoisie. From the Communists' perspective, the reformists deserted them not because they were doing lousy work that was a discredit to all leftists but because the reformists were anticommunist—a label that left-wingers find almost as repugnant as "racist."

The WVO members dismissed the criticisms of people like Len Stanley who had once been their allies and focused instead on the near-adoration of new recruits like Rand Manzella and Bill Johnson. That they had pampered the Cone workers and nailed Stanley and the Rubber Workers to the wall seemed immaterial. The praise was legitimate; the condemnation was not.

As the WVO's political isolation increased, so did its internal unity. Comrades became matchmakers, identifying likely candidates for marriage and encouraging their relationships. One such pair was Jim Waller and Signe Burke Goldstein.

Goldstein came to Greensboro in 1970 with her husband Carl and their two children. Both Goldsteins had been asked to leave university teaching positions because of their outspoken criticism of the Vietnam War. That was not the reason they were given, of course, but Signe Goldstein believes it is true.

When Carl was offered an art history professorship at the University of North Carolina at Greensboro, Signe decided to devote her time to antiwar work. With a few dollars and volunteers from the American Friends Service Committee and a local peace vigil group, Goldstein got reams of literature, a decrepit mimeograph machine, and a rundown storefront. The Greensboro Peace Center was born.

When the Peace Center folded in 1974, Signe was hired as a philosophy professor at Bennett College. She exposed her students to the Marxist classics and held study groups at her home in the evenings, as she had with Peace

Center volunteers. Among the writings she studied was the *Workers Viewpoint Journal*. "Studying made things clear," she said, "especially the WVO. I was impressed with their seriousness and the *Workers Viewpoint Journal* clarified complex issues."

Bennett was not pleased with Goldstein's injection of communist politics into the classroom, and in 1976 they asked her to resign. Her marriage disintegrated at about the same time. It was a difficult period personally and professionally, but politically it was the end of a long search. Goldstein heard Jerry Tung at the WVO-RWL polemics. That was, she said, "the turning point. I didn't have any question after that meeting that the WVO was the organization to move forward with the correct line."

Although not a member of the WVO, Goldstein got a job at Cone Mills to further develop her political commitment. She continued to study, and she wrote constantly in phraseology that is almost a primer of communist rhetoric. One essay proved to be the catalyst for the relationship between her and Waller, whom she had not met at the time it was written in early 1977. "On Bourgeois Love" read in part:

> A proletarian in personal relationships has no room for dishonesty. This is because its [the proletarian's] principal aspect is political unity, not self-interest, but also because it can fearlessly use the method of criticism and self-criticism to resolve contradictions and rectify errors. It has no need to maneuver. The bourgeoisie must constantly maneuver so as to conceal its actual aims and its lack of method for resolving contradictions. I think it is important to attack this particular screen which is intended to hide the utter bankruptcy of the bourgeoisie. . . .
>
> The point about honesty is not whether what we put out accords with our subjective and arbitrary reconstruction of "reality." It is whether it accords with objective reality. And it is impossible for the bourgeois to put out lines which accord with objective reality. Therefore, DISHONESTY IS A CLASS TRAIT. Those bourgeois who pride themselves on being honest are deceiving themselves about this too. They are dishonest in putting out their "honesty." They could only become honest by breaking with bourgeois ideology.[13]

For all its punishing prose and convoluted reasoning, "On Bourgeois Love" exemplifies the use of propaganda—whether for war, revolution, or religious fanaticism—simultaneously to give heroic character to the allies and dehumanize the enemy. Paul Bermanzohn said it more succinctly: "Love for the people had to include hatred of the oppressor."

Signe Goldstein shared "On Bourgeois Love" with friends in WVO circles. One of them gave a copy to Waller. Other friends, said Goldstein, "noted the similarities in our situations and life experiences. We were introduced and set up for a romance by our comrades."[14]

Metamorphosis 67

By the summer of 1977, Waller and Goldstein were talking marriage. They went to Chicago to introduce her to the Waller family. She later wrote, "Jim and I sat on the grass at the edge of Grant Park and discussed our future together. For a long time after we met he wouldn't tell me whether he was in the party or not. I didn't know for sure. But another comrade struggled [argued the point] with him that if I was going to think about marrying him, I had a right to know that. So after quite a bit of struggle he agreed to tell me—he was. He talked about future possibilities. We might be separated for periods of time. He could get an assignment and we would have to go anywhere. He made it seem to me at the time that I didn't count at all and some impersonal force, and not his love for me, would be controlling our destiny."[15]

Destiny for the WVO in North Carolina was laid out in an internal memo in the late fall of 1977. Titled "Plans for the Textile Industry," the memo told comrades of a program which would be carried out by 1979. It was not so much a textile industry campaign as it was a plan to take over textile organizing from ACTWU. The WVO was to "push ACTWU to take up a united front on right-to-work laws." They planned to have enough support in the mills to "prepare for a strike over contracts." They would win elections in union locals and on the union's decision-making Joint Board. A "Workers Center" would be established, a militant alternative to union halls.[16]

While the WVO publicly berated ACTWU for its weakness and corruption, it looked on the union's nationally organized J. P. Stevens boycott as a plum just waiting to be picked. In two years, the comrades were told, the WVO was to "be in the leadership of the J. P. Stevens boycott locally, statewide and perhaps nationally." The final point of the memo said that the WVO would be "in a position to force a united front with ACTWU to unleash a large campaign to organize the industry with TUEL in the lead."

TUEL is the acronym for the Trade Union Education League, an organization that did not officially come into being until one year after the memo was written.[17] Conceived at a WVO conference in September 1977, TUEL was to become a front group to which the Communists would recruit "advanced" workers, those who were not turned off by talk of revolution. Their presence would lend credibility to the promotion of TUEL as a caucus organized by workers from a number of unions, an essential part of the WVO's organizing strategy. "Make Systematic Preparation for the Dictatorship of the Proletariat. Build the TUEL," was the WVO's slogan. TUEL's purpose was to increase the WVO's legitimacy with the working class and to win new members to the party. Jerry Tung warned in 1978, "If the Party does not work in the TUEL in the correct way, TUEL chapters will sooner or later become autonomous."[18] But TUEL's power was to rest securely in the control of the WVO. Waller would become its national president; Sally Bermanzohn, its North Carolina president; and Bill Sampson, president of the Greensboro group.[19]

Although unaware of TUEL, the regional and national union leadership looked on the Cone situation with increasing urgency. Under the union contract, they were required to give full representation on all grievances filed by locals, whether or not the person affected was a union member. The WVO militants in the mills had, indeed, filed a barrage of complaints against Cone—some of which were valid, some of which were not. The union had to take them all, and the small amount of dues being collected at Cone did not come close to covering the costs.

The WVO was also using its members' election to union positions as a way to lend credibility to its more militant work. A Revolution Organizing Committee meeting, for example, would draw quite a few more people if the featured speaker was listed as a White Oak shop steward rather than as a member of the Workers Viewpoint Organization. It was unfair, exploitive, and hypocritical, especially in light of the WVO's attitude toward the mainline union. But the regional and national leadership was loathe to use the one tool that would allow them to restructure the locals and regain control: administratorship. It meant that the national would take control of the local's activities and suspend elections in the local. The union would use it only if the local became a threat to the union itself.[20]

Waller had worked at Cone's Haw River plant for nearly two years in mid-1978. Things were going very well: he and Signe had married early in the year; he had been elected shop steward, vice-president of his union local, and representative to the wage-negotiating committee for all five Cone locals. When he began at Cone, Waller worked in the dye house, the poorest-paid and least organized department in the plant. After several months, he got a transfer to the cutting room where grooves are cut into corduroy. The cutters were the most highly paid as well as the most unionized. Still, out of five hundred Haw River workers in the union's bargaining unit, less than 10 percent were active, dues-paying members.[21]

From the day he walked through the plant gates, Waller was outspoken about his revolutionary beliefs. That did not endear him to his co-workers or the weak union local. Like Bill Sampson at White Oak and Sandi Smith at Revolution, however, he proved to be a hard worker and a fierce advocate for the employees. He, too, went out of his way to help co-workers, whether on or off the job. They could not help liking him. They called him "Blackbeard."

The spring of 1978 brought Waller's first opportunity to serve on the union negotiating committee. It was time for the annual wage negotiations for Cone's five unionized plants in the Greensboro area. ACTWU's Julius Fry remembers the situation well. "Waller said that at Haw River the company didn't want to raise everybody's wages. They wanted to leave out certain ones, especially in the cutting room where he was working. When we got into negotiations, the company didn't make any such proposal."

What Cone offered was a small across-the-board increase at all five plants. ACTWU negotiated a settlement that was agreed to by all but one of the plants—Haw River. Instead, at Waller's instigation, the cutters who dominated the union local voted to strike. A strike was a key component of the WVO's strategy, Waller wrote later, to be used legally, as the Haw River strike was, or illegally "to smash the bourgeois democratic illusions of the masses."[22]

ACTWU gave union recognition to the strike because it was based on one of the few exemptions to the no-strike clause in Cone's contract: wages.[23] The strike lasted two weeks, with WVO members from Greensboro and Durham walking the picket line as they had at several other strikes that year. With Waller, they were able to increase the union local's membership, its dues-paying membership, to one hundred.

Then Cone announced that they would begin hiring permanent replacements for the striking workers. They made a final offer: if workers accepted the wage increase given to the other plants and came back to their jobs, the company would not start replacing. Most of the strikers left the line and went back into the plant. They knew that Cone was within its legal rights and that they would lose their jobs if they did not go back—jobs they could not afford to lose. Eventually all the strikers, including Waller, accepted Cone's terms and returned to work. Following the strike, when it came time to pay dues, union membership at Haw River fell back to less than fifty.[24]

It didn't take Cone long to find a reason to fire Waller. He had falsified his job application, neglecting to tell the employment office that he was a physician. ACTWU handled his arbitration, and during the lengthy legal process, Waller ran for president of his union local. As a discharged worker with a grievance pending, he had a legal right to do so. It was also a shrewd propaganda tool. Waller had been fired by Cone, the WVO maintained, but he had drawn so much support for his militant organizing that the workers elected him president anyway. They neglected to mention that Waller's election was a given. He was the only candidate.[25]

ACTWU was getting uneasy. The five Cone locals were as weak as they had ever been. Sampson at White Oak and Waller at Haw River had been able to generate brief flurries of union activity, but ACTWU needed to maintain a strong level of dues-paying membership in order to enforce the terms of the Cone contract. Thirty-five or forty out of two thousand workers, the average union membership at White Oak throughout 1977 and 1978, was not strong by anyone's standards. And some of the Cone locals were worse off than White Oak, lacking enough members to elect officers. Without officers, shop stewards, or grievance committees in those plants, the union was in very real danger of being sued for failure to adequately represent the workers.

There was also the matter of the Communists. If ACTWU officials had no direct proof that the WVO was manipulating the Cone locals in order to recruit workers to the party, they could be fairly certain that was what was happening. In its own memos, the WVO was clear about its motives. Waller wrote in 1979, "The reason we work in trade unions is to win and train the advanced to the Party one by one."[26]

Traditionally, organized labor has considered the union to be a goal unto itself, an organization that advocates for people who are otherwise unrepresented. Forces within a union that attempt to sway it from its mandate are as much a threat to the union, and thus the workers, as a team of corporate union busters. For Waller and the WVO, however, the unions were secondary to building the party. Trade union "misleaders" like Fry, "social props of the bourgeoisie," were to be "isolated and kicked out of the trade unions." The WVO would build independent unions and "cut angles to continue communist work under any circumstances."[27]

Their perception that the WVO was attempting to use the union for its own purposes led ACTWU officials to take over the administration of the Cone locals in January 1979.[28] For the purposes of the WVO and its propaganda, the timing could not have been better. Bill Sampson was running for president of the White Oak local; Waller was at Haw River. Under the administratorship, all elections were suspended. Noncommunist union members were confused and angry. "Members should have a right to vote for their leadership," said Bill Johnson. "This local should be *our* business."

The WVO leapt into the void. The administratorship was proof, they said, that Cone had ACTWU in its hip pocket, proof that the capitalists and the sellout union bureaucrats were in mortal fear of strong Communist union leadership. "Now's the time to seize the time," was the Communists' slogan. Time to organize the workers into an independent trade union under the militant leadership of the Trade Union Education League.

In the next few months, the WVO's actions in the mills as well as on the street would reflect the instructions of General Secretary Jerry Tung, who told the comrades of "the need to make thorough and systematic preparation for the dictatorship of the proletariat. And we must take it up with the 'unmerciful thoroughness' that Marx spoke of. Sole reliance on the legal forms without preparation for the illegal, violent forms will lead to serious setbacks."[29]

Tung's words were not set forth in an eyes-only document; they were spoken at a public rally—monitored, presumably, by agents of the government the WVO sought to overthrow.

"It's a whole level of contradictions," Howard Fuller said later, "that can only be explained by the fact that they really didn't understand reality: Talking about taking over the state and not realizing that, hey, if this is what you're really talking about, you better be ready for some serious reaction."

The WVO was not ready. That Tung would utter those words in public shows a tremendous sociopolitical dysfunction, a pattern of political organizing which drew its members into ever-tightening circles, distorting their view of themselves as well as of the outside world. For the party member, Hannah Arendt wrote in 1954, the world is divided into three camps: friends, foes, and "secret allies who merely cannot, as yet, summon up the necessary strength of mind and character to draw the logical conclusion from their own convictions."[30]

The delusion that swarms of secret allies wait only for the right campaign, the right issue, to stir their suppressed revolutionary tendencies led the WVO to shed all illusions of moderation in order to show a concrete definition between themselves and the corrupt bourgeois capitalists and reformists.[31] "They are," Arendt wrote, "so well protected against the reality of the non-totalitarian world that they constantly underestimate the tremendous risks of totalitarian politics."[32]

Arendt's theory was echoed by Richard Hofstadter in an almost haunting prediction: "The sidewalk Sorels who preach violence know very little about it, and sometimes prove pitifully ineffective in trying to use it. . . . The new prophets of violence are almost certain to become its victims . . . especially when their own romanticism carries them from word to deed."[33]

Part 2

Escalation

Chapter 5

> "It's not just a matter of sitting around singing songs like 'Pop Pop, Bam Bam, There Goes Another Nigger,' like the Klan does. We're more than that . . . much more."
> —Harold A. Covington, National Socialist Party of America

Testing the First Amendment

In 1977 and 1978, fascism appeared to be on the rise, as the Communists had predicted it would. And, again true to Communist predictions, reformists—the American Civil Liberties Union—appeared to promote the fascists through unqualified support for their First Amendment rights. To top it off, the news media, "puppets of the bourgeoisie," exhibited a morbid but unquestioning fascination for the publicity-hungry few who wore swastikas or pointy-hooded robes.

Frank Collin and his National Socialist Party of America were among the most notable beneficiaries of the publicity generated by the debate over free speech. In 1977, using the Chicago ACLU as a battering ram, Collin challenged the city's denial of a permit for him and his motley crew to demonstrate in Marquette Park.[1] While waiting on that one, Collin decided to apply for permits in some of the suburbs. Wisely, most of them ignored his letters of request, hoping the Nazi would simply forget about the whole thing or go somewhere else.[2]

One suburb did not, and perhaps could not, ignore Collin's request. The Village of Skokie, a predominantly Jewish town with a large population of Nazi Holocaust survivors, filed for a court injunction to prohibit Hitler's American progeny from ever setting foot inside the village limits. Seeing the publicity bonanza ahead, Collin went straight to the ACLU.[3]

The fall months of 1977 were also good times for Harold Covington. Between the end of August, when he announced his candidacy for Raleigh's city council, and the end of the year, the Raleigh newspapers alone had published more than a dozen articles about the twenty-three-year-old candidate

75

and his Nazi Party.[4] Even Collin had not been so successful in getting his political views aired in the media. Covington decided to run again, this time in the Republican primary for the state Senate. He did not like the Republicans any more than they liked him, but it got his name on the ballot and back in the news.[5]

Covington demonstrates well the differences between the Nazis and the Klan. Politically sophisticated and well-read, he studied not only fascist theory and history but also that of communism as well. He learned to milk the media. Unlike Virgil Griffin, Covington could articulate his positions, as repulsive as they were, like an old-fashioned orator. He was intriguing because he was so atypical of the down-and-out, ignorant Klan-type bigot.

Covington grew up in a moderately affluent family in Burlington, North Carolina, where he apparently had little contact with blacks. That changed when his family moved to Chapel Hill and he entered the town's large, integrated high school. Newcomers to almost any high school in the country are often subjected to teasing, sometimes harassment, from school bullies. And the paunchy, bespectacled, outspoken Harold Covington was no exception. "I have never been able to keep my mouth shut," Covington told a *Charlotte Observer* reporter in 1981.[6] "When I see something I don't like I just have to get up and say so, loudly and publicly."

What Covington saw, he claimed, were blacks "terrorizing and intimidating the whites." By his sophomore year, he considered himself the "school fascist." Some of the blacks responded with a vengeance. "Five of them attacked me in the bathroom. Somebody had left a Pepsi bottle on top of one of the urinals and I took it down. I was ready to die fighting. Well, I hit [one] and the other four ran out. And all of a sudden there I was standing alone in the bathroom with this bloody Pepsi bottle in my hand and I said, 'Goddamn, what do you know? They're not so tough after all!'"

Covington began reading about national socialism, and soon after graduating from high school joined the National Socialist White People's Party, which he claims sent him to South Africa in 1974. When he returned to the States, he switched his allegiance to the Chicago-based National Socialist Party of America.

Although based on similar ideologies, Klan and Nazi ideas about activism are very different. While Klans like Griffin's most often isolated themselves from the political world, Covington and his Nazis were decidedly revolutionary. Like a fraternal organization, the Klans rarely had any goals beyond increasing membership and getting publicity. The Nazis, on the other hand, sought to establish national socialism as the government of the United States. While most Klan members would at least give lip service to the rights of racial and religious minorities, Covington and the Nazis made no such concessions. The national socialist revolution would transform the United States into an Aryan nation—all minorities and "undesirables" would be deported.[7]

Despite their differences, the Klans and Nazis were identical in two ways: they were, for the most part, socially and politically impotent, and the only tool they had for disguising their impotence was terror. The robes, the swastikas, the vile rhetoric, and the aggression were targeted at those who had historical reasons to fear them. It was a cowardly power play, but it often worked.

In January 1978, the Illinois Supreme Court denied the Village of Skokie's injunction against Collin and the Nazis.[8] Skokie appealed to the federal courts, and the controversy became a national debate. Collin gloated at the distress he had caused among the nation's Holocaust survivors. He had struck a raw nerve in the people he most despised, and now he could just sit back and enjoy their agony while the ACLU and the court probed the limits of the First Amendment.

Harold Covington's campaign for state senate did not draw the media attention his previous campaign had, but it did force the local Republican Party to mail letters to its 15,000 registered voters urging those who might not have noticed that a Nazi was running on their ticket not to vote for Covington.[9] Still, he managed to get 885 out of 7,000 votes cast.[10]

Within a matter of weeks, Covington's name was back in the news. The Seventh Circuit Court of Appeals ruled in May that ordinances enacted by Skokie to ban the Nazi rally were unconstitutional. Collin immediately announced that he and his troops would march in Skokie on June 25. He then went to Raleigh, where he sought Covington's help in recruiting North Carolina Nazis for the event.[11] In less than a year, Covington had wormed his way into the national Nazi leadership. He would stand side by side with Collin, taunting the Jews of Skokie and the world. It was his chance to grab some of the national media spotlight. And it would give him an opening to grab power one day from Collin.

Covington, Collin, and a handful of their brownshirted followers did hold a rally, but it was not in Skokie. Two negotiators from the Justice Department's Civil Rights Division succeeded in persuading Collin that it was too dangerous to go to Skokie. Angry and perhaps violent counterdemonstrators planned to mass in the village, and there was no way the police could guarantee the Nazis' safety. Collin was not known for his bravery, and he had gotten what he wanted out of the Skokie controversy anyway. When the negotiators suggested an alternative—the plaza of the Federal Building in Chicago on June 24—Collin took it.[12]

On that day, Collin, Covington, and a few supporters were driven from Nazi headquarters in a police van. They walked through a police cordon to the plaza, where they were greeted by several thousand jeering, booing counter-demonstrators. They tried for fifteen minutes to speak over a portable public address system, but the booing never let up enough for the first word to be heard. The Nazis left the plaza the same way they had arrived—through the cordon to the police van and back to their headquarters.[13] It was not the scene Covington had envisioned.

The Skokie case did, however, cause some new interest in the North Carolina Nazis. Among the curious was a trio of Winston-Salem racists who were associated with a small local Klan: Wayne Wood, Milano Caudle, and Jack Fowler. Covington privately ridiculed the Klan; for him, they were, for the most part, Neanderthal types whose racism was knee-jerk rather then intellectual, like his. But he saw their potential value to the national socialist revolution: the Nazis would provide the brains; the Klan would provide the brawn.[14] He began courting Wood and his pals for the Nazi movement.

The Skokie controversy had repercussions beyond the Nazis. For the Workers Viewpoint Organization, the case was proof positive of one of their fundamental maxims: the constitutional guarantees of free speech, free press, and free association were mere illusions of democracy. When push came to shove, as it had in Skokie, the reformist ACLU used the bourgeois-controlled courts to give legal rights and world attention to a minuscule band of fascists. "Reformists promote fascism," the WVO said. "Reformists are a greater threat than the bourgeoisie." And, for those who could not or would not see the Skokie case as a victory for the First Amendment rather than the Nazis, it looked as though the Communists were right. The WVO prepared to deal with fascism in its own way.

Storm Clouds Gathering

Spring in Greensboro is a magical time of crocuses, redbuds, dogwood, and the GGO—the Greater Greensboro Open. In many ways the golf tournament typifies the image of Greensboro the city's leaders would like to see projected. Golf is a game of rules and boundaries, a game of affluence played on lush greens and fairways that never lack the proper care or nourishment. Network coverage of the GGO is Greensboro's annual telethon to promote its beauty and civility to a national audience.

In 1979, however, as the first crocus sent its first green shoot toward the warm late-February sun, the first in a series of changes in the rules of fair play began to occur, changes that would have a profound impact on Greensboro's clean-cut, fair-minded image.

The Klan was on the rise, as the WVO had predicted it would be. In times of economic stress, the Communists maintain, the monopoly capitalists promote the Klan and racism through their pawns in the news media in order to divide black and white workers and prevent the mass organizing that would topple the capitalist system and install the dictatorship of the proletariat.[15]

Sure enough, early 1979 saw a spate of articles and television reports on the upsurge of the Klan throughout the South. Some were important news stories; many focused on face-to-face confrontations—usually shouting matches—between Klanspeople and anti-Klan groups. Too often, though, the media used Klan stories as fluff pieces: interviews with self-proclaimed Klan leaders, complete with high-contrast photos of white-robed figures illuminated by a fiery cross against a pitch-black sky.

It was high drama, the kind of stuff that increases ratings and sales. So what if the local Klan leader could muster no more than a dozen card-carrying members? He dressed in an outrageous outfit and said outrageous things; he could draw a crowd.

It was pure hype and the Klan loved it. In the eyes of the media—and therefore the nation—they were no longer a Mickey Mouse, rag-tag band of social misfits. With their new media-supplied legitimacy, North Carolina's Klan and Nazis grew bolder in early 1979. And, in a strategy that would escalate throughout the summer, North Carolina Communists prepared to confront their racist enemies.

In February, the Federated Knights of the Ku Klux Klan announced that they would hold a one-day "historical" Klan exhibit at the Forsyth County Library in Winston-Salem. The outcry came quickly, and it was not just local. The Richmond-based Anti-Defamation League criticized the library board's liberal interpretation of its open-use policy, saying the board should "exercise discretion and good sense in determining the kind of public display exhibited on public property and supported from taxpayers' funds." A local NAACP leader said his group might send pickets to the exhibit if the library board refused to withdraw permission for the Klan's use of the facility. The board took no action.[16]

Neither the NAACP nor the Anti-Defamation League showed up for the exhibit. But two militant antiracist groups did: the Jewish Defense League and the Revolutionary Communist Party. There was a lot of shouting and threatening, but the Winston-Salem police quickly separated the groups and quelled the disturbance. There were no injuries and no arrests.

In the week before the library confrontation, Joe Grady, the Federated

Knights' grand dragon, announced that if protesters came to the library exhibit, he would "call in rednecks from all over the country" for a "right wing convention" at Winston-Salem's Benton Convention Center.[17] Grady later announced that the convention would be held in April, the first in a series of state-wide Klan recruitment efforts that would feature the first, last, and only pro-Klan propaganda film, D. W. Griffith's *Birth of a Nation*. Again, antiracist groups made their opposition known, and again the facility management refused to back down. Because of limited access to the center and the presence of scores of police, no confrontation like the one at the library occurred at the convention center meeting.

A month later, however, in Decatur, Alabama, a confrontation between antiracist demonstrators and a Klan group had disastrous results. The Southern Christian Leadership Conference (SCLC) had organized a march to protest the conviction of a retarded black man accused of raping a white woman. The man's retardation was so severe, the SCLC maintained, that he was incapable of driving the car in which the women said he had abducted her.

A hundred Klan counterdemonstrators, there to "stand up for white womanhood," arrived as the SCLC march began. A shot was fired, hitting a Klansman in the stomach. More shots followed—thirty-three in the twenty-eight seconds it took the police on the scene to gain control. Four people were wounded—two black and two white.[18] The SCLC called for another march the following week. They would not be intimidated by Klan violence.

Nelson Johnson and Paul and Sally Bermanzohn were on their way to a meeting in Houston when they heard of the shootings. They stopped in Decatur on their return trip. This time, they learned, not only would the march be protected by armed security but "self-defense patrols" would be established to guard the black community after the march. It was not the strategy of choice for the nonviolent SCLC, but the advocates of armed self-defense were undeterred. Johnson and the Bermanzohns participated in the march and worked with the defense patrols. It was heady stuff, to watch Decatur's blacks stand up to the Klan militantly and aggressively. It was dangerous, exhilarating—and politically correct.

One Man, One Gun

Glynco, Georgia, is the training site for special agents of the Federal Bureau of Alcohol, Tobacco, and Firearms (ATF). Among the graduates of the April-May class of 1979 was Bernard Butkovich, a Vietnam veteran, demolitions expert, and former investigator for the Michigan State Police, who was assigned to the ATF office in Cleveland, Ohio. Butkovich impressed his trainers with his skill in firearms and his physical stamina, which earned him the "Most Athletic" and "Distinguished Graduate" honors.[19] One of his trainers, Robert "Fulton" Dukes of the Winston-Salem ATF office, eyed Butkovich as a candidate for an undercover investigation that would involve a coordinated effort between the Winston and Cleveland offices.[20]

In October 1978, Dukes had received an anonymous tip that a Winston-Salem Klan member, Roland Wayne Wood, possessed a machine gun. Wood, a former porn shop owner with a record of misdemeanor and felony convictions, looks and acts like a heavyweight boxer who suffers the aftereffects of too many punches to the head. His six-foot-four-inch frame carries at least fifty pounds of fat, and most of his front teeth are missing. He is dull-witted and egotistical, an extremely dangerous combination.

The Winston-Salem police warned Dukes of Wood's violent tendencies, saying they considered him "one of the most dangerous persons in the area."[21] Then, in early 1979, Wood told the police that someone had tried to assassinate him by planting blasting caps under his car. The ATF investigation found that the caps were similar to ones used in a fatal bombing a year earlier. Dukes later testified that he concluded that Wood planted the blasting caps himself "to enhance his image with the Klan," but there is nothing in the record to indicate whether the ATF investigated the suspicious link.

Despite the police department's warning, despite the allegation that Wood had an illegal weapon, despite the possibility that he had some connection with the fatal bombing, the ATF did not begin a direct investigation of Wood until June 1979.[22] By that time, Wood and his friends Milano Caudle and Jack Fowler had split with Joe Grady's Klan in order to affiliate with Harold Covington's Nazis. Dukes received a tip, probably from Grady, that Wood was supposed to attend a Nazi rally in Parma, Ohio, on June 24.[23]

Apparently, under the preposterous presumption that Wood would take the automatic weapon across state lines and display it among a group of people he had never met before, Dukes contacted the Cleveland ATF office and requested an agent to infiltrate the Nazi meeting. Bernie Butkovich was assigned. He was to pose as a long-distance driver for McLean Trucking who had just been transferred to the firm's Winston-Salem headquarters. His orders were to meet Wood at the rally, get him to show his illegal weapon, and set him up for arrest.

Butkovich was an odd choice for the undercover job. His appearance—well dressed, clean shaven, blow-dried hair, classic Slavic features—was as unlike most truck drivers as it was most Klansmen and Nazis. And he did not use an alias, while any of his names—Bernard, Bernie, or Butkovich—was likely to trigger suspicion among a bunch of Nazi xenophobes.

Butkovich's cover as a truck driver was dangerously ill-prepared, so much so that he once told Wood that McLean provided the gas for his personal car, an old Pinto (McLean uses only diesel fuel).[24] The chance that marginally employed people like Wood or Caudle had worked as truckers was great, and yet the ATF allowed Butkovich to infiltrate the group in almost total ignorance of trucking work.

On June 24, with four ATF agents stationed nearby as backup, Butkovich walked across a large field to the White Power rally. As Harold Covington and Frank Collin railed into the microphones, Butkovich introduced himself and told his cover story to a few people in the small group of Nazis.[25] He saw neither Wood nor Caudle, both of whom, judging from the photographs he had been given, would have been unmistakable had they been there. Wood was a bearded giant; his sidekick was a foot shorter, usually shaved his head, and had the shoulders and torso of an ox. They were definitely not on the rally field.

Following the rally, Butkovich was told, there was to be a news conference at a nearby Howard Johnson's. He could meet Covington there and find out about the Nazis in Winston-Salem. Butkovich got in his car, radioed his backup team, and headed for the motel.

The news conference had hardly gotten underway when the doors to the conference room burst open and a couple of dozen hard-hatted, bat-wielding Jewish Defense League and Revolutionary Communist Party members began attacking the Nazis. Butkovich found a door in the back of the room, broke the lock, and escaped with a Nazi close on his heels. The police moved in immediately, but Butkovich and the Nazi drove around in the agent's undercover car for ten minutes until they figured the coast was clear.

When they returned to the motel, the Nazi introduced Butkovich to Covington and the agent told his cover story. Was there a Nazi unit in Winston-Salem? he asked. "We have a real good party leader in Winston-Salem," Butkovich remembers Covington saying. "They just formed a new unit. His name is Wayne Wood."[26] Covington wrote Wood's name and address on a napkin and handed it to the agent.

Butkovich left to rejoin his backup team. There, Dukes suggested that he make one foray to Winston-Salem at a later date "to try and finish this thing up."[27] The Parma operation had not come close to producing Wood's gun, but it had, Covington later said, left him with the impression that Butkovich had fought side by side with the Nazis against the Jews and Communists, an impression that firmly established the agent's credibility with the Nazi leader.[28] It would prove to be Butkovich's most important cover.

At the time of the Parma rally, Joe Grady was busy planning another showing of *Birth of a Nation*. He asked the Winston-Salem Nazis to come and sent out a news release announcing that the film would be shown at a recruitment meeting—one o'clock, Sunday, July 8, at the China Grove Community Center. The Workers Viewpoint Organization took notice.

At the Precipice

China Grove, just northeast of Charlotte, is typical of many small southern towns. Its twenty-five hundred people are either working class or poor, and the poor are mostly black. The blacks live on the edge of town in a subsidized housing area called Westside. Their segregation is geographically reinforced: only one road leads into Westside; a dense, horseshoe-shaped stand of pines surrounds the rest of the community.

The people of Westside were outraged when they saw posters going up all over town advertising that the Klan would use the China Grove Community Center to show *Birth of a Nation*. Local black leaders, including an imposing, outspoken young man named Paul Lucky, met at the Westside Community Center to discuss ways to stop the Klan not only from showing the film but also from using city property at all.[29] They elected a delegation to go before the town council to ask that the Klan's permit to use the center be withdrawn.

It didn't work. The delegation was told that the center was a public facility, open to all regardless of race or racist philosophy. Lucky countered that if the Klan had its meeting his community would march to protest it. The town council answered that since neither Lucky nor his group had yet applied for a permit to march, the town could simply deny any and all other permit applications for that day. Not to be outdone, Lucky announced that the black community would march "with or without a permit."[30]

Local members of the Southern Conference Educational Fund (SCEF), many of whom were working with ACTWU to organize a union at nearby Cannon Mills, became active in the early planning of the protest.[31] They brought together black and white mill workers, union activists, and local ministers to lend tactical and organizing support for a broadly based protest. There was no serious discussion of confronting the Klan at that time. The march was to be a vocal, nonviolent expression of opposition to the Klan's racism and lawlessness, as well as to the council's refusal to withdraw the Klan's permit. The blacks, especially, felt the need to show the Klan they were not intimidated.

The decision to hold a protest march did not meet with universal support in the black community. Some felt that it was better to ignore the Klan entirely, that a march would only fuel the Klan's sense of importance, that it would give the Klan undue publicity. And it could be dangerous. The few who wanted more aggressive action were quickly vetoed.

The people of Westside had held several planning meetings by the time Nelson Johnson and another WVO member showed up. "Some of us went down there and talked to people in the community and learned that they were organizing an initiative to respond [to the Klan meeting]," said Johnson. "There was a very strong political dimension to the discussion . . . to link [the rise of the Klan] very closely to the industry in that area, the textile industry, and the weakening of unity between people of color and white people. Our overall assessment was introduced into those discussions and I thought broadened people's scope and strengthened their resolve to persist in the direction they were moving in."

The WVO's "overall assessment," that the Klan was being promoted by the capitalists—Cone and Cannon—to divide black and white workers, was not a new concept for the people of China Grove. The SCEF and union organizers had concrete, firsthand proof that one of the primary union-busting techniques used in the area was race baiting. One company had gone so far as to put out a record, supposedly of an actual strike, in which strikers assaulted innocent nonstriking employees. Heavy black dialect was the hallmark of the strikers' voices.[32]

The concept the WVO brought into the discussion was that of aggressive, militant counteraction against the Klan, face-to-face. To the WVO, it was the only way to prove that blacks were no longer frightened, that the Klan's reign of terror was over. It was a short-sighted and manipulative strategy, and it violated two essentials of good organizing: any action should grow out of the community's own needs and desires; and if there is danger in the action, the entire community should be fully aware of the dangers and willing to accept the consequences.[33]

The people of China Grove had spent hours searching for a way to vent their feelings about the Klan, a way that met the needs of most of the community. Now a group of outsiders had convinced a majority of those who wanted to protest that a peaceful, nonviolent march was not the way to deal with the Klan. Look what happened in Decatur, they were told, and it seemed to make sense. But other than some talk about the need for armed defense patrols for the Westside community after the confrontation, there was little if any discussion of the very real potential for violence during the march and confrontation.

Several local ministers withdrew their support for the march, and the WVO responded with leaflets calling them "Uncle Toms" and sellouts to the capitalists. The SCEF organizers were appalled. Their painstaking work to bring together the mill workers, church leaders, and community people around a broad range of local issues was going down the tube, and they were powerless to stop it.[34] The WVO had mobilized a core of angry townspeople for a one-shot event and in the process decimated months of organizing work.

As July 8 approached, Paul Lucky's concern for the marchers' safety grew. He appealed directly to the chief of police, Richard Overcash, for a permit to march, as he saw that as the only way to control the situation.[35] A permit would have restricted the march to certain streets—away from the Klan—and Lucky felt that he and a few other local people could effectively handle any protesters who tried to move within range of the community center.

Overcash did not heed Lucky's warning directly. He again denied the group a permit to march. But later, after Lucky left, he requested precautionary backup support from the Highway Patrol, the Rowan County sheriff, and the State Bureau of Investigation. The film showing was scheduled to begin at one o'clock; Overcash asked the support units to be on hand before noon. China Grove's four full-time and four auxiliary officers were to be on duty no later than eleven; one would be stationed at the community center, two would monitor the group from Westside, and the rest would be on call.[36]

On Sunday morning, Signe Waller was nervous. Her anticipation of their planned second honeymoon, a trip to the beach, was dimmed by the prospect of what she and Jim might encounter in China Grove. Unlike the people of Westside, the Wallers were prepared, at least on a political and ideological plane. "We frankly wondered if we would be able to go [to the beach] at all," Signe later wrote.[37] "We admitted it was possible that one or both of us would be in the hospital, in jail, or even dead. I wondered how I would react if I saw Jim wounded. I had nightmares about it. But we knew it was correct to take a stand against the Klan, the scum of the earth that is spawned by the capitalist system."

Mike and Marty Nathan flipped a coin to decide who would go to China Grove and who would stay with their infant daughter, Leah. Marty stayed behind. She too was worried. "We agreed that it was a very dangerous thing. But we also felt it was a necessary danger. The Klan was out there. [Mike's] not very distant relatives had been killed by Nazis in Eastern Europe and he had a particular hatred of fascism. It was a question of fascism, racism that he felt he had to fight against."

And so they went, from Durham, from Greensboro. For revolutionary reasons, for personal reasons. To show the Klan they were not afraid—even though they were. The group included Mike Nathan, Paul and Sally Bermanzohn, Signe and Jim Waller, Cesar and Floris Cauce, Nelson and Joyce Johnson, Sandi Smith, and a dozen or so WVO associates, mostly white.

Nelson Johnson, who had stayed the night at Westside, was the only member of the WVO contingent on hand when the people of Westside began to gather at their community center early Sunday morning. By nine o'clock, Lucky counted eighty, many of whom were armed.[38] The guns, it was decided, would not be carried in the march but would be placed in a camper which would follow the group to the China Grove Community Center and back.

Lucky understood that the protest march was to leave Westside at noon. He later testified that shortly after eleven, at Nelson Johnson's request, he drove to Kannapolis to pick up some demonstrators who did not have a ride. No one was there. Lucky turned his car around and headed back to Westside. There was plenty of time; it was not quite eleven-thirty. He stopped at a friend's house and found two people who wanted to join the march.

The Westside Community Center was empty when Lucky and his friends arrived. He felt he had been had—sent on a wild-goose chase so that the WVO could start the march without him. Lucky ran to catch up with them. The chants became louder as he got closer: "Death, death, death to the Klan." "Decease, decease, decease the rotten beast." "The only solution is socialist revolution."

The group now numbered more than one hundred, and as Lucky made his way toward the front of the march, he could see that the newcomers were not from his community. They were mostly white.

A China Grove police cruiser pulled across Stevens Street at an angle to try to block the demonstrators, now within a block of the China Grove Community Center. One officer stayed with the car while the other tried to convince the group to stay back. They wouldn't listen. The officer spotted Lucky and asked him to use his influence to stop the marchers before they reached the Klan. "It's too late now," Lucky told him.[39] And it was.

Gorrell Pierce, a leader of the Federated Knights, saw the marchers as he was driving to the community center. When he arrived, he told his men, "If you've got a gun, you better go get it."[40] As they went to their cars to arm themselves, women and children who had come to see the film were instructed to take cover under tables in the building.

The march was rounding the corner; the people in the front of the line could see twenty or more men on the community center porch. A few wore robes, most had guns. In front of them was a brace holding two flags—the stars and stripes and the stars and bars.

A lone police officer stood on the porch cajoling the Klansmen to remain where they were as a Charlotte television photographer filmed the demonstrators surging toward them. The officers in the cruiser radioed Chief Overcash

In center of photograph, counterclockwise from left: Cesar Cauce (in white hat), Rand Manzella, Don Pelles, and Jim Waller. Note what appears to be a length of pipe in Cauce's hand, as in the man's behind him. Also note the towel wrapped around Pelles's forearm in preparation for a fight. China Grove, July 8, 1979 (Photograph from the *Salisbury Post*)

and then ran to the porch to do what they could to control the situation.[41] Sticks and clubs waved in the air punctuating the demonstrators' shouts: "Death to the Klan. Death to the Klan."

Joe Grady moved to the back of the porch, toward the door leading into the community center, but most of his men stayed up front. Wayne Wood, white power T-shirt barely covering his gut and a pistol stuck under his belt, struck an absurd karate-type pose while Milano Caudle waved his shotgun in the demonstrators' direction. The men behind them followed suit, edging toward the front of the porch, screaming obscenities and racial slurs in a futile attempt to drown out the chants.[42]

One of the WVO demonstrators, a six-foot, blond-haired, blue-eyed model of the Aryan ideal, grabbed the Confederate flag from its stand and torched it. As he reached for the other staff, Paul Lucky rushed to his side, snatching the American flag away. As he leaned it against the building, Lucky turned to the people from Westside. "This is our flag," he told them, "our America." He scolded the demonstrator: "This is dividing the people."[43]

The three police officers on the porch were trying desperately to move the Klan inside the building where the women and children were huddled in fear. The situation was near chaos. There was no way the officers could stop the demonstrators, some of whom were now at the edge of the porch swinging clubs and chains at its pillars. The men on the porch were all armed, most with shotguns. Several had their trigger fingers poised. If anything had startled them—a car backfiring—there would have been a bloodbath.

The officers began pleading with the Klansmen that there was no way they could control the demonstrators; the only way to avert disaster was for the Klan to retreat.[44] Slowly, the men pulled back into the center. The confrontation was over.

Cheering, the demonstrators began to move across the lawn toward the street. Caught in the wave of militance, Lucky walked into range of the Charlotte television camera and in poetic cadence offered a final verbal barrage: "If we have to *die* here, we'll *die* here. But there will *not* be any Klan—today, tomorrow, *never*. *Death to the Klan.*"[45] The camera followed Lucky as he strode after the group on its triumphant march back to Westside. He continued to punch the air with his fist, continued to shout, "Death to the Klan."

The community center area now clear, Grady emerged onto the porch. It was his turn to make a statement for the television audience. He talked about how the incident proved the Klan was right, that blacks were violent and lawless, that it was only the Klan's restraint and respect for the three police officers that prevented bloodshed. He should have stopped there, but his anger and humiliation were too great. "There *will* be revenge for this."[46]

As the Klan filed back into the center to watch the film, the Charlotte television reporter stood before the camera to recite his lead-in for the evening news. He said that the Klan planned to continue showing *Birth of a Nation*—an indication, he warned, "that scenes like the one that occurred here today may be repeated in the not-too-distant future."[47]

Oblivious to their brush with disaster, the demonstrators were jubilant on the return march to Westside. But suddenly someone spotted a car following

Wayne Wood (center) at China Grove, July 8, 1979 (Photograph from the *Salisbury Post*)

at a distance, a carload of white men, gun barrels sticking out the windows.[48] The doors to the camper at the back of the march opened quickly, and demonstrators began grabbing shotguns, rifles, and handguns. Then they made straight for Westside. The car turned down a side street and sped away.

An armed guard was set up around the perimeter of Westside, and people with walkie-talkies and citizens band radios patrolled the area. Some of the WVO people stayed through the afternoon, but by nightfall only one was left: Nelson Johnson. "I felt some responsibility simply because we had worked together to do the thing and everybody else was going home," he said. "We didn't see anybody try to come in, but we heard a lot of stuff on the CB radio . . . some Klansmen who said they scared the niggers off and different things about the boys from the west side. To my amazement, I didn't hear anything about the Workers Viewpoint organizers from the Klan. Their focus was on the people of the Westside community."

There was a strong feeling, Johnson said, that the Klan might retaliate during the night. And given their history as nightriders, it was far from an illogical assumption. Yet by Monday, all the WVO people were gone and Westside was left to fend for itself as best it could if the Klan showed up that night or Tuesday night or the next Saturday night.

Wayne Wood and Milano Caudle were not thinking about a night ride through China Grove, and they were not aware of any such thing as the Workers Viewpoint Organization.[49] Their anger was directed at Joe Grady, who they felt had left them in the lurch on the front line at the China Grove Community Center. Grady's cowardice did not sit well with Gorrell Pierce, either.[50] He wrested control of the Federated Knights from Grady and aligned himself with Wood, Caudle, and the Nazis.

If Mike Nathan was frightened before he went to China Grove, he was doubly so afterward. He was, Marty later said, surprised that the Klan had guns. "The Klan was pointing guns at unarmed people. For me, personally, because I didn't live through it, the impact of it was not so great. I never realized exactly how hairy it must have been. But I know that there were people who took it very seriously."

Apparently, though, not enough people took it seriously enough. The WVO focused its attention on three issues: the media's portrayal of the China Grove confrontation as a feud between opposing extremist groups; the charge by local people, the media, and others that the WVO was a Communist group; and the WVO's insistence that the Klan was not just a homespun group of racist terrorists but a tool of capitalist oppressors like Cone and Cannon. They

Milano Caudle (second from left) and Jack Fowler (in dark glasses) at China Grove, July 8, 1979 (Photograph from the *Salisbury Post*)

were so wrapped up in the overall political analysis that they neglected to scrutinize the Klan itself.

On July 13, a group called the China Grove Committee to Smash the Klan held a news conference at the China Grove Community Center.[51] Joyce Johnson and two other black women from the WVO were joined by two black men, the only China Grove residents present as "committee" members. They accused the town council, the media, and the police of being secret backers of the Klan and then announced that on July 21 a mass meeting would be held at the China Grove Community Center to discuss "the meaning of the rise of the Klan and . . . a comprehensive means to smash the Klan."

The meeting was held, but only a handful of people showed up, most of them from the WVO. Nelson Johnson attributed the lack of response to anti-communism. "At that time, the question of communism was being raised very

Wayne Wood (right) and Milano Caudle (with shotgun) confronting anti-Klan protesters at China Grove, July 8, 1979 (Photograph from the *Salisbury Post*)

strongly in the community. I think it had something to do with the lack of real broad participation in the initial demonstration and followup."

In a pattern that had by then become a hallmark of the Communists' involvement in an action, the WVO pushed the China Grove demonstration toward increasing militancy, leaving more moderate forces no choice but to withdraw. Then, when local people, including many of the demonstrators, began to question the militant strategy in light of narrowly averted violent consequences, to question the motives of the outside Communist organizers, the WVO pointed to the failure of the community to unite behind them as the reason for their lack of long-term success. "It always happens," says Nelson Johnson, "as soon as something very successful happens, there are ways that people figure out how to erode it, to negate it and turn it around." The attitude of the people of China Grove had swung 180 degrees. It was better to ignore the Klan, they now felt. Their change of opinion, Johnson said, "betrayed an incredible lack of understanding of this phenomenon we were encountering."

Johnson's refusal to give legitimacy to the concerns of the people of China Grove was a classic example of Leninist polemic techniques: "Reply to attack, not by defense, but by counter attacks."[52] This tactic, perhaps more than any other used by the WVO, served to widen the gap between the Communists and the people they sought to organize. To be told that one's concerns or criticisms "betray an incredible lack of understanding" is no less than an insult. The counterattack strategy may be superb in a political debate, but as an organizing tool it is self-defeating.

But the WVO persevered. If Piedmont North Carolina would not converge on China Grove for a "Smash the Klan" conference, perhaps a more urban setting was needed. Greensboro seemed ideal. Not only was it a center of WVO activity, Johnson explained, but "people would be less afraid . . . because there was no immediate history of this sort of thing [Klan activity] in Greensboro."

In classic WVO strategy, the aims of the conference would be twofold: political education and organizing. In this case in particular, Johnson said, political education was vital "to form the type of organizing we thought needed to be done." It would be the WVO's ballgame from start to finish. No pesky SCEF organizers, no weak-kneed preachers, no turf-conscious know-it-alls like Paul Lucky.

The national WVO was making major plans. In the three years since the Duke polemics, the organization had taken on new members and new issues with—it thought—astonishing success. In North Carolina alone, WVO groups included the Trade Union Education League, a committee to stop competency testing, Medical Aid to Zimbabwe, a variety of strike-support groups, and the as-yet-unnamed anti-Klan group. It mattered little that the people controlling these groups were always the same—Bermanzohn, Johnson, Waller, Smith;[53] they were spreading the revolutionary word and drawing supporters ripe for recruitment.

It was happening like that in many areas of the country. No longer confined to workers' organizing, the WVO, the national leadership felt, had established itself in the vanguard. They set the weekend of October 20 for the Founding Congress of the Communist Workers Party.

Their organizational strength was not the WVO's only basis for feeling that the revolutionary moment was upon them. They predicted an economic crisis of unprecedented proportions, a crisis engineered by the bourgeoisie to force the working class to its knees in order to exploit it for bigger and bigger profits.[54] They saw the Supreme Court *Bakke* decision, the so-called "reverse discrimination" case, as proof that the government was in league with the capitalists to take away the hard-won affirmative action programs for blacks. This, the WVO felt, would further divide black and white workers and make it almost impossible to unite the proletariat.[55] Lastly, the Klan was on the rise, a flying wedge for the ruling class, promoted by the media and protected by the state. To the WVO, the American public's choice was clear. On the right were the bourgeois capitalists and the Klan; on the left were the revolutionaries, the Communist vanguard that would overthrow the corrupt government and replace it with workers' rule—the only defense against oppression and exploitation. There was no middle ground.

Chapter 6

> Direct action is not intended to win particular reforms or to influence decision-makers, but rather to bring out a repressive response from authorities. . . . When confrontation brings violent official response, uncommitted elements of the public can see for themselves the true nature of the "system." Confrontation, therefore, is a means of political education.
> —Jerome H. Skolnik, *The Politics of Protest*

Racists United, Communists Divided

Harold Covington needed to broaden his power base. He had succeeded in pulling Wood and his pals out of Grady's Klan, and with Grady out of the way, Covington could continue to court Gorrell Pierce and the remaining members of the Federated Knights. If he could bring the like-minded racist groups together, if he could demonstrate to them his superior intellect, his superior speaking and organizing skills, he could win many of them to National Socialism.[1] Covington decided to organize a statewide gathering of Klan and Nazis, a media as well as recruiting event. They would put on a fine show: swastikas, robes and hoods, burning crosses, uniforms, boots and guns. Covington set the first Klan-Nazi rally for September 22 at a farm five miles east of Louisburg in the quiet, rolling farmland northeast of Raleigh.

In addition to the serious organizing and media work for the Louisburg rally, Covington was having a little fun in the late summer of 1979. Posing as Myron Silverstein, a traveling Jewish entrepreneur, Covington began writing letters to the Revolutionary Communist Party in Greensboro. He asked for literature, and after receiving it he would write back with questions about the party's interpretation of philosophy and of the political hostility between various New Communist factions. Significantly, he never mentioned the WVO.[2] On September 11, less than two weeks before the Louisburg rally, Covington broke his Myron Silverstein ruse. On Nazi letterhead featuring a two-inch wide black banner with a large swastika in the middle, Covington wrote: "You might be interested to know that, of all the Marxist groups I have attempted to bandy words with, you are thus far the only ones who have had the guts to answer my questions, especially about the Stalin purges."

He went on for over three typed, single-spaced pages, letting the RCP know in no uncertain terms that he had studied the communist classics, understood and despised what they were up to, and knew how to hold his own in a political debate, to which he repeatedly challenged them. He concluded:

> I have never yet met a Red who had the strength of faith to defend his Marxism with anything other than filthy words or an attempt at violence. (By the by, almost all of my men have killed Communists in Vietnam, and I was in Rhodesia as well, but so far we've never actually had a chance to kill the home-grown product, although we've put a few in the hospital and we nearly killed some of your people at China Grove last July—we had it all worked out with the cops that if you were dumb enough to try to attack the community center we'd waste a couple of you and none of them would see anything.) We will meet you on those terms if you want—don't ever try to mess with any of our rallies on private property or you will be killed—but I am curious to know if you have the courage of your convictions enough to put them to the test by meeting us on the field of reason.[3]

It is unlikely that Covington's "by the by" clause was dropped inadvertently into the letter. There is no evidence that any kind of deal "was worked out" with the China Grove police on July 8. Why would Covington fabricate such a story? The only explanation is that it was calculated to generate a response, a flurry of publicity, and a chance for Covington to grab the media spotlight.

Had Covington sent that letter to the WVO, Nelson Johnson said, "we would have taken it seriously." He and other WVO leaders had talked privately about the possibility of collusion between the police and the Klan at China Grove, and their literature consistently pointed out the corporate-media-government-police-Klan connections. With Covington apparently verifying the WVO's suspicions in writing, they would have, in Johnson's words, "gone public with it."

But Covington sent the letter to the wrong organization. The RCP ignored it, at least publicly. They knew that Covington had mistaken the WVO for them in China Grove, but the hostility between the two Communist groups was so great that the RCP did not consider passing the warning on to their rivals.

The Greensboro police were by now acutely aware of the bitterness between the WVO and the RCP. In August, two RCP members had attacked Signe Waller as she was selling Workers Viewpoint newspapers at the gate to Cone's White Oak plant. It was not the first violent episode between the two groups, nor would it be the last. Retaliation came swiftly. "We returned that afternoon and whipped their tails bad," a WVO leaflet later proclaimed. The police tried to investigate, but, despite their hatred of each other, neither group would cooperate in either identifying or filing charges against the other side. Instead, they hurled accusations at each other. The WVO rhetoric was strikingly similar to that they used against the Klan: the RCP were "scum elements," agents of the state, "mangy dogs" who "needed to be driven physically from the ranks of the workers."[4]

The police were not concerned so much about the rhetoric or even the politics of the groups as they were about what they saw as a marked increase in their propensity for violence.[5] High-level discussions within the police department began to focus on ways to avert another nasty situation. Surveillance was the tactic most often discussed.

Surveillance of the Nazis by the ATF was well under way. On July 26, Bernie Butkovich had pulled a battered orange Pinto to the edge of the unpaved street in front of Wayne Wood's house.[6] It was a four-room, white-shingled bungalow with a small detached garage in back—headquarters of the Forsyth County Unit, National Socialist Party of America. When Butkovich introduced himself to Wood, he was greeted warmly: "I've heard a lot about you from Harold. I really expected to see you before this."

They talked about Parma, about Nazi philosophy. And Butkovich talked about himself. Vietnam. Army demolitions expert. Driver for McLean Trucking. He needed a place to live, and Wood showed him the vacant house next door. The agent told Wood that it was a possibility, after he had gotten settled in a regular driving schedule. For the time being, though, he asked if he could simply list Wood's address on his Nazi application form. Then he could just stop by whenever he was in town to pick up newsletters and whatever else the Nazis mailed out. Wood was glad to oblige.

On reflection, Wood was a little unsure of Butkovich. He had a clean-cut college look about him, not at all what one would expect in a truck driver. And there was his Jewish-sounding name, Butkovich. But Wood doubted he was an undercover agent; not even the FBI would be dumb enough to send in a Jewish infiltrator. He made a mental note to keep an eye on the new recruit.[7]

Butkovich had met with Wood several times by early September. He sensed that Wood and the others were suspicious of him, but they continued to give him intriguing leads. On July 29, Wood mentioned that the NSPA had access to Thompson submachine guns—plural. Then, in a meeting at Nazi headquarters in Raleigh, Covington told the assembled group that Frank Braswell, a Nazi from Asheville, was about to get his pilot's license and planned to load his plane with steel ball bearings and drop them over black housing projects.[8]

Butkovich reported Covington's lead to his superiors, and shortly thereafter was sent to the Asheville area to see if he could make contact with Braswell. When he could not—he couldn't even find the road to Braswell's mountain hideaway—he returned to Winston-Salem to continue searching for the machine guns.[9]

Butkovich's search took some rather bizarre and potentially dangerous forms. In order to find evidence of illegal weapons, Butkovich "encouraged" his targets to produce or acquire them. According to Milano Caudle, "He asked us if we wanted selector switches [to convert legal semi-automatic weapons into illegal automatic ones], that he could get 'em if we wanted. He said he could train us in hand-to-hand combat if we wanted."[10] When Butkovich learned that the Nazis were feuding with Joe Grady, Caudle later testified, "he asked us if he [Grady] was giving us trouble. He was offering to see if we wanted Joe Grady done away with. He said if we didn't have the people to do it, he did. He also had the means. We said no."[11]

Butkovich denies ever talking about eliminating Grady, but Grady himself corroborated Caudle's story in 1985 testimony. Caudle phoned him, he said, warning that "a Yankee" wanted to kill him. According to Grady, Caudle said, "Old man, we don't agree politically, but I don't want to see you hurt."[12]

Wired

September 22, at a farm five miles east of Louisburg, the mood was festive. People smiled and sniffed the air downwind from the pit where a whole hog barbecued to near-perfection. Bluegrass blared over the loudspeakers, interrupted occasionally by the rousing strains of "The Ride of the Valkyries." Children cavorted in the dust and sand while moms and dads watched and chatted. It might have been anyone's family reunion or company picnic. Except for the robes and the swastikas, the guns, and the burlap-wrapped cross being soaked with kerosene.

To Covington's delight, the media were there in force, shooting roll after roll of film, cassette after cassette of tape. A baby dozed in its stroller; its tiny T-shirt said "Future Klansman." A pretty blond woman walked a Doberman on a short lead, posing for the cameras with a rifle held in front of her tight-fitting "White Power" T-shirt.[13] Bumper stickers read "Niggers Beware," and everyone, it seemed, carried a pistol or a shotgun or a rifle. The cross was almost ready to burn. It was nothing short of a photographer's paradise.

One of the cameras belonged to the Bureau of Alcohol, Tobacco, and Firearms. Butkovich had conned Wood into appointing him "official party photographer" for the event. He snapped group pictures, head shots, profiles.[14] Although his was supposedly a "one-man, one-gun" investigation, Butkovich assembled a photo collection that would be the envy of any of the old COIN-

TELPRO political surveillance teams. He got the Nazis: Covington, Wood, Caudle, Jack Fowler, Glenn Miller, Jerry Hatcher, and Roger Shannon. He got the Invisible Empire: Virgil Griffin, Jerry Smith, Chris Benson, and David Matthews. And he got the Federated Knights: Gorrell Pierce, his brother Roger, and Shorty Talbert.

Butkovich had incredible backup from the ATF for the rally.[15] A bureau plane made frequent passes over the rally field, and agents were scattered throughout the area in unmarked cars. They listened to Butkovich's conversations over a body transmitter hidden in his Nazi uniform. At least they tried to listen.

Transcripts of the tapes show that most of the talk was unintelligible.[16] Even Butkovich's voice was obscured by background noises—dogs barking, kids shouting, an idling car engine. Much of the recorded conversation was about the heat; one Klansman pointed out how lucky the Nazis were to be in uniforms instead of robes. There was some talk of guns, but about the only thing of significance was a portion of a discussion in which somebody said they—the Nazis—could buy anything they wanted from McIIargue's gunshop in Winston. "Tell 'em who you're with, too. Tell 'em you know Milano or Roger."

They discussed how difficult it was to polish the black Storm Trooper's boots and where to get neckties that would match the uniform. Someone said, "Milano's gonna have to get tailored shirts. He's got a neck like mine. No neck and a whole lot of damn body. Little bitty head, but nothin' in it." They laughed.

Butkovich instructed a woman named Peggy on how to use his camera so the Nazis could get a picture of the entire membership. Harold Covington said something about "Myron Silverstein." But most of what the transmitter picked up were sentence fragments and background noises. If Butkovich had been in any danger, the ATF would never have known. The batteries in his transmitter were operable for a maximum of six hours, and they had been running since he left Winston-Salem with the Nazis late that morning. By early evening, the transmissions had ceased. The rally continued until after midnight.

It was during the Louisburg rally that Covington coined a phrase which would later take on sinister connotations: the United Racist Front. The Communist survivors of the Greensboro killings alleged that the United Racist Front was a formal alliance, forged by Butkovich and Covington for the express purpose of attacking the anti-Klan demonstration.[17] Those who were present at the Louisburg rally claim otherwise. "We had never heard of anything called the United Racist Front," Milano Caudle said. "After the meeting, Harold was talking to two girl reporters and they asked him if it was a united racist front and he said yes. The next day it was all over the papers—Klan and Nazis to take over the world!"[18] An article using the newly coined term was clipped and added to the ATF's files, and the name "United Racist Front" was passed from agent to agent, agency to agency. Thus, a figment of a reporter's overactive imagination became fact.

The Challenge

The WVO was only vaguely aware of the Louisburg rally. Despite the widespread media coverage given to the Klan-Nazi gathering, the WVO leadership was either too wrapped up in planning the Communist Workers Party's founding congress or too wed to its overall assessment of fascism to question the implications of racist unity for their anti-Klan work.

"Based on some of the stuff we'd studied on the advent of fascism in Europe," said Paul Bermanzohn, "we thought that there were serious dangers in America and that we should try to deal with them head-on and not make like nothing's happening. Whether it's the Klan in North Carolina or Posse Comitatus in Wisconsin or the National Socialist Party in Chicago or Winston, it's the same crowd. It's a racist ideology splitting black and white people and preventing them from fighting the powers that be."

Marty Nathan agreed: "To me, it doesn't make much difference. A fascist is a fascist, no matter what uniform he wears. All those Nazis, almost all of them, had been in the Klan at one time or another. So to my mind, making that distinction ain't a whole lot of distinction to make. It's a pretty fluid bunch of murderers."

Their analysis of fascism, the similarity between the Klan and other racist groups, and the effect of organized racism on American society may have been valid, but their strategy for acting on their assessment was suicidal. To deal head-on with people they considered a "fluid bunch of murderers" without investigating the group's leadership, their motivation, their strengths and weaknesses, seems ludicrous.

They did not know of the split and the growing hostility between Joe Grady and Gorrell Pierce. They knew next to nothing of either the Nazis or Virgil Griffin's Invisible Empire. They knew a lot about the Klan in the 1920s, but little of the Klan in 1979—especially of its focus on communism as the ultimate evil. But most important, and most dangerous, they were woefully ignorant of the culture from which the contemporary Klan is drawn.

"The pathology of the white ghetto" is what southern philosopher Reverend Will Campbell calls it.[19] It is the same kind of antisocial behavior so prevalent in black ghettos. It is born of poverty and powerlessness, of humiliation and hopelessness. For many, the Klan and its ilk represent the only way a poor white person can say "I am somebody," the only way he or she can escape emotionally from the economic and social wasteland of American society. For a while, in the robes or security uniforms, they can be part of an organization they consider elite, an organization that carries an aura of mystery and danger and strength.

It is a sad commentary that idealistic liberals and leftists can easily understand how socioeconomic factors produce street gangs and thugs in the black ghetto but fail to recognize the same phenomenon among poor whites who join the Klan. To liberals, the blacks are oppressed and exploited; the whites are hate-filled and despicable. No one in his right mind would consider daring a Chicago street gang to "come out from under your rocks and face the wrath of the people." Yet that is precisely the challenge the WVO issued to the Klan in mid-October.

The WVO's first announcement of the November 3 march and conference received little notice. On its evening news of October 4, WGHP-TV in High Point briefly mentioned that a "Death to the Klan" march would be held in Greensboro. The group had, the reporter said, applied for and received a parade permit from the Greensboro Police Department. They had not.[20] But lying on Greensboro detective Jerry Cooper's desk was a memo from the department's administrative bureau asking for information on "communist groups."[21] Cooper had been on the police force since 1966 and an intelligence officer for two years before he was assigned to the Special Investigation Squad of the Criminal Investigations Division in 1979. He had used informants occasionally in the past, and he was now on the lookout for someone who could provide reliable information on the Communists.

Four days later, on October 8, the commander of the investigative bureau called Captain Larry Gibson into his office to find out if he knew anything about the "Death to the Klan" march. At the time, Gibson knew little of the WVO, except that they had been involved in the skirmishes with the RCP at White Oak. He had, however, a great deal of knowledge about Nelson Johnson, who spoke for the WVO on the television newscast. His fifteen years with the Greensboro police paralleled Johnson's years of activism in Greensboro, and Gibson blamed Johnson for much of the violence that occurred during the 1960s. "I felt concern about a confrontation between the marchers and police officers," Gibson said. "I felt uncomfortable about the whole thing."[22]

As the police planned their strategy for the November 3 march and their surveillance of the local Communists, the WVO was trying to inject new life

Landis - The Klan Tries to Rebuild its Shattered Image

August 25, 1979- Some Ku Klux Klansmen huddle nervously in a field at Bostian and Old Beatty Ford Rd. in Landis. They shout at each other for two hours to build up their image, which was shattered in China Grove. After seeing the coast is clear, they flash their rifles and beat their chests. The most vicious poison drips from their lips. They slander Jews as dirty and slimy. They say Black people "smell like billy gcats." One Klansman points to the darkness and says, "If there are any niggers down there that comes up here, I'll put a bullet between their eyes."

* * *

Just at a time when things are bad for all of us, when Black and White have more reason than ever to unite, the Klan is trying to confuse us by telling us our problem is each other. They are intensifying the conflict between different peoples in the working class, who are oppressed by the brutal system of capitalism.

SMASH THE KLAN WITH THE CORRECT UNDERSTANDING AND ARMED SELF-DEFENSE:

Historic Stand in China Grove Shows How to Fight the Klan

Hated symbol of the Klan goes up in smoke in China Grove

Just a month and a half earlier, the people of China Grove, along with the Workers Viewpoint Organization, chased these same scum Klansmen off the lawn of the China Grove Community Center. Armed with pipes, bottles, sticks and rifles, the people defended the China Grove Community. They burned the hated symbol of the Klansmen --their confederate flags. After deserting their flags, these "brave Klansmen" defended them by peeping out of the window as the flags went up in smoke.

For weeks, the media and newspapers had built up the Klan's showing of a racist film, while afterward, in one edition, they distorted the facts and meaning of the people's heroic stand against the Klan. Kicking the press out of our ranks at the rally after the demonstration was correct. The bourgeoisie (rich capitalist class which includes the Cannon, Cones, Dukes etc.) uses many forms to disguise and maintain their rule. They use the newspapers and media to make the Klan look strong and the workers look weak.

WVO leaflet announcing the "Death to the Klan" march on November 3, 1979

What made a difference in China Grove was the mighty force of the militant, armed and organized fighters, fighting in the people's interest. The combination of armed self-defense with the clear understanding that the Klan is secretly supported by the bourgeoisie is what put the Klan on the run and made the bourgeoisie tremble. WE AFFIRM THE CORRECTNESS OF HOW TO FIGHT THE KLAN AS SHOWN BY CHINA GROVE!!!

Take a Stand! Smash the Klan! Expose the Misleaders!

For a hundred years the Klan has beaten, murdered and raped. They have shot and lynched thousands of Black people, tarred and feathered Black and White union organizers, ridden in the night shooting into people's homes. How do we fight these dogs?

Do we stay home behind closed doors and tremble? Do we say ridiculous things like, "This is a quarrel between two hate groups?" Do we make public statements to the press saying we deplore violence and then do nothing? This is the way the Reverends Quick, Washington and Hamilton in fact covered for the bloody history of the Klan and misled people after China Grove.

Let's be clear -- what Reverends Quick, Washington and Hamilton did was to take the heat off the Klan and pave the way for the Klan to grow unchecked, allowing the Klan to put out their vicious hate teachings among brothers and sisters of the working class in Landis. This is what they objectively did, whether or not they intended it. These misleaders attacked the fighters of the Klan, including the Workers Viewpoint Organization, the Communist organization. The issue is whether you support the Klan or whether you fight against the Klan and what they represent. Reverends Quick, Washington and Hamilton are the most successful defenders of the Klan. They were able to do what the cops, press and local politicians couldn't do -- confuse, demoralize and disarm the community with their non-violent teaching.

The Klan Must Not be Allowed to Grow!

The Klan must not be allowed to grow! They have to be exposed for what they are --servants of the ruling bourgeoisie. They should be physically beaten and chased out of town. This is the only language they understand. Armed self-defense is the only defense. We uphold this stand in Tupelo, Decatur and all the places where the masses have beat back the Klan. We call on the people in China Grove and Landis to join with us to SMASH THE KLAN!

JOIN US NOV. 3rd IN GREENSBORO!
COME TO THE W.V.O. ANTI-KLAN CONFERENCE !

DEATH TO THE KLAN: PROMOTE ARMED SELF-DEFENSE OF THE COMMUNITY!!

CRITICIZE THE ROLE OF THE MISLEADERS!!

BUILD THE MULTINATIONAL UNITY OF THE WORKING CLASS!!

This leaflet by Workers Viewpoint Organization: For more info. call (919) 682-1014 into what it perceived as a withering anti-Klan campaign. Ironically exhibiting a racist attitude, an internal directive pointed to a problem in recruiting blacks: "Afro-American workers will tend to be drawn to this issue, although their understanding of what the bourgeoisie is trying to do will be limited and one-sided." But the main thrust of the directive was on how to revitalize the anti-Klan campaign with "red hot" slogans and a lively march on November 3. In summary, the directive stated, "the main content of the anti-Klan campaign should be militant, direct-action—a confrontation with the Klan would be best if we can get it."[23]

At the police department's October 10 staff meeting, Larry Gibson was directed to be on hand if and when the WVO applied for its parade permit.[24] He was to advise them that there would be two restrictions placed on the demonstration, restrictions that would be written on the face of the permit: "No weapons to be carried in plain view or concealed. Sign posts no larger than 2" by 2"."

The following day, still without a parade permit, Nelson Johnson and Paul Bermanzohn, along with several other WVO members, went to Kannapolis, to the gates to Cannon Mills, where they held another news conference announcing the "Death to the Klan" march. Accusing Cannon of promoting the Klan in order to divide workers, Bermanzohn and Johnson then launched into a barrage of headline-making anti-Klan rhetoric: "They can and will be crushed. They are cowards, nightriders who try to terrorize innocent people. They must be physically beaten back, eradicated, exterminated, wiped off the face of the earth." They bragged about China Grove and publicly goaded Grady and Pierce: "We invite you and your two-bit punks to come out and face the wrath of the people."[25] The headline on that evening's *Salisbury Post* said, "Communists Challenge KKK to Come to Rally."[26] The *Charlotte Observer* used the caption, "Group Seeks Confrontation with the Klan."[27]

Rooster and the Renegade

On Friday, October 11, Eddie Dawson decided to pay a visit to his pals in the "PD," as he calls it. Although his days as an informant were over, he frequently wandered the corridors of the police department looking for someone to shoot the breeze with. One of his favorite topics these days was the Communists in Greensboro. On this particular day he was talking with an old police contact when Jerry Cooper walked by. The officer suggested Cooper might like to talk with Dawson. As they shook hands, Cooper said to call him by his nickname, "Rooster," and the two then left for the detective's office.[28]

Dawson told Cooper that he had been an informant for the department and the FBI, that he could check on his reliability with his old contacts. Then he asked Cooper if he knew about an RCP meeting to take place October 14 at the Holiday Inn–Four Seasons. "Dawson said it might be a good idea to disrupt that meeting," Cooper recalled. "I told him we'd like to have information, but if he disrupted and violated the law he'd be arrested." Cooper never directly asked Dawson to inform on the RCP.[29] He didn't have to. If the police wanted information, Dawson would be happy to get it for them. Just like old times.

That afternoon nine RCP members were arrested at Hampton Homes, a housing project where the RCP was trying to recruit people for its meeting the following Sunday. According to the RCP, "The authorities were already worried about the influence of the RCP at Hampton Homes. . . . The afternoon of October 11, the police began massing near the rally site and made their move against the RCP spokesman. He was bodily dragged to a standing cop car and thrown on the hood. The crowd began chanting and booing the cops, who again freaked out and began chasing and arresting people."[30]

The police gave a slightly different version. They had received complaints from Hampton residents about excessive noise from the RCP's loudspeaker.[31] The police gave two warnings to the group to lower the volume to within city code. They were ignored, and the police moved in to arrest the person using the microphone. When he resisted, the RCP indeed began chanting, using words like "pigs" and "police brutality," words guaranteed to spark an angry reaction in a housing project hostile to the police. The nine were charged with disturbing the peace and inciting to riot.

The RCP arrests did little to ease the police department's fears about the upcoming WVO march. Probably nowhere in the country do police have amiable relations with the general populace of housing projects. Although the Greensboro department's record on racially motivated police violence is better than most, low-income communities still view the police with suspicion and hostility. If the Communists, whether RCP or WVO, were launching a strategy of aggressive organizing in the black community, the police would have to plan their coverage of those activities with extreme caution lest their presence inflame already existing police-community tensions to dangerous proportions.[32] And there did seem to be a pattern, at least with the RCP, of public agitation leading to arrest, which the group then used publicly to accuse the police of harassment, discrimination, and brutality. The police had come very close to losing control of the situation in the Hampton Homes incident; if the WVO was planning to route the "Death to the Klan" march through black neighborhoods, which seemed highly probable, there was a very real danger that a minor incident could erupt into violence if the police were not well prepared.

Jim Waller and Paul Bermanzohn were watching the RCP, too. "Jim and I were meeting about the November 3rd thing at the time," Bermanzohn remembered. "He'd come over to where I was working [the UNC-G Student Health Center] and part of our meeting would be to sum up the latest crazy antics of the RCP. There was a lot of anti-communism at UNC-G—that shit on the buildings [RCP members had spray-painted "Death to the Shah" on the new library]—they were really antagonizing a lot of folks. We thought they were giving communism a bad name. We were out there trying to do some good work and they were really screwing the thing up."

Bermanzohn does not remember what discussions he and Waller had concerning what to do about the RCP. "There's really very little you can do," he chuckled, "assuming we're not going to take them to court for defaming the good name of communism!"

There was nothing good to be said about communism in the Invisible Empire. Virgil Griffin had seen the *Charlotte Observer* article about the "Death to the Klan" rally. His newly elected assistant grand dragon, twenty-four-year-old Chris Benson, brought him a copy the morning of the Klan's state board meeting, October 14.[33] Griffin was steaming, and it did not take long for the rest of the group to share his fury. "I just read the part about 'we challenge these two-bit cowards to come out from under their rocks and face the wrath of the people,'" said Carl Nappier, the sixty-year-old treasurer of the board. "That was far enough for me to read. They was askin' for it as far as I was concerned."[34]

The feeling was unanimous. It was bad enough that communism was allowed to exist at all in the United States, worse that Communists could march openly in the streets. But they had crossed the line in calling the Klan punks and cowards, in daring them to a confrontation. Griffin called for a vote. Will the Invisible Empire go to Greensboro on November 3? All hands went up: Jerry Smith, a logger from Maiden and Griffin's personal bodyguard; John Pridmore, a textile worker from Lincolnton and exalted cyclops (president) of the Lincolnton klavern; Chris Benson and his wife Melanie, secretary of the board, from Charlotte; David Matthews, grand nighthawk, the head of security, even though he was considered totally disabled because of recent open-heart and chest surgery; Mark Sherer, a nineteen-year-old felon on parole from an armed robbery conviction, the Klan's state organizer or kleagle; and Nappier, who was also the exalted cyclops of the Hickory klavern.[35] Of the seven people present, only Griffin and Matthews had been in the Klan longer than a year. Most had been appointed to the board within the past two months.[36]

Griffin told the group he had an old Klan buddy in Greensboro, a friend

Escalation

who knew a lot about Communists down there. His name was Eddie Dawson. Griffin said he would invite Dawson to speak about the Communists at the Klan rally to be held in Lincolnton on October 20.[37] In the meantime, they should all go back to their klaverns to find out how the members felt about joining the protest. "Virgil mentioned we'd more'n likely get into a fight," Nappier said. "I said I was gonna pick out the biggest one and hit him as hard as I could."[38]

As Griffin's group continued its discussion of the "Death to the Klan" rally, Dawson succeeded in disrupting the RCP's meeting without saying a word. Although eager for new recruits, the young, racially mixed membership of the RCP was not anxious enough to welcome the aging white stranger into its midst. They delayed the meeting while the leaders discussed what to do about the suspicious character. Three hours later they canceled the meeting for "security reasons."[39] Cooper knew what had happened before Dawson contacted him the next day; he had been listening through a room divider in the adjoining conference room. He paid Dawson twenty-five dollars and told him to keep in touch.

Cooper did not have to wait long. Dawson called on October 16 asking if Cooper knew about yet another RCP meeting set for October 21. "I told him we knew of the meeting," said Cooper. "He again said it would be a good idea to disrupt this meeting. Again, I told him if he violated the law or disrupted he would be arrested."[40] Dawson thought for a moment. Griffin had called him the night before. Maybe Cooper would like to know about that. He told Cooper that he was going to Lincolnton on October 20 to talk to the Klan about the "Death to the Klan" march in Greensboro. "We'd certainly like to have information," Cooper told him.[41]

At three-thirty that afternoon, the police department received another call for assistance from Cone's White Oak plant to break up a fight between the RCP and the WVO. By the time the police arrived, the RCP had been chased off the plant site.[42] The RCP accused twelve WVO members of attacking four RCP leafleters with clubs. The WVO accused twelve RCP "cowards, armed with spiked clubs" of attacking two White Oak workers.[43] There were a few minor injuries but no arrests.

Who did what to whom at White Oak was not as important to the police as the fact that there had been more violence between the two groups. And they had yet to receive an application for a parade permit from the WVO. The next day passed, and the next. Finally, on October 19, Nelson Johnson walked into the police department. Captain Gibson was notified and took Johnson into his office. He told him of the restrictions on the march: no weapons in plain view or concealed, no sign posts larger than two-by-two. Johnson asked if the police had information about potential trouble with the Klan. "I told him I knew of none," said Gibson.[44]

The two sat down to fill out the permit application. Sponsor: Workers Viewpoint Organization. Person in charge: Nelson Johnson. Purpose: Political and Educational—to educate and organize opposition to the KKK and their secret supporters. Time: Sat. 11-3-79, 12 noon—2 p.m. Route: Starting point—Everitt Street and Carver Drive. Johnson had to get out a map and read the names of the streets the march would travel as Gibson wrote them down. Everitt to Dunbar to Lee to Benbow to Bragg—thirteen more streets before the termination point at Florida Street and Freeman Mill Road.[45] From the police perspective, it could not have been worse. The march would go through all but one of Greensboro's housing projects.

Gibson read aloud the standard clause at the end of the permit application, a release to the city from all claims, lawsuits, or judgments stemming from injuries or other claims that may occur during the parade. Again, Johnson asked if the police expected trouble from the Klan. Again, Gibson said he was not aware of any.[46] Johnson signed the application and left for New York, for the Founding Congress of the Communist Workers Party.

The delegation from North Carolina had been listening to Jerry Tung, studying his writings and working with him and the national WVO leadership for several years. In that time, they had seen the WVO develop into a tightly structured, highly disciplined organization. Its power structure ran from the top down: the Party Congress, which met to form the CWP in 1979, set national policy and programs; the party's Central Committee, of which Jim Waller became a member, was elected from the Party Congress; Political Bureaus were elected by the Central Committee to function between the party's biennial meetings; the bureau, in turn, elected delegates to Regional Committees and Standing Bodies, the local organizations.[47]

In 1979, the Southern Regional Committee was made up of Paul and Sally Bermanzohn, Jim Waller, Sandi Smith, Bill Sampson, and Nelson Johnson. The Standing Body was composed of the Bermanzohns, Johnson, and Waller. The decision to launch the anti-Klan campaign was not a national one; rather it was formulated by the Regional Committee after three of its members, the Bermanzohns and Johnson, returned from the militant second anti-Klan march in Decatur.[48] Although not directed by the national organization, the anti-Klan campaign was consistent with its overall goals: organizing within trade unions and in black communities. The North Carolina delegates were eager to announce their new effort at the Founding Congress.

That night, Johnson listened with Jim Waller and the Bermanzohns as Jerry Tung analyzed the road that lay ahead. They were mesmerized by the small

Chinese-American. Tung told them what they had been yearning to hear. The revolution was imminent. "This is the beginning of our countdown. The next three years, and particularly the next year, there will be a lot of sacrifices. Sacrifices like you have never sacrificed before. Tightness, discipline in a way you have never done before. Because the extent to which we can do that is the extent to which we can seize state power with a minimum of bloodshed. The extent to which we can help each other so that we will not lose our loved ones, and each other."[49]

Paul Bermanzohn later wrote that at that moment his head was spinning with excitement. In a little over three years, Tung had built the WVO from a loose collection of Communist cells to the Communist Workers Party. In three more years, Tung told the Congress, the party would be in a position to overthrow the government of the United States. Bermanzohn wrote, "Jim Waller and I looked at each other. 'I hope we can meet the test,' whispered Jim. We took Jerry's words seriously, for our experience was that what he said came true."[50]

Chapter 7

> An arresting fact about American violence, and one of the keys to an understanding of its history, is that very little of it has been insurrectionary. Most of our violence has taken the form of action by one group of citizens against another group, rather than by citizens against the State.
> —Richard H. Hofstadter, *American Violence: A Documentary History*

Ask No Questions, I'll Tell No Lies

Lincolnton. Saturday night. The Klan rally had gone well; if not as many people had come as Virgil Griffin would have liked, he had put on a good show for the couple of hundred who had come. Robes, flags, music, even horses. And, of course, the burning cross. Now it was time for the meeting. Members only. Jerry Smith and the security guards checked everyone in as Griffin made his way to the podium.[1] The green grand dragon's robes draped from his slight five-and-a-half-foot frame, making him look larger, stronger than he really was. He stood before the microphone and signaled Eddie Dawson to step forward. Not a particularly inventive or persuasive speaker, Griffin kept his remarks blessedly brief.

It was time to stand up for white people, he said. If you love your children, love your family, you will come to Greensboro to protest those Communists, "niggers," and race mixers. He introduced Dawson, whom he said he had known for eighteen years. Eddie had stood beside him when they both got beat up by the "niggers" at that Klan street walk in Morganton a few years earlier. Eddie has the facts on those Communists, Griffin said; he knows more about them than anybody.[2]

Dawson rose to the applause, his lanky six-foot frame dwarfing the grand dragon. He held up a poster that had pictures from the China Grove demonstration. It said DEATH TO THE KLAN in large red letters. The Communists had been giving the Greensboro police a lot of grief, he told the group. He talked about the RCP spray painting the UNC-G library, about their disrupting classes, about obnoxious posters all over the place. He said he had

Escalation

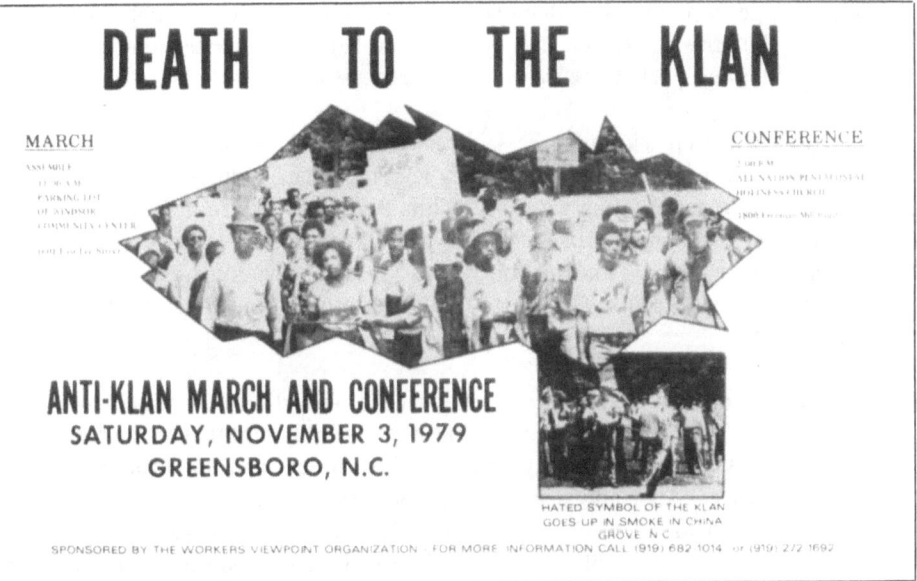

WVO poster announcing the "Death to the Klan" march on November 3, 1979

infiltrated some of the Communists' meetings—they were big "buck niggers," bigger than anyone in the room. And the "Death to the Klan" demonstration would be big, too. Six "nigger" colleges would send people there—students, faculty, football teams.[3] The Communists would bring in a hundred of their own, so there would be six or seven hundred people all together.

Dawson held up the "Death to the Klan" poster again, pointing to a photograph of the Communist demonstrator burning the Confederate flag at China Grove. "We're gonna be up against some tough ones," Carl Nappier heard him say. "He said he wanted some people who knew how to brawl. I was prepared for a knock-down, drag-out fight. I didn't know how we were gonna win cause of the numbers we were prepared to face."[4]

There would be wall-to-wall police, Dawson told them, maybe even National Guard. "Cops wouldn't have made a difference with a fistfight," Dawson said in a 1981 interview.[5] "There would have been a couple of heads bashed in."

The meeting was opened for questions. Someone asked about guns. Dawson said, "I'm not your father"; he said he couldn't tell anyone whether or not to carry a gun. He recited North Carolina gun laws: legal to carry guns in the open, but not concealed. "If you carry a gun, if you go out in the open with a bulge in your pocket, that place is going to be infested with police and you will be arrested. If you carry a gun, you better have your damn bond money in your pocket, cause you're gonna be arrested if you try any garbage."[6]

Griffin stood up. No guns, he said, no firearms. No women, either, said Nappier. Griffin shook his head, "If they're going to be members of the Klan, they can go to any meeting we have." Chris Benson suggested bringing eggs to throw at the Communists, and everyone started talking at once. Griffin banged the podium. Time to vote. Who votes *for* the Invisible Empire, Knights of the Ku Klux Klan to go to Greensboro on November 3? It was unanimous.[7]

"Death to the Klan" posters were being tacked up and handed out all over Greensboro. They listed the time and place of assembly for the march—eleven a.m. at Windsor Community Center on Lee Street—and the location for the conference—All Nations Pentecostal Holiness Church at Florida Street and Freeman Mill Road. On the back of many of the posters was an "open letter to Joe Grady, Gorrell Pierce, and all KKK members and sympathizers."

It called the Klan "one of the most treacherous scum elements produced by the dying system of capitalism" and added, "You are nothing but a bunch of racist cowards." The November 3 march and conference, it announced, were "to organize to physically smash the racist KKK wherever it rears its ugly head."

And then, "We challenge you to attend our November 3rd rally in Greensboro. . . . Grady, Pierce, all Klanspeople and your Nazi friends—you are a temporary pest and obstruction in our fight to end all exploitation and oppression. But, we take you seriously and we will show you no mercy."

It was signed: "Death to the Klan!!! Workers Viewpoint Organization."[8]

Four days after the Lincolnton rally, Eddie Dawson reported to Cooper. Dawson did not bother to tell Cooper that he had been the featured speaker at the meeting, just that he had answered questions. "Dawson said that Griffin told him to expect fifty or sixty to attend," Cooper said.[9] "He said that Griffin was trying to get help from the Klan in South Carolina, Pennsylvania and New Jersey. Dawson said he'd been asked about guns and had stated that it would be up to them. He said that the Greensboro police and the FBI would be at the rally, that if they carried guns they could expect to be arrested. I asked Dawson to keep me apprised of anything else he learned about the group coming to Greensboro." To keep him "apprised"; Cooper left the vital transmittal of information securely in Dawson's hands.

Two days later, on October 26, Dawson called again. "He'd been contacted by Griffin about a meeting October 27 near Raleigh. Dawson couldn't attend because it was his anniversary," said Cooper.[10] "He said the purpose of the meeting was to get Klan, Nazis and the Rights of White People together for the purpose of coming to Greensboro." Griffin told Dawson he would call again to report on the meeting, and Dawson told Cooper he would relay that information. Again, Cooper declined to probe.

Driving around Greensboro, Brent Fletcher spotted the "Death to the Klan" posters. Eddie would know about that, he thought, and he headed for Dawson's house. Driving around and visiting Eddie were about Fletcher's only pleasures in those days—other than drinking. He had been a Klan member in the mid-1960s, he said, "because I didn't have any friends and the Klan was about the only organization going then." He had served in Vietnam, had a leg and part of his other foot blown off, and lived now on his military disability, most of which went for booze.[11] Dawson had stuck with him through it all.

"Eddie told me Nelson Johnson was the head of it," Fletcher said. "He said the Communists were big, tough-looking, wouldn't back down from a fight. There'd been some trouble in a place called China Grove and he didn't understand why the police didn't arrest the Communists. He told me there'd be some men coming up from the Klan and possibly the Nazis."

Fletcher volunteered his house for the Klan's assembly point.[12] It was out in the county, had plenty of parking, and was easy to find: three miles south of the I-85–Randleman Road exit. He promised to raise the Confederate flag in the yard so people couldn't miss it.

Odd things were happening involving Sandi Smith. Following the China Grove demonstration, Jim Waller assigned her to move to the Kannapolis area, get a job in Cannon Mills, and begin laying the groundwork for a WVO organizing drive in the Charlotte area.[13] In mid-October there had been a fire in her trailer near Landis. Not a big fire, miraculously, but enough to make it uninhabitable. No one knew how it started, but there did not seem to be any evidence of arson.[14] Smith had become close friends with one of the local SCEF organizers, Daisy Crawford, and after the fire Crawford helped her find a house in Kannapolis, a much better place to live.

Then the FBI—or someone—came. Crawford could not remember exactly when it was, but it was before November 3. There was a knock on her trailer door and two white men flashed badges at her. Would she please help by identifying some photographs? they asked. She wanted to know why. They would not tell her. She stepped outside, closing the door behind her. There were three photos. Two of them were of men she did not recognize. The third was of Sandi Smith. Frightened, she went back in the trailer, told the men to leave, and slammed the door.[15]

Crawford waited and watched to make sure the agents were gone; then she went to a pay phone to call her good friend Lyn Wells at SCEF's Atlanta headquarters. "She was concerned that there was some kind of FBI probe going on around the union organizing or about China Grove," said Wells, "and that was pretty distressing to her. She felt harassed."

In fact, the FBI was not investigating Crawford or the union or China Grove. It was investigating the Workers Viewpoint Organization. An Associated Press wire story following the Kannapolis news conference had characterized the WVO as a group "advocating the violent overthrow of the government." The Charlotte FBI took notice and forwarded a memo to the Greensboro resident agency to initiate a national security investigation of the group.[16]

In 1985 testimony, FBI officials maintained that although the memo was sent, no investigation took place prior to November 3.[17] But given Wells's corroboration of Crawford's call before the shootings, it is clear that some agency—perhaps the State Bureau of Investigation, perhaps Cannon security—was attempting to investigate Smith.

Curiously, Crawford is the only activist who has ever reported being contacted by investigators prior to November 3.[18] But she never got the chance to tell Sandi Smith.

Virgil Griffin had to work the eleven p.m. to three a.m. shift on October 27, and so he sent Chris Benson to the second Louisburg meeting in his place. Jerry Smith and John Pridmore accompanied the assistant grand dragon. The meeting with Covington and the Raleigh-area Nazis went well. They agreed to meet the Klan in Greensboro on November 3; they agreed that no one would wear uniforms or any other identifying insignia; and they agreed not to bring weapons.[19] Eggs, Benson told them, were not considered weapons.

The discussion was not so amiable at the Hickory klavern meeting the following night. "Everybody wanted to go down to Greensboro and heckle the Communists since they did call us cowards," said Carl Nappier.[20] "So I got up and made a talk about leaving guns at home. I said, 'I've got as many guns as any of you's got and I ain't taking a single one with me.' And they said, 'Why?' And I said, 'If I went down there with a gun strapped on my hip, I'd be afraid of them, wouldn't I? I'm going down there to show them I'm not afraid of them. I'm going to holler and shout. The more noise we can make and keep their speakers from speaking, the better off we're gonna be. We'll probably have to fight.'"

But David Matthews and Eugene Roberson were not listening. "Eugene said, 'I'll kill me one. If they shoot, I'll shoot back,'" Nappier recalled.[21] "And David said, 'I always go prepared. You never know what'll happen.'" Nappier argued with them, and Matthews softened his stance. But Roberson was determined—damned if anyone was going to tell him no guns. The old man was about to start using his fists on the kid; instead, he pointed to the door and told Roberson to leave. He did.

The group started talking again. Some of the women were frightened. Geraldine Beaver and Linda Matthews, David's wife, decided not to go. That left Matthews, who offered to drive, Nappier, Beaver's daughter and son-in-law Rene and Terry Hartsoe, Ruby Sweet, and her sister Barbara Ledford.[22]

The Countdown

Morningside Homes and the other projects through which the anti-Klan march was to go were in the Greensboro Police Department's second district. District Two's Lieutenant Paul Spoon was assigned as event commander, to coordinate all police coverage of the march. Spoon, in turn, assigned Sergeant W. D. "Dave" Comer to provide on-scene coverage of the march, in addition to handling all routine calls in the district. Comer would have only six officers to work the district on November 3.[23]

During the week of October 26, Comer saw a copy of the "open letter" to the Klan. Twice he asked Spoon to assign extra officers for backup in case the Klan did show up; twice he was told he would have to rely on the six district officers. Comer asked a third time, and Spoon told him he would find out if the special Tactical Squad would be available for backup.

On October 30, however, when Comer asked the district commander, Captain Trevor Hampton, about the Tacts, Hampton said he was not aware that Spoon had made a request for them. The following day, Comer learned of Detective Cooper's informant-supplied information on the Klan's plans: eighty to eighty-five Klan members were coming; there was "a possibility" they would be armed. "I told Captain Hampton there was just no way we could handle all these events plus normal calls," said Comer.[24] The Tactical Squad was finally assigned to the march.

Comer was not the only one with the jitters on Halloween Day. The potential for violence on November 3 finally dawned on Ed Dawson. He phoned an old FBI contact, Len Bogaty, and asked his assistance in getting an injunction to stop the march. Bogaty told him that would be a matter for the city to handle, and he warned Dawson to stay away from the march if it could not be stopped. Dawson said he would have to go in order not to be accused of being an informant, to which Bogaty responded that he should keep in close contact with Detective Cooper and give him all the information he could get.[25]

It was now two days before the "Death to the Klan" march. Nelson Johnson had not yet received the parade permit, normally mailed within seventy-two hours of the application. He called a news conference for ten a.m. on the steps in front of the Police Department. Paul Bermanzohn joined him, along with three black women who held a fourteen-foot red banner that said "Death to the Klan." If the police were worried about the WVO and their march, the WVO was nothing short of paranoid about the police—with ample justification, they thought.[26] First, there were the restrictions on the permit, especially the ban on guns. In North Carolina, guns can be carried anywhere as long as they are not concealed. To prohibit guns "in plain view" during the march was probably unconstitutional, certainly highly suspect to a group that promoted "armed self-defense" against the Klan. Then there was the unexplained delay in issuing the permit itself. And, finally, the WVO complained that the police harassed and threatened to arrest people who were putting up "Death to the Klan" posters.

Johnson walked into the police department and demanded the permit. Captain Hampton told him that it was ready, and he advised him that Sergeant Comer would meet him at the corner of Everitt and Carver at eleven-thirty Saturday morning.[27] As they talked, Eddie Dawson was in another part of the police department. He had tried and failed to get an injunction; he told the city attorney, "Next time I want a favor from you, I'll bring you a bucket of blood."[28]

Johnson was already reading his statement to the media when Dawson walked out onto the steps. "We fully expect the police to continue their slimy tactics," Johnson bellowed. "We say to [mayor] Jim Melvin and the police, stay out of our way. The march will go on. The police hate us, we know it and they are out to get us. But the people of Greensboro are intent on driving out the scum KKK."[29]

Dawson approached Bermanzohn. "I played stupid," said Dawson.[30] "I said 'What the hell's this about? What's this sign—Death to the Klan? What are you going to do, kill these people?' And Johnson was just finishing with the TV people, and he walked over and the three of us was talking. He said, 'Those chicken people won't come off their hill.' So I said, 'What're you gonna do to them? Suppose they do, what are you gonna do to them?' And he said, 'Well, they won't.'

"The only other words that were spoken, they invited me down to the rally, their meeting or march or whatever. So I said, 'What if I want to join the Klan?' He said, 'In there with them pigs!' and he pointed toward the police station. And I walked away."

Dawson walked back into the police station, where he asked for a copy of the parade permit for the march. Even "Rooster" Cooper refused to help him on that one. Eventually, the city attorney told the police that they could not deny Dawson a copy of a public document, and he was given the permit, complete with the starting time and the parade route: Everitt Street and Carver Drive; twelve noon. Complete with the restrictions: two-by-two sign posts, no weapons in plain view or concealed.[31]

Two planning meetings were held on November 1 for the police to prepare for the march. The Klan, Cooper told them, and possibly some Nazis would hold a counterdemonstration at the end of the parade.[32] Word of possible violence had been passed to the minister of All Nations Church, the original site for the conference, and his board had withdrawn permission for the Communists to use the church facilities on Saturday. As far as the police knew, no alternative site had been found, but they assumed that the march would still terminate at Florida Street and Freeman Mill Road, where the group would probably assemble in a small shopping center parking lot for their speeches.

Given the CWP's intense and vocal hostility to the police and the poor police-community relations in the housing projects, a low-profile strategy was determined to be the only way the police could monitor the march without inflaming the existing tensions.[33] Sergeant Comer and two patrol officers were to accompany the march. Lieutenant Daughtry, Lieutenant Spoon and the police attorney were to follow it. The Tact squads, a total of nineteen officers, were to "leap-frog" as the march moved along its path. Stationed at intervals parallel to the route, but three to six blocks away, as the march moved beyond a Tact's station, it would move forward to a location well ahead of the march. Each Tact unit was to move from its primary to secondary location in the same manner until the march was completed.[34] They would not approach the demonstration unless requested to by Sergeant Comer.

It would have been a good strategy if Comer had known that the Tacts would not be on location until eleven-thirty. Spoon had told him that the Tacts would be *on duty* at ten. Because of the confusion over the march's starting time and location—posters said it would begin at eleven at Windsor Center; the parade permit said it would start at noon at Everitt Street and Carver

Drive—Comer assumed Spoon meant that the Tacts were taking the precaution of being at their assigned locations at ten.[35]

Ten o'clock was actually the time at which the Tacts and other officers were to be briefed by Detective Cooper. Sergeant Comer, the officer most directly responsible for protecting the march, was not asked to come to the briefing.

A Chance to Heckle

The night of November 1 was another Covington-inspired Klan-Nazi media event. The Nazis, along with Virgil Griffin's and Gorrell Pierce's Klans, were going to "roast" Joe Grady at a news conference at Wayne Wood's house.[36] Grady had publicly opposed the Klan-Nazi alliance. Griffin was unable to attend, but agreed to send Chris Benson, Jerry Smith, and Johnny Pridmore in his place.

Be sure to come in uniform, Wood told Bernie Butkovich. The agent had been working on the Wood investigation for more than five months and he was no closer to nailing the Nazi than he had been in June. There had been plenty of talk—fellow party members asking Bernie to teach them how to use dynamite and plastic explosives and how to convert semiautomatics to automatic and threatening to burn down the interracial dance hall[37]—but when Butkovich told them they would have to get the materials, nothing happened.

There was a new lead, though. One of the Nazis, Roger Shannon, had talked of having a Thompson stashed somewhere on his farm in Davie County. Butkovich offered to find some .45 caliber ammunition so they could try the gun out. Maybe then he could engineer a bust.

Covington was in the midst of his Joe Grady tirade and the WXII-TV camera was rolling when Butkovich entered Wood's garage. Butkovich always tuned out the speeches. His job was to identify people and listen for any mention of illegal weapons, something neither the Nazis nor the Klan were dumb enough to talk about in front of the news media. Griffin's Klan was not there yet, but the Pierce brothers and Shorty Talbert were, plus Covington, Wood, Caudle, Fowler, and Shannon.

The speeches were over and the television crew was about to leave when Benson and Pridmore, in robes, and Smith in his Klan security uniform arrived. The crew quickly set up again, asking the Klan and Nazis to engage in mock conversation while they taped the costumed spectacle for the eleven o'clock news. That completed, they went on their way.

To Butkovich, the mood seemed almost jovial as the Klan and Nazis made their plans for November 3. He did not take into account the fact that to these guys a knock-down, drag-out fight came as naturally as using the word *nigger* or that Wood and Caudle had talked gleefully about breaking one black man's leg and pistol-whipping another. All he was interested in was firearms, illegal firearms. Jerry Smith said something about pipe bombs, about how he had made one and tried it out and it sure would work good if thrown in a crowd of "niggers." But just then he was after Shannon, and Shannon had told him he could not go to Greensboro on Saturday. He would look into the pipe bomb stuff later.[38] It did not register with Butkovich that in less than forty-eight hours, Smith and the Klan and Nazis would go toe-to-toe with a crowd of Communists and blacks in Greensboro.

There was no talk of taking weapons to Greensboro. Benson said something about getting eggs, rotten eggs, but he also said Griffin did not want anyone to bring firearms. Then Butkovich heard Covington say something about a strict gun law in Greensboro—no firearms could be carried "into that city whether they're concealed or otherwise."[39] There was, of course, no such ordinance. There was only one document that contained that kind of stipulation—the permit for the march.

Pierce passed around a copy of the WVO's "Open Letter," which the other Klan and Nazis had not seen before. Butkovich read it and later characterized it as "goading the Klansmen on." Caudle said it sounded like the work of Nelson Johnson and that he sure would like a chance to heckle Johnson like he had been heckled in China Grove. Still, there was no talk of firearms. Butkovich told Wood he would try to come on Saturday. He knew he would not, for two reasons: ATF undercover regulations prohibited him from taking part in any potentially violent public event in which he might have to defend himself,[40] and the lead on Shannon's machine gun seemed to offer more promising investigative ground.

Following the news conference, the Klan and Nazis waited at Wood's house to see themselves on the news. Butkovich left to brief the ATF's Fulton Dukes. The Klan and Nazis were going to a rally in Greensboro to heckle Communist demonstrators, he told his supervisor; they were going to take eggs instead of guns. Smith had said something about a pipe bomb that would work good if thrown in a crowd of "niggers," but Butkovich did not think the threat was a serious one. He said later that he felt no need to report that information to the Greensboro police—that would have been Dukes' responsibility.[41] Besides, both Butkovich and Dukes later testified, all the people at the meeting had agreed not to carry "weapons."[42]

Butkovich asked Dukes to supply him with some .45 caliber ammunition. On Saturday, while everyone else was in Greensboro, he would take the ammo to Shannon's and try to get him to produce the Thompson. Dukes approved the plan and told him to pick up the .45s at the ATF office Saturday morning.

The Klan and Nazis were crammed in Wayne Wood's living room, drinking beer. It was time for the news. Then came the ultimate insult: the "Death to the Klan" story ran first. There was Nelson Johnson calling the Klan scum and cowards, the police slimy. It was too much. Jerry Smith pulled his pistol and pointed it at the television. He claims he said, "I oughtta shoot this television."[43] Benson claims he said, "I'll kill you, you son of a bitch."[44] Whatever the nature of Smith's outburst, his anger was shared by everyone in the room. The Communists had stolen their thunder not once but twice—in China Grove and now on the news. They were not going to let it happen again.

Eddie Dawson was tired of waiting. Griffin had told him that Benson would call to give him a report on the Klan-Nazi meeting in Winston. It was now nearly eleven-thirty, and Dawson had work to do. He had run off a stack of old Klan posters that he wanted to paste over the "Death to the Klan" signs. His original poster showed a silhouette of a man lynched from a tree; the slogan read: "DEATH! to the Traitors. COMMUNISTS, RACE MIXERS and BLACK RIOTERS, TRAITORS BEWARE. Even now the cross-hairs are on the back of your necks. KKKK.[45] It's time for old-fashioned American Justice."

The WVO used the word *death* in their slogan, but Dawson had second thoughts about using it in his. He pasted *notice* over the word *death*.[46] They would get the message. He drove into the projects, a solitary white man in a Cadillac, and he pasted up his signs.

The Eleventh Hour

The CWP organizers were confident on Friday night. Nelson Johnson had succeeded in a last-ditch effort to find a spot for the anti-Klan conference—it was in the Florida Street Shopping Center, an unused room adjacent to the Cosmos II nightclub. He would have to spend most of the night wiring it for lights and sound, but otherwise it was perfect.[47]

Allen and Dori Blitz were to bring in a group of Dori's co-workers from the Budd Trailer plant in Martinsville, Virginia.[48] They would come to the Wallers, where the Greensboro-area people were to gather for last-minute preparations: to make posters, banners, and leaflets and to sew insignia on the tan shirts and red berets of the Revolutionary Youth League, the children of the CWP.

In Durham, CWP members and supporters met at the Break the Chains

Old Klan poster that Ed Dawson pasted over the "Death to the Klan" posters on the night of November 1, 1979

Bookstore, a small party-owned business in a dilapidated building east of downtown.[49] Winos and other street people staggered past the door as the group discussed the next day's events and stapled posters on four-foot-long two-by-twos. Everyone was to meet at the bookstore at nine o'clock to carpool to Greensboro. It looked like they were going to have a good crowd, with several students from Durham's North Carolina Central University and Dori Blitz's co-workers from Budd. But something strange was going on with the police. The restriction on firearms was very suspicious. No one had ever heard of such a prohibition on any of the hundreds of marches they had been involved in. Why would the police disarm this march? Unless they planned to attack.

At about ten p.m. the phone rang at Jerry Smith's house. Half the Lincolnton klavern, complete with wives and kids, were there for a fish fry. Pridmore picked up the phone. It was Virgil. He wanted Smith and Pridmore to come by his trailer as soon as possible so they could drive to Greensboro and case out the march area.[50] Dawson would meet them at an all-night restaurant in Greensboro at two a.m. Leave now? Yes. Smith and Pridmore did as they were told.

As the Klansmen prepared to leave, people who lived along the parade route—Morningside and Warren and Hampton and Smith Homes—found a mimeographed leaflet stuck in their doors. It talked about police harassment and brutality in the projects, about arrests of black youth on trumped-up charges. It talked about how the police and city had disarmed the "Death to the Klan" march. It concluded: "We, the working class people have to depend on each other—we should not depend on the police. So, on Saturday, we want everyone on the march route to protect the march. We want you to sit on your porch or stand in your yard with your gun. . . . DEFEND THE MARCH WITH GUNS!!! DEATH TO THE KLAN!!!"[51]

Chapter 8

> We are what we pretend to be, so we must be
> careful what we pretend to be.
> —Kurt Vonnegut, Jr., *Mother Night*

The Road to Morningside

Virgil Griffin's children were ready for bed when Chris Benson knocked on the trailer door. Benson was to stay with the kids until their mother returned from her third-shift job at seven in the morning. The assistant grand dragon was then to meet the other Klan members at the Lincoln County Fairgrounds and ride with them to the rendezvous house in Greensboro.

They waited for Smith and Pridmore to arrive, talking sporadically. Benson knew Griffin did not quite trust him, and he was not particularly happy about the go-fer duties he had been saddled with—like babysitting.[1] But he was the assistant grand dragon; he got to wear the red robes and he got to stand in for Virgil sometimes. That was pretty heady stuff for a twenty-four-year-old newcomer, and it helped to make the mundane duties tolerable.

Pridmore banged on the door. "Jerry can't come," he told Griffin. The grand dragon scowled and started to berate Pridmore. Smith stood chuckling outside as the voices got louder and louder. He opened the trailer door and announced his presence with a full-blown belly laugh. Gotcha, Virgil.

Griffin finally started laughing, too. Then he tossed his car keys to Smith and went to the back of the trailer to take a shower and change his clothes. Before leaving for work, Linda Griffin had laid his outfit neatly across the bed: blue polyester slacks, white shirt, and his favorite red, white, and blue plaid sport coat—with a borrowed .25 caliber pistol in the pocket.

More guns were in the trunk of Griffin's car. Two belonged to Mark Sherer: a .22 rifle and a .44 black powder pistol. Another rifle belonged to Pridmore; he kept his .32 revolver strapped to his waist. Finally, there was Jerry Smith's sign. Stapled to the end of an old broom handle, it read, "James Earl Ray Is My Hero."

The phone rang. It was Cindy Hall. All of a sudden, it seemed to Benson, Griffin was in a hurry to get on the road. He told Smith to drive, and the three headed off into the night.

It hardly took any time at all to get from Griffin's trailer in Alexis to the good time gal's house in Stanley. Cindy Hall was ready, six-pack in hand. She got in the back seat with Griffin, and the foursome settled in for the two-hour drive to Greensboro, where Eddie Dawson was to meet them.

Scattered thunderstorms were moving through the Piedmont, and the drive took longer than anticipated. It was three in the morning by the time Smith pulled into a truck stop outside Greensboro. Griffin felt the bulge of the .25 when he dug into his pocket for phone change. He went to a booth and dialed Dawson's number.

"Meet me at the 'Your House' [restaurant] on High Point Road," Dawson said. The foursome piled back into the car, following the directions Dawson gave Griffin over the phone.

Dawson arrived at the restaurant several minutes ahead of Griffin and crew. His timing was fortunate. The storm had knocked out the power at the all-night coffee house, and the group would have had a difficult time finding it if Dawson had not been waiting in the parking lot with his lights on.

When Griffin's car pulled in, Dawson yelled out the window for them to follow him down the road to another all-nighter. It was nearly three-thirty when they all finally crammed together in a booth and got some coffee.

Dawson took a paper napkin and drew a map. Pridmore heard him say something about a six-lane highway, Windsor, a shopping center, housing projects. To him it sounded like they were going to confront the Communists at Windsor Shopping Center, located on a six-lane highway that went through the projects.

Griffin and Dawson told the others about the time they routed the Labor Party at the K-Mart, and they all laughed. When they had had their fill of strong coffee, they got in their cars and headed east on Florida Street. Even the darkness could not disguise the transition from middle-class white to welfare-supported black neighborhoods. At the intersection of Freeman Mill Road, Dawson pointed out the All Nations Pentecostal church, the original site of the anti-Klan conference. Across the street was the shopping center and the large parking lot where the march was to terminate. It was actually a much better place for the Klan's purposes: they could park in strategic getaway spots, their people could spread out and be less conspicuous, and they would not have to worry about the stigma of brawling under the Christian banner on church grounds—even if it was a black church.

It looked perfect. Dawson gave Griffin directions to the Orange Motel on I-85, where the grand dragon wanted to spend what was left of the night with Cindy Hall. Pridmore and Smith rode with Dawson as he eased his Cadillac through the Smith Homes housing project. They turned south on Randleman Road and several minutes later pulled into the driveway of the little house with the Rebel flag fluttering in the front yard.

Brent Fletcher went to the door and offered the three a slug from his half-gallon of vodka. They asked for coffee. Fletcher hobbled back into the kitchen and made some instant. Then he brought out a book on the Civil War and a collection of news articles and memorabilia from his days in the Klan. Pridmore unholstered his .32 and passed it around with the literature, just as casually. Those were the days, weren't they Eddie? Remember the Labor Party? We sure did show them, didn't we, Eddie?

Pridmore and Smith began nodding out. Fletcher pointed toward the bedrooms and told them to crash there; he would be sure to wake them early, he said. Dawson left, and Fletcher sat in solitude. Fletcher couldn't sleep, didn't really want to. He turned the radio on low, poured another vodka and coke, and looked back through his clippings. The words were blurry, but it didn't matter. He remembered the events, the old days. Friendship. Drinking buddies. Stand up for America—White America. He missed it, but it would be there again tomorrow. *Death to the Klan?* We'll show 'em, just like we did the Labor Party.

Durham. Dawn broke to the sound of rain and tiny Leah Nathan's demand for food. Mike stoked the wood stove as the infant suckled. The coldness of the kitchen was overshadowed by the chilling remembrance of China Grove.

Greensboro. Cindy Hall was hung over. She asked Griffin to come back for her later; she just couldn't go with him yet. Griffin took off, steaming. At Fletcher's he gave Pridmore the keys to his car and told him to get breakfast with Smith and then to get Hall from the motel. He asked Pridmore to cover for him, to tell people that Cindy Hall was his wife. "Hell no," Pridmore said, "I ain't claiming that ole gal." Griffin turned to Smith. "Uh-uh. I ain't claiming her neither, Virgil."

Hickory. David Matthews was anxious to get on the road, but by seven-thirty he had assembled only four other people. And three of those were women:

Ruby Sweet, her sister Barbara Ledford, and Rene Hartsoe, wife of Terry, the other man in the group. Where the hell was Gene Roberson? Matthews took off looking for him, the big-mouth who made such a stink about bringing guns. He returned without Roberson. No one knew where he was, and Matthews was seething. They were late, and they still had to pick up Carl.

Nappier was back in his dog pens when Matthews arrived. He locked the fifteen Dobermans in and grabbed two sets of brass knuckles from the house. He told Matthews that they needed to make one more stop. Max Hayes had called looking for a ride. As the car drove off, Nappier noticed the equipment in the back seat. A long-barreled shotgun rested in a rack behind the front seat, and on the floor was a pick handle and a set of "numchucks"—a deadly martial arts weapon made of two pieces of hardened, seasoned wood connected with chain. Nappier was not concerned about Matthews's shotgun; he always had one around. But the "numchucks," the pick handle, the brass knuckles—there'd be a good fight, thought the old man. They picked up Max Hayes; a hunting knife was strapped to his belt. A damn good fight, thought Nappier.

Lincolnton. At the fairgrounds, a small group of men gathered near Lawrence Morgan's yellow Ford van. Chris Benson's wife dropped him at the service station across the road. He got his pick handle and a five-foot length of logging chain from the trunk and walked toward Morgan. Griffin would be disappointed. There was just Morgan, Roy Toney, Lee McLain, Billy Joe Franklin, Harold Flowers, and Michael Clinton. Seven, including himself. Benson hoped Matthews and Nappier had had better luck finding people from around Hickory.

Inside the van were three lawn chairs and an assortment of sticks and Klan literature. Benson tossed in his chain and the pick handle, and the men made a rush for the six available seats. As they drove, Morgan and McLain passed their knives for the rest of the group to admire. They stopped once on the way to Greensboro, in China Grove, where they all chipped in and bought seven dozen eggs. Back on the road the mood was jovial. *Death to the Klan?* Try saying that with egg on your face, you Communist SOBs.

Greensboro. Eddie Dawson called Cooper at home. He told "Rooster" that Griffin arrived during the night with two other men and a woman and that they had brought a couple of guns. More people were to come in over the next few hours, Dawson said, and he asked Cooper if he wanted him to contact him again. Cooper gave Dawson a number that would put him through to the phone in his unmarked police car, then he finished getting dressed and headed downtown to meet Tracy Burke, a supervisor of the Tact squad. By then Dawson was already at Fletcher's.

Winston-Salem. Wayne Wood really wanted to stay home and watch cartoons with his son as he always did on Saturdays. But he was a Nazi, and he was not about to forego a chance to get even with the commies from China Grove. His wife was worried, and she didn't hesitate to tell him. "I'll be okay," he told her. "Really, I will."[2] And he was out the door.

Milano Caudle was waiting under the sign at the department store parking lot when Wood arrived. Milling around Caudle's blue Ford Fairlane were his stepson Junior McBride, his nephew Charles Findley, and Jack Fowler, a shaggy-haired, red-headed six-footer. Caudle was in the front seat pumping the brakes as the others watched for signs of life in the Fairlane's tail light. No luck. Fowler and Junior went up the street to a service station to get a new bulb. When they returned, Caudle opened the trunk to get a screw driver, and Wood spotted Caudle's semiautomatic AR-180 and a .357 Magnum. Maybe I oughtta get me a gun, too, thought Wood.

Gorrell Pierce had not shown up yet, but it was time to leave. There was not any need now for two cars, and so Wood suggested that Caudle follow him to his house so he could drop off the car in case his wife needed it. It took only a few minutes. Wood ran in the house and grabbed his shotgun and a teargas grenade from the closet. His wife stopped him at the door, pleading with him this time. "Don't you worry," he told her. "Don't you worry one bit."[3]

Greensboro. There had never been so many people in Brent Fletcher's house. He knew only three of them: Dawson, his old Klan buddy Jim Buck, and Griffin. But it didn't matter. They were his kind of people, whoever they were. And they just kept on coming. The two guys who had spent the night came back with a woman. She appeared to be with Virgil; at least, that was the way he treated her. Then came the baby-faced loner who carried a black powder pistol, and right after him came the car from Hickory with a few more women. Two couples came from the coast, Fletcher heard. And then there was the van from Lincolnton, a couple of guys from Raleigh, a carload from Winston. Fletcher quit trying to keep track of them. He let them look at his Civil War book and his clippings, which they all seemed to enjoy, and he went back to the kitchen to heat more water for coffee. And to fix himself another vodka and coke. The bottle was almost empty.

Across the road from Fletcher's, Cooper and Burke were parked behind a curb market. Using binoculars, Cooper got descriptions of all the cars in Fletcher's drive and on the lawn. He could not get all the license numbers, though. In North Carolina, plates are required only on the back of the vehicle; Cooper could not see the plates on the cars that were backed into the yard.

He and Burke left at about 9:45 so the detective would have enough time to run license checks before the scheduled briefing of the Tact squads at ten. Of the ten vehicles Cooper counted, he got positive identification on only four. He gave the printouts to the Tactical Division and went down to the assembly room, where fifteen Tact officers, two Tact supervisors, the commander of the district through which the march would travel, and the police attorney waited to hear Cooper's report. The report would be the basis for police strategy that day.

Cooper's part of the briefing was over in five minutes. He told the officers that he could not determine the number of people at Fletcher's, but that there were about ten cars in the yard. He told them that, according to his source, a few of the people had handguns. Again according to his source, the group planned to heckle the anti-Klan marchers along the route. They would throw eggs, he said. And the confrontation, if there was one, would occur at the end of the march.

Five minutes. Not enough time to ask the logical questions: If the march is not supposed to start until noon, why is the Klan mobilizing at ten? If the march is going to take two hours to wind through four black housing projects with a gang of rednecks heckling and throwing eggs along the way, isn't a confrontation possible, and even likely, long before the end? If two out of three Klan who arrived early this morning had guns, is it safe to assume that those are the only weapons in a group that now numbers twenty or thirty?

Five minutes. Not enough time to get the low-down on Cooper's source, such as Eddie Dawson's twice-expressed desire to "disrupt" Communist meetings, presumably on his own. If a sixty-year-old man talks about single-handedly disrupting a group of militant young people, what is he going to do with a bunch of armed Klan beside him?

Evidently, these questions were never asked. The police attorney ran through a litany of state laws under which the officers might have to make arrests: wearing masks or hoods on public ways, communicating threats, disorderly conduct, riot, going armed to the terror of the public.[4] The Tact officers were given their assignments, which stationed them from three to six blocks from the march route, and then they were given permission to eat lunch, with the admonition that they be at their posts by eleven-thirty.[5] One half-hour before the starting time listed on the parade permit; one half-hour after the time listed on the WVO's posters.

Countdown

10:30. Saturdays are almost always slow news days, especially in a town the size of Greensboro. As Jim Waters loaded his forty pounds of video equipment, he kept hoping his assignment editor at Channel 2 would come up with something else for him to cover. Anything else.

A protest march. Dull. Any novice could shoot it: closeup of picket signs and faces, fade back to show the group marching and chanting, thirty seconds or so of a talking head who tells the purpose of the march, back to the marchers. End of tape. Off to the next assignment. Dull.

Waters had covered the WVO news conference on Thursday. "Death to the Klan." The audio would be anything but dull on this one, he knew. But he was a photographer, a damn good one. He thought about the year he spent in Northern Ireland, about testing his personal courage and professional skill under fire. Waters was proud to have conquered the challenge, but he knew that he never wanted to experience war again. There had to be some middle ground, something less dangerous than war in Northern Ireland, something more stimulating than street marches in Greensboro, North Carolina.

10:35. The sky cleared, and the bright November sun began to warm the air. Signe Waller served her umpteenth cup of coffee to the newest arrival and passed around another plate of homemade coffee cake. Paul Bermanzohn once called her "the Elsa Maxwell of the movement. Nobody's ever left her house without something to eat."[6]

Jim Waller asked Dori Blitz to step outside with him. There could be a sniper along the march route, he told her as he handed her a .38 revolver. He had watched her in intense situations, he said, and was impressed that she never panicked and never backed down from a fight. He told her to take the gun, just in case.

Blitz had never fired a pistol before, and her pockets were not large enough to conceal a gun anyway. Waller got an old yellow rain slicker off a hook on the back porch and told her to wear it and carry the gun in the pocket. Then he showed her how to aim and fire. Armed self-defense—it was a major component of their anti-Klan strategy.

It was time to leave. They gathered leaflets and banners, song sheets and Workers Viewpoint newspapers, blackjacks and walkie-talkies. Waller and Bermanzohn drove straight to Morningside. Some followed; others stopped first at Windsor Community Center. To the demonstrators, the mood at Windsor was excited, even exuberant. To outsiders, like the news media and the police, the mood was defiant, sometimes angry.

10:40. Don Davis pulled his Chevy Nova to the far end of the Windsor Center parking lot to wait for his partner, *Greensboro Daily News* reporter Winston Cavin. He fidgeted with his cameras until he realized that he was the object of some hostile attention. "Pig stay away," a woman shouted, and soon others joined her in the chant. It was not the first time for Davis. His Nova was frequently mistaken for an unmarked police car. Cavin walked around the group to the Nova. The march's starting point had been changed, the reporter said. Davis felt that the demonstrators were jacking the media around, and he did not like it. But he had a job to do, as did Cavin. One of the demonstrators had given them directions to the new site, Everitt Street and Carver Drive. Off they went.

10:45. Eddie Dawson and Jim Buck were hunched over a map on Fletcher's kitchen table. Using the street names written on the back of the WVO's parade permit, they were trying to draw the march route on the map. But the streets through Morningside were narrow; some, such as Carver, are more like alleys and are not shown on city maps. Dawson and Buck were perplexed. Finally, they traced the route backwards, from Florida Street and Freeman Mill Road, through Smith Homes, Hampton Homes, and Warren Homes, to Morningside, somewhere along Everitt Street.

It was time to leave. People were scattered all over the house and yard, and it was not going to be easy to get them all together. Dawson walked into the back bedroom. It looked like a gun nut's paradise, with shotguns, pistols, and an assortment of other weapons strewn across the bed. Wayne Wood held up his teargas cannister and asked if he should take it along. "Look," said Dawson, "where we're going, the streets are real narrow, almost alleys. If you toss that thing *we'll* probably get the worst of it."[7] Wood put the cannister in his jacket pocket, along with a knife.

Out in the yard, Milano Caudle held up his AR-180 and told anyone who appeared interested that he could buy the guns for a mere $187. Jerry Smith spotted Chris Benson near Griffin's car. He walked over to the assistant grand dragon and ordered him to turn over his brass knuckles and his shotgun. Smith wanted all the weapons in the van, or so he told Benson.

Cindy Hall watched as the men moved from the back of the house out the front door. They all had guns, it seemed, and she became frightened. It was one thing to yell obscenities at commies, maybe even throw a punch or two. But guns? Nope, she wasn't going. Griffin said he would leave the .25 behind and laid it on a table. But Hall had made her decision. There were still all those shotguns and rifles being loaded into cars. She would wait at Fletcher's.

Griffin stormed out of the house and walked directly to Dawson. "How're we going to organize this thing," he demanded. Dawson and Buck would take the lead; they knew the town, and Buck had a CB in his truck. Six other vehicles were to follow, with Lawrence Morgan's van, which also had a CB, bringing up the rear.

Someone was missing. Fowler and Junior McBride had slipped off in Caudle's Fairlane to get a burger while the convoy was forming. People were already in the cars, however, anxious to get moving. Eight cars pulled out onto Randleman Road.

Cooper and police identification specialist John Matthews wound their way through the corridors of the police department to the underground parking garage, where they loaded their equipment into Cooper's unmarked tan Chevy Nova. Matthews had only one camera, one thirty-five millimeter lens, and five rolls of film. Cooper had his riot gear: a shotgun and a flack vest.

It took Cooper and Matthews almost twelve minutes to get from downtown to Fletcher's house. Most of the cars had left, but Cooper wanted to identify those that remained. Using his binoculars, he read off the numbers of the plates he could see. Matthews wrote them down.

Cooper and Matthews would have lost the caravan altogether had it not been for a lucky break. The caravan was about a mile down the road when Fowler caught up with them. They pulled into a parking lot and Fowler asked if someone would follow him back to Fletcher's so he could leave the Fairlane there—and the guns. "We've wasted too much time already," somebody told him. "Just fall in line."

As the cars made the turn from Randleman Road onto I-85, Fowler thought he saw Gorrell Pierce's blue truck headed toward Fletcher's. "Hold it," Fowler yelled into the CB. "Let's hold it here. I'll go back and try to catch Gorrell." Fowler made a U-turn and left the caravan on the access ramp. So they waited, not knowing that another car was rushing to catch up. Eight vehicles were parked along the ramp when Cooper spotted them.

The detective made a hard right to get on the road that parallels the access ramp and I-85. He attempted to contact Lieutenant Spoon, the event commander. The police radio operator advised Cooper that Spoon was out of contact. He asked about Lieutenant Sylvester Daughtry, the officer in charge of the Tact squads. Tracy Burke cut in, "He's still in the office."[8]

Burke and Cooper switched to Frequency 4, and Cooper reported, "Okay, you got eight vehicles parked and loaded on the ramp from down where we went this morning. They're on the ramp of 85 and 220 [Randleman Road]. It looks like about thirty or thirty-five people, maybe not that many, in the vehicles. They're just sitting on the ramp there waiting, all in the vehicles. So, we're gonna stand by here and kinda monitor them, see what they do."

It was 11:06.

Marty and Mike Nathan were at Windsor Center double-checking the medical supplies. Water, bandages, antiseptic, ammonia capsules, salt tablets—the normal equipment needed for a group of people walking a long distance. Jim Waller approached, asking which one would be responsible for covering the march. Marty felt she should stay with the students she had brought from North Carolina Central; Mike was nominated by default. He put the medical equipment in the trunk of his car and followed Waller back to Morningside.

Sergeant Dave Comer could hear the radio traffic between Cooper and Burke from his observation post down the block from the Windsor Center parking lot. He had checked the Morningside starting point earlier, but when he found no one there, he went on to Windsor. He found a group there, all right: a noisy, "Pigs-stay-away" group. Comer pulled back into a less obvious position and asked Cooper to repeat his information. "We got about eight or nine vehicles the opposite side parked on the ramp at 85 and 220, headed your direction," Cooper reported. "However, they're stationary at this time. We'll have further if they move in."

Comer tried to locate Lieutenant Spoon, and again Burke cut in. "Dave, I don't think he's in the car yet." Comer gave Burke the message instead: "For information, they're pretty hostile over here at Windsor, refusing to talk to us, what have you."

It was 11:12.

There was quite a respectable crowd assembled by the time Mike Nathan arrived at Everitt Street and Carver Drive. Not a whole lot of neighborhood people, though, except for some kids in football uniforms, their moms, and a slightly drunk man wearing a white fake leather jacket. Most of the WVO people were hustling around making last-minute preparations. Bill and Dale Sampson worked with Dori and Allen Blitz on the sound truck; Signe Waller was peddling WVO newspapers; Paul Bermanzohn and Nelson Johnson greeted the media. Most of the others stood in a semicircle in front of guitar-strumming Tom Clark, who led them in an off-key rendition of "We Shall Not Be Moved."9

John Matthews got a few shots of the caravan as Cooper reported to Burke and Comer over the radio. People were out of the cars now, pacing from car to car. The blue Fairlane cruised toward the front of the line, and everybody scrambled to get back into their cars. The Fairlane held back, waiting to enter the line, and finally jockeyed in just ahead of the yellow van.

"We're rolling now," Cooper told Burke, "headed that direction from this location. There's a total now of nine vehicles."

It was 11:13.

A demonstrator standing next to Tom Clark held a Klan effigy by its pointy hood. Around its neck was a sign that said, "KKK SCUM." On the ground was a can of charcoal lighter fluid, to be used at the appropriate dramatic moment to ensure a well-burning effigy. The adults sang as neighborhood kids in football uniforms joined the kids in the Revolutionary Youth League uniforms, who were to lead the march, in pummeling the dummy in the white sheet. "Just like a tree"—whap—"standing by the wa-ater"—blam—"we shall not"—ka-pow—"be moved." "Yaaaaay."

"Death to the Klan," a woman shouted into a megaphone. The demonstrators' clenched fists punched the air above their heads as the kids continued to torment the dummy. "*Death* to the Klan. *Death* to the Klan." The chants faded into a smattering of applause and a few whistles. The megaphone came alive again: "People, people, have you heard. Rev-o-lu-tion is the word. People, people, ain't it right. Death to the Kla-an is our fight."[10]

It was 11:16.

The caravan was now within a mile of Everitt and Carver, and Lieutenant Spoon was still out of radio contact. But the Tact commander, Lieutenant Daughtry, was finally on his car radio; Burke briefed him on the caravan's progress and Comer's situation at Windsor. Cooper broke in: "On 29 now, approaching Florida Street."

"Tracy," Daughtry asked, "are y'all in position?" When Burke responded that "most of us jumped out to get a sandwich or something," his lieutenant chided, "They got fourteen more minutes according to my watch. Rush 'em up."

Most of the Tacts were still eating at a fast-food place near the I-85 ramp where the Klan caravan had waited for Fowler, six miles from Everitt Street and Carver Drive.[11] Two of the Tact officers, however, both rookies on the special squad, had heard Cooper's report of the caravan's movement. Art League and Sam Bryant were already in the march area. Although they had been cautioned not to approach the demonstrators unless requested by the division or a Tact supervisor, they were curious. They headed for Everitt Street.

The rookies approached the demonstration site. It looked like a typical rally, nothing unusual. They turned left a block before Carver and drove on to their assigned location at Dudley High School, a few blocks south. The radio squawked, and they heard Cooper say that the caravan had turned onto Lee Street, just a block away.

It was 11:18.

Cesar Cauce parked Tom Clark's pickup on Carver at the corner of Everitt, almost completely blocking access to the alley-like drive. Several of the demonstrators walked over to help Cauce unload pickets and banners. Ed

Boyd of WTVD-TV in Durham let his camera roll as Cauce worked. There wasn't much else to do. Most of the other newspeople there were thoroughly exasperated and were talking to each other rather than the demonstrators. They had been told the march would start at eleven from Windsor, only to learn that it really would begin at noon from Morningside. To top it off, they had been insulted: Nelson Johnson accused "your" news media—directed at a High Point televison reporter[12]—of "promoting" the Klan, and Signe Waller refused to give another television reporter a complimentary copy of *Workers Viewpoint*. "They're only free for working people," Waller said. "What the hell do you think I'm doing here?" snapped the reporter, and she walked away.[13]

It was 11:19.

"Turning on Willow Road now," Cooper reported. Daughtry ordered Burke, "Let's hustle on in and get in those positions because they're moving before we anticipated." Burke replied, "We're on the way." A little more than a minute later, the caravan made the turn onto Everitt Street. Wayne Wood picked up the CB and notified those who might not have noticed, "We're heading into niggertown."

Finally, Lieutenant Spoon made radio contact with Daughtry. Totally unaware that the Klan caravan was almost on top of the demonstrators, Spoon asked Daughtry to meet him to discuss a message he had just received: the minister was refusing to allow the WVO to meet at his church. The decision had been made days earlier, a decision that everyone, including the WVO and Dawson, knew about. Everyone except Spoon.

It was 11:21.

Chapter 9

> "There are plenty of good reasons for fighting," I said, "but no good reason to ever hate without reservation, to imagine that God Almighty Himself hates with you, too. Where's evil? It's that large part of every man that wants to hate without limit, that wants to hate with God on its side. It's that part of man that finds all kinds of ugliness so attractive. It's that part of an imbecile," I said, "that punishes and villifies and makes war gladly."
>
> —Kurt Vonnegut, Jr., *Mother Night*

Massacre at Morningside

Ed Boyd walked to the northeast corner of the intersection to get a shot of a pile of "Death to the Klan" posters attached to picket sticks. "Help Celebrate the Founding of the Communist Workers Party" read the slogan at the bottom of the poster. Boyd heard something. It sounded like, "Here comes the Klan." That couldn't be right. He straightened up and looked to the left. There was a whole string of cars and trucks approaching from the east, coming very, very slowly. He focused on a tan pickup that seemed to be in the lead; then he panned to the left to catch the other cars as they came past him. A weird-looking guy in the back of a station wagon had his arm out the window. Zoom in. "Remember China Grove," Milano Caudle said to the demonstrators. A green sedan bore a Confederate flag plate on its front bumper. Zoom in. Fade back. The baby-faced passenger in the pickup behind the green car was working on something in his lap. He had a perverse kind of smile. Zoom in.

To his right, Boyd heard the now-familiar chant. "Death to the Klan." It started slowly, hesitatingly, and then got louder. He swung his camera back to the right just in time to catch a demonstrator hitting the trunk of a car with a piece of firewood, then another kicking at the rear of one of the Klan cars. Someone else came from the sidewalk to the left and kicked the car's side panel. People in the front of the caravan were starting to get out of their cars, and Boyd focused on them. Something caught his eye, up near a parked school bus. A puff of smoke. A split second later, he heard the retort. Guns. Boyd backed across the street, keeping the camera rolling but looking desperately for a place to hide.

Cooper was still on Willow Road, three blocks east of the Everitt-Carver intersection. John Matthews listened as Cooper advised Daughtry, "They're now at the formation point." Spoon interrupted, "You're talking on . . . What traffic you got going?"

"Okay," Cooper said, "we got about nine or ten cars on the opposite side has now arrived at the formation point for the parade and it appears as though they're heckling at this time, driving on by, uh, they're definitely creating attention and some of the parade members are, uh . . ."

Matthews nudged Cooper, "Heckling, hell. That sounds like gunfire." It was. In fact, by the time Matthews alerted Cooper, several shots had been fired.

Mark Sherer, the baby-faced nineteen-year-old in the pickup truck, had been inserting explosive primers on the black powder cartridges in his .44 when Boyd photographed him as the caravan approached. The line of cars came to a halt when Buck and Dawson saw a commotion in their truck's rearview mirror and stopped. Nine vehicles loaded with Nazis and Klan came to a dead halt on a narrow street in a black housing project. Demonstrators—black, white, Communist—swarmed into the street. Blocked by Buck's truck, under attack, the only escape for the caravan members was to fight back.

Sherer stuck his right arm out the truck window and fired his .44 at the ground. Not everyone heard the shot, but those who did started a frenzied chain reaction.

Benson, McLain, and Nappier got out of their car and started east on Everitt Street, in the direction the demonstrators were now running. Fletcher grabbed his shotgun from the floorboard and struggled to get out of the car. Sherer had the upper half of his body outside the truck's window, waving the gun with his right hand, pounding the roof with his left. "Show me a nigger with some guts and I'll show you a Klansman with a gun," he screamed.

Fletcher fired into the air. The reverberation sent demonstrators and neighborhood children scurrying for cover, most of them heading north on Carver. Yelling "Shoot the niggers," Sherer took aim at a couple of black figures on the south side of Everitt. They were children. Frozen in their tracks. Crying. He raised his arm above his head and fired.[1]

There was mayhem at the intersection of Everitt and Carver. The van and the Fairlane had stopped east of the corner when the line came to a halt. The ten men in the van piled out after Terry Hartsoe yelled that the car his wife was riding in, toward the front of the caravan, was being attacked by demonstrators. The path from the van to the car Hartsoe's wife was in was blocked by Tom Clark's pickup in the intersection; a pile of two-by-twos was sticking out the back. In the truck's cab, on the gunrack, was a loaded shotgun that Cauce had borrowed, along with the truck, from Clark. Jim Waller grabbed the gun off the rack just as half a dozen Klan and Nazis rushed into the intersection.

Demonstrator Frankie Powell, eight months pregnant, ran a few steps north on Carver when her right leg buckled. The forward momentum hurled her against the edge of the open truck door. Dazed and bleeding from a gash on her forehead, Powell couldn't make her body function. She lay on the pavement, barely conscious of the vicious fight going on above and around her.

Several of the Klan and Nazis were using the two-by-twos like axes, swinging at demonstrators in a full-force, over-the-shoulder chop. One rushed past Dale Sampson and other white demonstrators, cracking Sandi Smith on the crown of her skull, splitting the flesh in a huge T-shaped gash.[2] She staggered north on Carver. Sampson ran to her side, bracing Smith with her arms. Ahead of them were several children—panicked, confused. "Take care of the children," Smith said. "I can't run." Sampson herded the children up the street, and Smith took cover on the porch of the Morningside Community Center.

At the same time, Kate White and Floris Cauce were trying to help Frankie Powell to her feet. "We'll have to drag her," Powell heard one of the women yell. "Otherwise she'll get trampled." Limp, helpless, grateful, she felt hands take her by the arms and the back of her coat. She was moving. Thank God.

Harold Flowers was the last one out of the van. He was scared. Scared to fight; scared not to. Just as he reached the corner, a bearded man in a white checkered jacket came around the right front of the pickup. Flowers saw the glisten of gun metal. Bill Sampson was pointing the .38 right at him.[3] Flowers froze and looked into Sampson's eyes. The former divinity school student lowered the gun, turned, and ran back around the pickup to the west side of Carver Drive.

It was too late. "They've got guns," everyone was yelling at once. Wayne Wood ran back toward the Fairlane; Fowler was already fumbling with the keys, trying to open the trunk where their guns were stashed. Pridmore and Matthews scrambled through the van's cargo door. Matthews's heart was racing, and each breath felt like it would tear open the recent incision in his chest. He grabbed his shotgun and went back into the street, using the van's open passenger door for cover. Pridmore found another shotgun in the van. He had seen Waller and was sure the black-bearded man was going to shoot him. He started back toward the intersection with the shotgun nestled securely at his side.

Jim Waller and Roy Toney were in a life-or-death struggle over Tom Clark's shotgun. Toney had pushed the barrel into the air when Waller swung it at him, and now they were almost nose-to-nose, Toney clutching the barrel, Waller pulling and pushing the gun's butt and stock. One of them hit the wooden pump mechanism, ejecting a live shell and sliding another cartridge of buckshot into the chamber.

Demonstrator Jim Wrenn saw the fight and ran across Carver to help Waller. Cesar Cauce was still standing in the middle of the intersection, watching as the lead cars in the caravan slowly began to move out. He had no way of knowing that the Fairlane and the van stayed behind. He had no way of knowing that at that moment Pridmore and Matthews had guns in their hands, that the Fairlane's trunk was open and Wood's shotgun and Caudle's AR-180 and .357 were almost in the grasp of panicked, experienced shooters.

Cauce heard the commotion on the east side of the pickup. Armed with a two-by-two and a billy club, he went to check it out. He and Wrenn, along with several Klan, lunged at Waller and Toney at once. Someone's hand rammed the pump mechanism back and, in doing so, caught a piece of Waller's palm in the chamber, tearing it off. Waller let go of the gun, and Toney fell backward with it clutched to his chest. Wrenn was knocked on top of Toney, with Cauce and a couple of Klan flailing at each other across his back.

Wrenn and Toney were belly-to-belly with a shotgun between them. Toney thought he was going to black out. And he knew if he did he'd be dead. Toney heard voices: "They've got Roy." Wrenn heard voices: "Hit the ground." Suddenly the men on top of them were gone. Wrenn scrambled to his feet and made a dash across Carver to the front of the WXII-TV's station wagon, where half a dozen demonstrators and newspeople were hiding.

The pump mechanism on the shotgun Pridmore had grabbed from the van jammed; he was trying to rack it as he looked for the bearded man. He didn't see him. And, momentarily, he didn't see any reason to shoot.

Another shot. Sherer again, firing into the side of a parked car as the line of Klan and Nazis headed west on Everitt Street. "Move it, move it," Benson heard Griffin yell, and he ran back to the car, stomped the accelerator, and screeched away, leaving Nappier and McLain behind to fend for themselves.

Toney lay in the grass catching his breath and wondering what to do. There was the shotgun, right beside him. He lunged for it and pulled the trigger.[4] Shot number five.

Wayne Wood lifted his shotgun to his right shoulder. He sighted down the barrel and his index finger eased the trigger back, sending a load of birdshot into the side of the WXII car.

11:23.27

Cooper: "Shots fired, sounds like . . ."
Spoon: "Move the District Two cars into the area."

Escalation 139

Daughtry to Burke: "Move in."

Burke: "On the way . . ."

"I'm hit," screamed Frankie Powell. "I'm hit." The stinging in her back and legs was fierce, and she tried desperately to pull herself further under the front of the news car. She heard someone yell, "Protect the baby," and suddenly there was a pile of bodies on top of her. Like in a football game, she thought. Only this wasn't any game. There were now a dozen people trying to use the station wagon for cover. And somebody was shooting at the car. If they hit the gas tank . . .

Cesar Cauce was on his own now, trapped by Clark's pickup on the west, surrounded by half a dozen Klan. Sticks and fists were flying at him, but most of his attackers were small, one hundred and fifty to one hundred and sixty pounds, tops. Cauce was over six feet tall and weighed two hundred and twenty pounds. He tried to bull his way through the six of them and might have made it if they hadn't had sticks and clubs. One cracked him in the forehead, opening a two-inch gash and knocking him to his knees.

Crouched alongside the Fairlane, Jerry Smith began to move toward the fight by the pickup. Wood was to his right, slide-stepping west on Everitt with his shotgun nestled on his shoulder. Covered by Wood, Smith fired Caudle's .357 twice, and in a half-crouch, half-run, scooted between the parked cars to the sidewalk. Wood was next to him now, firing two more volleys of birdshot.

The birdshot hit Jim Waller from the right, peppering him from the shoulder to mid-calf. But for one pellet, he might not have noticed the sting until later. Until he was safe. One pellet, though, struck the shaft of his penis. He doubled over, gasping in pain. David Matthews saw the black hair, the black beard. "Nigger with a shotgun," he thought. He aimed at Waller's back, squeezed the trigger, and sent a full load of buckshot into his buttocks and the small of his back. But for one buckshot pellet, he might have survived. That one pellet tore upward from Waller's lower left back, through the left lung, through the left ventricle of his heart.

Dori Blitz was aware that Waller was near her. She was not aware that he had been shot, that the force of the blast propelled him forward several yards, that he collapsed behind her. Blitz was only aware that there were several men on Everitt Street. Shooting. One was moving up on Cesar, and it looked like he had pistols in both hands. This is it, she told herself. She pulled the snub-nosed .38 from her coat pocket. Waller's instructions came back: shoulder-point; wrap your right hand around the stock and get your trigger finger in position; place the butt in the palm of your left hand and wrap those fingers up and around to steady your right hand; hold both arms straight out, aim, and squeeze. Dori Blitz, birthright Quaker, fired shot number twelve, the first shot fired by the demonstrators.

11:23.47

"Heavy gunfire." Cooper moved his car onto Everitt Street and John Matthews focused his camera on the action around the yellow van. Cooper's car was still a hundred yards behind the van, at the bottom of a hill.

Spoon: "Pull all available cars in the city to the area of . . . , the Windsor Community Center."

Comer: "It's not at Windsor. I think they're at Everitt and Carver where . . . , the Tact Units are at. We're with the group at Windsor, no problem."

Where the Tact Units are at. If Comer had known that the Tacts *were not* at their assigned locations, he would have gone to Morningside as soon as Cooper radioed the Klan was on Everitt Street. But he didn't know. And he didn't move.

Thirty-seven seconds elapsed between Cooper's request to "send some units in here" to stop the stick fight and his announcement: "Heavy gunfire." League and Bryant, the two rookies on the Tact Squad, began to move when they heard Cooper's first call for assistance; Burke waited until Daughtry's order following "Shots fired." The rookies took the quickest route to Everitt Street; the Tact supervisor got on Route 29 at Florida Street and drove north. Past the Lee Street exit—four blocks from Everitt and Carver. Past the Gorrell Street exit—two blocks from Everitt and Carver. He was headed for Market Street, one mile north. He would have to double back on Gillespie Street, a three- or four-minute drive. He would be too late.

Jim Waters and Ed Boyd were within a few feet of each other in a parking lot on the south side of Everitt. Their cameras were rolling, microphones capturing the staccato of gunfire, lenses capturing one man, then a second, and a third stalking human targets. Don Davis, from beside his car to the east of the video photographers, had seen Fowler at the Fairlane's trunk, Pridmore covering him with a shotgun. Frame after frame moved through Davis's camera as Fowler opened the trunk and passed out weapons, a cigarette dangling casually from his lips.

Suddenly, Davis saw Pridmore reel to his left. Something had brushed Pridmore's shoulder; in a panic he jerked toward it and pulled the shotgun's trigger. The gun jammed. If it hadn't, Jack Fowler would have been blown away. The Nazi was in a direct line between Pridmore and Don Davis. The photographer hit the ground in an involuntary self-protective reaction.

Waters and Boyd continued to film. Smoke belched from the end of Wayne Wood's gun. Jerry Smith ran down the sidewalk with his .357 aimed at something near the pickup. Neither photographer could see it, but their videotape picked up the bright yellow slicker moving out of the background shadows toward Smith. Dori Blitz fired a microsecond before Smith shot at Cauce.

Escalation

Both missed. She emptied the gun at him, but Smith kept moving. With the now-useless gun at her side, Blitz moved back into the shadows and tripped over Jim Waller's body.

Cesar Cauce was on his knees in the gutter to the right of the pickup's rear wheel. The Klansmen around him backed off when they heard Smith and Blitz shooting. Now Smith had an easy target; he fired. Harold Flowers recognized the sound of bullet hitting flesh. The bullet struck Cauce just at the bottom of his neck, piercing his right lung, trachea, aorta, pulmonary artery, left lung, and spleen before exiting through his lower left back. He was still alive, fighting to get back on his feet.

Another figure moved from the shadows of the apartments toward Cauce. Armed only with a picket stick bearing a "Death to the Klan" poster, Paul Bermanzohn edged forward. He'd heard some shots, but his mind refused to comprehend. They couldn't be shooting at people.

On the other side of Carver, Bill Sampson had no doubt that the Klan was shooting at people. As Sampson raised his .38, Wood sent a final load of birdshot into the intersection. There were four wounded now under or in front of the WXII car. Sampson leaned over the hood of the station wagon and fired twice at the red-haired guy with the semiautomatic rifle. Fowler shot back. Twice.

Mike Nathan had seen Waller fall on the other side of Carver. He crept to the rear of the WXII car and started to dash toward Waller just as Sampson fired again at Fowler.

The Nazi eased the trigger back again. And again. A slug ricocheted off a car, and two slivers of copper pierced Nathan's left shoulder. Like Bermanzohn, Nathan still held a "Death to the Klan" picket in his hand. And in a split second, both doctors would feel the force of lead colliding with flesh and bone. Roy Toney had sent a second load of buckshot into the air in the midst of the shooting between Sampson and Fowler. All he wanted was to get back to the van, to get the hell out of this place. He saw Cauce in the grass trying to get up. One of the Klan near the pickup hoisted a six-foot-long two-by-two over his shoulder and brought it crashing down on Cauce's head. The force of the blow broke the stick in half, and Harold Flowers ran in front of Cauce to grab the other half before the Cuban could get it. On his knees and elbows now, Cauce turned his head toward the right and looked at Flowers. His jaw dropped and blood started pouring from his mouth as he collapsed face down into the grass.

Just get me out of here, thought Toney. He pulled the trigger for the third time, hitting Flowers in the shoulder and Paul Bermanzohn in the head and arm.

Boyd's camera was now focused on Cauce. He's gotta get up, Boyd kept

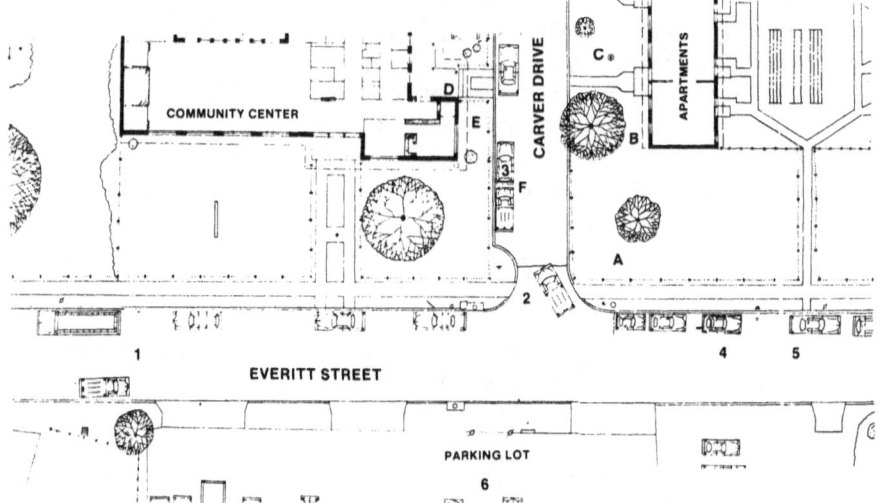

Map of Everitt Street and Carver Drive, adapted with permission from a larger scale drawing by Greensboro police detective Jim Ballance

Legend: 1, location of vehicle from which Mark Sherer fired the first shot; 2, area where Klan, Nazis, and demonstrators began brawling. Tom Clark's pickup truck, from which Jim Waller got a shotgun, is parked diagonally across the intersection; 3, WXII-TV news car where many demonstrators took cover during the shooting; 4, location of Milano Caudle's Ford Fairlane that carried the guns used by Wayne Wood, Jack Fowler, and Jerry Smith; 5, location of Lawrence Morgan's van that contained a mini-arsenal of shotguns, handguns, clubs, chains, and other weapons. David Matthews used the van's passenger door for cover as he fired four fatal shots; 6, parking lot where Ed Boyd and Jim Waters stood while videotaping the shootings. A, grassy area where Cesar Cauce died several moments after being shot; B, edge of apartments where Paul Bermanzohn was felled by buckshot; C, area where Jim Waller's body was found; D, community center porch where Sandi Smith was killed by a single buckshot pellet; E, area from which Bill Sampson was firing when he was fatally struck by buckshot; F, location where Mike Nathan was mortally wounded.

1, As the caravan moves into the demonstration area, Mark Sherer glances up as he loads a black powder pistol in his lap. *2*, Milano Caudle gestures at demonstrators and says, "Remember China Grove." *3*, Demonstrators swarm into the street as the Klan caravan passes. Just to the left of Bill Sampson's head (Sampson wearing checked jacket) a puff of smoke from Sherer's first shot can be seen. *4*, Leaning out of the truck cab, Sherer shouts and waves his gun. *5*, Caravan members (with sticks) clash with demonstrators in the intersection. *6*, Cesar Cauce stands alone in the intersection as demonstrators in the background flee for cover after more shots are fired.

7

8

9

10

11

12

7, At the left edge of the photograph, Jerry Smith runs toward the intersection with a handgun. Wayne Wood can be seen aiming his shotgun, as Junior McBride watches and Jack Fowler (right) loads the AR-180. *8*, Fowler is armed with the AR-180. *9*, Smith fires at Cauce, who is on the ground at the truck's right rear wheel. *10*, Cauce (center) has crawled into the grass after being shot. To his left in the background is Paul Bermanzohn. Roy Toney (right) is raising the shotgun he took from Jim Waller into firing position. *11*, Fowler, Smith, and Wood return their guns to the trunk as they prepare to leave. David Matthews (unseen) is still firing from the passenger side of the van. *12*, Mike Nathan lies mortally wounded in the street.

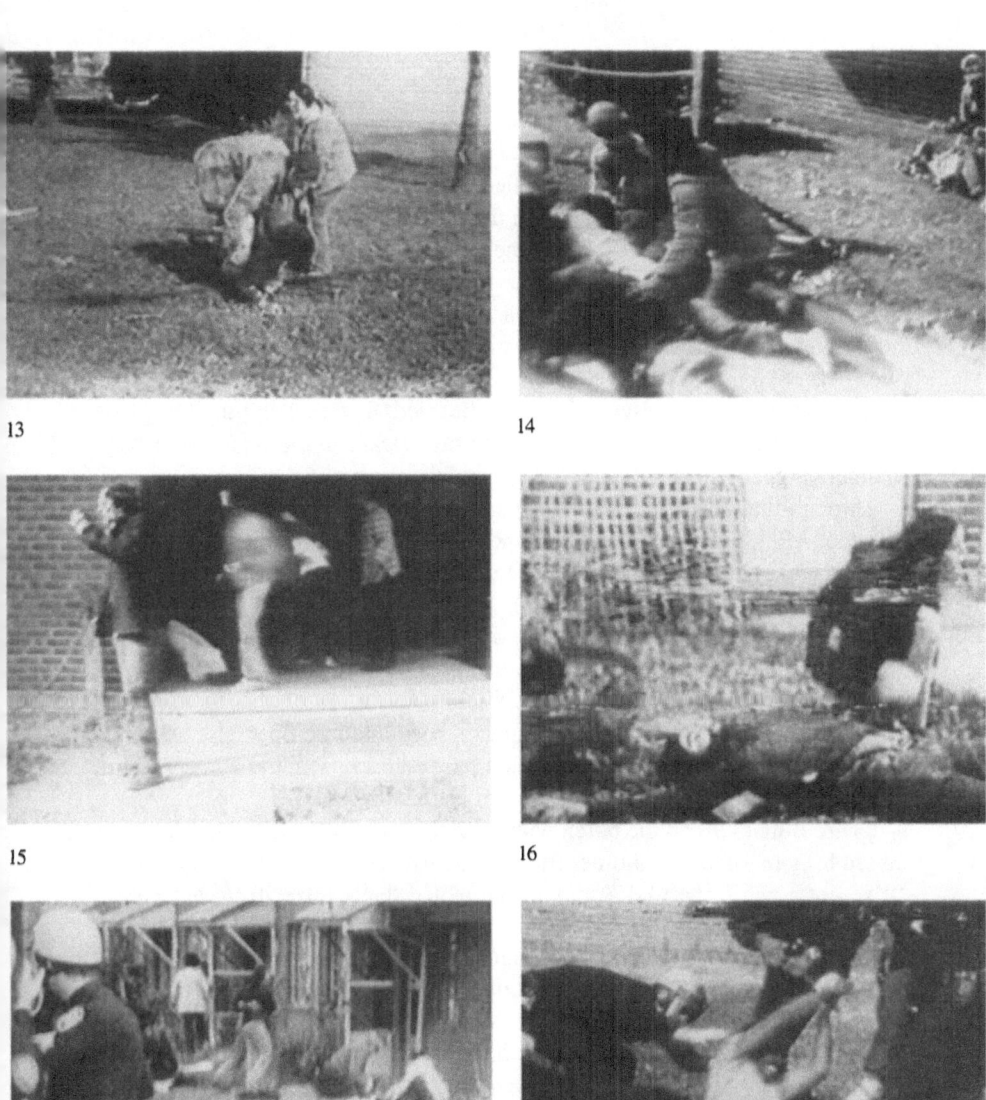

13, Allen Blitz and Sally Bermanzohn attempt to lift Cauce. *14*, Demonstrators and newspeople crawl out from under the WXII station wagon as Tom Clark (right corner) attempts to revive Bill Sampson. *15*, Demonstrators stand in shock at the community center porch where Sandi Smith's body is still propped against a brick wall. *16*, Signe Waller discovers Jim's body. *17*, Police and emergency medical teams work with the wounded. *18*, Nelson Johnson is arrested for inciting a riot. (Videotape stills on pages 143–45 are reproduced from videotapes by Ed Boyd, WTVD-TV, Durham, North Carolina.)

telling himself. Flowers, who had fallen a few feet from Cauce, pushed himself up and joined the other Klansmen fleeing toward the van. Jerry Smith was at the van's cargo door: "Let's get the hell out of here. C'mon Roy, before you get killed."

David Matthews stood beside the van's open passenger door, his shotgun at his shoulder, his eye focused down the barrel at the movement around the WXII car. Sampson shot twice more over the station wagon's hood, but Matthews's attention was diverted to the bearded figure attempting to cross Carver. To Matthews, Mike Nathan and his "Death to the Klan" sign were another "nigger with a shotgun." He pulled the trigger.

Through the viewfinder of his camera, Jim Waters could see Jack Fowler put the AR-180 back in the Fairlane's trunk. He looked so nonchalant. Waters's left eye was open, too. He learned in Belfast that closing the left eye for accuracy in focusing is a peacetime luxury. The action outside the range of the viewfinder could be deadly. Now the bright blue of Mike Nathan's jacket drew the photographer's attention to what his left eye saw. Then everything went red. "His face exploded," Waters said.

The blast of buckshot that tore Nathan's head and face open also shattered the windows of the WXII car. Sampson jumped back from the fender, as Jim Wrenn crawled into Carver Street to pull Nathan to safety.

Claire Butler was on the porch with Sandi Smith. She watched as Matthews raised his gun for the third time. Butler flattened herself against the brick wall. "I've got a gun," she told Smith as she pulled the revolver from her pocket and fired.

Matthews was watching Sampson and Wrenn. "Niggers with shotguns," he thought. He squeezed off another round, critically wounding Wrenn in the head and chest and piercing Sampson's heart with two buckshot pellets.

Rand Manzella heard his friend yell, "I'm hit." He cried out to Sampson, "I'm hit, too," and he crawled into the grass to try to help his friend, who was now on his back, groaning. Sampson extended his hand and slid the .38 across the grass toward Manzella.

Sandi Smith hunkered on the edge of the porch with her head between her knees. She was barely conscious, but she must have recognized Sampson's voice and understood that he was badly hurt. She lifted her head and began to turn it in Sampson's direction. The glisten of Butler's gun barrel caught Matthews's eye. Butler fired; he fired back. A single buckshot pellet hit Smith in the right temple and tore into her brain. Her head dropped back to her knees, eyes open, seeing nothing.

Carl Nappier was the only Klansman in the open now. He was on the sidewalk near the community center when he heard Sampson moaning. Maybe he could help. Manzella watched as the old man moved toward him.

He didn't watch long. Sampson was dying; Manzella had been wounded. He didn't wait to find out if the man coming toward him was friend or foe. He pulled the trigger twice. Nappier backed away.

Boyd and Waters had both heard a gun's hammer click repeatedly behind them. "Please don't," Waters begged, fearing that if the man shot at the Klan they would return his fire. Allen Blitz opened the derringer to find out why it wouldn't fire. It had the damn wrong-sized bullets in it. Blitz found a .38 and put it in. The sound of the derringer's chamber being closed was unmistakable. Boyd threw his camera down and dove for the back of his car as Blitz finally got off a shot.

Matthews fired one more time and then jumped into the van as it started to pull away. Harold Flowers couldn't believe what he heard: "I got three of 'em," Matthews said. "I got three of 'em."

11:24.29

Cooper: "Most of the fire is coming from the yellow van, coming from the yellow van. They're now leaving the scene."

Officers League and Bryant had pulled into a church parking lot just west of Everitt and Carver. Bryant stayed with the car while League took cover behind a cinderblock wall. Both saw the Fairlane as it roared west on Everitt, but Cooper had not said anything about a blue car. The yellow van. They could see it moving slowly toward them.

Someone in the van yelled, "There's Carl." Jerry Smith reached his arm out toward Nappier: "Hurry up, Carl, we gotta get the hell outta here." Nappier flew through the cargo door and Larry Morgan jammed the accelerator.

League stepped out from behind the wall and aimed his shotgun at the van's windshield. "*Stop. Police.*" He saw Morgan's eyes widen in shock and the van slowed momentarily. "What the hell you stopping for?" someone yelled at Morgan, and he hit the gas again. League aimed his gun straight at the driver this time. "*Police officers. Freeze.*" Bryant had pulled the police car across the intersection, and now he too had a shotgun pointed at Morgan. The van came to a halt and Morgan put his hands on top of his head.

11:25

Frequency 3 Operator: "Police Fire Emergency."
    Female Caller: "This the police department?"
    F-3: "Yeah."

Female: "Would you please send someone over here in Morningside Homes?"
F-3: "Yeah, they're on the way, ma'am."
Female: "They're over here shooting . . ."
F-3: "Yeah. We know it. They're on the way."
Female: "Oh, my God . . . Please . . ."
F-3: "Ma'am? . . . Ma'am?"

Part 3

Aftermath

Chapter 10

> The kind of violence now confronting us has occurred with regularity whenever a population committed to social change has confronted people committed to defense of the status quo. It seems we never learn.
> —Price M. Cobbs, M.D., William H. Grier, M.D., foreword, *The Politics of Protest*

Shattered

The first call to the Emergency Medical Services Station One was from a woman requesting ambulances and police at Morningside . . . rioting . . . people hurt.[1] A half-minute later, police communications requested ambulances at Everitt and Carver. Four ambulances were en route within fifty seconds after the first call, three minutes after Cooper radioed, "Shots fired." The paramedics had no protective gear—no weapons, no flack jackets. They had no idea what they were driving into, only that many people had been injured in a riot, a riot that could still be in full swing.

As the first ambulance cleared the police lines at Morningside, Tracy Burke was making his way south on Gillespie Street. At an intersection he noticed several carloads of white people and he recognized one of the cars he had seen earlier in Fletcher's yard. "You want to try to stop some of those other cars that were leaving, the other members?" he asked Lieutenant Daughtry. Daughtry either did not hear or did not understand the question. He told Burke to get a police van into the Morningside area. The line of Klan and Nazi cars pulled away as Burke radioed for the van. Then he proceeded south on Gillespie to Everitt. Sergeant Tracy L. Burke, the only officer other than Cooper to have monitored the Klan-Nazi caravan from start to finish, was the twenty-second officer to arrive at the shooting scene.[2]

Eighty-eight seconds from first shot to last.[3] No time at all. But the time it took the first ambulance to reach Everitt and Carver seemed interminable for the survivors. Tom Clark, blood dripping from his head, gave Bill Sampson cardiopulmonary resuscitation in a desperate attempt to keep the punctured heart beating. Sampson's T-shirt, pulled up to expose his chest, bore the Brown Lung Association's logo and slogan: "Cotton Dust Kills."[4]

Sandi Smith was dead on the porch, and Claire Butler was hysterical. After helping Frankie Powell to another area of the porch, Floris Cauce tried to calm Butler. She pulled Smith's legs from their hunkered position against her chest to a more normal slumped-sitting position. She then managed to persuade Butler that Smith was just unconscious. Then Cauce left the porch to see if there was anyone else she could help.

Sally Bermanzohn and Allen Blitz were at Cesar Cauce's body moments after the shooting stopped. They struggled to lift the huge man, yelling, "Someone please help us. Where are the doctors?" But it was obvious that Cauce was beyond help.

Mike Nathan lay alone in the middle of Carver Street. Those who approached him turned quickly away, repulsed at the sight. "I saw a body lying in the street. It had no face, just a mass of blood and skin," Allen Blitz said. He did not turn away. Instead, he took off his jacket and put it under Nathan's head. "It was a vain gesture to keep him from drowning in his own blood, to make him comfortable as he died."

Sally Bermanzohn found her husband lying in the grass next to the apartments. Blood was pouring from his head wound, and his right eye was so distorted by the pressure of blood flowing inside his skull that she thought the eye was gone. She found an old glove in his pocket and pressed it against the wound to slow the bleeding. He was conscious, and she talked gently to keep him calm. They heard someone say, "Sandi's dead. Jim's dead," and they both became agitated. Paul tried to get up, but all he could do was thrash on the ground. His left side was paralyzed, his right forearm ripped open by the gunshot. Sally worked to control her own panic and then began working on Paul again. "Relax, relax," she whispered.[5] His thrashing slowed and then stopped. He began drifting in and out of consciousness.

Dori Blitz stood inches away from the television camera. "The Klan did this," she hissed, "the cops and the Klan. The state protects the Klan and this makes it clear. They came in and opened fire on us and we fired back to protect ourselves."[6]

Further down Carver Street, Signe Waller knelt over her husband's body. Her face was distorted in anguish. Then she, too, saw a television camera. She pushed herself up as rage overcame her. Fist clenched in revolutionary defiance, she yelled, "Long live the Communist Workers Party. Long live the working class."[7]

The Getaway

Half of the eight caravan cars that escaped were following Fletcher back to his house. The two carloads of Nazis were on the way to Winston-Salem. Mark Sherer convinced the man he had ridden to Morningside with to drive him to an exit off I-40 where he could hide his .44, then drive him back to Fletcher's to get his car. Dawson and Buck were at a bar waiting for a news bulletin.

Cindy Hall waited at Fletcher's. She wanted a beer. Virgil had taken one away from her earlier in the day, and she knew she would be in big trouble with him if he found out she had been drinking at the house while he was gone. Suddenly Griffin was there. "He was excited," Hall said. "He said there was shooting and people falling. He said the law would be looking for everybody connected with the shooting."

Chris Benson and Max Hayes went outside and scraped Klan insignia off David Matthews's car. While they were working, Dawson and Buck returned. Dawson suggested that they all go to his house—he had a television and a phone, which Fletcher did not.

Buck headed off on his own. Fletcher had an important personal mission—he wanted to get another bottle of vodka—and would meet the group at Dawson's. Griffin rode in Dawson's Cadillac, leaving Benson to follow in his car with Hayes, Hall, and the three women from Hickory.

Dawson led the group into his den, turned on the color television, and told them they could use the phone. Max Hayes was not interested. "How the hell did they know we were Klan?" he asked. "I told 'em," Dawson replied. "I told 'em, 'You Communist SOB, you asked for the Klan, here we are.'"

Stunned into silence, Hayes asked himself, "Why the hell did he say that for?" They had been so careful, he thought. No Klan robes, no hoods, no paraphernalia. No way for the Communists to identify them as Klan—unless somebody told them. Unless somebody wanted them to know they were Klan. Unless somebody wanted to set them up.

Griffin was on the phone. "There's been a lot of shooting in Greensboro," he told his wife. "I don't know if anyone in the Klan was hurt or not." Linda Griffin began crying. Virgil couldn't stand it. "I'll see ya when I see ya," he said, and he hung up.

News bulletin. Four people dead. Ten wounded. The group at Dawson's still did not know whether the victims were Klan or Nazi, Communist, or innocent bystander. "Let's get outta here," said Dawson. "The police could be here any minute."

There was a knock on the door and panic set in. It was only Fletcher, freshly opened fifth of vodka in his hand. Buck was outside in his truck. Dawson suggested they all go to a motel room where they could think things through, and he told Buck to meet them at a motel on I-85. As Buck pulled away, Dawson told the others, "I've got a feeling Buck left to tell the cops," and he told them to follow him to a different motel. It was a diversionary tactic—Dawson needed to focus suspicion on someone other than himself—and it worked for a little while.

Fragments of Life; Fragments of Death

Everitt Street and Carver Drive were sealed off now. Within an area the size of a city block, police searched the street, the grass, trees, buildings, and cars for evidence. They charted the location of each item, from Tom Clark's shotgun thrown to the ground by Toney, to Mike Nathan's shattered glasses, to birdshot pellets and bullet fragments. They marked and initialed each item, beginning the laborious chain of custody documentation that the law requires for prosecution.

Four people were dead: Jim Waller, Bill Sampson, Sandi Smith, and Cesar Cauce. The state medical examiner had been called to take the bodies for autopsy. Ordinarily the bodies would remain at the scene until he took custody, but this was no ordinary homicide. A neighborhood had been terrorized. Fear and anger were building up to mass hysteria. Out of respect for the living as well as the dead, Charlie Porter, director of Emergency Medical Services, offered the use of Station One as a temporary holding place until the medical examiner arrived.[8]

It was not quite noon in Chicago, where Sidney Waller was taking care of last-minute details in his art shop. His daughter Jane was to pick him up in a few hours so they could fly to Greensboro for Jim's thirty-eighth birthday celebration on Monday.[9] That day would have been special for another reason: Jim and Signe had an appointment to talk with a specialist about having a baby.[10]

Sidney Waller was elated but concerned. He still could not understand why Jim had quit being a doctor, no matter how many times, how many ways he tried to explain. Nor did his father understand the radical political work Jim had become involved in. They would have some more arguments about it, Waller knew, but they would always be tempered with love and faith. Jim was so caring, so smart, so decent.

The shop door opened. Puzzled, Sid Waller asked, "Jane, it's not time to go yet, is it?" He heard the words, "radio . . . Jim . . . dead . . . Klan . . . Nazis."

Mike Nathan, Paul Bermanzohn, and Jim Wrenn were undergoing emergency brain surgery. Frankie Powell, Tom Clark, and several others were X-rayed, treated, and released. There was no point in trying to remove any of the birdshot pellets, they were told; probing for and removing the tiny pellets would be much more painful, much more damaging to the tissue, than leaving them in. They were given tetanus shots and prescriptions for mild pain-killers. Although there was no evidence of damage to Frankie Powell's baby, she was told to see her obstetrician as soon as possible.

Three of the wounded were in jail. Harold Flowers, hit by buckshot in the right arm and left leg, was taken to the hospital about an hour after his arrest, treated, and released into custody. Nelson Johnson was stabbed in both arms by an unidentified white man as he fled the stick fight at Everitt and Carver. He had been arrested for inciting a riot following the shootings. An angry crowd had gathered at the police line, and as he was arrested, Johnson began yelling, "The cops did this, the cops and Klan." Then, fists clenched, arms locked at his side, Johnson screamed, "We declare *war* on Melvin and the council."[11] The police swarmed him. When a demonstrator tried to pull them away, she too was arrested.

Rand Manzella was arrested with Sampson's .38 still in his hand as he knelt by Cauce's body. He had been wandering in a daze for several minutes without realizing he held the gun. Photographers took his picture—eyes glazed, jaw dropped, gun dangling from his hand. Finally, a police officer saw him. "Drop your gun and lie down," he ordered. Manzella could not move. Tracy Burke pushed him to the ground, took the gun, and handcuffed him. Burke advised him that he was charged with "armed to the terror of the public." The last person in North Carolina sentenced for "armed to the terror" was Eddie Dawson following his 1967 shooting spree in Alamance County.

Now Eddie Dawson sat alone in his den, staring at nothing, waiting for Rooster to call. He had taken Cindy Hall to the bus station after Griffin told her in the motel, "We might get five miles down the road before the police get us. There's no reason for anyone to know you were with Virgil Griffin in Greensboro because you weren't down there." She took the hint. Griffin gave her ten dollars and everybody left.

Jack Fowler had parked the blue Fairlane near Wayne Wood's house, sure that the Nazis would return. After fifteen minutes, though, he realized he could not wait any longer, not with the AR-180 in the car. He asked Junior McBride to wrap the gun in his jacket as he drove. They stopped near a rock quarry, and Fowler placed the gun behind some bushes.

If he couldn't take the car, he certainly couldn't take Junior; so Fowler drove to Caudle's. The Nazis were all there, all except Wood. "Wayne got killed down there," someone said. Six American Nazis stood in Caudle's yard and cried.

Fowler knew he had shot at two people. He did not know if they, too, were dead. This wasn't supposed to have happened. He had to get out, think, figure out what to do. Zigzag—he didn't even know the guy's real name—but Zigzag might let him hide out for a day or two. Jack Fowler said goodbye and started thumbing to Elkin, where the man known only as Zigzag lived with his wife and baby.

The Investigation

Saturday afternoon in Greensboro. Perfect Carolina autumn weather. Air so clean you want to gulp it in. Sky so blue you want to soar like Icarus into the blazing sun. The landscape is an artist's palette of greens and yellows, orange-rust-red-purple.

When his phone rang in Durham, Mickey Michaux thought it might be his daughter, on her way to spend the weekend with him.[12] It was not. Someone from the Greensboro FBI office gave him the startling news of the events at the rally. Then Michaux, the first black United States attorney in North Carolina, made the sixty-mile drive from Durham to Greensboro in forty-five minutes.

Tom Brereton's years as an investigator of white collar crime for the FBI have left him looking like a corpulent desk-bound executive, an image that does not hurt when he goes undercover as a flush-faced, joke-telling, second-generation Irish business manipulator. But as an FBI interrogator, Brereton is formidable.[13] For that reason, he was pulled off the golf course for an urgent message about a shooting at an anti-Klan march in a Greensboro housing project. Brereton knew immediately that there would be federal jurisdiction: a march is a constitutionally protected activity. He did not know on November 3 that he would be assigned chief investigator for the FBI and Justice Department's GREENKIL investigation; nor did he know that his work on the case would span four and a half years.

Jim Coman had planned to go to Clemson, South Carolina, to watch his alma mater, Wake Forest, take on the Tigers. At the last minute, he decided to stay home and watch the game on television instead. The Demon Deacons had just gotten on the field when the phone rang. Coman's boss, Guilford County District Attorney Mike Schlosser, gave him the news and told him to get down to the jail immediately.

Two things struck Coman when he first saw the suspects in the bullpen: they smelled so bad he thought he would gag, and one of them was wearing a Wake Forest cap. He wanted to strangle the guy.[14]

Twelve men would initially be charged with four counts of murder and one count of conspiracy to commit murder: Roland Wayne Wood, 34, Winston-Salem, Nazi; Coleman Blair "Johnny" Pridmore, 36, Lincolnton, Klan; Terry Wayne Hartsoe, 19, Hickory, Klan; Lisford Carl Nappier, 60, Hickory, Klan; Billy Joe Franklin, 33, Lincolnton, Klan; Jerry Paul Smith, 32, Maiden, Klan; Michael Eugene Clinton, 24, Lincolnton, Klan; Lee Joseph McLain, 36, Lincolnton, Klan; Roy Clinton Toney, 32, Gastonia, Klan; David Wayne Matthews, 24, Newton, Klan; Lawrence Gene Morgan, 27, Lincolnton, Klan; Harold Dean Flowers, 32, Lincolnton, Klan.[15]

A deputy sheriff booked the suspects, took their clothes, and issued orange prison jump suits. He overheard the man who had worn the Red Man cap tell someone, "They can't get me for all of them cause I only got three." David Matthews paused, "I wish I'd got them all."[16] Other than the deputy, only the shooters knew who they were. The film and videotape showing Wood, Smith, Fowler, Matthews, Toney, and Pridmore with guns was still being processed and reproduced for the networks, the wire services, and the police.

Lawrence Morgan was the first to talk, at two o'clock.[17] An FBI agent and a Greensboro police detective took his statement. Morgan said he drove his van to Greensboro with ten or twelve others. He knew only Smith and Franklin. He denied being a member of the Klan, denied there was any talk of violence on the way down. At Everitt and Carver, he said, demonstrators started hitting the van and everyone jumped out. Next thing he knew, someone shouted, "They're shooting," and two men grabbed shotguns from the van. He heard gunfire but did not see anyone shoot.

Question: "When they got out of the van and started getting weapons out, what did you think then?"

Answer: "It scared the shit out of me."

Roy Toney began to talk at 2:24. He came to Greensboro, he said, "to keep the American way." But unlike Morgan, Toney acknowledged that there had been discussions of violence in the van—fistfights. "I brought a pick handle with me and got out. This white guy stuck a shotgun in my face. I dropped the pick handle and grabbed the barrel of the shotgun. We were struggling and some of my friends came to help. Someone other than the guy who had the

Johnny Pridmore

Lawrence Morgan

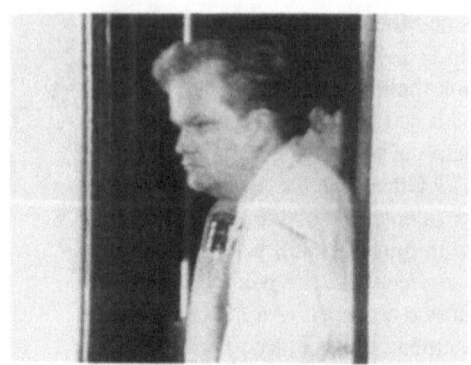
Roy Toney

David Matthews

Carl Nappier

Klan suspects are escorted by sheriff's deputies from the Guilford County jail to the courthouse for their arraignment on first degree murder charges. (Videotape stills are reproduced courtesy of Jim Waters, WFMY-TV, Greensboro.)

shotgun was hitting me in the face. I heard a gun go off and somebody said, 'Oh, my lord.' Then lots of shots went off. It sounded like World War II."

Toney denied shooting at anybody, but he admitted firing Tom Clark's shotgun twice into the air before he got back in the van.

At 3:35, Tom Brereton began interrogating Terry Hartsoe. He told about a Klan meeting at which they had agreed that the decision of whether to bring a gun would be left to the individual. He had not planned to bring his shotgun until David Matthews called that morning and told him to bring it. Hartsoe admitted bringing his numchucks, as well. The plan, he said, was if the Communists shot at them, "we were going to put them down." At first he insisted that the demonstrators had fired first, but later said the Communists had only sticks and boards. "I never saw any niggers with weapons. Only people I saw with weapons was the Ku Klux Klan."

Emergency Medical Services Station One was becoming a madhouse. Four corpses lay on gurneys in the corridor, waiting for the medical examiner's van to transport them to Chapel Hill for autopsies.[18] One of the police department's evidence specialists was assigned to guard the bodies, to observe the autopsies, and to collect, identify, and preserve all physical evidence found on, near, or in the dead people.

Floris Cauce was asked to come to Station One to identify her husband, on whose forehead someone had written what they thought his name was: SKIER.[19] The glass door to the corridor was locked, and the police and EMS personnel refused to let her in. She would have to identify Cesar through the door. To Floris Cauce, it seemed they were being unnecessarily cruel and arbitrary. All she wanted was to touch Cesar, to kiss him one last time. To say goodbye.

Dale Sampson and Signe Waller went to Station One, too. And they received the same brusque treatment. Finally, someone pulled a curtain across the glass door, making it impossible for the bereaved to get so much as a glimpse of their loved ones. For the grieving widows, this was harassment, anti-communism, further evidence of the conspiracy. It was intended to compound their grief, anxiety, and fear. So they thought, and so they told the EMS personnel, loudly, through the locked and shrouded door.

"It was not a morgue," EMS director Charlie Porter explained. The police evidence specialist was legally responsible for the bodies. They were evidence now, and he could not allow any unauthorized person to go near them. Not even a wife. Porter was frustrated by, but sympathetic to, the widows' anger. "It was just an ambulance base used to get the bodies off the street. I can understand how I would have felt if it were my family. But in the same token, I hope they can appreciate the position we were in. That was the only time in our history that we'd been in a position of being a morgue. We just weren't equipped to handle the family."

But no one at Station One could convince the families that they had not been singled out for particularly vicious treatment.

The Fugitives

The drive from Greensboro to Lincolnton was harrowing. Griffin kept telling the others that they could all be arrested for murder, that the police might stop them at any minute. He did not say it, but Chris Benson felt certain that Griffin wanted them all to stay with him because he did not trust them to keep their mouths shut.

They went first to Paul Smith, Jerry's father. Mark Sherer had arrived ahead of them, and he had already told the older Smith what he knew about what had happened in Greensboro. Smith said he had not heard anything from his son, and Rene Hartsoe started crying—for her husband, for Jerry, for everyone.

Griffin's constant jabbering about the possibility of the police catching them and charging them all with murder did not exactly help calm the situation. Then Sherer admitted that he had fired his gun at Morningside, that he had hidden the .44 but retrieved it after picking up his car at Fletcher's house. He fired the gun once more, then gave it to Paul Smith for safekeeping.

It did not take much for Griffin to convince Sherer that he should hide his car and flee with the Klan group. The cops, Griffin said, would find Sherer before sundown if he tried to go home. Sherer left his car and went with the group to Griffin's trailer.

The police could be waiting there, for all Griffin knew. And he certainly did not want to face his wife—she was too upset. He told Benson to park the car at the end of the drive. Then he told Sherer to walk up to the trailer, and if no one was there to get some food out of the refrigerator and cupboards. Finding neither cops nor Linda Griffin, Sherer filled a bag with groceries and returned to the car, and they headed back to Paul Smith's house for more supplies.

Blue lights up the road. Cops, right in front of Smith's driveway. They began to panic until they realized that there had been a car accident. Just an accident. Benson pulled into another driveway and turned the car around. There was another road that went around the back of Smith's property.

Benson and Sherer had to hike up a ravine and through the woods to get to the house. The others talked nervously as they waited in the car. "I think

Dawson set us up," said Ruby Sweet. Griffin nodded solemnly, "Yeah, so do I." The young men returned with more food, some blankets, two rifles, and a .32 revolver. As they loaded the gear in the trunk, Sherer told the group that his parents had a small cabin near Boone where they could hide out until they came up with a better plan. There weren't any other options.

The Vigil

At Cone Hospital in Greensboro, Mike Nathan and Jim Wrenn were out of surgery, hooked to monitors and life-support systems in the intensive-care unit. Wrenn was in critical but stable condition. Nathan was worse off. A major portion of his skull and brain had been devastated; the neurosurgeon, Dr. Steven Robinson, had been forced to remove a great deal of bone and tissue in order simply to clean and dress the wound.

Robinson's prognosis: "I saw no way he could survive. Period." Regardless, the intensive-care staff treated Nathan as though there were a possibility of a miracle. They gave him blood and fluids and kept him on a respirator. Robinson stayed at the hospital, just in case.

Marty Nathan and Kate White, Jim Wrenn's companion, would not leave the hospital, either. They stayed together in the waiting room of the ICU, one waiting for recovery, the other for death. Their fear was near-paralyzing. Not only were their loved ones in critical condition, but they believed that the surviving demonstrators, including themselves, were in grave danger as well. They *believed* the shootings were an all-out attempt to assassinate the CWP leadership; they *believed* that the killings were just beginning, that more goon squads were waiting to conduct more ambushes, or to strike, one at a time, in the hospital or on the highway or at home. They *believed* that the federal government would stop at nothing to eliminate the Communist Workers Party.[20]

One of the first things Marty Nathan did after arriving at Cone was to call the friend who was caring for Leah. She asked her to stay at the Nathan's house until she could return to Durham and to take care of Mike's mother, who was partially paralyzed from a stroke. She asked her to unplug the television and the radios, to hide the newspapers that would be delivered in the coming days, and to tell Mrs. Nathan that she and Mike had had car trouble. Marty knew that she and she alone would have to break the terrible news to Esther Nathan.

And then Marty Nathan waited. At first, she and White had only each other for company. As the day turned into evening, however, friends, family, and party members began to gather around the survivors. It would be many months before Marty Nathan, Signe Waller, Floris Cauce, or Dale Sampson knew solitude again.

Nightfall

Mickey Michaux and Jim Coman listened intently as each pair of investigators gave oral summaries of the suspects' statements. The complexities of the case grew almost geometrically with each report.

At nine o'clock, David Matthews told his story:

> "They said we were scum, that we were hiding under a rock, that we were chicken shit to come out and meet them head-on. Fine and dandy. We decided to come.
>
> "At first we was talkin about it and we took some guns. We heard that the Communists and the niggers was going to shoot us on the side, so we took some shotguns. We were cautious. So the niggers started shooting, and there was some spectators around and some Communists. So just like anybody with any common sense, anybody starts to shoot at you, you better defend yourself.
>
> "They were trying to protect theirselves and finally got stopped. Niggers and Communist Party, you could hardly tell who was the niggers and who was Communist.
>
> "We didn't take guns there just to kill people. There were some innocent people shot, I reckon, as I'm told anyway. But I was shooting at the niggers."
>
> Question: "I've been told that when you got back in the van, you said, 'I got three of them.' Did you make that statement?"
>
> Answer: "At that time, I thought I did. Yes."
>
> Question: "At that time? What was that statement, David?"
>
> Answer: "The people was dropping. I was shooting at them niggers that had riot guns."
>
> Question: "What statement?"
>
> Answer: "I thought I had hit the niggers."
>
> Question: "Okay. What statement did you make when you got back in the van?"
>
> Answer: "Well, to my knowledge, I seen niggers falling and all and I was out of shells and I thought that I had hit them."

Virgil Griffin's car bounced and rattled as it inched along an abandoned logging road. Seven pairs of exhausted, frightened eyes strained to search the darkness beyond the headlights for the hunting cabin that would be their sanctuary that night.

There it was—a tiny little cabin hidden in the woods, just two rooms, no electricity. But it was a lot bigger than the car they had been stuffed into for the past twelve hours. And it was safe.

Someone found a kerosene lantern. The eerie light flickered on Griffin's weathered face, making his hawkish nose even more pronounced. "Remember your Klan oath," he must have said a hundred times. Do not talk to the police, he instructed them. If you have to, deny you are in the Klan, deny being in Greensboro, deny carrying a weapon. Do not identify any other Klan member. The Klan has ways of dealing with rats. There is no hiding from the Klan.[21]

Remember your Klan oath. Most of the suspects in the Guilford County Jail did. Most of them said they did not know the people they were with, denied seeing the shotguns, knives, and ax handles in the van, and denied seeing anyone but the demonstrators shooting. A few of them refused to talk at all.

Carl Nappier, though, talked. He would be sixty-one on Monday. It would have been Jim Waller's birthday, too, but Nappier did not know that. He just knew he was an old man with a gimpy arm and a seventh-grade education, the exalted cyclops of the Icard Klan unit. And he knew he was in trouble.

Klan dues? Two dollars plus a ten-dollar joining fee. Membership? Thirty in his unit, down from forty-four. He named the people he rode down with and the people he saw with weapons. He told about demonstrators beating on the cars, about getting out and staring down a black man who held a piece of firewood and a box cutter, about seeing a wounded man and trying to help him only to have some jerk threaten him with a pistol. And he told about two statements he heard in the van before they were arrested. "The only comment that I heard was that there was three or four or five on Bill [Franklin] but I got 'em off. Jerry Smith said it. And then another guy said, 'I shot three. I shot at three of them.' That was David."

Nappier was upset, angry that the Klan had brought guns, and he talked a great deal about that. "Everybody wanted to go down and heckle the Communists since they did call us cowards, so I got up and made a talk about leaving the guns at home. We'd go down there, we'd take a club with us. If we had to fight, we'd use that, but leave the guns at home.

"This is a shining example of why I'm against the use of guns. There's three or four or five dead men laying down there, dead people laying down there and they shouldn't be there. They just shouldn't be there. There's three or four injured, and if I had got injured like I expected to get injured, with a stick or a club or something like that, I wouldn't feel so bad. But being shot—they don't deserve that. I mean, even if they are Communists."

Midnight in Morningside. Children who half-a-day earlier had walked to Everitt and Carver to see a parade had run home screaming. They had seen a bloodbath instead. Some continued screaming intermittently throughout the day and into the night. Some cringed in their rooms, afraid the shooting might erupt again at any minute. Some tried to put on a brave front of loud talk and laughter. Silence, they knew, would allow the terror of November 3 to overcome them.

Chapter 11

> We live in a society which . . . is programmed for fear. Just as fear is packaged to stimulate consumption, it is marketed to promote conformity.
> —Frank J. Donner, *The Age of Surveillance*

Under Siege

Greensboro was in a state of shock and confusion. City officials pleaded for public calm as they tried to explain the unexplainable. The breakdown in police communications on November 3 was obvious from the first police statements. The commander of District Two told reporters at a news conference that his officers were not aware of the Klan caravan's approach to the demonstration site until moments before the shooting began. Chief William E. Swing, speaking at the same news conference, contradicted the commander. The police, he said, knew that violence was likely to occur at the march; two units from the Tactical Squad had been assigned and a police detective had the caravan under surveillance from the time it left I-85 and Randleman Road.[1] Both said that officers were stationed within two minutes of the rally site, but neither could say why none appeared until the shooting was over.

Mayor Jim Melvin praised the police and pointed out, as he would again and again, that most of the people involved in the shootings were not from Greensboro. The killings, he said, were "an isolated, senseless, barbaric act of violence."[2]

Neither shock nor confusion nor grief deterred the CWP survivors from their immediate analysis of the tragedy. Their leaders had been singled out for assassination by the bourgeoisie. That was all they would say at first, until they got a chance to pull their ranks together and develop a strategy for moving forward. For a while, they even refused to talk about those who died at Morningside as people—as friends, lovers, anything other than martyrs to the cause.

Signe Waller's house became the center of the CWP regrouping. Fearful that government agents would storm the house to seize CWP documents, Dori Blitz burned Jim Waller's files. Tucked among his papers were love poems he had written for Signe. They, too, turned to ash.

After his release from jail on Sunday, Nelson Johnson became the head of the regrouping effort. The task before Johnson and the other CWP survivors was formidable. They had to set up an entire new leadership structure. They had to achieve political consolidation among widows and loved ones who were emotionally devastated and consumed with grief and fear. And they had to present a unified, well-thought-out analysis of the killings to the news media who were converging on Greensboro from around the world. The plan that emerged was strikingly simple: "We just developed a driving passion to go at the state," said Johnson. "No matter what it was, it was the state, it was the state, it was the state, it was the state."

Agent for the state? Sharpshooter for the FBI? Jerry Smith was neither. He sat in the interrogation room of the Greensboro Police Department and cried as Tom Brereton and Detective Herb Belvin applied the pressure. Smith admitted that he shot one time, at "a nigger with a shotgun"; he did not think he had killed anyone. Brereton wanted names—the people in the van, the people in the caravan, the people who organized the whole thing. Smith said he was afraid to name names, afraid of retaliation. Brereton shifted to another subject, then another. Then he honed in again; he wanted names.

"Sir, they'll get my family, I know they will."

"Yes, sir. We've discussed this before. Do you know the names?"

Smith wanted assurances that his family would be protected. Brereton started to reply. "If there's any indication of threats to your family . . ."

"Yeah, but it'll be too late then, sir. It ain't that I don't want to help you, you know that. I'll do anything I can to help you. But I can't help if it puts my family out on a limb, maybe in the grave."

Smith was sobbing. Brereton continued to push.

"When it comes out in court, everybody's going to know it," Smith pleaded.

"Yes, sir," said Brereton. "I'm sure that everybody already knows the people who organized this meeting. This is merely an opportunity for you to furnish some names."

"I'd rather write it."

"Okay, sir," and Brereton handed him a piece of paper and a pen. Smith wrote one name: Eddie Dawson.

As Brereton continued his interrogations on Sunday, Virgil Griffin sent Chris Benson and Mark Sherer down the mountain to get a newspaper. The articles were read over and over. Panic began to set in. "Virgil kept telling us we were going to be charged with murder," said Benson.

Barbara Ledford and Max Hayes wanted to go home. They would have to hitchhike; Griffin did not want to be seen near Hickory. Once again, he reminded them of their Klan oath, to deny seeing the shooting, to deny being in the Klan. Then he told everyone to get in the car. Ledford and Hayes would be left at the first paved road; the rest of the group would drive to another hiding place.

The Nazi fugitive, Jack Fowler, was safe at Zigzag's—for the time being. He had shaved his beard and dyed his hair black, in stark and probably obvious contrast to the paleness of his red-head's complexion. He did not know that his brother Rick, his friend Butch Johnson, and his cousin Jerry Pittman, a Winston-Salem police detective, were taking part in a manhunt for him.

Butch Johnson and Rick Fowler had gone to Pittman on Sunday. They were afraid for Jack, afraid some hot-headed cop or FBI agent would shoot him on sight. They thought they knew where he might be, and they hoped they could negotiate his surrender unharmed. Pittman called in several other detectives, and the two young men agreed to take them to the trailer where they thought Fowler was hiding.

Johnson got frightened as soon as he saw the officers who would accompany them—nine or ten men, all in plain clothes. They got in three unmarked cars and drove to the trailer. Johnson, Fowler, and Pittman were to go to the door; the officers would wait at their cars. Johnson looked back at them as he knocked on the door. The police were out of their cars, leaning across the hoods with shotguns leveled at the trailer door. Jack Fowler was not there. Johnson was relieved and angry. If he ever did find Jack, he would never, never tell the police. Johnson told another friend about the incident, told him that he was afraid the police would kill Jack on sight. Johnson did not know it then, but the friend knew Fowler was with Zigzag. He headed for Elkin as soon as Johnson left.

Tom Brereton and Herb Belvin started working on Wayne Wood. It did not take much. Once he started talking, he gave names and dates and everything else that came to mind. He told about China Grove, about the Louisburg rally, about the November 1 news conference, about Jerry Smith pulling his gun when Nelson Johnson scooped them on the news. He gave people's names, their nicknames, their CB handles. He identified guns. He talked about the panic that overwhelmed him and the others when they realized that the demonstrators had guns.

Brereton brought out a stack of photos, and Wood identified everyone he could. He stopped at one, saying the person had planned to come but had not. "I wished he had," said Wood. "I wouldn't of been in that truck I was in." He would have ridden with the man instead. Then he laughed nervously. He thought the man might be FBI, and the others did, too. The transcript of Wood's interview, prepared several days later, reads, "They think _____ is a Jewish name." Wood laughed again. "I felt like if the FBI was gonna come in, they'd use something beside a Jewish name."

Bernie Butkovich was at that moment on his way to the Greensboro Police Department. His ATF superiors had instructed him to cooperate fully with the Greensboro police, especially in their search for Fowler. Butkovich contacted Captain B. L. Thomas, head of the detective division. Early reports in the media had listed all the arrested as Klan from the Charlotte area, Butkovich testified in 1983, and he wanted to give the police the correct information. "Without exposing who I was," he told a federal grand jury, "I explained to him that I couldn't really discuss who I was or where I was from at that point, but that I wanted to relate to him the individual names that I knew."[3]

Late on the night of November 3, Butkovich did go to the police department and identify Wood, Fowler, McBride, and Caudle from police and news photos. By then, the ATF had advised Captain Thomas of their agent's identity, but neither Jim Coman of the district attorney's office, U.S. Attorney Mickey Michaux, nor the FBI had any idea who Butkovich was.

On Sunday, Butkovich went to Wayne Wood's house to see if he could get a lead on Fowler, Caudle, or any other Nazis. Wood's son told him that his mother was down the street at a friend's. When he found her, Paula Wood was livid. Butkovich testified that she said, "It's because of you and all those other Nazi people that my husband is in jail. He'll be in jail for life. Get out of here. I don't ever want to see any of this stuff. And don't ever come back."

From there, Butkovich went to Caudle's son-in-law. Milano Caudle was there, upset, stuttering, pacing, and shoving his hands in and out of his pockets. "Listen," Butkovich remembered him saying, "I don't mean to be an asshole to you. I don't mean to, like I don't trust you. Oh, we're all in trouble. Jack's a goner. We're all going to jail for life. It was never planned like that. We just went to the rally and all hell broke loose."

Butkovich tried to find out if Caudle knew where Fowler was, but it was fruitless. He then offered to go to the jail to find out what Wood wanted the Nazis to do, to find out whether they were wanted, to find out what Wayne's bail was—anything he could find out.

Butkovich called Captain Thomas and arranged to talk with Wood. The plan, he said, was to walk in the main door of the police department and ask a bunch of questions about the killings, and police detectives would grab him and take him back to an interrogation room. The lobby was swarming with reporters when Butkovich arrived. Bernie Butkovich, ATF agent posing as a truck driver, was wearing a Duke University T-shirt. Reporters ran to him. "Was he a friend of the people who were killed?" they asked. He said he was not there for that reason. The reporters persisted until the police realized what was going on and escorted him to the interrogation area.

Wood was half-crying, "whimpering a little bit," Butkovich said, when detectives brought him into the room. "What do you want us to do?" Butkovich asked. "The party members are waiting for instructions."

In sworn testimony, Butkovich said that Wood told him to burn down his garage, to make it look like the Communists did it in retaliation. Wood insists that it was the other way around, that in fact the ATF agent threatened to burn the garage. The fire was never set, but neither did Butkovich get any substantive information on Fowler or anyone else from Wood. He just cried, saying over and over again, "I'll never see the outside."

Detectives took Wood back to his jail cell. Butkovich waited in the interrogation room to give his report to Captain Thomas. The door opened and a pudgy, silver-haired man glared at Butkovich. It was Tom Brereton. "He pointed at me," Butkovich testified, "and said, 'Who the fuck are you?' And I looked up at him and I just smiled. He said, 'I'm going to find out who the fuck you are.' And as he turned around to walk out I said, 'Fuck you.' He stormed out of the room."[4]

So much for interagency cooperation. Despite an ATF policy which requires that local U.S. attorneys, FBI offices, and district attorneys be notified of any agency undercover operatives in their districts, it was days before Jim Coman and Tom Brereton found out who Butkovich really was. And Mickey Michaux did not know for months.

Butkovich left the police department, put on a body transmitter, and drove back to Winston-Salem. He had told Caudle earlier that he knew of a farm in Ohio where the Nazis could hide out. Now he was returning to bring them into the trap. Like the rest of the agent's six months of undercover work, however, this mission was thwarted. Caudle and Junior McBride had turned themselves in to the police before Butkovich made it to the city limits.[5]

The CWP made its first formal statement on Sunday: "This is a premeditated political assassination by the capitalist state. There is no way that the depraved psychopaths of the KKK and Nazis could launch an attack of this nature by themselves. It was clearly targeted at the leadership of the Party and all the comrades were shot in the head."[6]

Several, but not all, of the dead and seriously wounded did suffer head wounds: a single pellet through her temple killed Sandi Smith instantly; Paul Bermanzohn was in critical condition from his head wound, partially paralyzed but slowly regaining consciousness after extensive brain surgery; Jim Wrenn was on his way to full recovery despite several pellets lodged in his brain—he would be released from the hospital within the week.

A different kind of release would come for Mike Nathan. His brain had been "devastated" by buckshot, according to his doctors. It was only a matter of hours, a day at the most, before his heart would stop.

While Marty Nathan kept her vigil, the CWP discussed her husband and his impending death. He had been intimately involved with the Durham Communists from his undergraduate days at Duke, but he had never become a member of the WVO or the CWP. The CWP's Central Committee decided, and Marty Nathan agreed, that Mike would be inducted into the Party before he died. "I wasn't even there," Marty Nathan said of the induction. "It was my feeling that he would have wanted to be a member. It was appropriate."

At 10:45 Monday morning, Mike Nathan died a Communist. And shortly after the Committee to Avenge the CWP Five was born. "Avenge." No more illusions of moderacy for the CWP. "Under the direction and aid of the FBI," Monday's CWP press statement said, "the KKK and Nazis with military precision assassinated five members of the Communist Workers Party. . . . The murders of the CWP 5 is a clarion call to U.S. workers and oppressed people to rally around the banner of the Communist Workers Party to turn this country upside down to make these bloody capitalists pay for their crimes."[7]

The CWP would march again, they announced, to bury their comrades on Sunday, November 11. And they would march armed. The city responded by issuing a ban on all parade permits.

The Communists were undeterred. "We felt the state couldn't hold its position on the question of the march," said Nelson Johnson. "First, we weren't even thinking of applying for another permit. Secondly, we were going to march. Period. Whatever they were going to do, that was their decision. We were going to do what we were going to do."

City and police officials tried to meet with the CWP, but the Communists refused. They announced that the march would begin at a small rundown shopping center just east of downtown Greensboro, that the caskets would be carried through the streets by armed honor guards, that the Five would be buried at Maplewood, a previously all-black city-owned cemetery located a stone's throw from Morningside Homes. They refused to say what route the march would take.

The people of Morningside were horrified. Blood still stained the streets

Aftermath   171

and sidewalks around the Morningside Community Center. Police were everywhere, asking questions and picking up the remaining bits and pieces of evidence—a bullet fragment embedded in a tree, a piece of tooth found in a gutter. Reporters wanted to know how the residents felt. They responded that they felt invaded, under siege. They would not allow another march; never again.

In a prepared statement, the president of the Morningside Residents Council spoke for all eight of Greensboro's housing councils. "We are pleading for the peace and tranquility of our communities. As much as we are shocked, we are also angry that all this happened in one of our communities. Why must our communities be targeted for marches and demonstrations?"[8]

Exposed

A Klansman named Dawson had obtained a copy of the "Death to the Klan" parade permit two days before the killings, the *Greensboro Daily News* reported on Tuesday.[9] The police claimed that they were trying to find out who Dawson was, to find out if he was involved. A reporter tracked Dawson down: Edward W. Dawson, known Klansman, served time for terrorizing in Alamance County in 1967. Other than to deny that he was the one who got the permit and to deny any role in Saturday's tragedy, Dawson refused to talk.

Eddie Dawson had already given his statement to the police. He told the whole story from the Lincolnton rally through Griffin's getaway. Then he went home and tape recorded basically the same statement for the FBI. He did not understand why they had not called him yet, but he knew they would and he wanted to be ready.

On the day the Dawson story broke, the police department released an explanation of its actions on November 3, including transcripts of the police radio transmissions. Chief Swing displayed a chart showing that five police cars were at the scene within one minute after the surveillance car reported, "Shots fired."[10] He did not point out that the Tactical officers were ordered into position four minutes before Cooper radioed that shooting was going on.

Later that day, the Revolutionary Communist Party members made their bid for part of the media spotlight. They released Harold Covington's "we had it all worked out with the cops" (in China Grove) letter.[11]

Covington, Dawson, Cooper, Nazis, Klan, police—the evidence was falling into place. The CWP and its Committee to Avenge seized upon the various disclosures, and incorporated them into both their own analysis and their public statements. Their obsession with the state made it absolutely impossible for them to cooperate in any way with the police or FBI, either in the investigation of the killings or in the plans for the funeral march. The police and FBI, they charged, had engineered the assassinations; it was ludicrous, therefore, for the Communists to have anything to do with them. As late as Friday, they refused to tell the police what route the march would take to Maplewood.[12] To give the state that information, the CWP felt, would be akin to setting themselves up for another round of assassinations.[13]

The city was in an untenable position. It could not allow a group of hostile, armed people to march through the streets—especially through Morningside—but it had no legal means of stopping them, not after the city attorney discovered that no parade permit was required for a funeral procession. The question now was how to protect the marchers and the community from another violent confrontation. Reports were coming in from across the country that various Klan and Nazi factions planned to come to the funeral march.

Greensboro officials declared a state of emergency for the weekend.[14] That gave them the power to prohibit anyone from carrying firearms in the city and to conduct searches to ensure the prohibition. It also gave the city legal authority to control the march route. They told the CWP that the march would have to take the most direct and least residential route—east along Market Street to the cemetery's access road. A force of nine hundred National Guard, Highway Patrol, and Greensboro police would surround the march area, and the procession would not be allowed to veer from the established route.[15]

To Nelson Johnson and the CWP, the city's actions were further evidence of the state's desperate maneuvering to keep the masses from mobilizing in Greensboro to honor the fallen CWP martyrs. "They had publicly stated some of the security [measures]," said Johnson. "It was two rings; an inner ring and an outer ring with a corridor—a corridor of wall-to-wall police with guns. That's the ultimate in isolation that the city used to try to keep people out of it. Only the people who have the most fierce determination will come through all of that."

Isolation or protection, the city was indeed trying to keep people away. Announcements were given to all area media asking curiosity seekers to stay home on Sunday. They set up a rumor-control center and announced the hotline number. By Friday, nearly five hundred calls had been handled:[16] Is the Klan coming? My daughter planned to come home from college this weekend; is it safe?

One rumor, a terrifying one, appeared to be fact. Tom Brereton received a phone call from the Guilford County Sheriff's Department. A woman reported that a man had come to her house in a truck bearing U.S. Army

Aftermath 173

insignia from a base in Georgia. He had shown her grenades, claymore mines, and rocket launchers—enough, he told her, "to blow up the whole damn city." He was in Greensboro, the woman said, "to do what he had to do. The niggers and Communists had shown their true colors."[17] After talking with the woman, the man disappeared. Brereton notified the police, and Greensboro officials announced the situation to the public.[18]

On November 9, Bernie Butkovich turned in a sixteen-page, handwritten, sworn affidavit to ATF internal affairs investigators. Most of the statement was taken verbatim from his weekly field reports on the Wood investigation, but there were two significant changes from his notes on the November 1 Klan-Nazi meeting at Wood's. In the November 9 affidavit, Butkovich said, "I believe that while the media was there, there was discussion about the 'anti-Klan' demonstration to be held on Saturday, November 3, 1979, and the proposed counter-demonstration by the Klan." This, then, was the basis for Butkovich's and Dukes's decision not to notify the Greensboro police of the Klan and Nazis plans: "The fact that a confrontation would occur was a matter of common knowledge and received extensive local media coverage." Yet in the next paragraph of his affidavit, Butkovich said, "A Klan member indicated after the film crew left, that there was an open invitation to the Party . . . to go to Greensboro, NC to the 'communist demonstration' [anti-Klan rally]." And in a later deposition, Butkovich said, "This was the first mention of a Communist demonstration that I heard."[19]

Butkovich told in his affidavit of Covington's admonition against taking guns to the demonstration, but he left out a crucial paragraph from his November 1 notes: "Conversation with the Klan's Sergeant at Arms (dark hair, long sideburns, mustache, 5'8", 140 lbs., Klan tatoos) indicated that they had perfected a way of making fragmentary pipe bombs with striated water pipe, black powder and firecracker fuse. He indicated that he had made several and they would work good if thrown into a crowd." Based on Butkovich's affidavit, the ATF's Internal Affairs Division cleared the agent of any wrongdoing in connection with the November 3 shootings.

Sandi Smith would not be buried with her comrades. She was an only child, and her parents wanted her buried in her hometown. Services had been scheduled for Wednesday at St. Matthews Baptist Church in Piedmont, South Carolina. But the CWP wanted all the caskets, all the bodies, for Sunday's march. Smith's estranged husband, Mark, gave his authorization for her body to remain in Greensboro. It would be sent to her parents after the eulogy for the CWP Five.[20]

On Saturday night, the CWP agreed to meet with city and police officials. "At the point they shifted on the permit," Nelson Johnson explained, "we felt we were being put in a position of appearing unreasonable and dangerous to the community. Our point had been made. They were the ones who had to back off."

The CWP wanted assurances that people would not be searched when they came through the police lines. The police agreed not to conduct body searches, but under the state of emergency they reserved authority to search suspicious persons or vehicles anywhere in the city limits. The CWP then agreed that the honor guard's guns would not be loaded and that the police could inspect them prior to the march. "We were taking other measures to insure our safety," said Johnson. "We essentially telegraphed that to them through our discussion of their security. We told them that we could not be responsible for what happened to any of their people who were seen with guns standing on top of buildings unless we had a prior understanding of their identity. They agreed that they would wear orange or pink baseball caps."

A swamp near Camden, South Carolina, had been Virgil Griffin's hideout for the past week. After leaving Sherer's cabin in Boone, Griffin, Sherer, Benson, Rene Hartsoe, and Ruby Sweet drove to Griffin's sister's house in Camden. "She opened the door," he said, "and almost jerked me in the house."

Barbara Ledford had told Rene Hartsoe's mother that Griffin was holding the group at gunpoint, that he would not let anyone leave. Griffin's sister told him that Rene's mother had taken a warrant against him and that there was now an all-points bulletin on him and his car. Griffin gave the two women the keys to his car and instructed them to go to Rene's mother, "so she'd know what Barbara said was lies."

While the younger men unloaded the food and guns from his car, Griffin gave one final instruction. If the police stopped them, he told the women, "turn on the inside lights and put your hands on the dash so they know you don't have anything."

They spent one solid week in a cold, soggy swamp a mile's hike from anywhere. Griffin's brother-in-law brought them a tent and more food and blankets, but it was still rough living. On Tuesday, more supplies were brought, along with a copy of the South Carolina edition of the *Charlotte Observer*. "Mark read it seven or eight times a day," Griffin said. "Out loud."

Chris Benson was becoming a problem. He was scared. He grumbled about hauling supplies through the dense terrain, and he hated the swamp and wanted to go home. Sherer and Griffin began calling him "crybaby," which only antagonized him more.

The next newspaper they saw was Saturday's *Charlotte Observer*. It reported that President Jimmy Carter had assigned a team of twenty FBI agents to the case. And it said that they were searching for Virgil Griffin. He knew he could not stay in the swamp forever and that he would have little chance of escaping for long if the FBI was after him. Griffin told his brother-in-law to drive Benson and Sherer home. Then Griffin said, "Call Channel 9 [Charlotte] television station and tell them at ten in the morning I'll be there and to tell the FBI."

Earlier in the week, Harold Covington and Joe Grady had fed the FBI's worst fears about Jack Fowler. Covington said that Fowler was considered dangerous even by his associates among the Klan and Nazis. Grady said that Fowler had been at China Grove, that he probably recognized the CWP leaders he had seen there, and that he probably knew who he was shooting at on November 3.[21]

Jack Fowler was on the run. He left Zigzag's after his friend from Winston-Salem told him about the incident with Butch Johnson and the police. A long-distance trucker picked Fowler up on the interstate and agreed to provide him with food and a place to sleep in exchange for loading and unloading the furniture he was hauling. As they traveled through the central Great Lake states, the trucker told Fowler that he would have to return to North Carolina after the last leg of his run. Fowler asked to be left near Chicago, headquarters of the National Socialist Party of America.

The Final Mile

The CWP predicted five thousand people would join the march. The police estimated two thousand. By one o'clock, when the march was scheduled to start, there were perhaps two hundred people gathered in the parking lot on East Market. A good half of them were from the news media.[22] It was forty degrees and drizzling.

Police stood shoulder-to-shoulder along Market Street. They wore riot gear and carried shotguns. Stationed in one position, not able to walk around, they were already suffering from the chill. On the rooftops and the railroad trestle over East Market were the police sharpshooters in their brightly colored caps. The man with the claymore mines was still on the loose. And so was Jack Fowler.

Small groups of people made their way through the police lines, and the crowd slowly grew. There were no pat-downs or metal detectors, but officers did check large handbags and camera bags. Police stationed at the Lee Street exit off I-85 were more thorough, though. FBI sources had warned that a

CWP poster announcing the funeral march for the slain demonstrators on November 11, 1979

convoy of CWP vehicles coming from the east was laden with firearms. A roadblock was set up just beyond the exit ramp. Thirty-five people were arrested in the trap; forty weapons were confiscated.[23]

Word of the bust got to the CWP before the march started.[24] They were incensed. It was their understanding that the police would not search; now it was obvious that the police had lied. What else had they lied about? As people stood shivering in the icy drizzle, the CWP met with their lawyers and police negotiators in the warmth of a restaurant in the shopping center.

Two teeth-chattering hours later, a flatbed truck carrying a group of singers pulled into the parking lot. It was draped in red and black, with huge posters of the dead people. The singers led a chant: "A-venge, A-venge, A-venge the CWP Five." Then they began singing. "We are soldiers in the army. We have to fight, though some fall at our side." The cadence was curiously upbeat, if you ignored the words and the reason for the march and the military helicopters chop-chop-chopping overhead.

Hearses pulled up and five caskets draped in black were wheeled on gurneys into the street. Signe Waller led the procession, with friends and supporters pushing Jim's casket beside her. She carried a military rifle, her gaze fixed straight ahead, her jaw clenched in rage.

The march began to move east on Market Street. It had gone a block or two when to the right there appeared a break in the police cordon. Beyond was a field filled with National Guard. As the front of the march came parallel with the field, there was the unintelligible but unmistakable bark of a military command and the equally unmistakable sound of a hundred rifles being snapped into firing position. Past row upon row of M-16s with bayonets fixed, the marchers chanted, "A-venge, A-venge . . ."

It was dusk by the time the procession reached the cemetery. Nelson Johnson and the CWP leadership decided to cut the eulogies short. "We were racing against dark," Johnson said. The cemetery was surrounded by police and the helicopters continued to circle. "We didn't want to be out there in a situation like that in the dark. We had hoped we could get people out of town before dark." For many of the marchers, however, remaining there on the soggy ground as the temperature and the rain fell was unbearable. They walked back out of the cemetery in a steady line as the eulogies were given. Comrade Jim. Comrade Bill. Comrade Sandi. Comrade Cesar. Comrade Mike. Assassinated by the state. "*A-venge, A-venge, A-venge the CWP Five.*"

It was dark. The survivors were numb with cold and grief. There were no crowds now, no chants or songs, no cameras recording as they wearily trudged across the cemetery, through the gates, past the dilapidated houses along the access road.

Dale Sampson and Signe Waller (left) preparing to lead the funeral march on November 11, 1979 (Photograph by Ken Hinson)

As they approached East Market Street, they could see the lights and hear the idling motors of several buses the city had provided to return the mourners to their cars, parked more than a mile away. A chance to be warm, to sit down, to let go of their heavy rifles. No, said Nelson Johnson. "In the buses, you're in an enclosed area and the rest of the city is cut off from you. Our view was, you get in the buses and the whole search thing would start. We had already lost about forty pieces of armament, and they would have to estimate that if they were able to seize forty, they had to miss twice that much. They could just come in the bus and do it.

"If you were in the streets, they would have to have another pretext. We weren't going to take any measures that would sacrifice our political initiative. At the point which you're saying you're not afraid to die, there's nothing left. You just tell them that and get it over with."

So they walked the final mile, arm in arm. Numb with cold and grief. And fear.

Chapter 12

> The progressive mystique also served as a masterful weapon of social control. By promoting the appearance of enlightenment and tolerance, the mystique obstructed efforts to mobilize sustained protest.
> —William H. Chafe, *Civilities and Civil Rights*

To Find the Truth

Guilford County District Attorney Mike Schlosser assigned Rick Greeson to work with Jim Coman on the prosecution of the Klan and Nazis.[1] It was a smart move. Not only were the two Schlosser's most experienced murder prosecutors, but their friendship and respect for each other were so deep that not even the enormous stress of this complex and highly charged case could drive them apart. They were also the classic tough guy–nice guy team. Coman has the appearance and bearing of a bull mastiff; Greeson is slow and easy-going, gregarious, and quick to laugh.

Their appearances are somewhat misleading. Coman, now the special prosecutor for the state attorney general, was a meticulous local prosecutor and a passionate advocate for the victims he represented. Greeson once placed his job on the line in order to pursue an investigation that resulted in the resignation of a corrupt local sheriff. They share a passion for the law and a reputation for skill and integrity in its practice. "A prosecutor's job is not to convict," says Coman, "it is to find the truth."

Greeson and Coman knew the truth about the November 3 killings, and they would spend the next year in an unrelenting effort to convict six men of first-degree murder. The decision to go for a death penalty conviction would later be the subject of heated controversy, but for Greeson and Coman in November 1979, there was no choice. "That was a first-degree murder out there that day," insists Greeson. There were in fact two distinct types of murder on November 3. "You're guilty of first-degree murder if you go to commit any type of felony and it gets out of hand. In this case, it was a murder by people who came down willing to riot. The fact that these people were guilty of a riot and deaths ensued would make them guilty under the felony murder rule."

There was also premeditation involved, Greeson explained. "It doesn't mean that you have to plot it out and execute it. It just means that there's some thought beforehand—just time enough to say, 'Shall I do it,' and time to say, 'Yes, I will.' Here we've got a guy running up the damn sidewalk shooting a guy who's on his damn knees. And you've got a guy like Waller who's made a sponge, almost, with metal in his back.

"The only reason we had for not going for first degree was because the people were Communists. We refused to follow that train of thought. Legally and factually, these people were people, and they were brutally shot down. I can always explain why we went for first, but I could never explain going for second except for the fact they were Communists. And that's no damn reason."

"How could we have not tried them for first degree," Coman asked, "when four TV stations filmed it live? We could have just closed the books in Guilford County if we hadn't tried them for first-degree murder. I don't see how we could ever survive a challenge for selective prosecution if we hadn't tried them for first."

As the Greensboro police and the FBI worked to perfect the prosecutors' case, the pre–November 3 bungling and appalling lack of cooperation among the various agencies involved disappeared. The police identified, marked, and preserved thousands of pieces of evidence—the bullets and lead shot from the victims; the guns, knives, billy clubs, and ax handles; the yellow Ford van; the piece of Waller's palm jammed in the chamber of Tom Clark's shotgun. Except for the van, everything was sent to the FBI's lab in Quantico, Virginia, for microscopic and chemical analysis.

The knives and clubs would be examined for traces of blood, skin, or hair. The pistols would be test fired, and markings on the test bullets would be microscopically compared with bullets found in the victims or on the scene.

Proving which lead pellet came from which shotgun was another matter. Most people believe that anything fired from a shotgun is untraceable, and many of those who are aware that there is a tracing procedure are skeptical of its validity. Lead shot is really a hodge-podge of lead and other heavy metals, usually scrap. The testing procedure relies on the fact that in making any particular batch of pellets, a manufacturer uses whatever junk metal is available at that particular time. The composition specifications for lead shot are broad enough that the variance from one batch to another can be significant. Although batches of pellets are frequently mixed before being loaded into shells, each batch of loaded shells will have a recognizable mixture of lead composites. Thus, they can be traced.[2]

That is the theory of Donald Havekost, an FBI chemist who uses a procedure called neutron activation analysis. Havekost bombarded each pellet with radioactive isotopes. Since elements release radiation at different rates, Havekost was able to measure the amount of each element in every pellet he tested. He then compared the elemental composition of the pellets and grouped those that matched or were within acceptable limits. Finally, he examined an unfired sample of pellets from shells known to have come from the same source.

For example, at the time of his arrest, David Matthews had a purple Seagram's Whiskey bag full of unused shot shells, some of which matched the brand of expended shells found near where he stood during the shooting. Havekost compared pellets from these shells with pellets taken from the deceased and wounded and determined that they matched in elemental composition those recovered from Waller, Sampson, Nathan, Smith, and Wrenn. The tests took many months for Havekost to complete; his was the kind of painstaking work that led Jim Coman to characterize the investigation as a "textbook example" of prosecutor-police-FBI cooperation.

Two other aspects of the November 3 investigations, however, would prove to be examples of another sort. One involved another FBI analysis, the tracing of each shot fired that day from analysis of the sound tracks on the video tapes; its flaws would not become apparent for several years. The problems of the other were evident from Day One: the demonstrators refused to cooperate in the investigation. Since they believed that the state had engineered the assassinations, they found it virtually impossible to deal in any but the most rudimentary fashion with the law enforcement and court officials, the embodiment of the repressive bourgeois state.[3] Besides, some of their comrades were under indictment on charges related to the killings: Rand Manzella for "armed to the terror of the public"; Nelson Johnson, Allen and Dori Blitz, Lacy Russell, and Percy Sims for misdemeanor riot; and Willena Cannon for interfering with Nelson Johnson's arrest. There was nothing, the CWP thought, to prevent the prosecutors from indicting the rest of the demonstrators if they told everything—that they had dared the Klan to come, that they brought guns in violation of the parade permit, that they told people along the march route to defend the march with guns, that there was an internal memo saying, "A confrontation with the Klan would be best if we could get it."

The CWP needed legal help desperately, but they could not find it within North Carolina. The state ACLU rebuffed them, saying there were no civil liberties issues involved in either the shootings or the arrests of the demonstrators. And attorneys in private practice could not afford to be tied up in what was likely to be one of the most complex and controversial murder cases in North Carolina history.

Gayle Korotkin, a former Legal Aid attorney, came to Greensboro with a busload of CWP members and supporters from New York for the funeral march on November 11, expecting to return that night. She didn't. Although much of her work went unrecognized by the press and the public, she became the backbone of a legal team that grew in size, sophistication, and effectiveness as the case proceeded—from nothing to the Greensboro Civil Rights Fund.

Korotkin's diminutive size and intense shyness belie incredible stamina and determination. Her quiet voice retains a hint of a European accent, the legacy of six years spent with her parents on U.S. Army bases in Germany after World War II. The Legal Aid office where Korotkin worked was on the edge of New York's Chinatown, and she got to know some of the WVO people through their tenant-organizing work. She eventually quit Legal Aid to become a tenant organizer. She hates cars, loves to walk, and passionately believes that the U.S. government instigated the assassination of the CWP Five.

During the week after the shootings, as revelations about the police, the Klan, and Dawson hit the New York papers, Korotkin says, "I smelled a rat. I was a VISTA in Chicago when the Black Panthers thing happened. I woke up on December 4, 1969, and heard there'd been a shootout between the police and the Panthers. Later it came out that the police had planned it, it was a police assassination. And then it came out that there was a whole FBI anti-Black Hate Group plan."

A shootout. Early local news coverage of November 3 had been fairly straightforward, laying the ultimate responsibility for five deaths squarely on the heads of the Klan and Nazis and strongly condemning the lack of police protection for the march. As the days wore on, however, it became a "shootout."[4] The police leaked their "suspicion" that the CWP had fired the first shot. Furthermore, it was reported, an anonymous co-worker of Jim Waller's said he had had a conversation with Jim and Signe in which Jim said that his group needed a martyr to gain national media attention.[5] And, the co-worker alleged, Waller said they had a plan to achieve it. Although Signe Waller vehemently denied that any such conversation ever took place, the unsubstantiated story ran as fact.

Reporters clamored for human interest angles to the November 3 story. Some friends and family of the defendants were eager to comply, painting a picture of good ole boys who got caught up in a tragic situation, basically nice guys who had been provoked beyond endurance by the Communists' taunts. The Klan, they said, was no longer opposed to blacks, just Communists. The local reporters, in a rush to make deadlines and without editorial coordination of the overall news picture, neglected to dig beyond the patriotic image they had been given.[6] Had they bothered to check Wayne Wood's *White Carolina* newsletter, for instance, they would have found nary a word about communism, but page after page of scurrilous diatribe against blacks and Jews. They did not check, and the image of God-fearing white Christian Americans prevailed.

On the other hand, the CWP refused to talk about their friends and loved ones as anything other than dedicated revolutionaries who were assassinated by the state. "They could have said anything they wanted and gotten coverage, but they didn't talk about their people as humans," said one reporter. "The CWP would talk only in press conferences. There was open hostility—'You're part of the establishment.' We just couldn't get stuff like we got from the Klan."

Reporters were not the only ones who found it difficult to deal with the CWP on a personal level. Former friends and political allies were scorned. Lyn Wells of SCEF, health activist Tim McGloin, union organizer C. P. Ellis, and Cleve Sellers, the former SNCC leader, were among many who tried to offer condolences and to help organize a more broadly based public response to the killings.

"They [CWP] hadn't been able to muster any response," said Cleve Sellers, "not unless you call that dramatization with the empty guns a response. The funeral left a pretty sour taste in a lot of people's mouths. One, certainly the entire black community here in Greensboro was excluded from that—they chose to be excluded. And there were larger communities where people had real legitimate concerns about Klan violence that wanted to participate in some manner."

That was not the kind of response the CWP wanted—not at first. The kind of support they wanted was an unwavering commitment to focus efforts on their assessment that the killings had been a federally orchestrated political assassination. "Overall, there was an amazing silence on the left," said Marty Nathan. "That was because of the way the case was being presented in the media: we were the terrorists, we had infiltrated the mills rather than worked in them. People were capitulating to the whole provocation thing. They say to me that the CWP was abrasive and obnoxious and untrustworthy. I think the things acting on them were all those other pressures: being afraid to be identified with communism, being afraid of violence—some cosmic violence. They should have been able to see through a lot of that, but they weren't. I realize how great the pressures were and that they had everything against them not to join us."

Outside forces did not completely deter efforts to organize a more moderate response, however. Scores of individuals and organizations persevered, and it was that work that led many organizers to label the CWP as obnoxious, abrasive, and untrustworthy. SCEF's Lyn Wells came from Atlanta to work with local groups. "We knew that the CWP had problems in working with people who didn't hold their line," said Wells, "and that that would be an impediment to organizing people. We felt that this was a much more important thing than just their people being killed, but rather that five people had been killed by the Klan. This was the worst thing that had happened by the Klan in a long time."

Despite her reservations about working with the CWP, Wells tried to coordinate the organizing effort with them. She went to Nelson Johnson. He kicked her out of his house. "They felt that I was coming in to take over their show," she said. "And they very much viewed it as their murders of their people."

Wells turned to Greensboro's black leadership, activists like Cleve Sellers who put her in touch with church leaders and A&T students. Out of a series of hastily called meetings, a plan developed for a two-tiered response that would be appropriate for the majority of Greensboro's people who wanted to express concern. There would be a prayer service at one of the larger churches in the black community followed by a march to the steps of the Greensboro police department. "Some people were very leery of a march," Wells said. But the majority felt it was essential "because there were enormous questions about where the hell were the police during this thing."

The community-wide prayer service and march, scheduled for November 18, were never held. In tactics similar to those used to intimidate Frank Collin and his Nazis from marching in Skokie in 1978, the Justice Department's Community Relations Service convinced some of the local organizers that such events could be dangerous. "The CRS took the A&T students down to city hall," said Wells, "and showed them the kind of weapons the Klan had, showed them files on how dangerous Nelson and the CWP were. They never said, 'Don't go to the march,' they just said, 'We want to let you know what you're in for here.'"

The service was canceled, but activists continued to discuss the need for some kind of public demonstration in Greensboro. "The position I took," said Sellers, "was that we need more time, we need to set up a response that would allow people from outside the area to participate, too. That's when we began to talk about a national response. And then we sought to get SCLC [Southern

Christian Leadership Conference] and IFCO [Interreligious Foundation for Community Organization] involved." The newly formed National Anti-Klan Network had already scheduled a meeting in December in Atlanta, and Greensboro activists chose a delegation to attend that meeting to discuss the idea of a national event to protest the Greensboro killings.

The Informants

Eddie Dawson played his tape-recorded statement for the FBI on November 9. They met in a room at the Hilton Hotel near the regional airport. An FBI agent started asking Dawson questions after the tape ran out:

"Did you expect any violence?"

"Absolutely not, absolutely not."

"Was the game plan to disrupt?"

"To show strength."

"Any heckling, throwing eggs?"

"Absolutely not. Absolutely not. I think it was handled stinky. With all the advance notice they had—and I told them about some of the people. I expected when I turned that corner to see nothing but helmets, just a wall of city police."

Dawson then launched into a monologue on his history in the Klan. It was almost 6:00 p.m. when the agent terminated the interview. "We'll return to the office and view some photos and videotapes and see if you can identify anybody."

Dawson: "And get a cup of coffee?"

Agent: "And get a cup of coffee."

No charges were brought against Dawson. Nor were charges brought against Virgil Griffin or Mark Sherer, despite the fact that Chris Benson told the FBI that both men, convicted felons, had guns during their flight from Greensboro.[7]

Benson became an FBI informant following the shootings, but he provided little information and left the Klan in early 1980.[8] Another federal informant, though, provided a great deal of information, both before and after the shootings: Joe Grady, the Winston-Salem Klan leader who broke off with Wood and Pierce after China Grove. According to Milano Caudle, Grady helped to arrange Caudle's and Junior McBride's surrenders on November 4. In ATF documents, the person who negotiated the surrender is identified not by name but as "an informant."[9] That same day, Grady told the FBI that Jack Fowler had been at China Grove and that he was familiar with the WVO leadership.

"Grady intimated," said the summary of his November 4 interview, "that Fowler was aware of whom he was shooting during the confrontation."

The FBI talked to Grady again on November 14. The agent's report says, "Grady advised he was very much opposed to the Nazi Party, did not want the FBI to associate his Klan group with the violence prone Nazis. Grady stated that he even talked to the Alcohol, Tobacco and Firearms people (AFT) in an effort to set up some of the Nazis for arrest as he regarded them dangerous."

Harold Covington publicly supported the Klan-Nazi defendants. "What I regret is that twelve good men are in jail," he told the Associated Press.[10] When the FBI came to talk with him, however, he washed his hands of the whole deal. He had told his men not to take guns; he did not go to Greensboro on November 3 because he was trying to sell some stocks his grandfather had given him. Like Grady, Covington fed the FBI's worst fears about Jack Fowler. He told the agents that Fowler was a Vietnam veteran—he was not—and said that in his opinion Fowler was "extremely dangerous" and "should be approached with caution."[11]

On November 14, Jack Fowler surrendered to the FBI. His trucker friend had left him at an interstate "oasis" at Hinsdale, Illinois, twenty miles from Chicago. He phoned Nazi headquarters, he said, "and asked if I could take a shower and get some rest," but the Nazis wanted no part of him. Fowler sat by the phone booth, chain-smoking cigarettes and trying to figure out what to do. Three hours later he phoned Jerry Pittman, his cousin in the Winston-Salem police department, and arranged to turn himself in. He gave Pittman his new description—dyed black hair, no beard. Pittman asked if he was armed. Fowler answered that he had an unloaded .32 pistol stuck in his boot. Pittman told him to wait there, that he would call the FBI and have them send someone to take him into custody. Then Fowler waited again, watching each car that pulled off the interstate, hoping that the neatly dressed men who would arrive in the government-owned car from the Chicago FBI office would not shoot him on sight.

The Progressive Mystique

The Greensboro police department released its official version of "the anti-Klan rally," as the administrative report called it, on November 19.[12] The ninety-two-page document varied little from Chief Swing's initial statements about police coverage of the incident. It contained complete radio transcripts from both Frequency One, the channel used by officers not assigned to the march, and Frequency Three, that which all assigned officers were to monitor and use, from 10:52 to 11:32.

Despite the stark evidence of police ineptitude documented in the transcripts, the administrative report concluded that the planning and preparation were "adequate and proper"; that the 11:30 assignment time was "proper"; that the march organizers created "confusion . . . by having groups at two locations simultaneously"; that the "early movement" of the Klan also created confusion; that the police were not in position because the confrontation "took place forty (40) minutes prior to the scheduled march." The report concluded: "The police officers assigned to the march performed their duty in a professional and reasonable manner and there is no evidence to indicate that any officer hindered or interfered with the march."

There was, of course, never any question that the police "hindered or interfered with the march." The question was, Why weren't the police there? Rather than address the issue head-on, the administrative report side-stepped it, shifting the blame for the "confusion" onto the demonstrators. To many, the police report seemed nothing more than a whitewash.

One of the most significant facts that the police report failed to address was that Sergeant Dave Comer, the officer in charge of coordinating on-site police coverage of the "Death to the Klan" march, was operating under the impression that the Tact units were at their assigned posts at 10:00 a.m. Comer later told FBI investigators that he had brought up the discrepancy between the noon starting time on the CWP's parade permit and the 11:00 assembly at Windsor Center with his commander, Lieutenant Paul Spoon. Spoon, he said, told him to use his own judgment on where to place his officers. "He was never informed that the Tact Units would assemble at police headquarters and would not appear in the vicinity of the parade route until 11:30," the FBI report said.[13]

When Comer heard Cooper report that the Klan had arrived at Everitt and Carver and that there was a fight in progress, he did not think it necessary to move in to help control the situation. "All of his decisions on November 3," concluded the FBI, "were made with the belief that the Tact Units had taken their positions as of 10 a.m."

Other official reports followed the police report, most of which fell into the police department's pattern of blaming the victims. One memo from the North Carolina Human Relations Council noted that there had been other violent encounters between Klan groups and anti-Klan demonstrators. "While few of the violent counter-demonstrations [sic] have been ordinary citizens, most have been members of far-left groups seeking to exploit the issue of right-wing extremism in order to strengthen the forces of left-wing extremism. . . .

Their aim in confronting the Klan was not to strengthen American Constitutional Democracy, but to weaken it in order to further their own political goals." The CWP had confronted the Klan before, the memo stated, and "therefore, were aware of the dangers surrounding any anti-Klan demonstration."[14]

The Human Relations Council skirted the question of whether racism in any way influenced police planning for the march. The report acknowledged that many Morningside residents were concerned about the police failure to protect their community, but it concluded that the shootings themselves were not racially motivated. Thus, racism was no longer an issue.

Later, however, Bobby Doctor, director of the Southern office of the U.S. Commission on Civil Rights, addressed the question bluntly: "If the [Death to the Klan] march had been scheduled for a white community, I can't help but feel there would have been a stronger police response."[15]

Doctor's concern was immensely significant, and it was shared by most of Greensboro's blacks and progressive whites. To this day, city and police officials bristle at the suggestion that the racial or economic makeup of the community had any influence on the November 3 planning. Yet, by their own admission, one of the primary reasons for adopting a "lay-low" police strategy was the poor quality of police relations in the housing projects. Had the march been planned for a neutral area, like downtown or a middle-class area where there was little hostility toward the police, they surely would not have felt as much pressure to keep a low profile.

Those early reports essentially created a base of public sentiment into which a later critical official report was received. By May, when an eleven-member citizens' review board presented its findings after a five-month investigation, most of Greensboro had already made up their minds about who was responsible for killings on November 3.[16]

The citizens' report was strongly critical of the police in several areas: their reliance on an informant's claim that if a confrontation occurred it would be at the end of the march; their failure to station uniformed officers at both Windsor and Morningside; their failure to surround the caravan or the marchers when it became known that the Klan and Nazis were on the move. The committee found no evidence that the police conspired in the shootings, but it did find "some indifference by some police officers to the welfare of the CWP and the Klan."[17]

Greensboro's attempts to thwart the prayer service and a February 1980 march to protest the killings were particularly disturbing. The committee gave city officials a thrashing, calling them "out of touch with an appreciable segment of the community, both black and white." Human and race relations, the committee found, "suffered more from the aftermath than from the event itself."[18]

The report concluded: "If anyone had the impression that all was well in Greensboro, that concern for the poor and persons of limited access were being adequately addressed, November 3 and its aftermath clearly dispelled this notion."[19]

Official Greensboro politely received the citizens' committee report and promptly set it aside.

Recovery

For Signe Waller, writing was a catharsis, and she poured her personal and political feelings out on her typewriter. She went to Chicago in mid-November, where she stayed with Jim's father; the summer of 1977, when she and Jim had taken long walks in the park and talked about love and politics, was very much in her thoughts. "I'm sitting in Sidney's apartment looking out at Grant Park," she wrote. "My heart aches so, I want to die. It has been extremely painful to return here, but equally painful at home."[20]

In another essay, "About Jim," Signe wrote of his dedication to communism, his constant "struggle for the correct line," his "unsparing and thorough" self-criticism. His last five years "were the most valuable of his entire life. . . . He deepened his dedication, increased his selflessness, and by the time he stepped out there on November 3, 1979, he was a folk hero, a national hero. His spirit will be embodied by millions of people who will consciously try to live like him. . . . Comrade husband, we will avenge you. Forward to the Dictatorship of the Proletariat in the eighties!"

Signe Waller had turned her grief into strength, just as she had when she rose from her husband's lifeless body shouting, "Long live the Communist Workers Party."

Harold Covington was also in Chicago in late 1979, there to "seize the time," as the Communists would say. In Frank Collin's absence, the Nazis discovered "films, pictures and addresses of some little boys," Covington said, in Collin's room in the Nazi headquarters building. Covington responded by buying the building, "an urgently necessary tactic in order to remove my regrettable predecessor from the scene," he told party leaders in a confidential memo.[23]

On Collin's return to Chicago, detectives from Chicago's Youth Division placed him under arrest for taking indecent liberties with adolescent boys.

Aftermath 191

Collin, in astonishing stupidity, had taken photographs of himself and the boys he victimized. And he had left the evidence in Nazi headquarters. "Quite frankly," Covington bragged, "we handed Frank Collin to the cops on a silver platter."[24]

The coup was complete. In two short years, Covington had moved from being an unknown to the leader of the National Socialist Party of America. His name was not exactly a household word, but he intended to change that. A major political campaign was sure to bring him state-wide, perhaps national, media attention. Covington chose to run in the Republican primary for attorney general of North Carolina—as a Nazi. To the horror of the state's underdog Republican Party, Covington frequently and loudly proclaimed, "Scratch the surface of any Republican and you'll find a Nazi underneath."

As Covington goaded the Republicans, the son of Nazi Holocaust survivors fought to recover from a load of buckshot in his brain. Paul Bermanzohn had spent two weeks in Greensboro Hospital and another month at the Durham Rehabilitation Center. The physical therapy was excruciating, but as was so characteristic, Bermanzohn channeled every bit of energy he could muster into exercising the paralyzed left arm and leg. He would never regain voluntary movement, he knew, but he would have to work constantly to keep the muscles flexible, to prevent them from shriveling and contracting.

When Bermanzohn was finally released from the Rehab Center, his wife assumed a tremendous burden. They had a two-year-old daughter and another baby on the way. Paul was in a wheelchair, not yet strong enough to walk with a cane. They had no income and had to give up their apartment, setting up housekeeping in a friend's basement. Sally Bermanzohn's days were spent lifting, carrying, and pushing. When she did get out of the house, it was usually to struggle through the bureaucratic maze of Social Security and other social service applications and their inevitable delays.

The hardest thing for Sally, though, was to realize how Paul's injuries had changed his role as a father. "Paul really did share equally in raising [first-born] Leola," she said. "He would take her to meetings, and she's a very social kid as a result. He changed as many diapers as I did. They are very close.

"But after he was shot, he had no use of his left arm. How can you change a baby with one arm? How can you even hold a baby with one arm? Suddenly, from being an activist with a baby, I was pregnant, with a baby and a sick husband to take care of. I just had to do it all. It was very hard."

The FBI had attempted to interview both Bermanzohns while Paul was in the hospital. "I'm telling you, they beat me to the hospital," said Sally. "I remember a tall man in a three-piece suit telling me he wanted to help my friends. I just told him, 'Later.' I felt like they were involved. And they were. So why should I talk to somebody who's trying to murder my friends? Just because I don't believe that they're after me personally, they're certainly after everybody else. I didn't see it as an individual thing, I saw it as they were after *us*."

A few days later, agents appeared unannounced at Paul Bermanzohn's bedside in intensive care. He was stunned at their audacity. He was hooked up to life-support machines, trying to recover from the neurosurgery that had removed a portion of his skull and frontal lobe along with some—but not all—of the lead fragments that were embedded in his brain. But he was conscious and coherent enough to know what to do. He ordered the agents out.

Legal Nightmares

Jeff Farran was talking with a fellow attorney when the call came. It was the clerk of Guilford County Superior Court. Jack Fowler had surrendered, he was told, and was now in custody in the Guilford County jail. Farran had been assigned to represent him. "I was kind of nervous about it," said Farran, "because I thought he was one of the real bad-asses in the case. He was a Nazi, he had the AR-180 which a lot of people thought was a machine gun. And I didn't yet have the autopsies—Jack Fowler could have killed everyone out there as far as I knew."

Farran was unsure whether he should take the case. He had less than two years in his two-person private law practice after serving four years as director of the local Legal Aid office. Appointment to a case like this would mean a loss in income, and it would place a tremendous burden on his law partner, who would have to carry the practice alone. And there was the fact that Fowler was a Nazi.

As a Legal Aid attorney, Farran had seen the tragedy of racism on a daily basis—in employment, housing, education, medical care, city services; almost every aspect of his black clients' lives was affected by it. Now he was being asked essentially to give up his private law practice to defend a man who espoused the ultimate in racism. A Nazi.

It was Farran's Legal Aid experience that finally led him to accept the case. After weighing all considerations, he recognized what for him was the bottom line: "I believe that poor people have a right to lawyers. I worked for years in Legal Aid and never asked my clients' political philosophies. It was the same with Jack Fowler. He was indigent and needed a lawyer."

All of the fourteen Klan and Nazi defendants had been appointed legal counsel. Of the six who would be tried for first-degree murder, two were represented by the most prominent criminal attorneys in Guilford County. David Matthews was represented by Percy Wall, a quiet but shrewdly effective attorney who was active in the liberal wing of the local Democratic Party. Wayne Wood had the services of Robert Cahoon, a flamboyant courtroom personality whose skill in manipulating juries was legendary. From the outset, the defense attorneys agreed that their case would be based on self-defense.[24]

Greeson and Coman were confident that they could overcome the self-defense arguments. "With all the firepower [the Klan and Nazis] had," said Coman, "we felt we could knock that down. You go for who the aggressor was and who used excessive force."

In addition to the clubs, ax handles, and logging chain, two hunting knives, four shotguns, and three revolvers were found in the van. And except for Roy Toney, none of the Klan and Nazi shooters had been in mortal danger before they got their weapons and began firing at the demonstrators. When they went back to their vehicles, they had in effect retreated to safety. By leaving those positions they were no longer protecting themselves but attacking. They were the aggressors. It seemed so obvious—it was recorded on videotape.

But the tapes, as dramatic and seemingly conclusive as they were, did not show everything. The district attorneys knew that several of the defendants claimed to have seen demonstrators shooting handguns and shotguns at them from just north of Tom Clark's pickup truck in the intersection. The problem for Greeson and Coman was that the truck was parked at an angle in a direct line between the video cameras and the area where the defendants said they saw the demonstrators with guns. There was nothing visible on either tape to disprove the defendants' claims.

The district attorneys needed to prove that even if some of the demonstrators had guns in the intersection, they did not fire before the Klan and Nazis began shooting. There were two ways that theory could be proved.

The first was the eyewitness testimony of the surviving demonstrators, but the CWP and their attorneys were convinced that the state would turn on them and indict as many demonstrators as they could for the slightest infraction of the law on November 3. And there was the problem of their comrades already under indictment. The district attorneys had been candid: incriminating statements by the unindicted demonstrators could be used in court against those who had been charged.

The CWP took the candor as a threat. Marty Nathan explained, "Nelson and the Blitzes and Rand were all up on charges. The government was going to get them. They wouldn't have been telling us that the testimony we gave in the trial could be used against the six [demonstrators who had been arrested].

And Mike Schlosser didn't have to say to the media that most people in Greensboro thought the Communists got what they deserved. They never had any intent to portray the people as a real loss to society when they were killed."

What Schlosser actually said in a *Daily News* interview was that most people in Greensboro would agree with a recent letter to the editor in which the writer said that the Communists got what they deserved.[25] It was an off-the-cuff blunder that would hound Schlosser for years, but it was not atypical of his style as the county's chief prosecutor. As wise a decision as it was to assign the case to Greeson and Coman, and as necessary as it was to allow them to pursue their case without interference from the media and the public, Schlosser's assumption of the role of spokesperson was a mistake. He came off as abrasive and mistrustful. His demeanor helped fuel the CWP's notion that his office was part of the continuing conspiracy to destroy them.

Greeson had never encountered such a situation in a murder investigation. "They started negotiating from the very beginning for *their* cooperation. To negotiate down a [misdemeanor] riot charge in a murder trial would be incredible. And most of them didn't need any negotiating. But those who weren't guilty of any type of riot situation would not testify because of the fact that we may charge one of their comrades with rioting. We certainly weren't going to let them ride piggy-back—let those who were guilty of any type of a riot get off because another potential state's witness would not testify unless we gave them immunity."

The second way the prosecutors could determine the source and locations of the shots fired on November 3 was by analyzing the sounds produced by firing. The FBI's Technical Services Division had a sound analysis expert at the Quantico labs; Bruce Koenig's services had been requested by both the local FBI and the Greensboro police.

Using the sound track from Boyd's and Waters's videotapes, Koenig made a printout of the sound waves with which he could positively distinguish gunshots from other loud, sharp noises on the tapes. Then, by analyzing the echo patterns, Koenig determined the distance and direction from which the soundwaves from each shot hit the cameras' microphones. After charting the sequence and location of the shots, he viewed the tapes and matched specific shots with individuals who could be seen firing on the tapes.[26] Koenig's analysis would not be completed until the murder trial was well under way, but it would later be called "the most important and enlightening piece of evidence in this case" by the *defense* attorneys.[27]

Although a few of the demonstrators had given the police brief statements on November 3, it was early 1980 before Greeson and Coman were able to get statements from most of them. Gayle Korotkin and two other out-of-state legal volunteers advised their clients before and during the interviews. Korotkin did not like what she saw. "They acted like they were going through the motions. They asked minimally the right questions. They weren't overtly hostile. It was more like they were going through the formality."

Rick Greeson saw it in a different light. "We just couldn't get them alone. We offered to go off the record if they'd just talk. Their lawyers acted as a buffer and we couldn't ask the hard questions—why were you carrying a gun? Their lawyers would either tell us not to ask it or them not to answer it. They would give a statement, but we couldn't cross-examine them on it."

The cross-examination of potential state's witnesses, although often distressing for the witness, is absolutely essential to the prosecution of a case. A lawyer, whether for the defense or the state, must know the answers to those tough questions before he or she steps into the courtroom because the opposing side will almost surely ask them when the witness takes the stand. Surprise testimony from your own witness can destroy a case.

The CWP witnesses told where they were and what they were doing at Morningside when the caravan moved in. Few of them were able to make any positive identifications. They pressed the prosecutors to indict police officers and the rest of the caravan members for conspiracy to murder and to investigate their claim of high-level government conspiracy.[28] The district attorneys, though, felt that they had a single mission: to convict the shooters of first-degree murder. For them, nothing else mattered. "All we thought about were those five dead people," said Coman.

Greeson was particularly disturbed at the interview with Paul Bermanzohn. "It was like talking to a wall, except the wall talked back. It was scary. Absolutely, the party line took priority over those dead people. They died for that reason.

"There was no doubt. He didn't give a shit about our system of government and how we had to prove our case. That was *our* problem. That wasn't his problem, that wasn't the party's problem."

Mobilization

Greeson and Coman were not the only ones having problems with the CWP. Lyn Wells had spent weeks talking with North Carolina activists about the possibility of organizing a national march in Greensboro to protest the killings. They decided that the march should be held on the anniversary of one of the most significant events in civil rights history: February 1, 1980, the twentieth anniversary of the first sit-ins—at Woolworth's in Greensboro. The march, it was suggested, should be held the next day, Saturday, February 2.

"Everybody said it's a real good idea," said Wells. "But Mark Smith said, 'You've got to talk to Nelson about it.' I said I didn't want to do that again—last time he kicked me out of his house." Smith convinced Wells of the importance of discussing the idea with Johnson and the CWP before taking it to the Atlanta anti-Klan conference.

"Nelson didn't want to have anything to do with it. At all," said Wells. "He called us opportunists and ordered us out of his house again. Shortly after that we got word from the CWP that they wanted to participate. Of course, they wanted to lead it, but that wasn't going to happen, either."

The Atlanta conference brought together a broad range of moderate-to-left groups, some of which had not worked together in years. It took two nights of all-night negotiations before a proposal was ready to present to the entire conference. The main concern, said Wells, was that the march-organizing effort be structured in such a way that it could not be dominated by the CWP or anybody else. Each of the sponsoring groups, which included the SCEF, the SCLC, the Institute for Southern Studies, and the CWP, was given one seat on the steering committee and one vote. The coalition named itself "The February 2nd Mobilization Committee."

"We went over all the things that could go wrong in a thing like that and came up with rules for how people were going to conduct themselves." One of the cardinal rules laid down during the conference was that no one was to carry firearms during the march.

In a telex dated December 17 and code numbered "157"—civil unrest—the Charlotte FBI office notified Washington headquarters that, according to news reports, the SCLC and some forty other organizations had announced that a march would be held in Greensboro on February 2. It noted that CWP members were present at the conference and that Greensboro officials had asked the Bureau to advise them of any information they turned up about the potential for violence during the march. The Charlotte office stated that "no active investigation would be instituted by the FBI at this time, as the sponsors publicly deny violence is encouraged or anticipated."

In an administrative note at the end of the telex, Washington was advised, "Charlotte office has a full investigation of the North Carolina CWP and pursuant to the AG's [Attorney General's] guidelines will follow the participation of the CWP in the forthcoming march."

By early January, some of the organizers were on the verge of dropping the whole idea of a march. "We had to struggle with the CWP from the outset," said Cleve Sellers. "They wanted to control every aspect of the march, every single aspect. They felt like they had been the victims and everything started at that point.

"I told them, you can talk about the four little girls in Birmingham if you

Aftermath 197

want to talk about numbers. You can talk about Medgar Evers if you want to talk about leaders. So just don't do this, don't cut this off and say this is the beginning of Klan terror and Klan violence. The problem is that they postured themselves in such a way that you had to go at them."

One of the ways in which the organizers took control was to involve a large number of A&T students in the planning meetings. It was not only a matter of control. Sellers describes the A&T students as "one of the moving political forces in Greensboro. Numerically and politically, they knew the right from wrong, in essence."

"It was really almost unbelievable some of the tactics that were employed. [The CWP] would get up and villify people. They would get up and talk, taking up most of the time. We just made sure that we had enough people in those meetings that if somebody called for a vote we could either quash or get the vote in our favor."

But the CWP was intent on talking, on trying to divert attention from the Klan to the state. "People were saying, 'You're almost letting the Klan off the hook,'" explained Nelson Johnson, "but we were clear on what we were doing and we were not going to be driven off that, over to fighting the Klan outside of that context."

One of the more offensive tactics used by the CWP was implying that people on the Mobilization Committee were police agents. According to Sellers, "they brought in some fellow from South Carolina in the meetings. I was sitting in the back and he got up and went through this whole thing of pointing me out and saying I was a police informant."

Johnson denies that they actually accused people of being agents. "It was clear what was going on. It's not a question of you got it from the police, but it has objective content. If I was planning it, this is what I would want. People fought against that and began to say, 'You're saying I'm a police agent.' They wouldn't take self-criticism.

"I began to think about some of the things that I had read, some of the polemics that Lenin raised. All the words he used, like imperialist-bribed, imperialist-prejudiced. It seemed like overdoing it, but I was thinking, I can really see it. I can really see it like nobody's business. The consistency of a certain pattern of thought."

It was a pattern of thought that held its ground, however, a pattern of thought that said, in Sellers's words, "The best interest is to make sure that people who are concerned about Klan terror and racism have an opportunity to speak through their feet, to come to Greensboro and leave a message that we will no longer tolerate this kind of activity in any community. The Klan and Klan violence has to be stopped. That has to be said."

If the CWP—and the February 2nd Mobilization Committee, for that matter—wanted a clear example of police-state tactics, the city of Greensboro provided them with two. In the first, at a Mobilization Committee news conference in mid-January, reporters spotted two newcomers to the news corps. A check of the sign-in sheet showed that one said he represented the "Baptist Coalition." One of the reporters recognized him as a Greensboro police officer. It was a stupid and unnecessary ploy, and Chief Swing was forced to state that he had instructed his officers never to try such a stunt again.[29]

The second incident was equally stupid. Early on in the logistical work, the organizers realized that the demonstration would be very large and that they would have to find an appropriate indoor facility for the rally and speeches that would conclude the event. The Greensboro Coliseum was ideal—large, fairly close to downtown, and available on February 2. At least, that is what one of the organizers was told by the Coliseum management over the phone. When they went to fill out the application, however, the Coliseum did an about-face. The facility had been booked for a concert by a black promoter from Danville, Virginia. "We knew something fishy was going on," said Lyn Wells. "My sister-in-law was in the concert promotion business at the time. We asked her to find out what was going on."

The Coliseum manager told Wells's sister-in-law that he had no definite booking on February 2 and that if she had something solid, he would be glad to book her group. Wells then tracked down the Danville promoter and discovered that a concert he had booked earlier in the Coliseum had flopped and he had been left owing the city for the rental of the facility. By booking his concert for February 2, the city-owned Coliseum was simultaneously recovering his debt and thwarting the march-organizing efforts.

The Mobilization Committee filed suit to force the Coliseum to let them use the facility. The news media began to probe and found that the city was cosponsoring the concert to the tune of $14,000, an unprecedented deal on what the Coliseum manager acknowledged were "marginally successful" rhythm and blues concerts.[30] The Coliseum manager was repeatedly caught in conflicting and contradictory statements, yet neither he nor city officials would admit that the February 2 booking was anything other than an honorable attempt to attract more black promoters, and more black performers, for the entertainment of Greensboro's black community.[31] The court did not buy the city's explanations; a consent decree was issued and the February 2nd Mobilization Committee was granted the use of the Coliseum.[32]

The city's attempt to stop the march is hard to understand, unless it was pure political harassment. There certainly was no evidence that the march itself would be violent. FBI headquarters and field office files repeatedly referred to the Mobilization Committee's intent to keep the march "peaceful and nonviolent." Of the groups involved in organizing the march, only the

CWP was characterized as "extremely violence prone . . . entirely capable of violence during the February 2, 1980, march."[33] The files indicate that agents who had CWP members under physical surveillance believed them to be stockpiling weapons, but they included no evidence that any of the weapons was illegal or that they would be used for anything other than self-defense.

Neither was there much evidence that the Klan or Nazis planned to show for the march. Harold Covington had made some early statements about having a Nazi counterdemonstration, but he quickly changed his mind and announced a national "White Motorcade" through Greensboro on April 19, Hitler's birthday.[34] FBI telexes reflected only the "possibility" of two out-of-state Klan groups coming to Greensboro.[35]

In order to plan police coverage of the February demonstration, Captain Dave Williams, head of a new police intelligence unit, wanted to know which groups were coming, how many people they would have, and where they would be coming from. Williams's brand of intelligence gathering did not rely on second-hand information from informants or the FBI. He picked up the phone. "My philosophy is to call people and tell them who we are, what we're doing, and why we want the information. We ask them to cooperate—to help us out. Some people refused to talk with us and said don't call again. We didn't. But I've found most groups to be receptive, on each side of the political spectrum."

Williams's tactics were considered harassment by some groups, political intimidation by others. But they surely were less invasive and more reliable than sending out a swarm of informants to gather information.

Obstacles continued to crop up for the February 2 march organizers. At a January 28 news conference, Nelson Johnson was asked if the CWP would carry guns. The Mobilization Committee thought they had prepared all the sponsoring organizations for that question. The policy had been established in Atlanta: no guns. "We were afraid the CWP people were going to be baited," Lyn Wells said, and so they coached the groups on how to respond. "If the press asks, 'What does it mean, a peaceful, nonviolent demonstration?,' your answer was to be, 'A peaceful, nonviolent march, that's what it is.' Then if they ask if people are going to have guns, you were to say, 'We are telling people not to bring guns.' That's what we were supposed to be telling people. It just doesn't make sense to bring guns to a thing like that. [The CWP] agreed to that. But Nelson was asked once, twice, and the third time he said, 'I cannot tell any of our people ever again not to be armed. I will not tell people that.'"

Another all-night session was held, and at four in the morning the Mobilization Committee voted to expel the CWP from the march. The CWP vowed to march—armed—regardless.

Nelson Johnson (Photograph by Ken Hinson)

The city declared a state of emergency from Friday evening through Saturday evening. A force of three hundred National Guard, in addition to the Greensboro police, was assigned to the march.[36] Ambulances and EMS personnel—with newly acquired flak jackets—would leapfrog along with the Tact units parallel to the parade route.[37]

The march would have its own security force, as well. Cleve Sellers had recruited and trained two hundred A&T students to serve as parade marshals. "Their duty," Sellers explained, "was to keep the group together no matter what. If a sniper fired from a rooftop, it was safer to keep the group together than to let them spread out. Trust the police to take care of the sniper, just don't let panic occur."

In the absence of any emergency, the student marshals were to hold hands, enclosing the front of the march. "The assumption was that the CWP was going to try to siege up through the front of the march," said Sellers. They did. Twice the widows and their supporters pushed past the marshals and walked abreast well ahead of the march. "So we stopped the march," said Sellers, "just shut it down—and told them if they wanted to go ahead on that they should go ahead on, that we were trying to have something that was organized. And that we thought that kind of disruption made us too vulnerable for whatever might happen."

When the CWP fell back in with the march the second time, the student marshals blocked them from entering the front or middle ranks, forcing them well back into the crowd of nearly ten thousand people. The marchers completed the four-and-a-half-mile trek without further incident, but only about half the group entered the Coliseum for the rally and speeches. Again, the marshals had to surround the stage to keep the CWP from taking it over.

After the last speech was given, the marchers straggled back to their cars parked on the other side of town. The marshals—cold, exhausted, and frustrated—walked with them, keeping a watchful eye for last-minute trouble. Remarkably, there was none.

City officials, the field office told FBI headquarters, credited the lack of violence to the massive police presence.[38] A *Greensboro Daily News* reporter on the scene saw it differently. He wrote: "At one point the police began removing riot gear from the trunks of their patrol cars but put them back as it became obvious that the march's own marshals had the situation under control."[39]

Chapter 13

> Since no evidence of such a conspiracy will emerge, the accusers will exploit, as they have in the past, its nonexistence: Is it not obvious that a cover-up is part of the conspiracy and that the absence of proof demonstrates its effectiveness?
> —Frank J. Donner, *The Age of Surveillance*

Justice, Fragile Justice

In the months after the killings, the CWP sent scores of people to North Carolina for short- and long-term support work. It was an impressive effort, a mixture of compassion and political discipline. "Some had to leave," said Signe Waller, "but some took leaves from their jobs. Somebody was in charge of answering the phone, somebody in charge of cooking, somebody in charge of keeping the house clean. I remember a member of the Central Committee trying to help us deal with the grief, saying, 'You may not think so now, but you will find other pleasures in life, other things to live for, people to give your love to.' Very importantly, they were giving political direction to how we had to respond to this thing."

The political direction became more obvious to the CWP with each passing day. In early 1980, the prosecutors had reconsidered their legal case and dropped the conspiracy charges against all the defendants. "That Saturday night," said Coman, "we had probable cause to believe there was a conspiracy—the meeting at the house and so forth. After we got into it, we found out we weren't going to be able to make conspiracy."

Under state law, it was not enough for the prosecutors to show that the defendants conspired to commit an act that resulted in death. They had to prove that the defendants conspired to commit murder. "We would have needed somebody to say, 'We put the guns in the cars because we wanted to kill somebody,'" Coman said. The evidence simply was not there. What was there, Greeson and Coman believed, was firm evidence of first-degree murder and felony riot, and those were the indictments presented to the Guilford

County grand jury. True bills on both counts were issued for David Matthews, Jerry Smith, Jack Fowler, Wayne Wood, Johnny Pridmore, Lawrence Morgan, Roy Toney, Junior McBride, Harold Flowers, Billy Joe Franklin, and Terry Hartsoe. Carl Nappier, Lee McLain, and Michael Clinton were indicted only on riot charges. Milano Caudle, who had been charged only with conspiracy, was dismissed from the case.

The district attorneys' failure to pursue the conspiracy question further confirmed the CWP's theory that the prosecutors were part of the state's elaborate cover-up apparatus. The dismissal of charges against Caudle was, according to the CWP, especially damning to the state. The AR-180 used by Fowler and the .357 used by Smith were Caudle's guns, brought in his car along with Wood's shotgun. In the CWP's opinion, Caudle was a key figure in the overall conspiracy to assassinate their leadership.

Signe Waller, on behalf of all the widows and survivors, filed a motion for a special prosecutor. "I didn't have any illusions that Schlosser was an impartial prosecutor trying to pursue justice," she said. "I knew he was part of the god-damn-fucking cover-up, that he knew what had happened, he knew who did what and he was glad the Communists got what they deserved."

The CWP wanted an independent prosecutor, somebody they could believe had no part in the conspiracy or cover-up. They believed that William Kunstler could do the job, and Kunstler agreed to have his name presented to the court. "We didn't even get to argue that in court," said Gayle Korotkin. "Schlosser told the judge he wouldn't even consider it and the judge wouldn't allow oral argument."

The court had now joined the prosecutor. For the CWP, it was yet another confirmation of the existence of widespread conspiracy. The forthcoming trial, Signe Waller said, "was going to be used to further attack us, just like they did by killing us, by slandering us by saying we martyred ourselves, by accusing us of being perpetrators of the crime—that we provoked it." The demonstrators began talking to their lawyers about the legal repercussions of refusing to testify.

The murder trial was about to begin. No matter what or how hard they tried, it seemed that city officials could not confine the ghosts of November 3. In the seven months since that day, the international news media had descended on Greensboro three times—following the shootings and for the funeral and February 2 marches—and each time they had poked holes in Greensboro's progressive image.

There were no images, no illusions in the Guilford County Courthouse, though. The prosecutors and the CWP witnesses were at a standoff. The demonstrators held firm to their decision not to give full statements to the prosecutors unless they were all granted immunity; the prosecutors did not feel they could make any bargains until they knew what the demonstrators had to say. And Greeson and Coman had strong indications that the demonstrators were not going to testify even if immunity were granted. "We kept asking their attorneys in advance, 'Will they cooperate?'" said Greeson, "and they'd say, 'We can't guarantee it.'"

As the trial date approached, the district attorneys made a decision that made any cooperation by the CWP impossible. Rather than grant immunity or drop the misdemeanor riot charges against Nelson Johnson, Allen and Dori Blitz, Rand Manzella, Lacey Russell, and Percy Sims, the prosecutors asked the grand jury for felony indictments against the six. "We wanted to do it all along," said Coman. "We held off hoping that we were going to get some kind of cooperation from them. But when it appeared that nobody was going to cooperate, then hell, there wasn't any reason to hold back going to the grand jury."

"Once we got into the case and viewed the films, it was obvious they were guilty of felonious riot," said Greeson. "There was no question that the two Blitzes fired a weapon, no question that Percy Sims verbally told those people to get out of their cars, there's no question that Lacey beat on the trunk of that car—without which none of this would have happened. Allen and Dori fired in defense of others, but whatever happened, they did participate in a riot."

To the CWP, this was one more addition to the mounting evidence of conspiracy and cover-up. "We knew the trial was going to be used to further promote anti-communism, to try to attack us," Signe Waller said. And if they did testify, "we knew that we would constantly be held in contempt. We would have been trying to tell the story about our work in the mills and all that. And that would have been ruled out of order—contempt of court—because the only charges were this guy pulled the trigger in these few seconds."

Waller was probably right. Had the CWP witnesses insisted on presenting their comprehensive analysis of the conspiracy to the jury, they would have been ruled out of order. And had they continued to violate the judge's instructions, they would have been held in contempt. "The point is," said Coman, "we were not running a Congressional investigation into what went on. We were trying to prove that these six people killed somebody. And we were trying to do it with the evidence that would establish our position. If there was some conspiracy, that's for another area of inquiry."

Coman and Greeson were having problems with another potential witness, as well: Eddie Dawson. On June 13, three days before jury selection was to begin, Dawson called Mike Schlosser. He had found out that an article was to be published soon in the *Greensboro Daily News* naming him as the informant in the Klan. On top of that, he understood that the defense was about to subpoena him. He was worried, and he wanted Schlosser's help. Schlosser told Dawson to meet him at his house later in the day; then he asked Greeson, Coman, and Captain Thomas to participate in the meeting.

When Dawson arrived, the five men got in one car and drove to a secluded park near Schlosser's house. "At first he said, 'The defense is going to subpoena me and I want you to quash that,'" said Coman. "I said, 'Look, man, we don't owe you shit. You volunteered to provide information, you're the one who got yourself into this pickle and if you get subpoenaed by the defense there ain't nothing we can do. You've got to honor the subpoena.' Then I went on to tell him that Cooper was going to testify and in all likelihood we were going to name him immediately at the outset of the trial as the informant.

"He went batshit and started making all these threats—telling me if I didn't get the subpoena quashed and if we brought his name up as the informant he would say plenty that would make the Greensboro Police Department squirm, that he had tape recordings of all these conversations. I told Dawson in some rather explicit language what he could do, I told him, 'Look, if you get called to the witness stand, I don't give a shit what you say about the Greensboro Police Department, but you better tell the damn truth. And we're not helping you get out of any damn subpoena. If you try and run, we'll help them find you.'

"I'd be a liar if I said it came out directly—'I'm going to lie if y'all don't help me.' He did not say that, but it was a veiled threat. This is the kind of stuff he kept saying: 'I gotta worry about me and I gotta say what's going to help me.'"

The prosecutors had enough to worry about without Dawson. After the grand jury issued the indictments, Greeson and Coman chose to combine the trials of the four defendants who were most visible on the videotapes: Fowler, Smith, Pridmore, and Morgan. Although Wayne Wood was also very prominent in the tapes, they decided to hold off on his trial because, as Coman said, "he'd been super-songbird" in his statements to the police and FBI. If they could get convictions on the first four defendants, the prosecutors felt certain that the others would be found guilty, as well.

The defense attorneys had a different strategy, however. They planned to move to include Wood and Matthews in the first trial, which would accomplish two crucial defense goals: increasing the number of defendants on trial would raise the probability that the jury would be confused about who did what to whom, thereby making acquittals more likely; and bringing in Wood and Matthews would mean that the defense team would be led by two of the state's most skillful criminal lawyers, Bob Cahoon and Percy Wall.[1] The motion to include Matthews and Wood in the trial was one of the first filed by the defense. Although the prosecutors argued vigorously against it, the motion was granted by Judge James Long.

In addition to Cahoon, Wall, and Jeff Farran, representing Fowler, the defense team included Hal Greeson for Johnny Pridmore, Neill Jennings for Jerry Smith, and Robert Douglas for Lawrence Morgan. Six defense attorneys versus two prosecutors. The legal teams were lopsided not only in physical courtroom presence but also in the number of peremptory challenges of prospective jurors. While there is no limit to challenges for cause—for persons who have made up their minds about guilt or innocence—each side had 14 peremptory challenges per defendant. Peremptories are used to dismiss persons who the attorney feels would not be sympathetic, for whatever reason. On the four alternate jurors, however, the prosecution was given a total of four challenges, while the defense had four challenges per defendant. That gave the state a total of 88 peremptories; the defense had 108.[2]

Both the prosecution and the defense knew that jury selection would be crucial to winning the case. But the defense had another advantage. By going for a conviction on first-degree murder, which could carry the death penalty, the prosecutors had virtually eliminated the kind of persons who would be most likely to convict a group of Klan and Nazis who had killed Communists. Well-educated professionals, liberals, and blacks—precisely the kinds of persons who were least likely to be swayed by the predictable manipulation of anti-Communist sentiment by the defense—are highly represented among opponents of the death penalty. Greeson and Coman worked long hours with a local psychologist to establish a profile of the kind of person who would be most likely to convict. What they came up with was a profile of the death penalty opponent: educated, middle-to-upper class, liberal, black.

Over two thousand Guilford County residents were asked to appear for jury selection. Each was sent a letter explaining the nature of the case and the expected duration of the trial—several months. More than 70 percent asked to be excused for hardship reasons. Of the 616 potential jurors who were examined, 377 were excused for cause. Nearly a third of those excused said they were opposed to capital punishment, but the majority said they were convinced that the defendants were guilty.[3]

Coman felt that there were underlying reasons. "The people who fit into our bracket didn't want to be on the jury. They had more excuses than Carter had Little Liver Pills. As soon as we would ask the key questions—Do you know anything about it?—they'd shoot up their hands and say, 'I saw it on TV. They're guilty. Nothing I hear in this courtroom's going to change my mind.' And they were gone.

"You wouldn't believe the painstaking efforts Rick and I took to get the kind of people we wanted on the jury, to say, 'Hey, you realize that's not evidence. The only thing you can consider is what you see in the courtroom. Do you understand that?'

"'Yeah, but I was sittin in my living room drinking a Budweiser . . .' We'd say, 'Listen to me, will you?' You'd go through this whole thing trying to get people to say, 'Okay, I realize I saw it and I've got an opinion, but I can assure the court that I'll be fair and open-minded and I'll reach for a verdict based on what I hear in this courtroom.' And the sons of bitches wouldn't say that. They wanted out.

"Of all the people we passed to the defense, they were able to get rid of forty-nine for cause, which meant by the time we passed them they'd changed their mind on a fair trial."

Of the ninety-four blacks in the jury pool, none was excused by the state. Sixty-three were dismissed for cause—two-thirds of them because they said they were unable to judge a Klan member objectively. Of thirty-one blacks passed to the defense, fifteen more were successfully challenged for cause. Thus, it took only sixteen of the defense peremptory challenges to assure an all-white jury.

With only half of the jury selected, Greeson and Coman had just twenty-eight challenges left. They had seated only one juror who came close to their profile. His name was Octavio Manduley, a college graduate who worked as a chemist for P. Lorillard. But Manduley was also a Cuban exile who had fought with the Americans at the Bay of Pigs to overthrow Fidel Castro.[4] Gayle Korotkin, sitting in the courtroom as the CWP's legal representative, was horrified. An anti-Communist Cuban with CIA connections—the conspiracy, she felt, had now penetrated the jury. She passed the word to the demonstrators.

With six jurors and four alternates left to choose, the prosecutors changed their selection strategy. They would look for younger people who might be more open-minded, less intimidated by the prospect of serving on this jury. Juror number seven was William A. Browning. "In my opinion," said Coman, "there was only one person who deliberately lied to get on that jury. Browning. His answers—if somebody sitting up there answering those questions was somebody I wanted, Browning was it. But when the defense questioned him he said he felt sorry for them [the defendants], that he could see how somebody could be sitting over there and he could even see himself sitting over there."

"I about shit," said Greeson.

Gayle Korotkin was writing furiously in her notebook. Almost every juror fit an anti-Communist or pro-Klan stereotype: exiled Cuban, defense sympathizer, former Marine master sergeant and Vietnam vet, friend of a Klan member who once went to a rally, one who thought the Communists caused the incident.[5] All of the jurors expressed some degree of anti-Communist sentiment. Greeson and Coman knew that in Guilford County, North Carolina, in 1980, the chances of coming across a prospective juror who was neutral toward or supportive of communism were slim to nil. Their strategy was to probe through the political bias for reason: Do you believe people should be killed for their political beliefs? Is it less of a crime to kill Communists? They were ugly questions, but they had to be asked.

One Uncovered; Two Undercover

On July 14 all hell broke lose. *Greensboro Record* reporter Martha Woodall broke the Butkovich story. From interviews with Covington, Wood, Caudle, and Gorrell Pierce, she had pieced their suspicions together and tracked Butkovich to his Cleveland ATF office. ATF officials were forced to confirm that he had been on an undercover mission in North Carolina, but they refused to comment on the Nazis' allegations that Butkovich had encouraged them to use automatic weapons, that he tried to get them to train in the use of plastic explosives, or that he urged them to bring guns to Greensboro on November 3.

What the ATF officials did tell Woodall was that the undercover operation was run in full accordance with agency policy. That policy, she was told, dictates that the local police and district attorney, the FBI, and the U.S. attorney be fully briefed as the operation occurs, and that it be monitored closely at the agency's highest level.

Woodall checked with the police, the district attorney, and the Greensboro FBI office and received a "no comment" from all three. When she asked U.S. Attorney Mickey Michaux whether he knew there was an undercover ATF agent among the Nazis before November 3, however, he was stunned. He had known nothing about it.[6]

An ATF agent provocateur among the Nazis. The CWP was convinced and skeptical at the same time—convinced that Butkovich was the mastermind of the assassination; skeptical of the Nazis' claim that he had set them up. In a news release the following day, the CWP said:

> What was disclosed confirmed entirely the analysis of the CWP since November 3—that the murders of the CWP 5 were political assassinations planned at the highest levels of the federal, state and local government, and that a massive coverup is being carried out.

By spilling the beans, the Klan/Nazis now hope to say they were first set up, then they were provoked and that they acted in self-defense.
We say to the scums: tell more, tell it all, tell the whole truth if you dare.[7]

Neither the CWP nor the Nazis were aware that as the trial began, two more undercover ATF investigations of the Nazis were under way. One involved an informant in the national Nazi hierarchy; the other involved an undercover agent from the Asheville, North Carolina, ATF office.

Public outrage had forced Harold Covington and his Nazis to abandon their plans for a "white motorcade" through Greensboro on Hitler's birthday. He changed the site to Raleigh and billed it as "the largest white racial demonstration in the past decade."[8] By early April, however, he was again forced to drop his plans for the motorcade. Publicly, Covington claimed that he canceled for two reasons: first, the Raleigh city council had enacted an ordinance prohibiting guns within five hundred feet of a parade or demonstration; second, he had received information that Communists planned to attack the motorcade. Rather than jeopardize his followers' lives in a public setting, Covington announced, the Nazis and the Klan would hold a "Hitlerfest" at a farm in Johnston County, south of Raleigh, where the racists would be free to handle their own security in their own way.[9]

The real reason Covington abandoned the idea of a public motorcade was found in a memo from the St. Louis, Missouri, ATF field office: on April 4, a party informant, identified as CI/203, told the ATF that Covington had "confided" that he would have to cancel the motorcade. The informant said that Covington told him "if he can only gather twenty vehicles for the motorcade he will look dumb. . . . Covington said that in order to save face . . . he is going to announce that it is being cancelled because he believes the Revolutionary Communist Party is going to attack the motorcade."[10]

The ATF files show only one party leader in St. Louis: Michael Allen.[11] The St. Louis file contains little information about illegal guns, though. Taken at face value, in fact, it looks more like a COINTELPRO file. Allen supplied the ATF with Nazi membership lists, organizational rules and structure, and "eyes only" memos to party leaders from Covington. One of those memos detailed his method for ousting Frank Collin, which he dubbed "Operation Bobby Brown."[12] Covington told the Nazis he would sign the headquarters building over to the party "when the situation stabilizes." Instead, he put the building in a blind trust to conceal his ownership.[13]

His takeover of Nazi headquarters and national leadership was not Covington's only coup in 1980. In May, he won an astonishing 43 percent of the vote in the Republican primary for attorney general.[14] Flabbergasted is too mild a word for the reaction of the state's Republicans. Throughout the campaign they had publicly disavowed any connection with or support for Covington, warning voters that there was a Nazi on the ticket. They had cautioned party members against inadvertently or ignorantly pulling the first lever, marked "Covington," and admonished them to vote for the real Republican and well-qualified candidate, Keith Snyder.[15]

The Republicans' postelection assessment, which was shared by political columnists and editorial writers around the state, was that the 43 percent had voted in ignorance, that Snyder was not well-known in the state, whereas the surname Covington was prominent in North Carolina history.[16] Some speculated that the voters might have been aware that there was a Nazi on the ballot, but mistakenly assumed it was the Germanic-sounding Snyder.[17] For whatever reason, voters at Greensboro's Windsor Center, a mile from Morningside, voted four to one in Covington's favor.[18] Covington, of course, had his own pat answer: "Most conservatives are closet Nazis."[19]

Later in 1980, Covington and Snyder would be linked in a stranger fashion. Until 1976, Snyder had been the U.S. attorney for the Western District of North Carolina in Asheville. In 1974 and 1975, Snyder was involved in a cooperative investigation by the FBI and ATF into informant-supplied allegations that Virgil Griffin and Frank Braswell, then known as *the* Nazi in North Carolina, were in possession of illegal weapons. According to FBI documents, the two agencies repeatedly requested that Snyder indict the suspects. Each time, Snyder put the case back in the investigators' laps, telling them that he needed more evidence than an informant's word to present to a grand jury.[20] No charges were ever brought.

In September 1979, though, Covington led another ATF undercover agent to Frank Braswell, as four months earlier he had led Bernie Butkovich to Wayne Wood. Michael Sweat, an agent from the Asheville ATF office, presented himself to Covington as Mike Swain, a swashbuckling mercenary who was eager to commit illegal acts in furtherance of white supremacy. He told Covington he had a source for automatic weapons. He said that for $20,000 he would perform an assassination. And he said that if the need ever arose, he had a plane and could smuggle fugitive Nazis to South America.[21]

To even the most dim-witted extremist, which Covington definitely was not, that kind of talk could mean only one thing: a setup. Rather than tell Sweat to take a flying leap, though, Covington simply said he was not interested. But, he told the agent, he knew someone who might be: Frank Braswell, Covington's only competition as the top Nazi in North Carolina.

Two days prior to the breaking of the Butkovich story, Sweat made contact with Frank Braswell. Braswell phoned Covington to check on Sweat; given the go-ahead, he began talking to the agent. The Nazis had a plan, Braswell said, to "make an example of Greensboro" if the Klan and Nazi defendants were convicted.[22] Thus, another ATF undercover operation was launched, one that would result in conspiracy convictions for two of the people who led Martha Woodall to the Butkovich story: Milano Caudle and Gorrell Pierce. Braswell was also convicted.

Ironically, then, Snyder, who as U.S. attorney was unable to find enough evidence to indict Braswell, was almost defeated for his party's nomination by Covington, a Nazi who brought two ATF undercover agents into his own party, resulting in the convictions of two of his rivals.

Chapter 14

> So we stand: as in every crisis since life began, confronting both good and evil in our nature and in our world.
> —Lillian Smith, *Killers of the Dream*

Nothing but Contempt

It took five weeks to select twelve jurors and four alternates. The prosecutors used all but three of their challenges; the defense had seven left.[1] Gayle Korotkin presented her analysis of the jury to the demonstrators, whom Greeson and Coman, still hopeful of some level of cooperation, had subpoenaed as witnesses. Korotkin said that she and the other legal workers "helped make it clear to the demonstrators that the trial was going to be a farce. There had been a range of options presented to them about what defenses they could claim for not testifying. They refused all halfway measures. Even those who weren't CWP members, those who had the heaviest family responsibilities, were so outraged by the whole process. They just weren't going to compromise with that process, to give credibility to that process."

In addition, many of the demonstrators felt that their testimony was not needed. Signe Waller said, "There were enough witnesses from the community that were willing to testify. There were the videotapes. There was enough evidence that could be reconstructed from the event—more than is present in any other murder trial. There was enough evidence to convict all the people in the caravan and the fourteen men a thousand times over.

"They didn't need our testimony to get evidence they had no other way to get. It was a correct political decision to try and show the way by not participating in that."

But there was testimony the widows and friends could give, testimony the district attorneys could not introduce without them. They could have helped

Aftermath

the jury get to know the victims as people—loving, hardworking, idealistic human beings. They could have told about Jim Waller's poems to his father, about Sandi Smith's love of children, about Cesar Cauce the love-struck newlywed, about Bill Sampson's corny jokes and songs, about Mike Nathan, on call to his Lincoln Health Center patients twenty-four hours a day, seven days a week. Under the rules of evidence, that was the kind of testimony the prosecutors could not bring in from any other source. And it was crucial. Without it, the prosecutors could only refer to the victims by name or by the grossly impersonal legal term, "the alleged victims."

"They could have helped us tremendously," said Greeson. "If we can't humanize the victims and make that human's life worthwhile, we are not going to be able to get convictions." Coman agreed: "It would have made [the jury] have some appreciation for a guy like Mike Nathan laying in the street with his head blown off instead of them looking at him as some kind of commie–cur dog who got what he deserved."

The trial began on August 4, but by then the demonstrators' decision had been made: they would not testify. Secretly, the demonstrators made another decision. "I knew something was going to happen," said Gayle Korotkin, "but I didn't know what. Somebody had said to me, 'No matter what happens, don't do anything. Just watch.'"

As Judge Long entered the courtroom on opening day, Korotkin looked around and saw Marty Nathan and Floris Cauce. They quietly took their seats as Long motioned the bailiff to bring the jury in. When they were seated, Long began his opening remarks.

Nathan stood up, shouting that the trial was "a sham," that the federal government was responsible for the five deaths.[2] Bailiffs grabbed her and covered her mouth with tape as the judge ordered that the astonished jurors be taken from the courtroom. They did not know who she was—not yet.

Long had Nathan brought before the bench and told her he would cite her for contempt of court. He ordered the tape removed so that she could speak in her defense. "I will never remain silent while the bourgeoisie brings fascism and world war on the heads of the American people," she shouted.[3] The defendants looked at each other and tried to stifle their laughter as the bailiffs took her from the courtroom to the Guilford County jail.[4]

When the jury was reseated and Long again began his instructions, Floris Cauce stood up and repeated the scene, leaving a vial of foul-smelling oil on the floor. The jury filed back out, and Long sentenced Cauce, as he had Nathan, to thirty days in jail.[5]

Greeson and Coman could not believe it. "I don't question the fact that they grieved for their husbands," said Coman, "but they sacrificed justice for the cause. It was more important to keep the goddamn cause going than it was to convict the killers."

This was an oversimplification, perhaps, but for the CWP the distinction between the shooters and the engineers of the assassinations had to be made. "Look what was happening at the time," said Marty Nathan. "There was absolutely nobody but the CWP, the widows and a very small number of people that were actually saying it was the federal government—murders by the government of five people—and nobody, particularly the district attorneys, had any interest in that. What we did was an attempt to break through that to define other issues.

"There were other attempts to bring the issue before the people—the egging of presidential candidates in the 1980 elections. I shouted down Rosalyn Carter in Winston-Salem. There was the Democratic National Convention [where Signe Waller slipped through an elaborate security system and set off a string of firecrackers during Jimmy Carter's acceptance speech]. I think it had to be done. I have no regrets for it."

On August 21, Bruce Koenig submitted his sound analysis of the shots recorded on the November 3 videotapes. He had been able to document the time and sequence of all thirty-nine shots fired. He pinpointed the location of all but three: the third, fourth, and fifth shots, which he simply listed as "not calculated."[6] The Greensboro police and the district attorneys asked for an explanation.

Shots three, four, and five were—in legal terms—the most important shots fired that day. The claim of self-defense rested almost entirely on the defendants' claims that they got their guns out only after demonstrators began shooting at them from north of Clark's pickup truck in the intersection. Without any demonstrators to testify to the contrary, the prosecutors' only hope of successfully challenging the self-defense argument depended on Koenig proving that the shots came from somewhere else. At the time, they were not aware that Sherer had fired shots three and four. Even if they had been, Sherer refused to testify, and there was no way to force him to take the stand. He was in prison, his parole revoked after he and Virgil Griffin were convicted for a cross burning in January. The threat of contempt for refusing to testify was meaningless to him.

Greeson and Coman decided to take a chance. They had gone through all the technical and boring testimony of the police chain-of-custody witnesses on the guns and other weapons, the pellets, and the bullet fragments. The state medical examiners had described the victims' wounds and given their expert testimony on the causes of death. FBI chemist Donald Havekost had given his

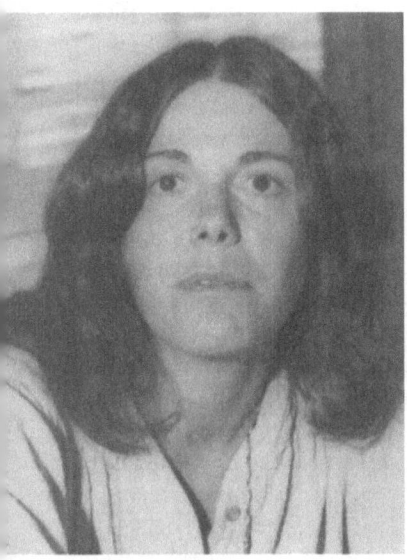
Signe Waller (Photograph by Ken Hinson)

Dale Sampson (Photograph by Ken Hinson)

Floris Cauce (Photograph by Ken Hinson)

Marty Nathan (Photograph by Ken Hinson)

excruciatingly detailed explanation of how lead pellets are manufactured and how he was able to determine which pellet in which victim was fired from which gun. All the boring, confusing, and crucial technical evidence was in. It was now time for eyewitness testimony.

The district attorneys chose Tom Clark, the guitar-strumming demonstrator whose pickup made it impossible to see whether any shots were fired from the intersection. Clark himself was clearly visible on the tapes, running across Carver from in front of his truck to the back of the WXII news car at about the time the three shots were fired. If he would, he could tell the jury whether or not he saw or heard anyone shooting in the intersection. He could identify his dead friends, give them names, make them real people to the jury rather than "alleged victims."

Clark was brought to the witness stand. Rick Greeson handed him a photograph of Jim Waller's body and asked Clark if he could identify him. Silence. Greeson asked again. And again. "Yes," Clark finally replied, "of course I know him. He was killed in a government conspiracy and this trial is just an attempt to cover it up."[7]

The normally soft-spoken Greeson was almost out of control. He slammed the photographs on the bar in front of Clark, his voice raised in anger. "Is this Jim Waller?" Silence. He asked again and then again. Judge Long ordered the jury out of the courtroom and asked Clark if he understood that he was committing contempt if he refused to testify without asserting his Fifth Amendment rights. Clark said, "I've nothing but contempt for these proceedings."[8] Bailiffs took him from the courtroom.

Greeson was devastated. Never in the sixty murder trials he had prosecuted had he encountered a situation in which the family and friends of the victim had not done everything in their power to help the prosecutors. But here was a case in which they had not received a single phone call or a single letter from a mother or father or sister or brother of the Five. And their widows and friends, it seemed, were intent on sabotaging the case against the killers.

"It's just a sad commentary on things," Jim Coman said, "that the best friends those people had in death were me and Rick Greeson. And we didn't know any of them. We did everything we could to bring their killers to justice. And I don't believe that Marty Nathan or Dale Sampson or Signe Waller or Floris Cauce can look in the damn mirror in the morning and say that."

The jurors were equally bewildered by Clark's refusal to testify. One juror remembered the incident with sadness.[9] "It made me think, how stupid, that guy could do good here. We need to hear from him. Why won't he go ahead and use the system? We know the system has faults, but use it anyway. Tax it to the limit."

Self-defense

The defense had an advantage now. They knew that the prosecutors could not risk bringing another hostile demonstrator to the stand. At every opportunity, they raised the question with the jury: If the demonstrators didn't fire the guns in the intersection, as the defendants say they did, why won't they come forward with the truth? Although one of the jurors was convinced that the defendants were guilty as charged, that kind of question had an impact. "It's not too difficult to plead your case if you don't have anyone on the other side to say that's not the way it was."

On September 3, Bruce Koenig issued a supplementary report with his opinion on the three shots: "The location of the muzzle blasts of gunshots 3, 4, and five all probably occur north of the intersection of Carver Court [sic] and Everitt Street, Greensboro, North Carolina, though no exact location could be determined."[10] North of the intersection. The defense attorneys had their case: self-defense.

Koenig's report came in just as the prosecutors were about to conclude their presentation of evidence, and the defense attorneys wanted desperately to introduce the sound analysis as evidence on their clients' behalf. But Koenig's report was derived exclusively from the videotapes, and this put the defense attorneys in a legal quandary. In order to introduce Koenig's sound analysis from the tapes into evidence, the defense would have to enter into a stipulation with the prosecution: they would have to agree to admit the videotapes—the most dramatic evidence for the prosecution—as substantive evidence.[11]

Under the rules of evidence in North Carolina courts at that time, photographs could be used only to illustrate eyewitness testimony; they could not be admitted as evidence on their own. Because Koenig was not an eyewitness, he would not have been allowed to testify on the basis of findings made solely from the videotapes in the absence of a stipulation to admit the tapes as substantive evidence. Greeson and Coman were confident that the tapes coupled with Koenig's report would work in the prosecution's favor. "That audio report was more for us than it was for them," said Greeson. "They started out telling the jury, 'We're going to prove to you the Communists fired the first shots.'"

The sound analysis showed not only that the first two shots were fired from the front of the caravan but that shots three, four, and five were fired during the stick fight in the intersection.[12] They could have been fired by the Klan and Nazis as easily as by the demonstrators. But even if the three shots had been fired by the demonstrators, the videotapes and the sound analysis proved that there were no demonstrators shooting when Wood, Smith, and Matthews began their fatal barrage.

Other than those shots, Koenig's report confirmed the prosecution's evidence on the location of each of the remaining thirty-six shots.[13] "That thing was so much for us," said Greeson. "It showed that when the defendants said somebody was firing at them, the film showed nobody was there and the audio showed nobody firing from there."

The prosecutors quickly agreed to a stipulation admitting the tapes and the sound analysis as substantive evidence. On September 24, Koenig took the witness stand for the defense. Like Bob Cahoon, Koenig had learned how to impress a jury. In answering questions, he turned toward the jury box and spoke directly to them. He smiled as he explained in simple, but not condescending, terms the complex procedures he used to reach his conclusions. His conclusions, he told them, were based on scientific principles, infallible scientific principles. His self-confidence was overwhelming.[14]

When asked if he could be more precise about the locations of shots three, four, and five, Koenig stood before a scale diagram of the Everitt-Carver area. It encompassed an area of six hundred feet east to west and three hundred feet north to south of the intersection, including the truck at the front of the caravan from which Mark Sherer fired the first shot, the yellow van at the caravan's rear, the parking lot from where Waters and Boyd filmed the shootings to the south, and the northern end of the half-block-long Carver Drive.

Using an acetate overlay and a grease pencil, Koenig drew a square within the larger diagram. He drew a line from the edge of the community center on the west to the edge of the apartment building on the east. His north-south lines went at ninety-degree angles from the corners of the buildings to the northern curb on Everitt Street, which made the fourth line of his box.

Koenig told the jury that the reason he would say only that the shots in question "probably" came from that area was that it was one of two places on the diagram from which shots would not produce traceable echo patterns. The other area was at the front of the caravan. But he was "ninety percent certain" that the three shots came from somewhere within the box he had drawn on the overlay.

When Koenig returned to the stand after a lunchtime recess, though, the defense attorneys pressed him to be more specific about where in the relatively large box the shots had been fired. Koenig again took the grease pencil. This time he drew an inverted cone that lay north of the pickup and was centered over Carver Drive—precisely where the defendants said they first saw demonstrators firing guns.

In his testimony, Koenig had not only changed the size of the area in question but increased the probability that the three shots had been fired from the smaller cone-shaped area to ninety-nine percent. Coman was incensed, but he and Greeson were still confident that, overall, Koenig's testimony would do more for the prosecution than for the defense. Greeson led Koenig through what the *Greensboro Daily News* called a "friendly cross-examination,"[15] focusing on shots fired by the Klan and Nazis: shot one, Mark Sherer; two, Brent Fletcher; six, Wayne Wood; seven and eight, Jerry Smith. The first shot positively linked to a demonstrator was number twelve, fired by Dori Blitz as Smith ran down the sidewalk shooting at Cauce.

Legally, Koenig's testimony was in the prosecution's favor. For the jury, however, said one member, "it served to confuse you as much as anything." The defense had opened saying that the demonstrators fired first; Koenig contradicted that, but said that three shots were fired from north of the pickup. The defense attorneys said they were fired by demonstrators; the prosecutors said there was no way to prove that. "After a while," said the juror, "it gets so confusing you just want to say, 'Get on with it.'" And that is exactly what the defense attorneys wanted the jury to feel. The more confused a jury gets, the more likely they are to find reasonable doubt.[16]

Greeson and Coman still had reason for confidence, though. The defendants were going to take the stand. "If you can get a defendant on the witness stand," Coman said, "you have really helped your cause tremendously because then you get to cross-examine him. And that jury wants to see what he's got to say. If you can catch that fucker in a lie, nine times out of ten you're going to win the case. And if you catch him in two or three lies, you've got it made."

There were two important witnesses that neither the prosecution nor the defense would call to the stand: Eddie Dawson and Bernie Butkovich. According to Greeson, it took "an act of Congress" for the prosecutors to get an interview with Butkovich. "What was primary on my mind at the time, I wanted to know why the hell we didn't know the Nazis were coming to Greensboro."

"The feds don't tell DAs shit," Coman complained. "After it's over you might get a call, but they don't tell you shit."

What the prosecutors were told was that Butkovich went undercover among the Winston-Salem Nazis to investigate allegations that Wood and Caudle were gunrunning to white hate groups in Ohio. This is a bit different from the one man (Wood) and one gun (the Thompson submachine gun) Butkovich now says he was investigating, but the prosecutors had no reason to question that aspect of his statement. What they were after was evidence that could help convict the defendants of first-degree murder.

"What we found out," said Greeson, "and it's typical of the feds and the main reason we didn't use him, is that he didn't think anything was going to happen."

"As far as he knew there wasn't going to be any bullshit with weapons on November 3," Coman said. "He wasn't interested in it because it wasn't part of his damn investigation. They were gonna come here and jeer at some commies—big deal. The guy had a single purpose: 'I'm down here to make a federal case on gunrunning.' That's all he gave a shit about."

Butkovich did tell the district attorneys about Jerry Smith and the pipe bomb, but he insisted that he never believed Smith's comments had any relation to the anti-Klan demonstration. And since no pipe bomb had been confiscated on November 3, it appeared that Butkovich was right.

Eddie Dawson was even less cooperative when Greeson, Coman, and Captain Thomas met him for a second time. They met in a motel room; Dawson refused to walk into the Guilford County Courthouse while the trial was going on. "We met him out of strategic self-defense," said Greeson. "They had zeroed in during the trial to make it sound like Dawson was a provocateur and actually led these people into a trap. After talking to him, we found out he wouldn't have done a damn thing to dispel that."

"'Reluctant witness' doesn't come close to describing his reticence," Coman said. "I got a little ugly with him and told him we could subpoena his ass. He said, 'The most you could give me is thirty days. I could make thirty days standing on my head.' We'd already had the damn charade of trying to put Tom Clark up. What in the hell would it have looked like to this jury if we now bring in Dawson, supposedly to dispel the lies they've been telling about him being the ringleader, and he won't answer questions? He would have undermined our own case."

The prosecutors knew that even if Dawson did testify, he could not be much help to their case. But they did want the option of calling him if the defense started making points the prosecutors would have to rebut. They told Dawson to think about it overnight. Because they would be in court, they asked him to call Captain Thomas with his decision in the morning. After Dawson left, said Coman, "we all said, 'That son of a bitch, he'll go to jail first.'"

The next morning, according to Dawson, "I called the captain. He didn't say hello or kiss my ass or nothing—just, 'Very good, Ed. I knew we could count on you.' I said, 'Whoa! How do you know what my answer is going to be?'[17]

"'Well,' he said, 'we figured you'd stay with last night's decision.' I said, 'Yeah, I'm not coming.' I just wanted to make sure we understood one another 'cause he caught me offguard. Just, 'Good decision, Ed.'"

The way Dawson describes the conversation, he gives the impression that there was something sinister in Thomas's comments, that perhaps Thomas did not want him to testify in order to protect the police. Coman, who has worked closely with Thomas for years, looks at it as typical of the captain's sarcastic manner. "You screw something up and he says, 'Way to go, Jim. That was real good work.' I took [his comment to Dawson] not as, 'Hey, atta boy, Eddie,' but as, 'You been a class-A asshole all along. Why not now?'"

The defendants took the stand. Pridmore and Morgan were convincing in their claims that although they could be seen with weapons (Morgan had a hunting knife), they neither killed nor injured anyone. Fowler admitted firing the AR-180 four times, but he said he was aiming at Dori Blitz and could not explain how a fragment from one of his shell casings pierced Nathan's shoulder.

Wood insisted that he was shooting into the air to try to scare away demonstrators with shotguns. Jerry Smith claimed he had been hit on the head during the stick fight and could not remember running up on Cauce and firing into his neck. David Matthews told the jury about seeing "niggers with shot guns," and he admitted shooting at them.

The prosecutors used the videotapes and sound analysis to impeach the defendants' testimony on cross-examination. "We ate those guys up," said Coman. "They would say, 'Yeah, there's black men there with shotguns.' We'd stop the film. 'Where are they?' The audio report—there weren't any shots from there. We caught them in so many lies.

"[Neill] Jennings gets up there and tells the jury, 'My client [Jerry Smith] says that he didn't do it, that he got hit over the head and blacked out. But if you find that he didn't black out and didn't know what he was doing, then he did it in self-defense.' Rick and I said, 'Hey, we're going to eat that shit up.'"

The prosecutors were convinced that the jury would see the guilt of Matthews, Wood, and Smith in particular—beyond any shadow of a doubt. Most of the jury, anyway. They knew that Browning, juror number seven, would be a problem. Not only had he stated in court that he had sympathy for the defendants, but frequently, when the district attorneys would examine a witness, Browning propped his chin in his left hand with the middle finger raised along his cheek. Coman was sure he was giving them the finger, and he asked Judge Long to watch for it. But Browning's left side faced away from Long, and the judge was never able to catch him in the act.

Some observers give Browning the benefit of the doubt, saying it may have been his habitual way of propping up his head and only inadvertently a sign of disrespect. A fellow juror disagreed: "I know I don't think so. There was friction between Browning and everybody. He just didn't belong with the group." The juror saw a chance encounter between Browning and one of the defendants in the courthouse snack bar that was especially disturbing: "Browning looked at him and gave him a thumbs-up."

The defense called their final witness on October 13. His name was Rexford Stephenson.[18] He was the anonymous co-worker of Jim Waller's who told the *Greensboro Record* about the conversation in which Waller said the Communists needed a martyr and they had a plan to get one. Stephenson told the jury that he and Waller had the conversation shortly after the China Grove confrontation. According to his testimony, he warned Waller that the Klan was nothing to fool around with, that next time someone could get hurt. Waller responded, "We are prepared for violence." Stephenson said he intensified his warning to say that someone could get killed. "That's what we need, a martyr," he said Waller told him.

According to Stephenson, Waller was "a dangerous and violent man . . . capable of using a gun against those who disagreed with his views." There was no way the prosecutors could rebut Stephenson's testimony. The only witness to that conversation—and the only person who could contradict his statement—was Signe Waller.

The closing arguments were predictable. Greeson and Coman relied on evidence and testimony to show how the Klan and Nazis came prepared for a fight. They showed that they could have avoided a fight by simply staying in their cars. They went over and over the tapes and the sound analysis to show that when the defendants retreated to their cars to get the guns, they could have escaped. To most observers in the courtroom, they proved felony riot and first-degree murder.

The defense focused on what could not be seen on the tapes and on who did not testify. The defendants sat quietly, respectfully, as they had throughout the trial, and nodded when their attorneys said they had come to Greensboro to protest communism, to stand up for the flag and America. They were just "good ole boys" who had been provoked beyond endurance and then attacked by gun-wielding Communists. And those Communists were now afraid to take the witness stand and testify under oath, afraid to tell the truth.

Honoring the Dead

In the midst of closing arguments, on November 2, the CWP held a memorial service for the Five at Maplewood Cemetery. There were no helicopters this time, no National Guard. Just riot-equipped Greensboro police and a small

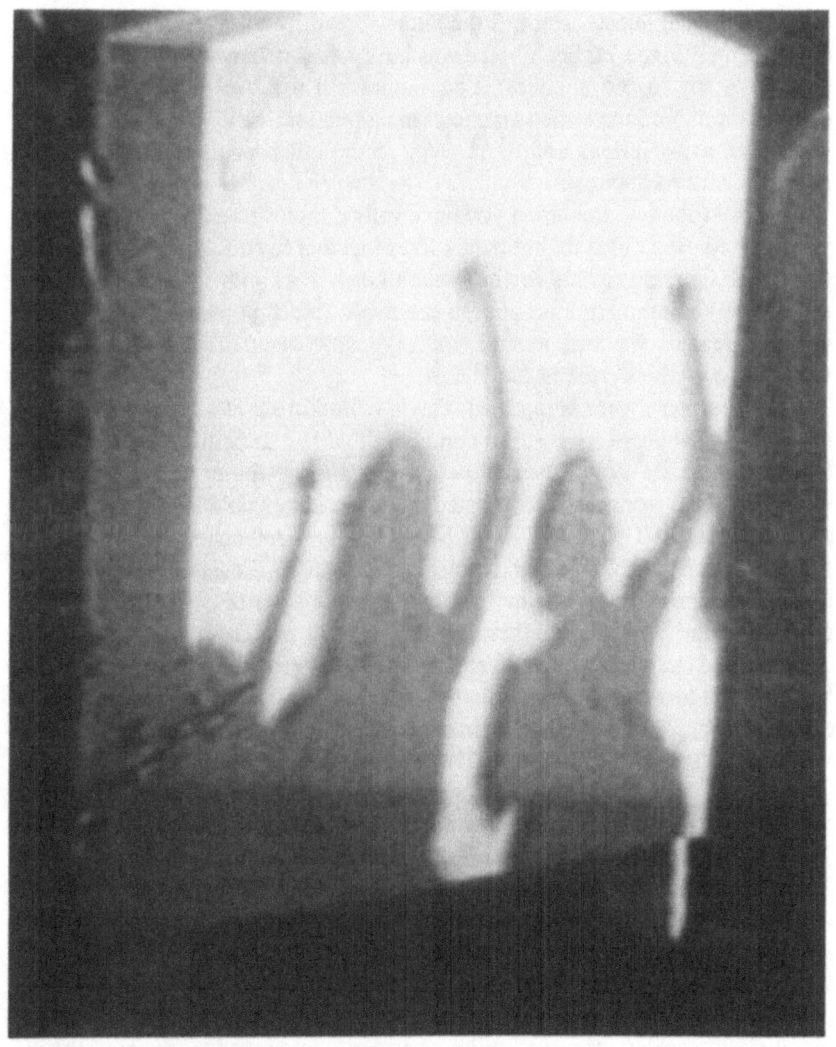
Silhouettes of clench-fisted mourners at the tombstone of the slain demonstrators (Courtesy of Jim Waters, WFMY-TV, Greensboro)

crowd of invited guests. Each of the widows read a eulogy; they were tearful but strident.[19] Signe Waller's voice was husky, and it sometimes broke as she read: "We say to our enemies: You cannot kill us. You have tried bodily assassination. You have tried character assassination. You have only exposed yourselves as weaklings and fools. We, on the other hand, are stronger and more determined than ever.

"We pay tribute to the blood you have spilled, beloved martyrs. . . . Just as you inspired us in our brief but happy lives together to struggle hard alongside you for our common goal, you continue to inspire us with strength and courage. . . . We commemorate you on the eve of the first anniversary of your glorious deaths. We will avenge you. We vow to march forward to final victory—to workers' rule in the U.S.A."[20]

As the eulogies were being read, Gayle Korotkin sat at a typewriter working on the final version of a civil complaint that had to be filed the next day. On November 3, 1980, the statute of limitations would run out and the widows and the wounded and arrested demonstrators would lose their right to sue for damages. The complaint listed eighty-eight defendants, ranging from Eddie Dawson and Bernie Butkovich, to the Klan-Nazi caravan members, to the governor of North Carolina, to the Greensboro police department, to the chief of security at Cone Mills.[21] The civil suit asked for $48 million in damages and charged that the defendants took part in a conspiracy going as far back as 1968 to surveil, harass, disrupt, and finally assassinate "militant, anti-racist labor organizers who were attempting to organize both black and white workers." After November 3, 1979, the complaint charged, the defendants undertook a massive cover-up to protect the conspirators. Korotkin finished typing the fifty-one-page complaint and rushed it to the clerk of court's office just before it closed. It was titled *Waller* v. *Butkovich*.

On November 7, Judge James Long read his charge to the jury. He explained the law on first-degree murder, on felony murder, on felony riot. He told them to deliberate on each defendant separately, and that for each one they should consider the full range of verdicts: guilty of first-degree murder, premeditated; first degree, felony; second degree; voluntary manslaughter; involuntary manslaughter; not guilty. And Long instructed them carefully on self-defense: the defendant must have been under mortal attack, must not have had any avenue of escape, must have responded with a force equal but not superior to the attacker's.[22]

As the jury was escorted to their deliberation room, the CWP held a news conference in the courthouse corridor. "The Klan/Nazis will get off with a slap on the wrist. . . . The verdict was sealed last June when the government collaborated with the Klan/Nazis' lawyers to carefully select a reactionary all-white jury. The verdict was sealed when District Attorney Schlosser refused to charge any of the forty Klan/Nazis with conspiring to assassinate the Communist Workers Party 5.

"We say and now death to all forty Klan/Nazi murderers!"[23]

The jury began its deliberations; the lawyers, the judge, the defendants, and the news media began a courthouse vigil waiting for the verdict. Neither they nor the Greensboro police were aware that a group of Nazis had talked with an Asheville ATF agent about setting off explosives in Greensboro, perhaps at the courthouse, if their comrades were convicted.

Throughout much of the trial, agent Michael Sweat continued to meet with Frank Braswell to find out how the Nazis planned to "make an example of Greensboro." The ATF's targets now included Braswell's wife, Patsy, Milano Caudle, Gorrell Pierce and his brother Roger, and James "Shorty" Talbert. According to the ATF, the group evolved a plan to put homemade napalm in fifty-five-gallon drums which they would place in four locations in and around Greensboro. If the Klan and Nazis were found guilty, they would set the explosives off by remote control at four in the afternoon, just as people began getting off work. One drum was to be placed downtown, one at a shopping center, one at a gasoline storage facility near the airport, and the last at a chemical manufacturing plant. Sweat told them he would obtain forged passports and fly the Nazis to South America when the mission was complete.[24]

The Nazis claim that they were suspicious of Sweat all along and that they made up the bomb plot to see how far he would go with such an absurd story. On October 8, Patsy Braswell told the agent that they knew they had been infiltrated; on the fifteenth, the Nazis told him that they were delaying the plot indefinitely because they heard that the Klan and the Communists had disruption plans of their own. That was the last direct contact the agent had with the Nazis; they refused to talk with him. The ATF requested approval for a wiretap to be placed on Braswell's phone. Approval was granted.[25]

But apparently no one in the ATF thought to alert Greensboro authorities that the city could be in grave danger when the verdicts came in.

The jury began deliberating on Monday, November 10. The first vote, taken on Tuesday, was seven to five to convict.[26] Browning led the argument for self-defense, and succeeded in persuading two jurors to switch.[27] The vote was now seven to acquit, five to convict. One juror did not buy it: "It stuck in my throat. When a guy comes in with all kinds of weapons and gets in a fight and comes out shooting, and they say you're acting in self-defense, that's just not right. If you're acting in self-defense, you don't go behind the car and get a cigarette [as Wood did] and shoot."

The jury was deadlocked throughout the week, but by Friday the vote had shifted: nine to acquit, three to convict. When they reconvened on Monday, a tenth juror switched. "Octavio [Manduley] was next to me and holding out," said the other holdout for conviction. "He said, 'No matter what, I just cannot accept what they did in my town.'" By early afternoon, however, Manduley too had been convinced to vote for acquittal.

Eleven people bore down on the holdout. "I'd been browbeat for three or four hours. If I stuck to my vote, it would be a hung jury. I guess I was at my wits' end. And I thought, maybe everybody sees it this way."

Shortly before five o'clock on November 17, Judge Long reconvened court. The jury had reached a verdict. Octavio Manduley handed the verdicts to the clerk and stood as they were read aloud. *State of North Carolina* versus *Jack Fowler*: First-degree murder in the death of James Waller. Not guilty. First-degree murder in the death of Sandra Smith. Not guilty. First-degree murder in the death of Cesar Cauce. Not guilty. First-degree murder in the death of William Sampson. Not guilty. First-degree murder in the death of Michael Nathan. Not guilty. Felony riot. Not guilty. The charges were read on each count for each defendant. Thirty-six times the clerk read the verdict: not guilty.[28]

The CWP had its statement ready: "This disgusting verdict will outrage the American people. This is a green light for Klan and Nazis to run the streets of this country to terrorize and kill. . . . There is no justice under capitalism. We demand people's justice. *We demand: Death to all 40 Klan, Nazi and government assassins.*"[29]

Chapter 15

> In negotiations or whatever, you must rally them, focus their attention, do agitation and propaganda to maintain their interest. Then take advantage of the enemy's mistakes to rally the masses and bring them out again for another high tide in the mass movement.
> —Jerry Tung, *The Socialist Road*

Illusions

The acquittals spawned massive public outrage. Loud demonstrations and silent vigils occurred throughout North Carolina and in many other parts of the country. Greensboro Mayor Jim Melvin issued pleas for restraint, put the police department on full alert, and appeared on national news programs to try to save what was left of Greensboro's progressive image.[1] Public calls for a federal investigation were rapidly growing into demands, but as they had throughout the past year, Greensboro officials could only respond with platitudes: the jury had spoken and it was now time to put the sordid affair to rest.[2]

The liberal-to-far-left community rejected the city's response out of hand. Five people had been brutally slain in the streets and yards of Morningside Homes, and the shooters had not received so much as a fine for littering. People who had scoffed at the CWP's conspiracy theory were forced to admit that something very sinister was going on, something that was looking more and more like a conspiracy.

From almost the day after the shootings, small groups of people—mostly older black activists and white Quakers—had been meeting in Greensboro. Although most did not feel that the killings were part of a conspiracy to assassinate the CWP's leadership, they felt stymied and angered by the city's refusal to deal with the questions of the police department's racism and indifference toward unpopular groups.[3]

Community activists were quite accustomed to the city's efforts to thwart even the most benign attempts to deal directly with social ills. But they felt that the November killings were too large an issue, and the facts too well known, for city officials successfully to divert attention in some other direction. They had assumed that the case would be decided in the Guilford County Courthouse, not in City Hall, that the defendants would be convicted, and that justice would be served.[4]

When the acquittals were announced, many community activists began to question whether there had been some sort of manipulation of the judicial process. It seemed inconceivable that the shooters could have been acquitted without it. The informal discussion groups joined forces to organize a community response; they called the coalition Citizens for Justice and Unity (CJU).

The CJU's first public event was a "witness" in the plaza of the Guilford County Governmental Center. They had hoped that in using such a Quakerly event they would inspire Greensboro's religious community to join in the call for justice.[5] Their success was limited in that respect, but they did develop a large and active core of people who worked on a number of community issues, including the call for federal intervention.

The CWP echoed the demand for a federal investigation, despite their belief that the federal government engineered the assassinations. Foregoing the strident rhetoric of the past, Nelson Johnson sent a letter to progressives around the state: "Thousands are pinning their hopes for some small expression of justice on the Federal Government. We too hope the Federal Government will bring civil rights charges against the Klan and Nazis. There is no question as to whether civil rights violations occurred; they did. There is no question as to whether there is sufficient evidence to bring charges against the Klan/Nazi killers now; there is."

Johnson quoted federal civil rights conspiracy statutes and then asked, "Why is the Federal Government hesitating on bringing civil rights violations charges? The truth is that charges of conspiracy to violate civil rights would immediately implicate the Federal Government itself."

Only "mass pressure," Johnson said, "will keep the Government from covering up the case even if charges are brought."[6]

The CWP's call for a federal investigation was a strategic move to help bridge the chasm to more moderate leftists and liberals. As in the past, they laid the blame for their political isolation on a government campaign to discredit the Communists, to promote the image of the CWP as, in Johnson's words, "a left terrorist lunatic fringe group . . . a small band of ideological nuts locked in their own ideological world, out of touch with the real world."[7]

Without broadbased support, the CWP had little chance of sustaining the costly, long-range effort to expose the conspiracy through the civil suit. With the help of a few long-time friends, most notably Dr. Neil Prose, who had worked closely with Mike Nathan, and the Reverend Philip Zwerling, Bill Sampson's Harvard roommate, the CWP organized the Greensboro Justice Fund in the spring of 1980.[8] The Justice Fund, which took over from the short-lived Committee to Avenge the CWP 5, was set up as a tax-exempt group to do education, organizing, and fundraising work around the civil suit and other issues arising from the killings and their aftermath. Neil Prose was the fund's director; Marty Nathan, its spokesperson.

One of the first organizations formally to align with the Justice Fund was the Washington-based Christic Institute, a small group of activists and organizers who centered their work for social change in religious and spiritual values.[9] They had come together to work on the Karen Silkwood case and refined an impressive style of coalition-building and fundraising through tightly organized legal and educational work. In August, the institute sent its newest staff member, Lewis Pitts, to Greensboro to look into the allegations of conspiracy in the killings.

Pitts was a lawyer who had spent the past few years traveling throughout the country to provide legal services to antinuclear protesters. His price was room and board. The years of battling the combined forces of the government's Nuclear Regulatory Commission and the nuclear corporations had left him embittered toward the legal system and the capitalist state. When the institute had first sent him to Greensboro, Pitts considered himself a self-made revolutionary who had forsaken the practice of law. After looking into the case, he returned to Washington and asked the institute to assign him to Greensboro, as a lawyer for the Greensboro Justice Fund.

Pitts's return to legal work was inspired, he explained, by Gayle Korotkin and the other lawyers who were representing the Communists. "They told me, 'Look, man, cool out. [Revolution] takes utilizing all forms of struggle, which includes legal, particularly when the legal system is used to convey the illusion of democracy and fairness.'"

In apparent contradiction to the CWP's strategy during the state trial, the lawyers told Pitts, "We need to do work in the legal system but do it in a new way—to have a co-equal component of the legal work to be public education. Go through the steps of the system and when the system starts failing you, make that a point to the public so they don't have any illusions about it."

Using the system to point out its failures and contradictions was hardly new strategy. It was the hallmark of the movements for nonviolent social change, from Gandhi to King. But the Justice Fund had a distinct advantage in focusing on the legal system in this case. Almost every individual or agency they would criticize was a defendant in their civil suit. As objects of pending litigation, the defendants were under strict legal advisement not to make any public comment on issues related to the suit. Thus, the Justice Fund was the sole source of information among the parties to the civil suit. Whether the fund's allegations were accurate or not, the defendants were powerless to respond.

The Christic Institute put a restriction on its involvement in the civil suit. The Communist Workers Party would not be the named plaintiff. "We figured it would be a lot easier to get broad support if it wasn't the CWP versus the United States," said Pitts. They would bring the suit on behalf of individuals—Waller, Cauce, Smith, Sampson, Nathan, their surviving spouses, the wounded and arrested demonstrators. In framing the language of the suit, it was decided not to describe the plaintiffs as Communists. "Communist was a label," Pitts said. "We said, 'Let's go at what you do if you're a Communist.' The essence of why the people got attacked was the day-to-day work they were doing—labor organizers who were trying to better the plight of working people and bring black and white people together. So why not make that the basis for the suit?" And so the victims and plaintiffs were characterized as "militant anti-racist labor organizers"[10]—the suit was titled *James Waller et al.* versus *Bernard Butkovich et al.*

The Federal Case

The Justice Department filed its response to the CWP's civil suit. It sought dismissal, in part, on the grounds that "reduced to its simplest terms, the plaintiffs' claim can only be that, when federal investigative officials become aware of a purportedly calculated nonfeasance on the part of local law enforcement authorities, they have some duty to act so as to prevent or mitigate the resulting damage. This view does not comport with the duties of federal officers as established by law, nor does it comport with sound notions of federalism."[11] In icy, crude legalese, states' rights took precedence over human life. The feds had no duty to protect citizens whose local police turned their backs on impending attack.

"You've got a Catch-22 situation," said then–U.S. Attorney Mickey Michaux. "If you come in there, then you've got federal interference. If you don't, you've got a problem where everybody's careless. Legally, I don't think there's a duty to tell you that if you walk out that door you're going to get shot. I have a moral obligation. But I've found that it's very difficult in many instances to get certain people to act in a moral capacity. They don't want to see any gray areas. They want either a black or a white situation. I think that's the perception the federal government has of itself. That's why I couldn't stand to work for the federal government."

Michaux had had enough. He had been peripherally involved in the case in the beginning, but bowed out when the state assumed jurisdiction in prosecuting the Klan and Nazis. But if Michaux stayed out of the case, the Justice Department and FBI did not. On the Monday after the shootings, the department assigned Michael Johnson, its most experienced attorney in the Criminal Section of the Civil Rights Division, to coordinate the collection and analysis of evidence and to serve as liaison between federal investigators and the state prosecutors.[12] Johnson's chief investigator was Tom Brereton. Within two days after the acquittals, Johnson came to Greensboro to lay the groundwork for a federal investigation into civil rights violations. He and Brereton proceeded slowly, cautiously, and very quietly.

Michaux knew of the civil rights investigation, but his disillusionment with the Justice Department's particular brand of justice had become overwhelming. He was a Jimmy Carter appointee, committed to Carter's attempts to focus the Justice Department on human rights and civil rights. But with Ronald Reagan coming into office, Michaux was certain that any human rights orientation in the Justice Department would be scrapped.

Michaux called a news conference for May 5, 1981, to announce that he would resign in June. He also wanted to announce that he had requested authorization to begin prosecution of the Klan and Nazis under federal civil rights statutes. "I called the Department and they asked me not to do it," said Michaux. "I told them how long I had left in office and they assured me that an answer [to his request] would be forthcoming before I left."

Michaux's resignation was announced to the media; his recommendations and request for authority to prosecute were sent directly to the chief of the Criminal Section, Civil Rights Division.[13] The investigation and legal research, Michaux said, convinced him that "a firmly established factual basis for federal prosecution does exist." Michaux cited two sections of the United States Code—Title 18, Sections 241 and 245 (b)(4)(A).

Section 241 was the statute Nelson Johnson cited in his letter to North Carolina progressives. It sounded tailor-made for the November 3 situation: "If two or more persons conspire to injure . . . any citizen in the free exercise or enjoyment of any right or privilege secured him by the Constitution . . ."[14] Michaux agreed: "I am firmly convinced that a literal reading of Section 241 will sustain any prosecution and conviction in the context of a conspiracy to deprive a group of constitutional rights based on ideological rather than racial basis."

In outlining the legislative history and legal precedents of Section 245, Michaux acknowledged its major drawback as applied to this case: the conspiracy must be racially motivated. Michaux felt that the racial factor could be overcome, however. "Proof of the racial element (if necessary) may necessitate the trial of the matter becoming a history class on the racist philosophies of the Ku Klux Klan and the American Nazi Party, then connecting such philosophies to their opposition to communism."

Michaux returned to Section 241, clearly his preference and, again advocating its use, took a farewell swipe at the Reagan administration: "It would indeed be hypocritical for the Administration to express concern about the rise of violent crimes and its effects on our citizens, or the right to life of the unborn, yet stand idly by when five human beings are gunned down in front of television cameras by fanatical members of hate groups solely because of their ideology." He called on the Reagan Justice Department to "vigorously and exhaustively prosecute violent acts of terrorism perpetrated against . . . citizens" who should not "be subjected to 'vigilante justice.' "[15]

Michael Johnson would not disagree with Michaux's conclusion on the necessity for federal intervention, but he did disagree, and told Michaux so before he sent the May 5 letter, with the U.S. attorney's analysis of Section 241 as well as his contention that prosecution under Section 245 could become a "history class" on Klan and Nazi ideology.

The problem with Section 241 did not lie in whether the deprivation of rights was based on either ideological or racial grounds. Johnson explained, "241 has to be understood from its historical context. The language of the statute seems to apply to anybody. But 241 was passed around 1870 to enforce the 14th Amendment [which] states, 'No *State* shall' deny due process or equal protection of the laws.

"The Supreme Court's interpretation of the statute says there has to be some state involvement to prosecute under 241. Unless you have action by a state agent to further the conspiracy, you have no cause of action."

Asked if that would not apply to Dawson and Butkovich, Johnson replied, "If you could prove—beyond reasonable doubt—that Bernard Butkovich was part of the conspiracy, or that the police sought Dawson to provoke the Klan as an object of the conspiracy, then 241 would have applied. But if you don't have that evidence, it does not apply. For criminal purposes, it cannot be happenstance."

By implication, Johnson's response indicates that neither his nor the subsequent grand jury investigation turned up sufficient evidence that Dawson or Butkovich acted "under color of law" to interfere with the anti-Klan march. And even if state involvement had been a factor, it would have been extremely difficult to prosecute under Section 241.

There is no doubt that the CWP—in its actions and pronouncements before, during, and after the July confrontation in China Grove—acted on the belief that the Klan had no right to exist, much less enjoy the constitutionally protected rights of free speech and assembly. By their own admission, the CWP conspired to "oppress, threaten [and] intimidate" the Klan at China Grove to keep them from "the free exercise or enjoyment of any right or privilege secured . . . by the Constitution."[16] And their rallying cry for November 3 was "Death to the Klan." To ask a grand jury to indict the Klan and Nazis under Section 241 for their actions on November 3 without seeking indictments against the CWP for their actions at China Grove would have left the prosecutors wide open for arguments to dismiss based on selective prosecution.

"It wasn't a matter of choosing which statute to prosecute under," said Johnson. "It was finding one that applied." As his legal research and interviews with witnesses intensified, it began to look more and more as though Section 245, enacted in 1968 to correct some of the legal problems in 241, was the criminal statute under which prosecution should be brought.

Johnson focused his investigation on the combination of subsections legally cited as 245 (b)(4)(A) and (b)(2)(B): "Whoever, *whether or not* [emphasis added] acting under color of law, by force or threat of force wilfully injures, intimidates or interferes with, or attempts to injure, intimidate or interfere with . . . any person because of his race, color, religion or national origin and because he is or has been . . . participating in or enjoying any benefit . . . or activity provided by any State or subdivision thereof" or any persons who conspire to "intimidate such person or any other person or class of persons from . . . participating, without discrimination on account of race, . . . in any of the benefits or activities described [above shall be guilty of an offense against the United States]." The benefits referred to include "any . . . service, privilege, program, facility or activity provided or administered by any State or subdivision thereof."[17] The city's permit for the anti-Klan march was such a benefit.

The clauses "because of his race" and "because he is . . . participating without discrimination" appear to leave this section as problematic as Section 241. The evidence that the Klan and Nazis went to disrupt the march because it was an integrated activity was circumstantial at best. Every one of the Klan and Nazis maintained from the beginning that they went to Greensboro to confront Communists who had taunted, goaded, and threatened them. There was substantial evidence, though, that the racists *thought* the WVO was a black or predominantly black Communist organization.

There had been at most fifteen whites among the hundred or more anti-Klan demonstrators at China Grove. In his Lincolnton speech, Ed Dawson warned the Klan that they would face "big buck niggers" and hundreds of students from Greensboro's "nigger" colleges. The "Death to the Klan" poster Dawson circulated at that meeting had a photograph of the China Grove demonstrators—almost all black. Caudle and others at the November 1 Klan-Nazi meeting knew that Nelson Johnson wrote the "Open Letter" challenging them to come to Greensboro, and it was Johnson who appeared on the eleven o'clock news with three black women holding a "Death to the Klan" banner. And Jerry Smith brought his "James Earl Ray Is My Hero" sign, a clear attempt to intimidate or provoke blacks.

That kind of evidence would be admissible in federal court. Mickey Michaux's "history class" would not. Under federal rules of evidence, organizational philosophies can be introduced only so far as they relate to the defendant on trial and the specific charges under which he or she is being tried. "Criminal cases are against individuals," Michael Johnson explained. "They apply to individual conduct. The only way you can bring [political philosophy] in is if the defendants adhered to those beliefs and acted upon those beliefs." Thus, the Klan's history of intimidating and killing black people and civil rights workers could not be used as evidence against the Klan assailants in Greensboro unless a direct link could be proven between that history and the actions for which the defendants were on trial.

The foundation for federal prosecution was fragile. "There is not a one-sided street in this whole affair," Johnson said. "There were things done by people on both sides." Johnson and Tom Brereton had to dissect every aspect of the events that led to the November 3 shootings and put them back together in a legal framework that would withstand the burden of proof "beyond a reasonable doubt." They had to investigate the demonstrators as closely as they did the Klan and Nazis. It was not a political witchhunt; it was vital to the successful prosecution of the case. They could not afford any surprises in the courtroom.

True Stories

The CWP's educational effort broadened further in early 1981. Sally Alvarez, a party supporter, produced a sixty-minute color film called *Red November, Black November*. Funded in part by the Justice Fund, the professional-quality film illustrated the evidence of conspiracy and provided the first glimpse into the personal lives as well as the revolutionary work of the Five. If it had not been apparent before, the trial certainly proved how essential it was for people to understand that the victims were decent human beings, the kind of folks they would like to have known.

Aftermath

The premier showing of the film was held on March 1 at a small theater in the Greensboro Coliseum complex.[18] In addition to a visible crew of Greensboro police officers, the CWP had its own security patrolling the area with walkie-talkies. Despite the security concerns, the atmosphere was festive, with over two hundred people joining the widows and November 3 demonstrators for the premier.

In the corridor, a reporter spotted a familiar face. She approached him cautiously. "How ya doin?"[19]

"Pretty good, pretty good. And yourself?"

"Okay. Kinda risky coming out here tonight, isn't it?"

"I just want to see what they're saying about me. It's open to the public, and I'm part of the public."

Someone signaled that the film was about to start and the two walked to the ticket booth. "Two?" the reporter was asked.

"No, no. We're not together." She paid for one ticket and walked quickly to the theater entrance. Tom Clark was taking tickets.

"Who was that man you were talking to?" he asked.

"Ed Dawson." She went inside and took a seat near the back, wondering what would happen next. The widows and families were all in the front row, oblivious to the gaunt, gray-haired man taking his seat at the end of a center row. Voices could be heard in the hallway outside. Moments later Sally Alvarez walked down the aisle. She stopped at Dawson's seat and looked straight into his eyes. "You are not welcome here, Mr. Dawson," she whispered. "Please leave quietly. We will return your money." Dawson did as he was told.

As the film began, the word spread quickly through the audience. Ed Dawson was here. Walked right past all the police, all the security. It was an outrage. The murmuring settled down after a few minutes. There were the videotapes, the horrible videotapes, and many in the audience were reliving their own personal horror of November 3. The narrator talked about Ed Dawson and Bernie Butkovich, the Greensboro police, the FBI, the ATF—and political assassination.

There were moving, personal interviews with the widows and co-workers. Jim and Sandi and Mike and Cesar and Bill were given life and substance, humor, and compassion. When the film ended and the lights went up, the families and friends of the Five were not the only ones with tears in their eyes.

Another piece in the CWP's educational campaign was not so moving. *The True Story of the Greensboro Massacre*, a 254-page paperback book, was Paul and Sally Bermanzohn's contribution to the educational effort.[20] It, too, focused on the lives of the Five. But the Bermanzohns' heavy-handed focus on the revolutionary aspects of their work, their friendships, even their play, was suffocating. Their friends came across as one-dimensional party drones.

In their zeal to portray the Five as heroes, the Bermanzohns exaggerated, embellished, and distorted.[21] Paul Bermanzohn would once again learn the hazards of revolutionary overstatement: *The True Story* would be introduced by the defense in the federal criminal trial to impeach his testimony.

Shortly after the premier of *Red November, Black November*, a federal grand jury in Asheville indicted Frank and Patsy Braswell, Milano Caudle, the Pierce brothers, and Shorty Talbert with conspiracy to firebomb Greensboro. The Nazis hollered "entrapment," but the ATF wiretaps showed that they had continued to discuss the plot over the phone even after they had severed communication with Agent Sweat.[22]

The Braswells, Caudle, the Pierces, Talbert, Wood, Fowler, and Collin—it seemed that the Nazis were under attack from all quarters. The NSPA had been in turmoil since February when party dissidents, including Frank Braswell, had attempted to expel Harold Covington. Covington had responded by purging the dissidents. Now, however, Nazis around the country had become convinced that Covington was acting in some kind of undercover capacity to annihilate the National Socialist Party of America.[23]

Covington had to act quickly. He called a news conference in Raleigh and announced that he was going underground. The reason he gave was that John Hinckley, the would-be assassin of Ronald Reagan, had been linked with the Nazis, a link that Covington himself confirmed the day before he resigned. It was no longer safe to be a publicly recognized Nazi, Covington told reporters. He would continue his racist organizing, but not as head of the National Socialist Party of America. He named Michael Allen, the St. Louis ATF informant, as his successor.[24] Then he quietly slipped into South Carolina and anonymity.[25]

The trial of the six Nazis for conspiracy to bomb Greensboro began in Asheville in July. The jury heard tapes from the body transmitter Sweat had worn.[26] They heard Frank Braswell threaten to murder Guilford County District Attorney Mike Schlosser, and they heard Sweat suggest that they should murder "unenlightened" people like *Greensboro Record* reporter Martha Woodall, as well. They heard Sweat instruct the Nazis on how to make large quantities of napalm; the Nazis later decided to use conventional explosives—seventeen *thousand* tons. As the last tapes were played, however, the jury heard Sweat urge the group to proceed after they told him they wanted to postpone the bombing plan because a source warned them that the Greensboro police were on the alert for possible terrorist activity. Sweat told them, "What you were talking about doing is a piece of cake. A moron could do it without being caught." His contacts in South America would be angry, he told the Nazis, if they did not follow through. "I already told these guys we got money coming down. I don't want to shit in my own nest."

The jury spent the entire next day listening to the tapes from the wiretap on Braswell's phone. In twenty-eight days the tap recorded 1,702 calls; the Nazis had continued to talk about the plot until the defendants were acquitted.[27] On November 17, Braswell called Pierce: "We played a helluva game. Do you know what brought the verdict? That's right. They don't like napalm." Later he talked with Caudle: "We said enough that they knowed we wasn't going to take it lying down."[28]

There was no evidence that Braswell or any of the others had obtained the materials necessary to carry out their plan. Not so much as a firecracker. And although Sweat and other ATF agents testified that they took the plot "seriously," they had never bothered to get a search warrant, not even when the jury began deliberating in the Greensboro Klan-Nazi trial.[29]

Braswell had an almost unimpeachable witness to verify his contention that he knew Sweat was an undercover agent he had known as Mike Swain—former assistant U.S. Attorney Bruce Briggs. Braswell had come to his office, Briggs testified, in July 1980 and asked if he knew anything about a mercenary named Mike Swain who claimed to have a paramilitary training camp in Mitchell County. Briggs had never heard of Swain, but he agreed to let Braswell know if he heard anything. A few weeks later, he did. Briggs testified that he warned Braswell that Swain was an infiltrator—he did not know for whom.[30]

Braswell, testifying on his own behalf without counsel, told the jury that after talking with Briggs, he tried to ease Sweat out of the group. They were frightened, he said, and had to proceed cautiously because the agent frequently threatened to blow up the Braswell's house if they were not "honest."[31] He testified that after they finally broke contact with the agent, the Nazis continued to talk about the plot over a phone they knew was bugged. It was a game, he said, a tease to rile whoever was listening on the other end.

The Nazis' plan was beyond absurd, an explosives expert testified. He estimated that seventeen thousand tons of explosives would cost in the neighborhood of $4 million; to transport it, the Nazis would have needed 850 tractor trailers.[32]

The jury was instructed on federal conspiracy law. The evidence had to show that the defendants agreed to a plan and agreed to participate of their own free will. The evidence had to show that at least one defendant committed one overt act to further the plan. The evidence did not have to be physical—a jar of napalm or a stick of dynamite; it merely had to be an act. Participation in a meeting to define the plan was such an overt act under the law.[33]

On the second day of deliberations, the jury announced it was deadlocked—ten for conviction, two for acquittal. A mistrial was declared.[34]

The Nazis asked for free transcripts of the trial in order to prepare their defense for the retrial. They never got them. They returned to court in September without the transcripts and without lawyers. After four days of testimony, they were convicted of conspiracy. Frank Braswell, Gorrell Pierce, and Milano Caudle were each sentenced to five years and $10,000 fines. Patsy Braswell, Roger Pierce, and Shorty Talbert received two years suspended and three years probation.[35] They immediately filed an appeal.

Five days later, Harold Covington was issued a passport in Miami, Florida.[36] According to FBI documents, he then returned to South Africa.[37]

Part 4

Answers

Chapter 16

> *Informant on TV*: In an appearance earlier this week on the television show "Lie Detector," former police informant Edward Dawson passed a lie detector test with his assertion he did not provoke the shooting deaths of the anti-Klan demonstrators in Greensboro.
> —*Charlotte Observer*, February 24, 1983

Spy-Speak

In October 1981, the Durham-based Institute for Southern Studies released a thirty-two-page special report, "The Third of November." The institute did not have the resources to conduct an in-depth investigation, but the staff agreed that they could still produce a valuable resource by compiling a detailed chronology and analysis of the incident from China Grove through the trial.

The project began a few weeks after the acquittals. Then, in January 1981, one of the staff members got a tip. Ed Dawson had tried to get the city to provide him with legal representation in the CWP's civil suit. He had been rejected and he was angry. Dawson might be ready to talk.[1]

And talk he did, for four solid hours. He talked about the old days in the Klan, about his arrest for terrorizing, his informant days with the FBI, and how he got involved with Rooster Cooper.[2] He told about going to the Lincolnton rally, about getting the CWP's parade permit and arranging the rendezvous at Brent Fletcher's, about calling Cooper twice (not once, as Cooper maintains) on the morning of November 3 to report on how many people were at Fletcher's and how many had guns. On the second call, Dawson said, he told Cooper there were "twelve to fourteen people there and they had guns, everybody had a gun."

Dawson admitted leading the caravan to Everitt and Carver, where he shouted, "You asked for the Klan, here we are," and then driving off when the fighting began. He admitted helping Griffin and his people flee from Fletcher's to his house to the motel and finally out of Greensboro.

He said he would not talk about the Greensboro police, but then started dropping tantalizing hints. "I got some good answers for you. You know, the dates and a couple calls, I'm not going to disclose those to anybody. But I got tapes on three of them." And Dawson told about the meeting with the district attorneys and his subsequent phone call to Captain Thomas, when he was told, "Very good, Ed. I knew we could count on you."

While not subscribing to the CWP's conspiracy theory, the members of the institute staff who were veterans of the civil rights and antiwar movements knew from experience how governments and police and prosecutors had historically worked together to block investigations of assaults on leftists. Dawson's story seemed to fit the mold.

"Our intent in this report," the authors stated in the introduction, "is not to prove any conspiracy but rather to provide a record of what happened in a way that illuminates a host of remaining questions which must be answered before anyone in good conscience can place Greensboro in its proper perspective."[3]

The report focused on the role of the police, the prosecuting attorney, and city officials in "managing and mis-managing the events surrounding the killings."[4] The edited transcripts of the Dawson interview were printed in a seven-page appendix.

In late 1981, "The Third of November" was clearly the most comprehensive public document on the shootings. But it was flawed, particularly the section dealing with the trial. Relying too heavily on day-to-day news coverage of the trial, the institute researchers failed to probe beyond appearances. Mike Schlosser was accused of "systematically weaken[ing] the prosecution" in going for first-degree murder, in dropping the conspiracy charges, in selecting an all-white jury, in "trading" Koenig's sound analysis to the defense, in failing to call Dawson or Butkovich to the witness stand, and in not allowing the political philosophies of the Klan and Nazis to be brought out in court.[5]

When interviewed for the report, Schlosser refused to talk about substantive aspects of the trial—he was then a defendant in the CWP's civil suit. The one issue he did agree to talk about was the dismissal of conspiracy charges, but his answers were curt and unenlightening. "There was no evidence of conspiracy to murder," he said.

Asked if the fact that the Klan and Nazis brought guns did not show that they planned to attack the demonstrators, Schlosser replied, "The Klan always carries guns." Why didn't he call Dawson or Butkovich to the stand? "Butkovich didn't witness anything that would have helped us. Dawson's testimony wouldn't have helped us either."[6]

To the institute staff, Schlosser's curt and unenlightening answers equaled evasion, deception, and cover-up. "By dismissing the possibility of a planned assault with a flippant observation such as 'The Klan always carries guns,' Schlosser gave the defense attorneys the opening they needed: self-defense."[7]

Despite its flaws, "The Third of November" was as close to definitive as anything published to date, but the institute staff recognized that their research had raised more questions than it answered. "The actions of various parties can still be explained in more than one way, some more palatable than others."

To "encourage the probing effort," the institute report recommended that the Civil Rights Division act promptly to prosecute the Klan and Nazis; that Congress investigate the role of the Justice Department and ATF in handling the case as well as "the adequacy of federal statutes to protect citizens when local officials fail to uphold the exercise of their constitutional rights"; and that the people of Greensboro demand an independent investigation of governmental actions in the case.[8]

Armed with the report, Citizens for Justice and Unity renewed its call for federal intervention. Institute staff members came to Greensboro to help build organizing momentum from the interest generated by the report. But other than the CJU and the Justice Fund, people in Greensboro were reluctant to take a public stance on the case. "People deplored the killings but didn't have it in them to stand up," said one CJU member.[9] "This was such an unpopular cause to be related to—people didn't think beyond CWP, Klan or Nazi."

To break through those barriers, the institute persuaded its president, Julian Bond, to come to Greensboro to offer "a third voice," a straightforward call for justice in a tragedy that was neither the inevitable outcome of Communist provocation nor a conspiracy to assassinate the CWP Five.[10] Bond met with the CJU, black community leaders, ministers, and A&T students who later agreed to organize a series of events intended to demonstrate that there was, in fact, strong support in Greensboro for federal intervention. There were public forums and private meetings with Justice Department officials and members of Congress. A number of local ministers allocated one Sunday to address the issue of justice in Greensboro to their congregations; church members signed petitions which appealed to the Justice Department and Congress to pursue federal remedies against the Klan and Nazis and to the Greensboro City Council and Human Relations Commission to pass resolutions supporting the citizens' call for federal action. By early 1982, the CJU and the ministerial effort had succeeded in getting resolutions passed in both the council and the commission and in getting hundreds of citizens to sign the petitions.[11]

It was an impressive organizing and educational campaign, but it had little effect on the course or speed of the federal investigation.

In March 1982, a federal grand jury was empaneled in Winston-Salem to establish if there was sufficient evidence to issue indictments against those involved in the November 3 shootings. The demonstrators and their attorneys were skeptical. "We never had any illusions about the grand jury," said Lewis Pitts. "We had to demand it, we had to force it, we had real spats with [the Justice Department] even before it was convened."

In pre–grand jury interviews with Michael Johnson and other Justice Department attorneys, Pitts got the distinct impression that "it was going to be a witch hunt. It appeared to us they were just trying to get at the people they thought were [CWP] activists and anti-Klan demonstrators. We were very concerned that they would drag them in and ask about how did you get there and what are your politics and how many demonstrations have you been to. We made it clear we were going to object to them going into that."

There was another major concern: Michael Johnson had told the Justice Fund lawyers that the grand jury might indict some of the demonstrators. "We began to wonder whether this was an attempt to use the biggest issue that was used against the CWP in the Klan trial," said Gayle Korotkin. "It was an attempt to sort of promote non-cooperation. Given the historical role of grand juries and given the administration's obvious view toward the left in general, we didn't need the Justice Department to tell us the threat of potential prosecution was there."

Johnson bristles when asked to talk about his dealings with the Justice Fund lawyers and the demonstrators. Under Justice Department restrictions, he cannot talk about it in detail, but Johnson insists that the early meetings dealt with the Justice Fund's request that the demonstrators be granted immunity from prosecution in exchange for their testimony. Like the state prosecutors before him, Johnson was legally and ethically bound to advise anyone who might be the subject of the grand jury's investigation of the possibility. It was not a threat, it was a fact.

The Justice Fund's determination to protect its clients from possible indictment made Johnson's job all the more difficult. In his opinion, it was the CWP's "non-cooperation" and not the Justice Department's "foot-dragging" that made the investigation interminably long. "For those people to claim they were responsible [for forcing the grand jury investigation] is ego-self-gratification," Johnson said. "The reason things weren't happening faster was because they were holding back."

Whether the anti-Klan demonstrators were holding back or not, they were the first noninvestigatory witnesses to appear before the grand jury. Most of the twenty-six demonstration witnesses gave news statements following their testimony.[12] For the most part, they were pleased with the way the jurors received their testimony. They said that they were allowed to talk about their union and organizing work and their commitment to bring black and white people together and to eliminate racism and violent racist groups like the Klan and Nazis. But they continued to hammer away at Michael Johnson's and Tom Brereton's roles in the proceedings.

Johnson, they maintained, delayed the grand jury investigation for over two years; he had threatened demonstrators with prosecution and he had not begun to interview anti-Klan demonstrators until—suspiciously—the day before the report by the Institute for Southern Studies was released. Brereton testified in the state trial that in the mid-1970s he had employed Ed Dawson on a few occasions to do carpentry work on his house. And he was responsible, the Justice Fund alleged, for erasing thirty minutes of Jerry Smith's "taped confession." Actually, the erasure was done by Detective Herb Belvin, who inadvertently recorded over the first side of Smith's November 3 interrogation tape. The incident was thoroughly investigated by Greeson and Coman. They concluded that what had been erased was the reading of Smith's rights and preliminary attempts to get him to talk. It is clear from the transcripts that Smith spent the majority of the interview crying and expressing fear for his family. Belvin was teased unmercifully for his mistake by those who knew about it. They called him "Rosemary," after Richard Nixon's secretary.[13]

Conspiracy Amended

In May 1982, an amended complaint was filed in *Waller* v. *Butkovich*.[14] Tom Brereton and the Justice Department were added to the list of defendants for their alleged role in covering up the original conspiracy. Joining the list of attorneys for the plaintiffs was the ACLU, once the scourge of the CWP for its unwavering support of the constitutional rights of all Americans—Klan and Nazis included.

Drafted by the ACLU, the amended complaint was tightened significantly. The primary exclusion was about seven pages of allegations of a decade-long conspiracy against the plaintiffs by various federal, state, and local agencies, including the Greensboro Chamber of Commerce, southern textile mills, and the Ku Klux Klan and Nazi Party. The 1982 complaint focused on the conspiracy leading up to and the cover-up following the Greensboro shootings.

As in the original complaint, however, the allegations of conspiracy in planning the attack seemed excessive. "A plan was mutually agreed upon by the Klan and Nazi defendants and agents of defendants Greensboro Police Department, BATF, and FBI, including Dawson and Butkovich. . . . This was a plan by which an attack on plaintiffs and other members of the targeted classes would be made, the police defendants would not prevent or provide protection from the attack, and the informant-defendants Dawson and Butkovich would facilitate and participate in the attack."[15]

As specific as the allegations sound, according to Lewis Pitts, the plaintiffs were not required to prove that the defendants actually met and laid out a plan. "We don't allege conspiracy to murder, although that's what appeared to happen. It was a conspiracy to violate the civil rights of those people, and an objective of that conspiracy was also to cover it up.

"My feeling is that it was a little more conscious than 'let's put in proximity these volatile issues and people and hope something will happen.' You could have the owners of Cone Mills just having a conversation with certain people. With the Carter administration, you've got Southern connections. There could be a few words passed—'this stuff's really getting to be a pain in the ass down here, can you take care of that?' That gets passed to a high level official who's not involved in the day-to-day political surveillance and they pass it to someone who's in like the ATF and they take it over. Then it becomes more deliberate and a conscious plan. That's the crowd that does the dirty work."

Proving conspiracy in the civil suit would not be as difficult for the Justice Fund lawyers as it would be for the federal prosecutors in the criminal civil rights trial. The burden of proof in a criminal trial is on the prosecutor to prove "guilt beyond a reasonable doubt"; in a civil trial the plaintiffs must only prove their case by "a preponderance of the evidence."

Still, there were odd discrepancies in the wording of the amended complaint which raised questions about the credibility of other allegations in the document. Contrary to evidence that was well-known at the time, the complaint alleged that Sandi Smith was killed "by a carefully aimed shot that struck her between the eyes."[16] Sampson and Nathan, it said, were "hit by carefully aimed shots which struck between the eyes, in the head or in the heart." Bermanzohn, too, was struck "by a shot between the eyes."[17] Autopsy and medical reports introduced in the state trial show that not one of those victims was shot between the eyes.

Another allegation that does not match the evidence deals with the arrests of several demonstrators following the shootings. "The defendants . . . attempted to divert attention from their complicity in and responsibility for the attack and resulting murders. Acting without a warrant or probable cause, defendant Greensboro Police Department . . . arrested plaintiffs Johnson, Cannon and Manzella immediately after the attack on baseless charges."[18] As understandable as the demonstrators' hysteria was on November 3, the police had little choice but to arrest them. A neighborhood had been terrorized, and fear and anger were sweeping through the community. In that volatile setting, the police had little choice but to arrest Nelson Johnson for inciting a riot when he began shouting, "We declare WAR." They had little choice but to arrest Willena Cannon for interfering with an arrest when she fought them as they tried to take Johnson into custody.[19] And they had no choice but to arrest Rand Manzella for being "armed to the terror" as he wandered through the yards of Morningside with a gun in his hand.

The strongest part of the complaint rested in its sixth cause of action. It charged the Greensboro Police Department, its informants, the FBI, and the ATF with "having knowledge of the existence of a conspiracy . . . and having the power to prevent it or aid in preventing the same, neglected and failed to do so. Those wrongful acts and omissions were the proximate cause of plaintiffs' injuries and constitutional deprivations."[20]

On June 3, Bernard Butkovich was escorted by an ATF lawyer past reporters to the grand jury room. He gave the jurors a brief personal history: Vietnam vet—Special Forces explosives expert, investigator for the state of Michigan paroles board, received ATF training at Glynco, Georgia, in the spring of 1979, where he was awarded distinguished graduate honors and was voted "most athletic."[21]

The Wood investigation, he testified, "was originally planned [as] what we refer to as a one-man, one-gun investigation. Should Mr. Wood arrive [at the Parma, Ohio, rally], it was presumed he would have the machine gun. It was presumed that the investigation would terminate at that time with an arrest."

When Wood did not appear in Parma, Butkovich testified that Fulton Dukes "may have mentioned" going to North Carolina one time "to try and finish this thing up." He told the jury that he met with Dukes and John Westra, the agent in charge of ATF operations in North Carolina, in Asheville on July 25 where they discussed, but made no decision on, whether he would be allowed to attend public functions as a Nazi.

Butkovich did not tell the jury about Westra's instructions to stay away from party functions where there was a possibility of violence, but he did go into some detail about the Nazis' vehement hatred of blacks and Jews. He told them of unsuccessfully attempting to investigate Covington and Braswell regarding illegal weapons and cigarette and alcohol smuggling.

Butkovich testified about a conversation he had with Wood in September 1979, shortly after the *Winston-Salem Journal* ran a feature article on the local Nazis in which Wood claimed—falsely—that they had a paramilitary training camp in Davie County. Wood told Butkovich that the Nazis really should set up such a camp in order to train for the overthrow of the government. Wood suggested that they could use cut-up broom handles to practice lobbing sticks of dynamite. Butkovich said he told Wood that they would have to practice with the real thing, and the agent asked him if he could get dynamite, caps, and plastic. "I have no problem getting dynamite," he quoted Wood as saying, "and I have no problem getting caps. I'll take care of that. But I may have a problem getting military plastic explosives."

The grand jury did not hear from Butkovich about Jerry Smith's November 1 statement regarding pipe bombs that "would work well if thrown into a crowd." He said there was no discussion of taking guns, clubs, brass knuckles, tear gas, or mace to Greensboro—only rotten eggs. "I decided that the possibility of looking into firearms violations were virtually non-existent for the rally, so I departed and made contact with the undercover team."

Butkovich said that his mission on November 3 was to try to locate another Thompson said to be in the possession of a Nazi from Davie County. He told the jury what he did when he heard of the shootings, about talking with Wood in the interrogation room, and about his encounter there with Tom Brereton.

When it came time for the jurors to ask questions of the witness, one was particularly curious about the agent's cover as a truck driver. "Were you a casual employee at McLean?" the juror asked.

"That's correct. That was the terminology used," answered Butkovich.

"Who gave you the terminology?"

"It came from the case agent and in turn came from McLean Trucking."

"And it was casual road driver, long distance?"

"Correct."

"You wasn't leased to McLean?"

"I don't know that much about the workings of McLean."

"That's what I thought."

Targets

In July, as the Klan and Nazis took their turns on the witness stand, the FBI was trying to find Harold Covington, for a couple of reasons. First, according to a memo to FBI headquarters, the Bureau wanted to know about Covington's letter to the RCP in which he said he "had it all worked out with the cops" at China Grove.[22] Second, the FBI had come across one page of a two-page letter Covington purportedly wrote to the North Carolina attorney general, Rufus Edmisten, in April 1980. In the letter, Covington told the attorney general that he had information regarding high-ranking North Carolina officials in connection with November 3.

"Upon my demise," Covington wrote, "or upon the introduction of any legislation restricting or denying our right to freedom of speech, freedom of association, the right to keep and bear arms, etc., a manila envelope containing a statement by myself will be placed in the hands of the Greensboro 14 defense attorneys and the press and news media. This statement, sworn and notarized, will contain a complete and accurate account of everything I know regarding the 3rd of November incident in Greensboro, naming names, dates, etc. I do not believe that you, Mr. Schlosser, or Governor Hunt, or . . ."[23] There was nothing else on the page.

The FBI sought authority from headquarters to extradite Covington from South Africa so that he could explain the two letters to the grand jury. And there was another reason. The Nazis, headquarters was told, were accusing Covington of being a CIA agent or a link between AFT agents, and they charged that he was being protected by the federal government. Authority to extradite was necessary, the memo said, "so that the CWP and Nazis would not be able to use his non-appearance as a coverup claim."

The federal investigators also had a problem with Wayne Wood. He had accused Butkovich's case agent, Fulton Dukes, of attempting to influence his grand jury testimony. Wood told of a meeting between himself, Dukes, and Joe Grady in which he said that Dukes told him that if they "stuck together" and did not lie about the ATF agents, "everything would be okay."[24]

A polygraph examination found Wood's answer to be deceptive regarding his allegations about Dukes, but neither the polygraph examiner nor anyone else could explain the amount of knowledge Wood had about the ATF's investigation of him if Dukes had not given him the information.[25] He said that Dukes told him he was Butkovich's superior and that the investigation started because of pictures of Wood with an automatic weapon. Moreover, Wood knew that the blasting caps that had been found under his car were similar to those the ATF found in the fatal 1978 Kernersville explosion. Wood also knew that on November 3, Butkovich was supposed to establish undercover contact with Davie County Nazi Roger Shannon to investigate the Thompson .45.

Michael Johnson sent a memo to the Justice Department asking authority to investigate Dukes. Wood's information about the investigation "could not have come from a public source," Johnson wrote. "There is information which indicates that Special Agent Dukes may have made serious disclosures of the grand jury inquiries, as well as ATF investigative files to a potential defendant in the grand jury proceedings."[26] Johnson cannot comment on anything that occurred in the grand jury, other than to say, "I know of no allegations that were not thoroughly investigated by the grand jury."

There were two other possible sources of Wood's information: Joe Grady and Roger Shannon. If Wood was one of the people Grady told the FBI he "set up" for the ATF, then Grady could have been the one who got the picture of Wood with the machine gun, and he might have been the person who put the blasting caps under Wood's car. As frequent as Grady's contacts were with Dukes, he could have known or logically assumed that Dukes was Butkovich's superior.

Butkovich contacted Shannon at least once prior to November 3 trying to get him to produce his Thompson. He offered to buy .45 caliber ammunition so they could practice shooting the weapon. And on the evening of November 1, Shannon told Butkovich that he would not be able to go to Greensboro on November 3 because he had to work a late shift. Butkovich told Shannon that he was not going, either, and made plans to go to his Davie County farm on Saturday afternoon.

Whether that was the evidence presented to the grand jury will probably never be known, but Dukes was never prosecuted for interfering with the grand jury; he remains an ATF special agent in Winston-Salem.

The grand jury recessed in September, at about the same time the FBI received a cable from the U.S. Embassy in Pretoria, South Africa. Harold Covington was no longer in the country. The FBI tracked him to Canada and then lost him again.[27] Permanently. In Chicago, the National Socialist Party of America was as good as dead. Its office was closed, and Michael Allen, like Covington, had disappeared.[28]

The year 1983 saw the first in-depth study of the November 3 shootings by a major news organization: Public Broadcasting's "88 Seconds in Greensboro."[29] Like the institute report, it focused heavily on Ed Dawson, who agreed to appear in the documentary. Reporter James Reston, Jr., used Dawson's interviews to effectively probe both the police performance on November 3 and the larger question of using informants and infiltrators in law enforcement.

"88 Seconds" also gave a sympathetic and unquestioning personal portrayal of the five victims and of their organizing work in North Carolina. One segment sent brown lung activists reeling in disbelief and anger. Paul Bermanzohn and Marty Nathan were shown giving a mock breathing test to an unidentified mill worker, and a photograph was shown of Bermanzohn and Jim Waller standing with several disabled workers under a banner that read, "Carolina Brown Lung Association." Reston credited Bermanzohn and Waller as "founders" of the organization.

When asked to comment on that segment of the program, Lacy Wright just shook his head and changed the subject, but Len Stanley did not hesitate to express her feelings. "They got that picture that was shown on TV from Chip [Hughes, her husband]. He gave it to Sally because we thought Paul was going to die. It was like a memento. We saw it on TV and couldn't believe it. They act[ed] like all along they had been organizers of the whole brown lung effort. That simply isn't true. They scorned it and spurned it as bourgeois reformist.

"But that's what happened before. They used people's hard-won, painstaking legitimacy and credibility to go in and whip it away from them by taking it over. It's just not fair. It's incredible opportunism."

Like the works that preceded it, the flaws and gaps in the program were more than overcome by the issues and questions it raised. It commanded a national audience and, according to one CJU leader, "it forced the people in power in Greensboro to recognize that this was an issue that would not die."[30]

Armed with credible organizing and educational tools like "88 Seconds" and "The Third of November," the Justice Fund and the November 3 survivors refined their communications skills. Their effectiveness was compounded by the legal restrictions placed on all the city, state, and federal defendants in the civil suit and on those involved in the grand jury investigation. With only one side of the story being promoted—vigorously—through the media and public forums, the CWP Five were transformed from isolated revolutionary extremists into persons who were basically do-gooders but who happened to be Communists, now called the Greensboro Five. In an editorial piece, *Washington Post* columnist Colman McCarthy likened the victims to idealistic VISTA volunteers or American religious women working for social reform in Central America.[31]

The Justice Fund itself took on a new identity in early 1983: the Greensboro Civil Rights Fund. The two organizations existed simultaneously for a short while, but eventually the Justice Fund was "put to sleep," in Marty Nathan's words, "because it was too confusing having two organizations."

The fact that Nathan, Lewis Pitts, and Gayle Korotkin were the most visible people in both organizations did not ease the confusion. To most observers, it appeared as though the CWP simply adopted another new name, as it had scores of times throughout its brief history. But there were significant differences. The primary focus of the Civil Rights Fund was to raise money for the civil suit. A lot of money.

"We could have done it with the Justice Fund," said Nathan, the director of public education for the Civil Rights Fund, "but there were problems with funding—primarily foundation funding—with both the Christic Institute and the Justice Fund asking for money for the same suit. We knew we had to raise a million dollars. The board of the Justice Fund was mainly leftist with no relationship to foundations. But we had mounting support from the church and civil liberties communities. That gave us both the political support and the opportunity."

The Civil Rights Fund was incorporated as a project of the Christic Institute. "We asked people who'd been supportive to come on the board," said Nathan. The board included Nathan, Christic Institute staff members, activists from the national offices of several large religious denominations, and leading civil libertarians. It was an impressive list, but the plaintiffs retained ultimate control over the civil suit.

Eight separate legal organizations or law offices, including the ACLU and the Christic Institute, were listed on Civil Rights Fund's letterhead as its legal counsel, which gave the appearance of a well-balanced team that reflected a range of political and legal perspectives. "We deliberately pulled together a broad coalition for the legal team and a fairly broad coalition for the board of directors," said Pitts, the fund's project director. "What we're relying on is that reasonableness of all the participants to appreciate the quality of your decision when you pitch all these people together and come out with a rational decision. I want to be tugged from the left. I want to be tugged from the right. If there's not friction, then we made a mistake. We've fooled ourselves that there's a diversity that doesn't exist."

But there was a difference in the legal decision making. According to Pitts, "If somebody starts acting like a jackass, then the plaintiffs have the right to get rid of them. They can fire the lawyers. And if the rest of the lawyers think some organization is out of tune, we can go to the plaintiffs and say, 'You're being crossed up here.'"

The likelihood of that happening was slim, though. Pitts and Gayle Korotkin did almost all of the legal work. The other organizations and individuals listed as legal counsel had little, if any, role in the day-to-day pursuit of the case.

In February, the grand jury reconvened, offering two who fled with Virgil Griffin, Chris Benson and Max Hayes, immunity from prosecution in exchange for their testimony against any Klan of Nazis who might be indicted.[32] They accepted. Mark Sherer was offered a plea bargain. In exchange for pleading guilty to taking part in a conspiracy to violate the demonstrators' civil rights and for testifying truthfully in federal court about his role in the conspiracy, he would be granted immunity from prosecution on a host of other charges that could have been brought against him—conspiracy resulting in injury or death, conspiracy to obstruct justice, and parole and firearms violations. Sherer signed the guilty plea on March 24.[33]

By mid-April, the word around the Winston-Salem federal courthouse was that the grand jury was about to issue indictments. Pitts made several attempts to get word to the jury that he had "important information" to present to them. What he had was an undated, unsigned "briefing paper" which gave a thumbnail sketch of the ATF's internal investigation of Butkovich's role in the Nazis prior to and following the shootings.[34] The last line on page five of the six-page paper said, "The Federal Bureau of Investigation (FBI) was kept apprised of the significant investigation developments as they occurred." The wording of the document made it unclear whether the FBI was apprised of the Wood-Nazi investigation or the ATF investigation of Butkovich, but Pitts felt it meant the former, and he was sure it would persuade the grand jury to look into the allegations of closely coordinated federal involvement in the killings.

The federal prosecutors would not tell Pitts whether the briefing paper was already included in the evidence before the grand jury, and they would not allow him to take it before them. On April 20, Pitts and Nelson Johnson went to the grand jury room during a lunch recess. They knocked on the door. An unidentified woman let them in. They left moments later after being told that the jury foreman was not there and that if they had new information it should be given to the prosecutors.[35] Pitts and Johnson were talking with the prosecutors when Tom Brereton stormed into the room. He told the pair they were under investigation for attempting to influence the grand jury—a felony—and he ordered them out of the courthouse.

Johnson and Pitts deny that they actually made contact with any of the grand jurors. They did talk with someone in the jury room, however, and, given the tight security around the proceedings, it is more than possible that the woman in the room was a member of the grand jury. As a lawyer, Pitts should have known better than to put himself in such a position, but the incident provided another opportunity for Pitts and Johnson to charge the prosecutors with refusing to investigate their allegations of government involvement in the conspiracy. "Quite frankly," Johnson told reporters in the courthouse, "nobody wants to discuss the information in my documents—that is what the issue is here."[36] Neither Brereton nor the Justice Department prosecutors could respond.

The following day, nine of the Klan and Nazis were indicted under Section 371, Title 18, of the U.S. Code, charging a general conspiracy to violate federal law.[37] The defendants in *U.S.* v. *Griffin* were Virgil Griffin, Ed Dawson, David Matthews, Wayne Wood, Jerry Smith, Jack Fowler, Roy Toney, John Pridmore, and Milano Caudle. They were also charged with violating two subsections of 245: (b)(2)(B)—a conspiracy to violate the civil rights of persons because of their race or religion; and (b)(4)(A)—a conspiracy to violate the rights of persons because they were participating in an integrated activity.

Matthews, Wood, Smith, Fowler, and Toney were also charged for actions under the code that resulted in injury or death. And Wood was charged under a separate subsection, interfering with interstate commerce, for wounding one of the television photographers who had hidden with the demonstrators under the WXII news car. Finally, Dawson and Griffin were issued separate indictments for conspiring to interfere with the federal investigation.

The indictments were the result of the longest-running grand jury investigation in Justice Department history. Approximately 140 witnesses had been heard and countless pieces of evidence examined.[38] The indictments were hailed by most observers, including the Civil Rights Fund. They expressed hope that a federal jury would find what the state jury had not—guilt beyond reasonable doubt—but they continued to criticize the federal government's role in the investigation.

"It's clear to me," said Pitts in 1983, "they didn't do any good-faith investigation of government complicity. The way they handled that ATF memo. I didn't have any confidence that this grand jury was the cat's meow. It was only called because it was forced by public pressure. They've now got under their belts the longest and most detailed grand jury investigation in the history of the Justice Department, and it's still half a loaf. We still don't know the answers about the government." As skeptical as the anti-Klan demonstrators and their lawyers were about the federal procedures, though, they were bound to honor their commitment to cooperate fully in the forthcoming federal trial. They had demanded it.

On May 13, a court order was issued which temporarily crippled the Civil Rights Fund's ability to continue its public education around the case. Supreme Court Chief Justice Warren Burger assigned a retired federal judge from Minnesota to preside over *U.S.* v. *Griffin*. The judge immediately issued a sweeping gag order which prohibited all Justice Department lawyers and investigators, all defense attorneys, and all witnesses from making any public statements regarding the case until its conclusion.[39]

Although this was perhaps the largest judicial assault on the First Amendment in North Carolina history, the state's major news organizations remained strangely silent. The Civil Rights Fund was the only organization to attempt a legal challenge. Eventually the order was modified to allow fund attorneys and spokespersons to talk about the civil suit, but they were still prohibited from talking about matters relating to the federal criminal trial—an admittedly difficult distinction.[40]

Shortly after modifying the gag order, the judge became seriously ill. He was replaced by Thomas A. Flannery, a retired federal judge from Washington, D.C.[41] One of Flannery's first actions was to expand the gag order to include not only witnesses who had been subpoenaed but "all potential witnesses."[42] His attitude toward the news media's right to access to the proceedings and the public's right to know was further illustrated by an order requiring all news personnel to register with the clerk of court for permanent press passes and restricting the number of passes to twenty-five. North Carolina's media again passed up the opportunity to protest the restrictions.

For a short time, the news media's attention was diverted to Asheville, where, in September 1983, the six Nazis stood trial for a third time on the bombing conspiracy charges. The first trial had ended in a hung jury; the Nazis were convicted on retrial, but won an appeal based on the Justice Department's refusal to give the defendants transcripts from the first trial. Now, for the second time, a jury convicted them of plotting a crime they could not possibly have carried out.[43]

As fall progressed into winter, a dramatic and probably damaging change took place in the prosecution of *U.S.* v. *Griffin*. At a pretrial hearing in late 1983, Justice Department attorney Dan Bell took the lead prosecutor's seat at the prosecution table. With him were attorneys Norajean Flanagan and Greg Linsin, and Tom Brereton. Michael Johnson sat alone on a bench behind the prosecution table, a spot normally taken by paralegal assistants.[44]

Johnson had spent nearly four years with Brereton investigating every aspect of the case—every allegation, no matter how absurd; every fact, no matter how difficult to uncover. The last eighteen months had consisted of fourteen-hour days, with half a day off on Sunday. No one knew more about the people, the evidence, and the issues surrounding the November 3 shootings than Johnson and Brereton. Bell, Flanagan, and Linsin knew significantly less.

Norajean Flanagan was officially assigned to the case in January 1982, but because of her involvement in other Justice Department matters, she did not effectively join the team until that July. Dan Bell joined the team in September 1982, after the grand jury recessed; his participation in the investigation was limited to the jury's wrap-up sessions in the spring of 1983. Greg Linsin was assigned in September 1983.[45] By then, the Justice Department knew that Michael Johnson would not be the person to prosecute the case.

Johnson refuses to discuss the reason for his withdrawal from *U.S.* v. *Griffin*, but he makes it clear that he wanted very much to continue as head of the prosecution team and he does not disguise the pain he still feels over his departure. Johnson took a Justice Department assignment as an assistant U.S. attorney in Little Rock, Arkansas, leaving the prosecution of one of the most complex civil rights trials in history in the hands of newcomers.

Chapter 17

> They got what they wanted: the attention of the world.
> —Jim Cooley, opening argument, *U.S.* v. *Griffin*

Trial Two

The United States versus *Virgil Griffin* began on January 9, 1984.[1] Security in the Winston-Salem federal courthouse was extremely heavy. The street entrance was sealed so that everyone entering the building could be searched by guards at the plaza entrance. On the second floor, tables, a walk-through metal detector, and a half-dozen U.S. marshals formed a barrier between the elevators and the large hallway adjoining Courtroom 2-A.

Shortly before nine o'clock, David Matthews and several other defendants were waiting their turns to go through the metal detector. Matthews placed his keys and pocket change in a plastic dish and slid them across the table to a marshal on the other side. The metal detector's warning buzzer sounded as he walked through, and marshals surrounded him. Matthews stood with his arms outstretched at shoulder level as they passed hand-held detectors over his body. Buzz. He took off his brass-buckled belt and walked through the uprights again. Buzz. He took off his ring and his Playboy tie-tack. Buzz. A marshal pointed to Matthews's back pocket. He scowled, slid his hand into his pocket, and handed the marshal a pouch of Red Man Chewing Tobacco, foil-lined. The metal detector was doing its job.

Judge Thomas Flannery had ordered that jury selection would be held *in camera*—closed to the public. No reporters. No spectators. The Greensboro, Winston-Salem, Raleigh, and Charlotte newspapers, which had not challenged the original gag order, now joined forces to challenge Flannery's closure of jury selection. It was too late.

Reporters were allowed in when court formally convened to listen as each pool of thirty nameless jurors was asked preliminary questions. Had they heard anything about the case? Flannery asked. Every hand went up. Did they know any of the defendants or attorneys? None did. The judge then told the group that he would question them each individually, out of the presence of reporters, the public, and other jurors. He told them not to discuss the case with anyone and not to read or listen to anything about it in the news. "What's reported in the media may be inaccurate, biased, misleading, highly prejudicial, and inadmissible in trial," Flannery warned. The reporters looked at each other and grimaced.

The courtroom was cleared for Flannery's *voir dire* questioning of the jurors. In the hallway, marshals ordered spectators off the floor and reporters into a windowless witness room. The news corps complained loudly. The head marshal—he refused to give his name—came down hard: stay in the witness room, door closed; no loud talking; ask permission to go to the bathroom; if you leave the floor while court is in session, you cannot return until it adjourns. When he left, a reporter gave him a name: "Attila." They all laughed, loudly.

Waiting for court to reconvene in open session, the reporters read, talked about "Attila" and totalitarianism, and doodled in their notebooks. One started snooping through the drawers in the room's conference table. She found a paper clip, a candy bar wrapper, a corner torn from a legal pad and folded into a neat square. She unfolded it. Tiny hand-printed red letters formed the words, "Better dead than Red."

It took twelve days for Flannery to select a pool of seventy qualified jurors from which the defense and prosecution would pick twelve jurors and six alternates. Flannery had heard the newspapers' arguments and denied their motions to open jury selection. Overruled on appeal, the judge eventually ordered the court reporter to make transcripts of the *voir dire* available to the public in the clerk of court's office. The transcriptions took more than six weeks to complete.

Although the eighteen seated jurors were selected in open court, Flannery allowed the lawyers to issue their peremptory challenges in secret. As each prospective juror's name was called, the attorneys for both sides huddled at their tables, whispering their recommendations to each other. When they had made their decisions, they wrote them on forms and handed them to the clerk, who in turn gave them to the judge. Without comment, and without acknowledgment of which side might have used a challenge, Flannery either excused or seated the juror in question.

All eleven blacks in the jury pool were excused. The twelve jurors and six alternates who remained appeared to represent a good cross-section of middle-class white America, although the majority were over forty. Another common trait, which became noteworthy as the trial progressed, was their seriousness.

They listened attentively to each word that was spoken; they leaned forward to look at each piece of evidence; they gave equal attention to the prosecution and the defense attorneys. There seemed to be no question that they would decide this case on its merits, without regard to the controversy surrounding the trial.

Jury selection transcripts show yet another common denominator among the jurors: their astonishing lack of knowledge of contemporary issues and events.[2] A preliminary questionnaire had weeded out all prospective jurors who had formed an opinion in the case, but there seemed to be no middle ground. Few of those questioned in *voir dire* knew anything beyond the fact that a shooting occurred and people died.

The jurors' knowledge of the Klan was minimal—they wore white sheets and burned crosses—and a significant number were not even aware that the Klan was a racist organization. More men than women had heard of the Nazis, but this was primarily through military service in World War II. Even then, they equated Nazism more with Germany than with the virulent racism and anti-Semitism that led to gas chambers and concentration camps. The WVO and the CWP were virtually unknown. One juror asked if they weren't the same as the Nazis.

In a case in which racist motivation would be a key factor in the determination of guilt or innocence, the jurors had little if any understanding of the extremist views of the organizations that brought the defendants to Greensboro on November 3. Mickey Michaux's recommendation that the trial be a "history class on the racist philosophies of the Ku Klux Klan and the American Nazi Party, then connecting such philosophies to their opposition to communism" was rejected out of hand. Flannery ordered that there would be no testimony or evidence regarding the philosophies of any of the groups involved. His ruling was so broad that the name "United Racist Front" could not be mentioned in testimony regarding the September Klan-Nazi meeting in Louisburg.

Flannery read his opening statement to the jury. He explained federal conspiracy law and instructed them on the points the prosecution would have to prove—beyond reasonable doubt—in order for them to convict the defendants on the substantive counts of the indictments: the defendants must have acted to intimidate by threat of force; they must have acted willfully; they must have been motivated by the race or religion of the victim and by the victim's involvement in an integrated activity authorized or administered by the City of Greensboro; and the actions of Matthews, Wood, Smith, Fowler, and Toney must have resulted in bodily injury or death. On Count 14, the government had to prove that Dawson and Griffin conspired to prevent others from cooperating with or testifying truthfully to federal investigators.

Dan Bell took a little over an hour to explain how the United States intended to prove four points to the jury: that the defendants "plotted to use force" to disrupt an anti-Klan parade which was protected by the Constitution and authorized by the City of Greensboro through its parade permit; that the defendants were driven by two motives—to vent racial hatred and to get revenge for the disruption of their meeting at China Grove; that the Klan and Nazis gathered at a house near Greensboro, set up an armed caravan, and gunned down twelve people and killed five; and that the two "ringleaders"— Griffin and Dawson—conspired to prevent other Klan members from talking with the police and FBI.

Predictably, the defense attorneys focused on two issues: their clients went to Greensboro to protest communism, not to violate the demonstrators' civil rights because of their race; and they shot only after they were attacked by a mob of stick-wielding Communists shouting, "Death to the Klan." Self-defense.

As it had in the state trial, testimony in *U.S.* v. *Griffin* began with chain of custody witnesses. All who testified in the first phase of the trial played some role in Bruce Koenig's audio analysis—Ed Boyd and Jim Waters, the police officer who took measurements of the Everitt-Carver area, the person who made the scale map of the crime scene. Eighteen chain of custody witnesses were examined and cross-examined before Bruce Koenig finally took the stand.

Polished and egotistical, Koenig performed like a pro. When it came to locating shots three, four, and five, however, he gave different testimony from that he had given in the state trial. There were two areas from where shots did not produce sufficient echo patterns to trace, he told the jury. One was the cone-shaped area north of the pickup on Carver Street. The other was west of a school bus parked on Everitt Street, just beyond where Mark Sherer and Brent Fletcher fired the first and second shots. When prosecutor Greg Linsin asked Koenig on redirect examination whether he was asked to consider the area west of the school bus in preparing his analysis for the state trial, Koenig replied, "No, sir."

He testified that the map he used in the original test was folded along a line east of the school bus, that he had not been asked to consider anything beyond that point. Linsin asked, "If I ask you today, are you ninety-nine percent certain that shots three, four, and five were fired north of Everitt and Carver?"

"No, sir. I'd have to include the area of Everitt and Carver and this area west on Everitt past vehicle 39 (the school bus.)"

When a reporter called Rick Greeson and Jim Coman for their reactions to Koenig's change in testimony, the district attorneys were furious. No, they had not limited Koenig in any way. On the contrary, they had asked him to consider every inch of the area, every possibility. If asked to rebut Koenig's testimony in the federal trial, Coman said, "I would have to say that Koenig wasn't truthful."[3]

The next witness was Mark Sherer. Impeccably dressed and groomed, Sherer looked more like a handsome campus heartthrob than the Klan member and convicted felon he was. But that sanctimonious smirk Ed Boyd filmed as Sherer rode into the "Death to the Klan" site was still present as he took the stand. He looked eager to confront Dan Bell, confident that he could confound and frustrate the Washington lawyer.

Sherer had withdrawn his guilty plea in the opening days of the trial. In order to force his testimony, Flannery granted him immunity from prosecution for self-incriminating testimony he might give in this trial. He was not, however, immune from prosecution for perjury or contempt of court in this proceeding.

In his grand jury testimony, Sherer admitted firing three shots on November 3: two into the air and one into the side of a car as the caravan pulled out—shots one, three, and four. Now Sherer claimed that he only fired once into the air and once into the car. Bell read from his grand jury and FBI statements and asked him if they were truthful. "They were true at the time," Sherer replied.

He insisted that his gun jammed the second time he tried to fire into the air, that he knew he actually fired twice because before leaving the gun with Jerry Smith's father, he fired it once to clear the chamber. When he got the gun back several months later, there were still three rounds in it. Bell read from his previous testimony: "I felt I shot at least one other time into the air."

"Did you make that statement and was that a true statement?" Bell demanded.

"I honestly do not recall making those statements. I do not deny that I made those statements."

Again and again, Bell challenged Sherer on discrepancies between his prior statements and his testimony in court. Again and again, Sherer slipped past the implications of perjury: "Due to the fact that I was sometimes confused about how many shots I fired, I can't specifically recall what I said."

Bell asked Sherer about the escape to the mountains, then to South Carolina. He asked if Griffin had not repeatedly warned the group to "remember your Klan oath." He showed Sherer a copy of the Klan oath, and he read the portion dealing with secrecy: deny being in the Klan, don't identify anyone in the Klan, don't tell the police anything. "I do not recall any of the specific wording," Sherer said.

"Did you swear to a Klan oath?"

"I simply do not recall."

"Did you take an oath that you would die rather than violate the oath?"
"I simply do not recall."

On cross-examination by Griffin's attorney, Fred Harwell, Sherer's demeanor changed dramatically. Two shots, he was positive, only two. Griffin had not threatened or intimidated him into fleeing with the group; he merely "mentioned" that they would be arrested if they returned home.

Harwell showed him another copy of a Klan oath. "This is the three-page document identical to the oath I took," said Sherer, his memory suddenly restored. He read two paragraphs from the third page to the jury: "The Klan swears allegiance to protect and defend the governments of the United States and the state to death, to help, aid and assist officers of the law." The secrecy portion of the oath, he said, dealt only with the Klan's "signs, words, and grips."

On redirect, Bell got Sherer to admit that he lied to the FBI in their early questioning of him. But he went on to say that he had also lied to the grand jury. "I allowed my testimony to be colored, swayed, twisted and molested," Sherer maintained. He said that Bell had "browbeaten" him into pleading guilty. "I was threatened with prosecution on five offenses plus firearms charges."

Finally, Bell sought to impeach Sherer's credibility before the jury. Flannery instructed the jurors to consider this testimony "only so far as it affects his credibility. It is not to be used as evidence against any defendant."

Bell asked, "Beginning in mid-November, 1979, through January, 1980, did you ever conspire to kill anyone who might testify [in the state trial]?"

"No, I did not conspire with myself or anyone else in this case. I stress the word conspire." Sherer insisted that there had never been any overt act committed in furtherance of a discussion he had with other Klan members regarding "one person who might turn state's evidence" in the state trial.

Bell asked him if it was true that he had obtained a weapon during the course of the discussions about murdering the witness. "I did transfer a weapon between myself and another person," said Sherer, "a shotgun with an eighteen-and-a-half-inch barrel." Sherer denied that the transfer of the shotgun constituted an overt act under conspiracy law. "The conversations used the term 'sniper attack,'" he explained, "which means long-range. This weapon had a range of sixty feet—totally useless for a sniper attack."

Sherer ended his courtroom appearance with his know-it-all sneer still on his face. As he walked past Virgil Griffin, slouched sullenly at the end of the defendants' bench next to the gate through the bar, Sherer lifted his hand from his side and gave the grand dragon the thumbs-up.

The other Klan witnesses who testified for the prosecution were not as hostile as Sherer, but three who appeared on the same day were so bizarre that reporters and observers—and probably the jury—left that day's session feeling that they had witnessed something unearthly.

The first was Carl Nappier. He sat in the witness chair and propped his withered arm against the rail, looking directly and intensely at the attorneys as they questioned him. He told his story without hesitation in his mountain dialect and down-home vernacular. Asked why he was now testifying for the prosecution when he had testified for the defense in the state trial, Nappier responded, "I was called by both the defense and the prosecution at this trial and I was kinda confused about that. But not for long. I figure I'm just here to tell what I know. I'm not for or against anybody."

He came across as somebody's grandpa—totally believable. When he started talking about going to Greensboro with the idea of fighting the biggest anti-Klan demostrator he could find, however, when he talked about how he would prefer to fight barehanded against someone armed with a knife rather than a club, those who were listening were forced to confront their own ability to judge human character. If he was as honest as he appeared to be, then grandpa had a streak of viciousness.

The next witness looked like he stepped right off a horror movie set. Flannery ordered the jury out of the courtroom while Eugene Roberson, the Klan member who argued with Nappier about bringing guns and then failed to show up, was led to the witness stand. The judge wanted to question him out of the jury's presence in order to determine whether he was competent to testify.

Spectators looked at him and immediately lowered their eyes and slowly peered back. He wore a T-shirt with the slogan "Gas, grass or ass. Nobody rides for free." But that was not what put the courtroom observers into shocked silence.

Sunglasses mercifully covered Roberson's eyes, but his mouth, nose, and ears were horribly disfigured—jagged ridges of scar tissue pulled his face in several directions. There were four-inch tufts of matted hair sticking straight out from either side of his head. Other than that, his scalp bore the same kind of scars as his face.

Reporters leaned up to the bar and whispered to Tom Brereton, "What the hell happened to him?"

"Acid."

"The Klan?"

Brereton whispered that a year earlier, Roberson's wife had discovered he was running around on her. She dumped acid on his face while he was sleeping.

Flannery asked Roberson his name, the date, and where he was and what he was in court for. His answers were satisfactory, and so the judge told the marshal to bring the jury back. They had to walk within a few inches of the witness stand in order to get back to the jury box. Eighteen faces looked, looked away, looked again, then looked around the room in disbelief.

Roberson testified in a thick-tongued monotone about a conversation he had with David Matthews after the Icard Klan meeting. Nappier had argued with them about bringing guns to Greensboro, Roberson testified. "Carl said everybody's looking for a fistfight rather than a gun fight. After the meeting, David said, 'If they got guns we won't have anything to defend ourselves with.'

"I said, 'Somebody's liable to get killed or locked up.' And he said, 'Well, that's the purpose of it.'"

Roberson testified that he hid out in a motel on November 3 in order to avoid going to Greensboro with Matthews.

Matthews's attorney Jim Cooley conducted the cross-examination. It soon became obvious why Flannery had decided to test Roberson's competency before allowing him to testify before the jury.

"Do you remember a conversation Mr. Harwell [Fred Harwell, Griffin's attorney] and I had with you in the presence of your mother?" the attorney asked.

"Yup. I sure do," answered the witness.

"And do you remember telling us that you went to Greensboro on November 3rd with another man?"

"Yup. I sure do."

"Do you remember telling us that Jesse Jackson was there and that you pushed him down when the shooting started and saved his life?"

"Yup. I sure do," Roberson chuckled. "You interviewed me without the presence of my lawyer."

"Did you tell us you saw a black man point a gun at Carl Nappier, that you saw a civil rights worker stick a gun in a Klansman's throat?"

"Yup. I sure did." Roberson was almost giggling now. "I didn't have to answer you truthfully because I didn't have a lawyer."

Cooley looked at Harwell. They had been had. The witness was excused.

The final actor in the "trio macabre" was Ruby Sweet Miller. She was as pathetic as Roberson was horrifying. Short, fifty pounds overweight, wearing a summery pink and purple nylon dress in the dead of winter, Ruby Sweet looked as though she would die of fright before she reached the witness stand. Her hair was thin and stringy, dirty like her white ankle socks. She could have walked out of the pages of a case study on Appalachian poverty and malnutrition.

Ruby Sweet Miller—she had gotten married since November 3—could hardly speak, she was so scared. Despite Flannery's constant reminder to "speak up," her voice rarely rose above a whisper. And most often her answer was, "I don't remember."

The prosecutor pressed her for answers. Don't remember. Do you remember testifying before the grand jury? Yes. Did you tell the grand jury thus-and-so? Yes. Was that true testimony? Yes. On and on it went with Dan Bell pulling out the words that Ruby Sweet Miller was terrified to say out loud.

On the night of November 2, she and Linda Matthews ("she was like a sister to me") cried and prayed together after David told them that people could "get killed or hurt" the next day. After the shootings, Virgil Griffin kept the group together to avoid "the law." He threatened to beat her and the others if they violated the Klan oath by identifying Klan members to the police or by admitting that they had guns.

Jim Cooley and Fred Harwell led the cross-examination. They understood, they told her, she was upset and confused, she was on pain medication and "nerve pills." The Klan never intended to attack or hurt anyone on November 3, did they? No. Virgil didn't order you to go to the mountains or threaten to beat you? No.

Cooley asked about her pre-grand jury statement to Tom Brereton and Norajean Flanagan: "Did they ask you lots of questions?"

"Yes."

"Did they ask questions over and over?"

"Yes."

"Did they tell you you were lying?"

"Yes."

"Were you scared?"

"Yes."

"Were you crying?"

"Yes."

"Did you have to leave the room?"

"Yes."

"Would you have done anything to get out of that room?"

"Yes."

"So you signed the statement."

"Yes. After I got through talking to them I took an overdose of pills and tried to kill myself. I couldn't take it anymore."

Pathetic Ruby. Gruesome Gene. Vicious Grandpa Nappier. They were a slice of humanity from a culture few people have seen, and fewer still understand—the pathology of "Klan Country," North Carolina, 1979–84.

Answers   265

First Appearances

"The United States calls Bernard Butkovich to the stand." There was an audible gasp from the spectators. Butkovich looked relaxed as he sat in the witness box. Dan Bell guided him through what was by now a recital to Butkovich: Special Forces—Vietnam; ATF training; the one-man, one-gun investigation of Wood; Wood's and Caudle's anger at being left in the lurch at China Grove; the November 1 news conference at Wood's house, where the Klan talked about no firearms "concealed or otherwise."

Asked about Jerry Smith's pipe bombs, Butkovich added a new twist to his previous statements: "He said they had a very good fragmentary effect because of the striations [grooves cut in the pipe] and would work very well if thrown into a crowd of niggers." Not one of his official reports or sworn statements included the clause "of niggers."

Butkovich said that under ATF regulations, he could not give the information about the pipe bombs to local police. He testified that he did give the information to Fulton Dukes. On cross-examination by Wood's attorney Roy Hall, Butkovich was asked whether he heard any plans for violence discussed at the November 1 meeting. "What I heard was that there would be no firearms taken," he replied.

"Have you ever reported any planned violence for November 3rd?"

"Yes, sir. To Special Agent Dukes regarding the pipe bombs."

Jeff Farran, again appointed to defend Jack Fowler, asked Butkovich about a May 1982 sworn statement he gave to Tom Brereton in which he was asked whether the conversation with Smith was "in any way related to the group coming to Greensboro."

"No," Butkovich testified at the time, "it was not."

Butkovich explained to the court, "Knowing what I know now, I testified accurately and truly. At that time." He sounded like he had been to the Mark Sherer school of doubletalk.

Neill Jennings, Smith's attorney, asked the agent why he had not said anything about the pipe bomb in his grand jury testimony. "If I was asked, I testified to it. If I was not asked . . ."

Like Butkovich, Rooster Cooper had given his story so many times before testifying in the federal trial that it had become a rote recitation. On November 3, he said, Dawson called him one time, at eight-thirty in the morning and told him that Griffin and two other men had arrived, that they all had handguns. "He emphasized the fact that Griffin arrived and they had plans to ride the parade route and heckle the marchers. If there was any face-to-face confrontation, it would be at the end of the route at Florida Street Shopping Center."

Cooper said Dawson described Griffin as "a hothead, that we needed to pay particular attention to him." Even with that warning, Cooper testified, his briefings to the Tacts and other officers at ten o'clock focused on the assumption that violence would somehow be staved off until the end of the march. His assignment was "to monitor the parade route, anyone who might be coming into the parade route, and to let the officer working the parade know of anyone coming in."

But Sergeant Dave Comer, the officer in charge of the march, did not know that the Tacts were not in position when Cooper reported that the Klan caravan was moving toward the demonstration site. Comer did not testify in the federal trial, and Cooper's testimony did not shed any light on the failure of the police department to keep its coordinating officer fully briefed on the police strategy for the day.

Cooper did tell the jury why he did not move in to the rally site when fighting broke out. His car was unmarked, he said, without a siren or blue light. "I was dressed in blue jeans and a windbreaker and looked like ninety-five percent of the people out there. I felt at the time that the best thing I could do for my safety and Mr. [John] Matthews's safety was to stay in the vehicle and report what I saw."

The first demonstrator publicly to testify about the November 3 shootings was Frankie Powell. The pattern established during her testimony would be repeated throughout the direct examinations and cross-examinations of all the demonstration witnesses. On direct examination, she was given the opportunity to explain how she got involved with the WVO—through union work; why she opposed the Klan—because of their history of violence against her race; why she went to the "Death to the Klan" march—she might not have marched because of her pregnancy, but she was determined to attend the anti-Klan conference at the parade's conclusion. She was asked to identify various leaflets; without going into detail about their content, she explained that she did not agree with everything the WVO said in the leaflets, but that she felt it was extremely important to distribute them to get people interested in the conference.

Powell was asked why she brought her derringer (used by Allen Blitz to fire two of the final shots) in violation of the parade permit. She reiterated that she had not decided whether or not to join the march, but that she knew she would attend the conference. It was her habit, she testified, and it had been for years, to carry her gun if she might have to go home alone after dusk.

She was asked to identify her friends from the videotapes. Tears welled up in her eyes as she watched the shootings on the small monitor adjacent to the witness box. She turned her head away when the monitor showed the bloody aftermath, looking at the screen only when Greg Linsin asked her to identify someone.

The defense attorneys made Powell read line by line from the leaflets she could identify. "We are against non-violence and pacifism," she read, "and for armed self-defense. We should beat the hell out of the Klan wherever we find them. These dogs have no right to exist.

"We took the Klan on in China Grove and we'll take them on again. We invite the scum Klan to come out and face the wrath of the people."

"I didn't agree with that," Powell insisted, saying that she passed the leaflet out as a way of "telling people to come to this conference."

"You are a plaintiff in a $48 million civil suit arising from this case, aren't you?" asked Fred Harwell. "The defendants here are also defendants in your civil suit—for money damages. You want them convicted, don't you?"

"Yes."

"You are an avowed Communist, aren't you?"

"No, sir."

"Isn't it true that in the civil suit you are identified as a Communist?"

"I don't know the wording of the complaint. I am not now and never have been a member of the CWP."

Harwell read from the complaint: "Frankie Powell is a Communist, a labor organizer and/or an advocate of equal rights for black people who was seriously injured on November 3."

Judge Flannery interrupted, "It says 'a Communist . . . and/or an advocate for equal rights for black people.'"

Harwell continued, "If they are convicted, it is likely to result in monetary compensation in your civil suit."

"I don't know what the jury will find. I do know that I do want these people convicted."

Tom Clark and Allen and Dori Blitz all went through the same kind of questioning. Jerry Smith was visibly agitated when Dori Blitz took the stand. He moved from his seat on the far side of the courtroom to the bench nearer the witness box, glaring at this Communist, this woman who was not afraid of a fight, this Communist woman who emptied her gun at him.

But it was Paul Bermanzohn who put all the defendants on the edges of their seats. He was The Enemy—a Jew-Communist who agitated blacks, a Jew-Communist who called the Klan scum, a Jew-Communist who had everything they did not and never would: intellect, good looks, highly valued profession, communications skills. His paralysis had not stopped him from furthering his medical career; he was now a psychiatrist. His paralysis was physical and limited. Theirs was economic and social—and total.

Bermanzohn's direct examination was uneventful. It lasted only fifty minutes. Norajean Flanagan took him through brief descriptions of the China Grove confrontation, the November 1 news conference where he met Ed Dawson, the restriction on the parade permit against firearms, his arrival at Everitt and Carver, the arrival of the Klan and Nazis, and the shooting that left him paralyzed and five of his friends dead. It was moving testimony, made all the more so by the visible reminder of his injuries—a constant tremor in his left arm. Roy Toney sat nervously pulling and chewing on his moustache as he listened to the man he was accused of shooting.

When Fraley Bost, Toney's lawyer, got up to cross-examine Bermanzohn, the atmosphere of the courtroom changed drastically. After a few preliminary questions about China Grove, Bost asked him if the demonstrators were armed when they went to the China Grove community center. "I saw no arms," Bermanzohn replied.

Bost walked back to the defense table and picked up a copy of *The True Story of the Greensboro Massacre*. He held the book out towards Bermanzohn. "That's not what you said in your book," Bost challenged. He read from page 39: "They [the Klan] did not want to start a fight in the presence of a resolute, united and armed populace." Bermanzohn was forced to agree that he made that statement.

"Did you see any guns on the way back?"

"I don't recall."

Bost showed Bermanzohn a page from his grand jury testimony in which he responded to the same question, "Yes, there were several weapons, several weapons and shotguns on the way back to the community center."

Then Bost asked if he hadn't purchased a .38 caliber handgun on the morning of the China Grove incident. "I have no recollection of stopping on the way to China Grove, much less of purchasing a gun, sir."

An ATF firearms transaction record was handed to the prosecutors. It was obvious they had not seen the document before; they passed it to Brereton, who appeared as unfamiliar with the form as his colleagues. When they had finished examining it, Bost introduced it as evidence for the defense. It showed that Paul Carl Bermanzohn purchased a .38 special at Colonial Gunshop in Hillsborough on July 8, 1979. Bost handed the form to Bermanzohn and asked if he could identify the signature. "Yes, sir. That's my signature."

After a few more questions about planning for the "Death to the Klan" march, Bost picked up the book again. "It says here that Bill Sampson got behind a station wagon with a gun as the caravan drove through," he said. "You saw that?"

"Much of the book is based on what people told me," Bermanzohn responded. "We did the best we could considering my physical condition and my wife having a baby."

It appeared that the prosecutors were as unprepared for cross-examination on the book as they had been for the introduction of the ATF form. Flanagan raised an objection to Bost's using hearsay to impeach her witness. After a ten-minute bench conference, Flannery excused the jury so the attorneys could argue their points openly and so that he could question Bermanzohn directly.

Bost read from page 22: "As the caravan approached, he pulled out his gun and positioned himself behind a station wagon." He turned to the judge. "It says here that Bill Sampson was a leader of the defense team."

Flannery looked at Bermanzohn. "Was he?"

"I was told so."

"Who was in charge?"

"Dr. Waller."

"He's deceased."

Bost asked, "Who else was on the defense team?"

"I don't know," said Bermanzohn. "I testified as to what I saw, I wrote about what I was told."

Flannery asked whom he talked with. "Dale Sampson, Tom Clark, Frankie Powell, Dori and Allen Blitz, Don and Ros Pelles. The book is largely based on what they told me."

"But you can't remember who told you specific things," said Flannery. It was a statement rather than a question.

"You testified you didn't expect violence," said Bost. "That's not what you said in your book." He read from page 42: "The Windsor Center is at a central intersection in Greensboro, an easy place to get to, but also an easy place for the Klan to attack from a speeding car and get away. For this reason we planned to have the bulk of the march start at Morningside Homes."

Flannery called a recess so that he could read pertinent sections of the book before making a ruling on the prosecutor's objection. When he returned twenty-five minutes later, he said he would sustain the objection regarding any material in the book that was not based on the author's personal observation or knowledge.

In the jury's presence, Bost questioned Bermanzohn's direct knowledge of key statements made in the book. Bermanzohn testified that all but the change from Windsor to Morningside were based on what people told him, what he read in the newspaper, or what he understood was testified to in the state trial.

Fred Harwell challenged Bermanzohn with the implication that he stood to make a lot of money from the civil suit if the defendants were convicted in this trial. He then went through a stack of twenty-five WVO leaflets and internal memos and asked Bermanzohn to identify each one. They were not read to the jury, but after Bermanzohn was excused from the stand, many were introduced as evidence for the defense. Included was the leaflet circulated along the route that said, "We want everyone on the march route to protect the march. We want you to sit on your porch or stand in your yard with your gun." Also introduced was the internal directive which said, "A confrontation with the Klan would be best if we could get it."

The prosecutors found one witness who was able to overcome a portion of Bermanzohn's testimony. Mark Andrew Stone had taken over the Colonial Gun Shop after his father died. He testified that his father filled out the original ATF firearms transaction form for Bermanzohn's gun purchase. The original, which he brought to court, showed the purchase date as July 8. Stone said that his father frequently got confused about dates, and that this was definitely a mistake. July 8 was a Sunday; the store could not legally open before one o'clock. The prosecutors wanted to introduce the ATF form as evidence, but Stone refused to hand it to the clerk. He explained that ATF regulations require the store owner to keep the original. Flannery told him to give the form to the clerk. When he protested again that federal law required him to keep the original, Flannery leaned toward the witness and said, "*I'm* federal law around here." Stone handed the form to the clerk.

Interspersed with the demonstrators' testimony were more chain of custody witnesses, the medical examiners, and the physicians who treated the victims. Their testimony led to that of Donald Havekost, the FBI's neutron activation analyst. He was on the stand for the better part of two days, explaining to the jury how he conducted his tests and reached his conclusions. Then he gave his analysis of every single piece of lead or bullet fragment found at the scene or recovered from the victims. The word *boring* does not begin to describe Havekost's testimony. Although it was obvious that he had expended a great amount of effort on his analysis, his testimony was so highly technical that most jurors, observers, and courtroom personnel were unable to maintain attention after the first hours.

There was one light spot in Havekost's two days on the stand, though. Greg Linsin handed him a glass test tube containing a baggie with two lead fragments removed from Jim Wrenn's brain during surgery. In order for the fragments to be introduced as evidence, they had to be taken from the vial for Havekost to properly identify them. He uncapped the container and tilted it so that the baggie would fall into his hand. It would not come out. He shook the vial and tried again. Then he tapped it against the witness box. A juror passed

Havekost a metal nail file to use for a probe. That did not work, either. Dan Bell handed him his red pocketknife. The baggie remained at the bottom of the vial.

After several more unsuccessful tries, Linsin took the vial from the witness and asked Tom Brereton to work on it while he went to another area of questioning. Brereton tried sticking his finger in. It was not long enough. He shook it some more and tapped it against his palm. Linsin and Havekost seemed to be the only people in the courtroom who were not watching the spectacle. Brereton tried pencils and pens, then his finger again. This time it looked as though the test tube had taken a permanent grasp on the finger, as well. Fifteen minutes passed. A recess was called. Twenty-five minutes later, Linsin announced to the court, "We have solved the technical problems," and he handed the baggie and fragments to Havekost. The giggling in the courtroom quickly subsided as Havekost resumed his monotonous testimony.

Chapter 18

> We can count on injustice in human affairs.
> —Albert Camus, *Neither Victims Nor Executioners*

For the Defense

The prosecutors presented seventy-seven witnesses and an overwhelming array of technical evidence: charts, graphs, models, analyses, and the videotapes—run in forward, reverse, slow motion, stop action, and with elaborate Hollywood-produced highlights. No one would venture to estimate the cost of obtaining evidence and prosecuting the case, but $1 million is probably a conservative figure.

The prosecution's Klan witnesses—most of them—gave striking testimony about their intent to fight the Communists in Greensboro and of Griffin's, more so than Dawson's, attempts to keep people from talking to investigators. The anti-Klan demonstrators gave the jury an understanding of their idealism and their dedication; their testimony gave the dead people meaning and substance. As the CWP had feared all along, however, their cross-examination provided some of the most important evidence for the defense.

The defense attorneys opened with several low-key witnesses—a police officer who found a nightstick beside one of the victims, another who said the Klan and Nazis were "cooperative" when arrested at the scene. Virgil Griffin was the first defendant to testify. Throughout the trial, he sulked and pouted at the end of the defendants' bench, but from the witness box he tried to project an image of the earnest patriot, a man who had spoken out against communism for the entire twenty-one years he had been involved with the Klan.

Griffin's testimony contradicted that of almost every Klan witness who went before him. He told the jury several times and in several different ways that in talking with other Klan members about coming to Greensboro, he always said, "We're going to stand in silence and watch the parade. I told them they may spit on you and call you scum. I told them not to say anything. But if they hit you, hit back."

Griffin said that he only fled from Greensboro in fear of being arrested, but that he never intended to interfere with any investigation. He maintained that the only instruction he gave the fugitive group was to tell the truth when they were questioned. He insisted that he turned himself in to the FBI as soon as he found out there was a federal investigation.

Dan Bell did a skillful job of getting Griffin to impeach his own testimony. Using the Klan oath that had been introduced as a defense exhibit, Bell read the clause in which members "promise and swear . . . to help, aid and assist officers of the law." He asked Griffin if he was honoring that part of the oath when he hid out in the swamp. "I knew that men had been arrested for murder and I didn't want to get arrested for murder," Griffin said. In a belligerent tone, he continued, "If they [the police] had come to the creek, I would have answered their questions."

Bell's impeachment intensified, using Griffin's statements to the FBI—in which he refused to identify Klan members—and his grand jury testimony—in which he admitted taking an oath "not to name anybody in the Klan"—to discredit him before the jury. Griffin's hostility increased in direct proportion to Bell's introduction of contradictory statements and witnesses, but he held his ground, denying that he went to Greensboro to disrupt, denying that he threatened witnesses or told them to lie. The one point that he was unimpeachable on was his contention that he did not know until the day he left the swamp that federal investigators were involved in the case. It was crucial to his defense.

Ed Dawson, Wayne Wood, and Milano Caudle did not testify in their defense. Dawson, whom Tom Brereton dubbed "88 Statements in Greensboro," had never taken the stand in any of his previous trials. He was loath to break that tradition. And considering that much of the evidence against him in this case had come to light through his interviews with the Institute for Southern Studies and on "88 Seconds," it was probably wise to deny the prosecutors the opportunity to get him talking before the jury.

Wood, who dozed off in court at least once a day, was far from an ideal witness. He had always insisted that on November 3 he shot only into the air and then only to scare the gun-wielding demonstrators away so that he and his friends could escape. A polygraph test he took in June 1982, however, showed "deception" on his answers to questions regarding whether he knowingly shot at people and whether he recognized any of the people he shot at.[1] Waller and Clark were in the open when Wood fired at them. They had been at China Grove, as had most of the demonstrators who were hit by Wood's birdshot as they took cover in front of the WXII station wagon. The prosecutors could not introduce the polygraph as evidence in the trial, but they would certainly find a way to cross-examine him about it if he took the witness stand.

Caudle did not need to testify. As his lawyer, Leon Porter, pointed out in his opening statement and his arguments to dismiss, Caudle's name had scarcely been mentioned during the entire proceeding. The evidence showed that he owned the car in which Fowler and McBride rode to Morningside Homes and that he owned two of the guns used in the shootings. He had been angry about China Grove, but in the November 1 meeting all he had said was that he would "like the opportunity to heckle the Communists like we been heckled." On driving into the rally site, Caudle shouted, "Remember China Grove," which the defense attorneys claimed was actually, "I remember you from China Grove. I'll be there [meaning the Florida Street Shopping Center, the attorneys said], will you be there?" No matter how many times they played the tapes, only the words "remember China Grove" could be heard distinctly. But it did not matter. None of the evidence showed that Caudle conspired to do anything but go to the march and "heckle," and there was no evidence to show that he had even gotten out of the car, much less injured or threatened anyone at the rally site.

David Matthews's testimony was as close to self-incrimination as a defendant could get, short of a flat-out confession. Jim Cooley asked why he brought his gun. "From what Ed Dawson told us, I thought it was just a lot of political talk about Death to the Klan. But as a Klan, I'd never been to a Communist rally. I was worried. I didn't know whether they'd just talk or not." So he came prepared.

Matthews admitted firing five times. He placed figures on a scale model in the spots where he said black men (he did not use the word *niggers* in the federal courtroom) were firing shotguns at him—the spots where Waller, Nathan, Wrenn, Sampson, and Smith were hit. "When they started shooting at us, I knew then that it wasn't political talk," he said. "They were trying to kill us."

Over defense objections, Dan Bell used Matthews's November 3 police statement to impeach his credibility before the jury. They heard that he went to Greensboro to "agitate with the Communists and niggers," that he could "hardly tell who was the Communists and who was the niggers" at the rally, and that after the shooting he said, "I got three of 'em."

Jerry Smith stuck with his amnesia story. He remembered firing one shot from near the Fairlane, but had no recollection of running down the sidewalk and firing three more times at Cesar Cauce. When asked about the pipe bomb,

Smith insisted he had had one conversation with Mark Sherer about a bomb Sherer had built, but that he had never discussed it with Butkovich or anyone else.

Fowler, Pridmore, and Toney gave fairly persuasive testimony. Fowler told the jury he had been "saved by the Lord" during the time he spent in Guilford County jail. Jailhouse conversions are often self-serving and sometimes fraudulent. Fowler seemed to be the exception. There was an air of serenity about him. Whether listening to testimony, smoking a cigarette in the corridor, or testifying in his own behalf, it was hard to identify the Jack Fowler in the federal courtroom with the hulking figure on the videotape who fired a semiautomatic rifle at human targets.

Fowler testified that he saw two demonstrators near the pickup, one with a shotgun and one with a handgun. "I felt like I was going to have a heart attack with my heart jumping out of my chest," he said. "I ran back to the Fairlane." He admitted firing twice at the man with the shotgun and twice at Dori Blitz after she shot at Jerry Smith.

Jeff Farran did such a thorough job on direct examination that there was little testimony Norajean Flanagan could challenge Fowler on. She introduced a few contradictory statements he made before the grand jury, but there was nothing major. And the fact remained that the injury Fowler caused was the result of a ricochet.

Roy Toney and his attorney, Fraley Bost, did a courtroom demonstration of the fight between Waller and Toney over the shotgun. It was a superb tactic. When Bost stuck the gun barrel at Toney's throat and racked the chamber, everyone in the courtroom knew exactly how the defendant felt on November 3. "I thought I was dead," he said.

The two staged a mock struggle for the gun, and Toney fell to the floor. "I was seeing stars and wondering where were my friends and where were the police," Toney explained. "I thought if I blacked out this guy's going to blow my head off. That's what I thought." And the people in the courtroom understood. They understood, too, when Toney testified that he fired the gun two times—into the air, he thought—as he ran back to the safety of the van. "I thought if I fired, they would get out of there and leave me alone."

Although John Pridmore's name was mentioned in court more frequently than Caudle's, there was no evidence that he fired the shotgun he was photographed with on November 3. He had been involved in several of the planning meetings, but none of the witnesses accused him of making the kind of inflammatory remarks that Smith and Matthews had.

Courtroom observers began to make predictions on the verdicts: Caudle—acquit; Pridmore—fifty-fifty; Toney, Fowler, and probably Dawson—convict on the general conspiracy; Wood, Matthews, and Smith—convict on conspiracy resulting in injury or death; Griffin—convict on the general conspiracy and interfering with the investigation.

Washout

The defense attorneys presented their own expert witnesses to contradict the testimony of the FBI's Bruce Koenig and Donald Havekost. Both witnesses, a sound analyst and a metallurgist, testified that they had studied the FBI data and concluded that Koenig's and Havekost's tests were so flawed as to be meaningless. The sound analyst said that according to his analysis of the tapes, there could have been as many as forty-two shots fired on November 3. But, he said, it was scientifically impossible for anyone, "even me," to pinpoint the precise location of the shots. He did say that shots three, four, and five could not have come from as far away as the school bus.

The metallurgist challenged Havekost's use, in many instances, of a single element to determine matching pellets. "One element is not satisfactory to characterize the material," he said. An accurate match would require three and preferably four separate elemental matches.

It was a classic scientist-versus-scientist standoff. "If it's a washout on experts," Farran said later, "that benefits us. The government has the burden of proof." Rex Stephenson, the dramatic final witness in the state trial, was not allowed to testify in federal court. Out of the jury's presence, Judge Flannery said that, in his opinion, there was no evidence to show that Jim Waller made the statement about needing a martyr and having a plan to get one in connection with November 3. The defense attorneys argued that although the conversation was not related to the anti-Klan demonstration, they wanted to use Stephenson's testimony to show Waller's state of mind—an exception under the hearsay rule. "You have ample evidence of his state of mind," said Flannery. "He gave Dori Blitz a gun and showed her how to use it. And he had a shotgun."

Jim Cooley argued vigorously to introduce Stephenson's testimony, but could not sway Flannery. After nearly half an hour of arguments, the judge cut the attorney off. "I've made up my mind," he said. "It's highly prejudicial."

Flannery allowed the testimony of another witness under the state of mind exception to the hearsay rule. Larry Lemons was a co-worker of Bill Sampson's at White Oak. Lemons considered Sampson a friend, although he was not in the union and did not share his political beliefs. Sampson had come to his house on the evening of November 2. They talked, Lemons said, "about softball, politics and the rally the next day. I asked him why were they doing this. We hadn't had any trouble with the Klan in Greensboro."

Farran asked Lemons if Sampson had given any indication of his state of mind regarding the possibility that the Klan would come to the rally. "I said to him as he was leaving, 'I wish you wouldn't go,'" Lemons responded. "He said they'd be ready for them."

Clair Butler was the only demonstrator to testify for the defense. It was an extremely uncomfortable position, not only because of who would benefit from her testimony but because of what she had to admit. Until she testified, no one other than the attorneys knew that her actions on November 3 may have drawn the gunfire that killed Sandi Smith.

Butler told the court that she brought a .357 handgun to Greensboro, as was her practice whenever she traveled. She left the gun in her car at the rally site, but got it out when she became concerned because there were no police present. The gun was stuck in her belt when she ran with Sandi Smith to the community center porch after the shooting started.

Butler testified that she never saw Bill Sampson fire his gun, but "I was aware that he was shooting. I don't know how I was aware." When she looked out from the corner of the porch, "I saw a man shooting and pointing a gun at me. It was a long gun. He was shooting down Carver Street and turned towards me. I pulled back and I couldn't see him. I told Sandi I had a gun and pulled it out and fired in his direction."

Butler was not sure whether she fired once or twice. What she was sure of was that immediately after she fired, Sandi Smith "looked out and said, 'Stay back.'" That was when the fatal pellet hit.

A total of 120 witnesses testified before Judge Flannery told the jury, "That finally concludes all the testimony in this case, ladies and gentlemen." Court was recessed for the weekend, with closing arguments set for the following week.

On Monday, April 9, Dale Sampson, Signe Waller, Floris Cauce, and Marty Nathan were allowed as spectators in the courtroom for the first time. As potential witnesses, they had been prohibited from attending court during testimony. Now that the testimony was concluded, they sat with Gayle Korotkin in the second row behind the prosecutors' table—Korotkin's post throughout the trial. Moments before the formal opening of court, the clerk made an announcement: "This is to advise you that Judge Flannery has ordered that the courtroom will be locked during session." There was no explanation.

The closing arguments were as contradictory as the evidence and testimony that preceded them. There was ample prosecution evidence that the defendants went to Greensboro to disrupt the anti-Klan rally and that they expected violence. There was ample evidence that those who were charged with injuring or killing people had done so. There was ample evidence that Virgil Griffin encouraged or threatened Klan members to evade "the law."

One crucial point for the prosecution was not made in closing arguments, however: that, based on the China Grove confrontation, on Ed Dawson's characterization of the Communists as "niggers," and on Nelson Johnson's role as spokesperson prior to the shootings, the defendants *believed* that the group they would confront in Greensboro would be predominantly black.

The defense attorneys attacked the prosecution's weaknesses: the defendants did not go to Greensboro because the demonstrators were participating in a racially integrated activity; they went to protest Communists who had goaded and provoked them. As it had in the state trial, the defense focused heavily on shots three, four, and five. They challenged Koenig's change in testimony; Hal Greeson, who represented Johnny Pridmore in both trials, told the jury it was not true that Koenig was given a folded map in the state trial. Then the defense attorneys pointed to the testimony of several witnesses who said they saw demonstrators with guns in the intersection or heard gunfire from that area.

Flannery's charge to the jury cut through the discrepancies in the closing arguments. His instructions were explicit and detailed. He told the jury that in all but Count 14—the obstruction of justice charge against Dawson and Griffin—the government had to prove four elements beyond a reasonable doubt: one, the defendants must have wilfully conspired to interfere; two, they had to use force or the threat of force; three, the activity that was interfered with must have been administered by the City of Greensboro; and, finally, the United States had to prove that the defendants acted because of the race or religion of the participants and because they were taking part in a racially integrated activity. He explained that race did not have to be the sole factor, but that it had to be a "substantial motivating factor—one without which the defendants would not have acted."

Self-defense, Flannery said, could only be considered "if the government has proved all other elements." If they reached that point in their deliberations, he instructed, the burden of proof was on the government to show that the defendants did not act in self-defense. He told the jury to consider whether the defendant was the aggressor or provoked the confrontation. "One who intends to provoke cannot claim self-defense," he said.

Flannery told the jury to consider whether the circumstances at the time led the defendant to believe he was in imminent danger of death or bodily harm and whether his actions were directed at his perceived assailant.

On Count 14, Flannery told the jury that the government had to prove that Dawson and Griffin conspired through "misrepresentation, intimidation or threat of force to prevent others from communicating with federal agents regarding a violation of federal law." He stressed that the question before them was not whether the defendants conspired to interfere with a state or local police investigation. They had to have known or believed that the witnesses were about to give information to an FBI agent or other federal investigators.

It took Flannery a little over two hours to read his charge to the jury. At 6:40 on the evening of April 12, he told them, "I've never been more impressed with jurors than in this case. You have performed above and beyond the call of duty." He told them to get a good night's rest and return to the jury room at 8:30 the next morning.

During the three days the jury was out, they returned to the courtroom only three times to review evidence. On the first day, they asked to see two of the videotapes and Koenig's chart showing the sequence and location of the shots. The clerk of court showed them how to use the video equipment, and they were left alone in the courtroom to discuss their own analyses of the tapes.

On Palm Sunday, April 15, the jury sent Flannery a note requesting further interpretation of Count 14. In open session, the judge explained that they had to find that the defendants conspired to prevent or delay information to federal law officers. "Federal," he emphasized, "not simply state or local."

A few hours later, the jury sent Flannery another note. He opened court at 4:08 and read the jury's question for the record: "Do we have to know beyond reasonable doubt that the defendants in Count 14 had to know they were evading federal officers?"

Flannery answered, "The government has to prove beyond reasonable doubt that the defendants conspired to prevent persons from contacting federal investigators. They are not charged with evading or conspiring to evade arrest."

An hour later the verdicts were in. Forty-eight times the clerk read the name and the charge. Forty-eight times he read, "The jury finds the defendant not guilty."

Marshals blocked the exits as the judge and jury walked out of the courtroom in silence. Virgil Griffin raised his arms above his head and gave a jubilant thumbs-up. David Matthews and Jerry Smith sobbed uncontrollably. Asked for a comment by reporters, Ed Dawson's jaw dropped and he began to stutter. Finally he got the words out: "For once in my life I can't think of anything to say." Milano Caudle embraced a reporter; crying, he said softly, "I'm sorry for those that was hurt and those that was killed."

Cross-burning at 1981 Klan rally (Courtesy of Jim Waters, WFMY-TV, Greensboro)

Lewis Pitts, Gayle Korotkin, and Dale Sampson sat tightly together at the far end of a courtroom bench. Reporters were wedged into the throng of defendants, their families, and attorneys, trying to get comments. No one paid attention to the three in the corner, the three who represented the dozens who agreed to test the federal judicial process. In losing, they won. Another acquittal. Another injustice. More proof of the cover-up. More proof of the conspiracy.

When the doors finally opened to the corridor, reporters ran to phone the headline in, then returned for more quotes. There was nothing surprising or particularly profound. The defendants and their families were grateful. Pitts, Sampson, and Korotkin expressed shock and outrage. Dan Bell spoke for the prosecution team: "It's obvious we disagree with the verdict and are very disappointed in it. But under our system of justice, the jury does have the final say. That's all I have to say."

Virgil Griffin alone was defiant. "I feel like I died and went to heaven. Now I can go to a Klan rally again." He announced that the Klan would have a statewide victory celebration the following Saturday at the farm near Louisburg. "No matter what the Communists may say"—Griffin sounded like a Muhammad Ali mimic—"the KKK is here to stay."

A total of forty-eight people, many of them children, showed up for Griffin's victory party.[2]

Chapter 19

> I remember you said freedom and
> responsibility are like Siamese twins: they die
> if they are cut apart.
> —Lillian Smith, *Killers of the Dream*

Judgment

Finally the aftermath of November 3 spent itself. Six years and three days after the shootings—November 6, 1985—Greensboro Civil Rights Fund attorneys and the plaintiffs in *Waller* v. *Butkovich*, the $48 million civil suit, announced a settlement: the City of Greensboro consented to pay $351,500 to the estate of Michael Nathan.[1]

The settlement came nearly five months after the conclusion of yet another three-month trial in which, for the first time, local and federal law enforcement officers were made to account for their actions before, during, and after the shootings.[2] The *Waller* jury's verdict, which came several hours after the jurors made an initial, heart-stopping announcement of a deadlock, fell far short of the plaintiffs' claims for $48 million in actual and punitive damages against sixty-five defendants under federal conspiracy and state wrongful death and assault and battery statutes.

The jury refused to award any punitive damages and denied all claims under federal conspiracy laws, voting only to hold eight defendants liable for the injuries to three plaintiffs. In the wrongful death of Mike Nathan, the jury held liable event commander Paul Spoon; Detective Jerry Cooper and his informant Ed Dawson; Mark Sherer, who fired the first shot; and those who fired the wounding and fatal shots—David Matthews, Jerry Smith, Wayne Wood, and Jack Fowler.[3] They also held the four shooters liable for assault and battery on Nathan, Paul Bermanzohn, and Tom Clark.

The jury set total damages at $394,959.55: $351,500 for the wrongful death of Nathan; $3,600 for assault and battery on Nathan; $1,500 for assault and battery on Tom Clark; and $38,359.55 for assault and battery on Paul Bermanzohn.

The city threatened to appeal; the plaintiffs had already filed another $48 million civil suit against Cooper's supervisor and several more ATF and FBI agents. But the simple fact was that the Civil Rights Fund did not have the money either to pursue the civil suit or to battle an appeal. And for the city's part, an appeal would have been at least as costly as a settlement.

So, for perhaps the first time in the history of the case, the plaintiffs and the city achieved a compromise. The appeal was dropped, the civil suit was dropped, and the city paid only the damages for which the jury held Spoon and Cooper liable. Like the *Waller* jury's apparent compromise to break the deadlock, the settlement did little to illuminate the complex issues and questions raised during the thirteen-week trial.

Although much of the evidence and testimony in *Waller* had been presented in *U.S.* v. *Griffin*, the atmosphere in the Winston-Salem federal courtroom was decidedly different in 1985. U.S. District Court Judge Robert R. Mehrige infused the court with a carefully balanced mixture of seriousness and openness, in stark contrast to the dour, paranoid court of Judge Thomas Flannery.

Inside the court, Mehrige frequently chastised attorneys for sloppy legal work or irrelevant questioning of witnesses, but he would just as often offer them guidance through sticky points of law or crack jokes to break the tension. He treated the six-member jury and six alternates as revered friends, praising them lavishly for their careful attention, apologizing for and asking them to disregard his occasional outbursts at attorneys, and inquiring daily about personal matters—one juror's cold, another's Lamaze classes, another's soccer team. The jurors, in turn, hung on every word Mehrige said. One of the most frequent instructions he gave was that they would be shirking their sworn duty if they allowed labels—Klan, Nazi, Communist, police, or federal agent—to influence their judgment of witnesses or their determination of the facts.

That was an admittedly difficult instruction to follow given the thinly veiled hostility between the plaintiffs and their attorneys and the defendants and their attorneys. There was an invisible but omnipresent barrier between the right side of the court, where the widows and survivors and their supporters sat behind the Civil Rights Fund attorneys' table, and the left side of the court, where attorneys for the FBI, ATF, and City of Greensboro and volunteer attorneys for the indigent Klan and Nazi defendants were flanked by row upon row of police officers, federal agents, and Klan and Nazis.

The plaintiffs' hostility was easily understood: they held each of the people across the aisle directly responsible for the deaths of their loved ones, and, in their minds, the defense attorneys' primary function was to shield their clients from justice.

The attitude of the defense attorneys was cynically characterized in a cartoon tacked discreetly behind a door in one of their offices. On one side were a bunch of clowns turning cartwheels, making faces, and waving a banner that said, "WE WANT PAPER!" In the center, a disgusted Judge Mehrige sat behind his bench with his chin propped in his hands and his eyes rolled upwards. On the front of his bench was a sign: "Defendants, please take a number"; the next number was 568. At the other side of Mehrige's bench, one lawyer-type said to another, "No, it's not the circus. Those are the plaintiffs' lawyers in the *Waller* v. *Butkovich* case."

The Klan and Nazi defendants, with one notable exception, kept whatever feelings they had toward the plaintiffs under wraps. They were as flabbergasted as everyone else in the courtroom, though, when Wayne Wood came in during jury selection wearing a T-shirt with the slogan "Kill a Commie for Mommie"; on another day he wore a shirt that said "Eat Lead You Lousy Red." Wood announced to the court that he would not participate in the proceedings if a "nigger" sat on the jury, and everyone, including his former comrades, heaved a sigh of relief when a black man was among those selected.

Wood made one more appearance in court, however, when he was called to testify. This time he wore a three-piece suit—with five little skulls pinned to his breast pocket. He gave a Hitler salute while taking the oath with his right hand hovering over the Bible.

Wood's fanaticism was boundless. He testified that he could not recall stating in deposition that Jews were "the root of all evil." When asked about an anti-Semitic ditty he used to sing for the Nazis, however, he laughed and began singing to the refrain from "Jingle Bells"

> Oh what fun it is to have
> the Nazis back in town.
> Rat-a-tat-tat
> Rat-a-tat-tat
> Shooting all the kikes . . .

Mehrige ordered the federal marshals to take the jury out, and then he adjourned court for the weekend.

It was the Third of May. The moon was full.

Wood's performance was a gut-wrenching contrast to that of the witness who had preceded him: Paul Bermanzohn. The abnormal gait from his left-side paralysis had caused a stress fracture in his right foot. Bermanzohn testified from a wheelchair.

He described his injuries on November 3 and the long months of painful physical and emotional recovery to the jury. His present physical state, he said, was "very marginal. Breaking a bone in my foot put me in a wheelchair. If something happened to my right arm, I'd be sunk."

If Bermanzohn saw Wood smugly waiting his turn to testify, his face did not show it. He did, however, make several references to his parents' terrifying experiences during the Holocaust. And although he was forced to acknowledge that much of the CWP's pre–November 3 posturing, as well as his book, was "overstated" and "grandstanding," his testimony coupled with his physical presence was deeply moving. He set the stage for Wood to convict himself with his own stupidity.

Wood may have been the clear winner of the Hoisted-by-Your-Own-Petard Award, but Bernie Butkovich made a run for it himself. His responses to questioning from the plaintiffs' attorneys were so blatantly evasive that Judge Mehrige was forced to excuse the jury in order to lecture him: "What I want is the truth. I don't want the truth to depend solely on the form of the question."

This is the kind of exchange Mehrige objected to:

Q: "Did you buy a Nazi uniform?"
A: "No."
Q: "How did you acquire a Nazi uniform?"
A: "Agent Dukes bought it."
Q: "Were you with him?"
A: "Yes."

Butkovich's testimony improved somewhat after Mehrige's lecture, but neither his words nor his demeanor did anything to enhance his image or that of the ATF. He came across as an egotistical automaton who could not or did not want to see beyond the specific task at hand. His portrayal of the ATF left the impression of a bunch of Keystone Kops, too wrapped up in James Bond fantasies to recognize the need for such mundane things as extra batteries for the body mike Butkovich wore to the Klan-Nazi rally in Louisburg.

Conclusions

Overall, the testimony from ATF and FBI agents, as well as the police, painted a picture of law enforcement officers that was vastly different from the "leave no stone unturned" image presented on television and in the movies. There was no coordination between agencies. The feds said that they could not legally intervene in local matters. A similar attitude prevailed among the police: the patrol officers could not intercede with the Tacts, who could not question the role of the detectives, who took their orders from higher-ups, who were not fully informed because neither they nor their underlings bothered to probe or coordinate. It was, essentially, a 1980s version of the Nuremburg Defense: nothing was done, or the wrong things were done, because no one knew what anyone else was doing and it was not their responsibility to know.

As discomforting as the officers' testimony was, there was little to show that there was any intent or conscious effort to deny the demonstrators' civil rights. Their lack of communication, coordination, and precaution was deplorable, but not, for the most part, illegal.

In holding Cooper and Spoon liable, though, the jury seemed to be saying, "The buck stops here."[4] They recognized that Cooper's lack of concern for and control of Ed Dawson's actions and Spoon's callous disregard for his duty as event commander were proximate causes of the bloody melee. And at last, at long last, six people had the social and political maturity to see beyond pseudo-patriotic anti-communism to hold the shooters responsible for the terror and carnage they unleashed.

Yet in awarding damages on behalf of only three of the sixteen plaintiffs, and in denying any punitive damages, the jury seemed to be sending another message. Nathan, Bermanzohn, and Clark brought no weapons to the scene (Cesar Cauce brought Clark's shotgun along without his knowledge), nor were any of them involved in the fight that preceded the shootings. By denying all claims of those who had and denying punitive damages even to those who had not, the jury seemed to be saying that in some way they must be held accountable for the violence they helped to incite.

The jury's judgment was an imperfect ruling in a case fraught with confusion and contradiction. Their decision was frustrating to many because, like the CWP in the late 1970s, people tend to want absolute answers, to have everything separated into neat packages that we can identify as Good or Bad, Innocent or Guilty, Us or Them. But in a democracy, especially, we must recognize the fallacy of seeking absolutes. We must uphold the rights of even those whose views we abhor if we are to preserve those rights for ourselves.

Yet with those rights come responsibilities. The CWP had a right to demonstrate. But did they have a right to challenge the Klan to a confrontation? The Klan and Nazis had a right to counter-demonstrate. But did they have a right to bring guns?

The police had an obligation to preserve the rights of the demonstrators and the counter-demonstrators, as well as those of the housing project residents.

Once they knew a confrontation was imminent, did they not also have the duty to tell both the Klan and anti-Klan demonstrators what they knew and to impose strict controls on the location and movement of the demonstrations?

Federal officers are prohibited by law from interfering in local police matters. But where does their mandate to avoid interference end and their responsibility to protect citizens begin? Do they really have to wait until a violation of federal law has occurred before they can offer assistance?

The use of informants and undercover agents is particularly problematic. Few would disagree that infiltration is sometimes a necessary investigative tactic. Yet there is a clear distinction between monitoring for possible criminal activity in extremist groups and encouraging that activity. Extremist group informants, whose allegiance must always be suspect, cannot be allowed to dictate the terms of their work. And it should go without saying, but tragically did not, that an undercover agent should never take his target's word as gospel. In Greensboro, hostile, competing factions escalated self-righteousness and paranoia to the point that they were blind to the forces they were dealing with. Mistakes, errors in judgment, and prejudice fed upon each other until they clashed with explosive, deadly force.

The confrontation was preventable, and yet in many ways it was inevitable. It was an isolated incident, and yet the ingredients that combined at the flash point are part of the fabric of American society. Controversy will always breed extremists; frustrated extremists will often turn to violence. Civil authority will always have to act as a barrier, to walk the delicate and dangerous line between ensuring people's right to dissent and preventing dissension from escalating into disaster.

In Greensboro, the classic right-left-civil triangle degenerated into a circle of hate-filled intolerance. Klan, Communists, cops—they saw each other only by their labels, labels which represented threatening entities rather than human beings. Denying the humanity of your adversaries, as any Marine combat instructor will tell you, is the first step in training soldiers to kill.

In November 1979, this lack of consideration for the participants as real human beings blinded the police to forewarnings of impending violence. It blinded the anti-Klan organizers to the explosive atmosphere they had generated. And it blinded the Klan and Nazis to any way out of the confrontation other than "get them before they get us."

Because there are no pure heroes in this story, it is easy to dismiss the Greensboro killings as an isolated incident, the product of a host of fools clashing in one tragic moment. It is easy to say that the events of November 3 have little relevance for the majority of Americans who are neither revolutionaries nor fascists nor officers of the law. But those groups are only *representa-*

tive of the forces that exploded in Greensboro, forces that lurk within all of us, forces that, in the 1980s, have been manipulated by opportunists from Washington to Hollywood into a nationalistic fervor that endangers the world.

If there is any lesson in the events of November 3, 1979, in Greensboro, it is that when we forsake the ability to judge others for who they really are, we begin to lose our own humanity as well. We become demagogues, willing to destroy innocent lives on the altar of self-righteousness. We thus become the evil we attempt to suppress.

Perhaps, by stepping back to look at the sixteen-year history of the people and events that shaped November 3 and its aftermath, we can also look into ourselves, as individuals, as a society, and as interdependent children of Planet Earth. Perhaps, in doing so, we can become attuned to the slow evolution of disaster in the making and join hands across national and ideological boundaries to stop it before it consumes us.

Epilogue

A Racist Self-destructs

In the house where the Klan and Nazis rendezvoused on November 3, in the presence of a woman friend and her two children, Brent Fletcher put a pistol to his head and blew his brains out. A reporter phoned Fletcher's loyal friend, Ed Dawson, and, speculating that Fletcher had been despondent over his involvement in the killings, asked Dawson if he didn't feel responsible for his friend's suicide. Dawson was outraged at the suggestion, and he let the reporter know it.

At sixty-six, Ed Dawson continues to work as an independent carpenter. Always rail-thin, he has become painfully so; the age lines on his face have deepened into fissures. The battered blue pickup that carries his ladders and tools has aged no less gracefully than Dawson. Like its owner, it reflects both allegiance to and disdain for the Klan: its horn blares "Dixie"; the hood ornament was replaced with a replica of a charging steed which once probably bore a Klansman in flowing robes—now a Snoopy dog has been wired to the horse's back instead.

During the six years of litigation following the shootings, Virgil Griffin's power base evaporated. His attempts to reorganize in the western parts of the Carolinas have resulted in a few rallies, but attendance has been sparse. Klan types in North Carolina in the mid-eighties are looking for militaristic, "Rambo"-like leaders. They have found them, but not in Virgil Griffin.

Epilogue

In God We Trust

Jack Fowler has become a born-again Christian. He married and adopted his wife's two children, and on weekends they go into Winston-Salem neighborhoods to talk with people about Jesus and to encourage them to go to church. Fowler works at the same tire recapping business he worked for in 1979, and he hopes one day to go into business for himself. When he talks of social issues, it is apparent that racism and anti-communism still cling to his character, but the hatred has dissipated in the face of God, family, and work.

Fowler's longtime friend, Milano Caudle, is now serving five years in federal prison for his conviction in the 1980 bombing conspiracy. Caudle never professed the salvation of Jesus. Yet he, like Fowler, is deeply committed to his family. Unlike most of the defendants, he never brought his family into the courtroom to give a show of support. There was always the danger that something could happen, he felt, and he would not expose his wife and children to the risk. Caudle was one of the few defendants who expressed remorse for the Greensboro tragedy and sympathy for the widows and survivors. Yet he remains a racist.

Wayne Wood, too, remains a racist—a sacrilegious racist. His Identity Ministry is a Nazi front, a cowardly, exploitive, tax-dodger's shield. It is, like many so-called ministries today, a clever and convenient way to use the First Amendment as camouflage for racist, undemocratic, and totally un-Christian organizing.

Johnny Pridmore does not claim any religious conversion; he clings to his lifelong belief that God made the races different and that's the way it ought to stay. He laments that he and his wife cannot afford to send the daughter who was born during the 1980 trial to a private, all-white school. Despite his racist views, Pridmore was always open and personable—quite unlike his colleagues Virgil Griffin and Jerry Smith. The recruitment of Pridmore into Griffin's Klan was in all likelihood the major reason for the growth of membership in 1979. People who would have rebuffed the surly grand dragon were attracted to Pridmore.

These men have not escaped unscathed. A part of each of them is imprisoned in the hell they helped to create.

The CWP Is Dead; Long Live the CWP

Shortly after the conclusion of the 1985 civil rights trial, the CWP held its third party congress.[1] Only it was not the CWP anymore. As the North

Carolina Communists had so many times in their brief history, the national organization adopted a new name—the New Democratic Movement—and a new character.

Socialist revolution was no longer their professed goal. It was placed in a political time vault and wedged—unseen and undiscussed—in the foundation of the new organization. Like "The Internationale," which was sung for the "last" time at the congress, the NDM's revolutionary goals would be resurrected only when the organization achieved "cultural hegemony" in the United States.

The movement's stated social ideals were noble: "a society of peace, freedom, justice and prosperity. A society which makes real the principles of the Constitution and the Bill of Rights." The congress established detailed platforms on issues ranging from the economy to the environment, from equality to culture, from the new international order to family and community. The NDM's positions were, for the most part, in line with the contemporary mainstream Left. In reality, wrote one NDM member, they had found in both the name and the platform "a marketing device" that would have eluded them as long as they openly declared themselves Communists.[2]

The change in identity and strategy was transitional; that is, to be used until the NDM achieved a sufficient power base to once again declare itself for what it was when it was the CWP: revolutionary, Communist, and intent on taking over the United States. The strategy was three-fold.

The first part of the plan was to gain political power on the local and state level through elections. NDM members would not necessarily be running for office themselves, but they would provide organizational and fundraising support for progressive Democrats and independents. Raising thousands of dollars overnight by phoning members, as Jerry Tung told the congress the CWP did in Jesse Jackson's primary presidential campaign, was a sure way of catching the attention of traditional political leaders and gaining credibility for the group, thus bringing them into the political mainstream.

The second part of the plan was to once again use labor unions as a springboard to power. Unlike their union work in the late 1970s, the NDM campaign would not focus on mobilizing workers for revolution. Rather, they intended to gain control of the unions' pension funds, which make up a significant source of capital for American financial institutions. The pension funds would thus open an avenue for controlling the institutions themselves.

With power in state and local government, in the unions, and in a few financial institutions, the NDM would be in a position to lower interest rates and provide loans to "community controlled" businesses. That would force other lenders to do the same. Those that could not compete would be bought out, creating a domino effect which would ultimately lead to NDM control of the financial plum: American Express. "We'll still pay the top managers salaries of two or three million dollars," Tung told the congress. "We don't mind paying an American Express president to beat out VISA or Mastercard and take over for us."

The final part of the plan was nationalization, or "public ownership," as Tung preferred to call it, of the American economy. Public ownership was more clearly defined in the congress's resolution on the economy. "The direction of this work must stress 'worker and community' control. This may often mean control by the NDM in order to position ourselves or workers in order to influence and direct investment decisions, thus building model enterprises and promoting the superiority of publicly owned business."

But would the NDM be *publicly* controlled? In its public documents, the NDM proclaims that its membership is open to anyone who upholds its overall goals of peace, justice, and equality. In his speech to the congress, however, Tung said, "We differentiate between the membership and the leadership of the NDM." The NDM, therefore, is no more open than the CWP was. Party membership was open only to those who were invited by the inner circle; the rest were cast as "supporters" until they proved themselves through their ideology, dedication, and tireless work. The NDM's distinction between leaders and members would create a similar political caste system, with decision- and policy-making resting securely in the inner circle.

The NDM's plans for takeover seem preposterous. But perhaps, in some elements at least, they are not. Like so many of the Communists' campaigns, this one would generate repression, for that seems to be the only way America has learned to deal with insurgency, and Communism thrives in repression. NDM-backed candidates would be the subjects of a flurry of Red-baiting, which in this era of ultra-conservatism could spark a move for the return of loyalty oaths and other tests of "patriotism." Attempts to take over union pension funds would generate a backlash from both the unions and the corporations. And if by some wild set of circumstances the NDM gained a foothold in any financial institution, much less American Express, it would be in a position to cause considerable dislocation in the American economy.

The success of even part of their plan would be worth much to the NDM in propaganda value and organizing mileage, but it is unlikely that even with their new "democratic" identity the NDM will become a significant force in American politics or society. Most observers feel that the CWP would have withered to nothing long ago if it had not had the outrage over the Greensboro killings and subsequent acquittals to build organizing momentum. CWP members are too well known in their communities to change their stripes at this point, and their transformation is scoffed at by most of the moderate leftists from whom they would draw their support.

The New Revolutionaries

During the course of the post–November 3 litigation, the widows and survivors who once shouted "avenge" and "death" were awakened to the realities of effective organizing in the United States. And their experience may have been a primary influence in the creation of the NDM. They discovered that without the support of organizations they once scorned as "bourgeois reformist," they would never be able to obtain the financial and legal backing necessary to pursue the civil suit. Pragmatism took precedence over politics.

Marty Nathan and Dale Sampson were the Civil Rights Fund's most prominent spokespersons and fundraisers, generating support from the ACLU, the NAACP, the Congressional Black Caucus, and the National Council of Churches, to name just a few. They recruited consultants for public relations and direct-mail fundraising. They raised $600,000 for the civil suit, and in the six months following its conclusion, Sampson raised another $80,000 to pay the balance of the trial debts.

Both Sampson and Nathan got married shortly after the trial; their husbands are cousins. While Marty Nathan and her husband, Elliot Fratkin, traveled to Africa to conduct research for his doctorate in anthropology, Dale Sampson and Elliot Levin became the parents of a baby boy.

Signe Waller, who had wanted so desperately to bear Jim's child, lost her father suddenly and her mother slowly in the years between the shootings and the civil suit. She had great difficulty finding work, but in 1985 began teaching again at Winston-Salem State University. After years of hosting countless meetings, news conferences, traveling lawyers and organizers, Waller lives in relative solitude in the house she once shared with Jim.

In the summer of 1986, Nelson Johnson made a startling announcement.[3] He was no longer a Communist, he said. He planned to enter Union Theological Seminary in the fall to become a Baptist minister. Johnson gave a sermon at one of Greensboro's largest black churches, and his message, couched in liberation theology, was praised by the minister and congregation. But mainstream Greensboro remains skeptical: What better place to mobilize and organize blacks for the revolution than from the pulpit?

Paul and Sally Bermanzohn live in New York with their two daughters: sociable first-born Leola and Sandi, a fighter like her namesake, Sandi Smith. With the children in school, Sally has become involved with the local PTA.

Paul practices psychiatry at Maimonides Hospital, named after the twelfth-century Spanish rabbi and philosopher who, like Jesus, counseled to reach out to the poor. Bermanzohn, who could easily be making a six-figure salary in private practice, makes $50,000 annually at Maimonides.

Resolution

The litigation stemming from the Greensboro killings may have ended, but a legacy lives on. Scholarships in the names of Mike Nathan and Sandi Smith have been established at Duke and Bennett, respectively.

And the fight against racism and racist violence will continue, although not in the overtly confrontational mode of 1979. After placing half the settlement in a trust fund for young Leah Nathan, Marty divided the balance among the other widows and plaintiffs. Most of them returned all or part of their share to establish a fund for victims of racist violence in the South.

Preliminary plans called for the reactivation of the Greensboro Justice Fund, to be administered by the widows and Southern civil rights and religious leaders. But by mid-1986, a year after the reformation of the Justice Fund was announced, there was little to indicate that the fund was operating. Lewis Pitts, an attorney for the plaintiffs who remains their consultant, was unsure of the fund's status.

It was a good concept—to provide financial and legal assistance, not so much in highly publicized cases, but in instances in which the victim may have few if any resources to draw on. Part of the fund was also to be made available to groups trying to organize and educate on the issues of racism and racist violence.

It would be a fitting legacy if the spirits of Jim Waller, Mike Nathan, Sandi Smith, Cesar Cauce, and Bill Sampson could thus continue to confront the ghosts of racism that haunt the South.

GREENKIL Revisited, 2009

Amid a flurry of song, prayer, and ceremony, the survivors of the Greensboro killings and their allies basked in the glow of what they hoped would be a validation of their martyrdom. It was May 25, 2006. The event was the closing ceremony for the Greensboro Truth and Reconciliation Commission (TRC), which was based on similar commissions investigating human rights abuses in South Africa and East Timor and the first such body in the United States.

Unlike the majority of such commissions worldwide, the Greensboro Commission was not the product of a coordinated effort between survivors of past systemic human rights abuses and subsequent moderate governments. This was survivor-initiated, survivor-led, "pure survivor advocacy," as one insider labeled it. In that light, one would suppose that the TRC's findings would echo the charges that the survivors had been promoting throughout the twenty-one years between the end of the civil suit *Waller v. Butkovich* and the 2006 ceremony:

- the five demonstrators had been assassinated in a vast conspiracy between the Klan and Nazis, the Greensboro police, federal law enforcement, and Cone Mills;
- a subsequent cover-up was orchestrated by the police, city officials, and the local news media; and
- the local district attorneys sabotaged the murder trial of the Klan and Nazi shooters by excluding blacks from the jury while accepting avowed anticommunists.

Remarkably, the commission's findings did not exactly toe the party line.

But it wasn't for lack of prodding and manipulation by the Communist Workers Party (CWP) survivors and their advocates.

Nearly thirty years have passed since gunfire erupted at Everitt Street and Carver Drive. For many in Greensboro it has seemed like a Thirty Years War. The conclusion of the 1985 civil suit left Greensboro city leaders, law enforcement, CWP survivors, Klan, and Nazis alike exhausted and the community itself increasingly polarized. If people thought, in 1985, that the controversy had been settled, that the protagonists would patch their wounds and get on with life, they had not reckoned with the survivors' determination.

Nor had they recognized the transformation of the Greensboro Justice Fund's leadership—Marty Nathan and Nelson Johnson in particular—from dogmatic Maoists to highly effective, though still radical, organizers. In what the old CWP would have reviled as "revisionist history," the leadership toned down the less palatable aspects of its conspiracy accusations and recostumed the "militant antiracist labor organizers" of the civil suit as "unarmed anti-Klan demonstrators," "labor and civil rights activists," and "community organizers."

Before ceasing funding in early 2008, the Greensboro Justice Fund made small grants to leftist grassroots groups throughout the South. Because of its geographical influence, the fund became the primary vehicle for building both support networks and legitimacy for organizing around the Greensboro "massacre." Marty Nathan worked for more than twenty years as its executive director—an unpaid, volunteer position for most of her tenure. From the fund's inception, widows and other comrades involved in the 1979 shootings dominated the fund's board and advisory group.

With Nathan and most other survivors living elsewhere, local advocacy fell to the few who remained in Greensboro: demonstrators Nelson Johnson and Willena Cannon and longtime allies Ed Whitfield and Lewis Brandon. Naturally, much of their effort centered on keeping the memory and issues of November 3 alive through anniversary marches and public forums in which they further sanitized their role in the "Death to the Klan" activities while continuing to pummel the city of Greensboro and its police department with accusations of conspiracy to assassinate the CWP leadership.

For their part, city officials maintained the silence that had been required during the lengthy litigation. One can only speculate as to how things could have changed if Greensboro leaders had taken the initiative at the conclusion of the trials and simply and sincerely apologized for the failures that led to the tragedy. Instead, their silence left the stage open for the survivors to take over the story's production, and their spit-polished version of events surrounding November 3 became accepted as fact for writers, playwrights, documentarians, and an ever-increasing number of journalists and historians of local, national, and even international stature.

The Justice Fund had learned the power of name-dropping early on. Recruiting a few respected progressives to its advisory committees lent legitimacy to its cause and made persuading others to shelve their skepticism easier. Changing the message from "Avenge the CWP Five" to "Support the Justice Fund" didn't hurt either. Signe Waller later reflected that excoriating critics had often been self-defeating. "Our stiff-necked polemical stance," she wrote, "made united fronts difficult and isolated us from potential allies in the mainstream. . . . After November Third we reaped what we had sown." The problem was that the fund remained selective regarding with whom to relax its political stance. Those who were persuaded by the survivors' version of November 3, and especially those with impressive credentials, were on the receiving end of warmth, openness, humor, and generosity that were both charismatic and genuine. Those who remained unconvinced were either ignored or browbeaten with well-rehearsed arguments.

In the meantime, Nelson and Joyce Johnson were doing what they did best: organizing. After Nelson graduated from Virginia Union School of Theology in 1989 and served as assistant pastor in one of Greensboro's mainstream black churches, the Johnsons built on credibility garnered in like-minded religious circles to establish the independent Faith Community Church. Soon thereafter they and their supporters founded an outreach center that combined counseling and services for the homeless with community organizing and agitation on economic and justice issues, including November 3 anniversary events. It was called the Beloved Community Center.

If ever anyone doubted Nelson Johnson's organizing ability or the impressive behind-the-scenes talent of his wife, Joyce, the couple's effectiveness through the Beloved Community put that to rest. Still, they were unable to overcome the widespread distrust of Nelson Johnson that lingered among Greensboro citizens, including many in government, law enforcement, and the media. For them, it seemed nothing he could do would redeem him—he was, in their eyes, responsible for the 1969 fiasco at North Carolina Agricultural and Technical State University (A&T), responsible for the 1979 killings at Morningside Homes, responsible for keeping the community in racial turmoil.

Johnson was undeterred. He continued to step into the limelight through local organizing campaigns, most notably through a predominantly black ministers' group called the Pulpit Forum and its involvement in a union wage effort at a Greensboro Kmart distribution center. There were turf battles, but Johnson's style of organizing drew supporters out of the woodwork, white and black alike. By 1996, no less than Greensboro's mayor, Carolyn Allen, was publicly siding with Johnson and the Kmart workers, "urging," she said, "Kmart to enter serious negotiations with their employees."

As the twentieth anniversary of the killings approached in 1999, the Justice Fund and Beloved Community organized "A Night of 1,000 Conversations on Justice," which was held in the homes of local supporters, several of them newly recruited moderate community activists. Featured at these "conversations" was a collage of news videos edited to enhance the illusion that the Klan and Nazis drove up to an innocent-looking demonstration, unloaded a trunk full of guns, and opened fire, killing demonstrators in what appeared to be an unprovoked slaughter. The conversations themselves were led by Beloved Community–trained facilitators, whose talking points kept the discussions focused on what they called "the City's part in the violence and the media's role in the subsequent coverup."

On the anniversary itself, a survivor-inspired play, *Greensboro: A Requiem*, by Emily Mann, made its local premiere at the University of North Carolina at Greensboro. One reviewer wrote: "The subject is the murder of unarmed demonstrators in the small town of Greensboro in North Carolina . . . in a caravan drive-by massacre." The *New York Times* called it "an American hate story about right-wing violence and government duplicity."

The CWP survivors and their allies had effectively refined their stories into one loud, clear voice, repeating—until it became inviolable—the story of beleaguered radical do-gooders set upon by stereotypical southern racists and police and government conspirators. In many ways it was standard political advocacy—portraying their story in the way that showed them most favorably. But by suppressing and distorting crucial information they crossed the line into hucksterism. The survivors' recollections and analyses of events surrounding November 3 may have been forged in the "correct line" of 1979, but that did not give survivors license to ignore evidence that emerged in the ensuing years.

Those few who tried to bring the full story to light were roundly condemned as opponents and "demonizers" by the survivors and their allies; they were accused of blaming the victims, of being apologists for the city and the police, and of giving a "green light to racists." Although many people in Greensboro recognized the survivors' revisionist effort for what it was, fewer and fewer were willing to step forward to contradict the "massacre" rhetoric. Thus, critics backed off and a growing number of sympathizers were drawn in.

Those who became November 3 adherents through "A Night of 1,000 Conversations" and the twentieth-anniversary activities were brought together for further discussions, which included talk of opening yet another investigation or staging a mock trial. It is not clear at what point the concept of a truth and reconciliation commission was proposed, but by late 2001 the Justice Fund and Beloved Community Center had applied for and received a twenty-thousand-dollar start-up grant from the Andrus Family Fund, a New York–based foundation that had just begun funding truth and reconciliation activities. They were calling it "The Greensboro Massacre Reconciliation Project."

In April 2002 the two groups submitted another grant proposal to Andrus for a three-year, $330,000 grant. The project's name was changed to the more palatable Truth and Community Reconciliation Project, with the project's goal being "truth seeking, reconciliation and healing." The proposal's description of the 1979 killings was short, pithy, and typically incomplete: "40 Ku Klux Klansmen and American Nazi Party members drove into a legally planned anti-Klan march and attacked it, killing five demonstrators and wounding 10 others."

The proposal's authors noted that coverage of the three trials "saturated" the city for six years, yet concluded that the news media "did little to provide a sense of truth, justice or reconciliation." They pointed to "the continuing and profound public ignorance of the known facts and [t]he limits of our own knowledge of the role of government and industry officials in the killings." They acknowledged "deep divisions and antagonism" in the community but sidestepped any responsibility by claiming the divisions were based on "unresolved issues of the Massacre itself and the economic and race-based contention from whence it was born."

Within a few months the first installment of the Andrus Fund grant was on its way to the Beloved Community. In describing the project in its 2002 annual report the Andrus Fund said the commission "would attempt to address the conflict in Greensboro surrounding the killing of five labor and civil rights demonstrators."

Despite its apparent acceptance of the survivors' description and analysis of events, Andrus stipulated that another organization it had recently provided seed money for, the International Center for Transitional Justice, serve as an active project consultant. The Transitional Justice Center was staffed by people who had a long history of involvement with truth commissions around the world. The center made recommendations to the project that included forming a national advisory committee to lend the effort legitimacy, as well as a local task force to organize the community to support the plan.

Seeding boards, committees, and coalitions with stalwarts is a hallmark of what Leninists call "democratic centralism," in which the rank and file may debate issues and policy but only a small leadership cadre makes the final decision. This is the "correct line." No further discussion is allowed. The project's National Advisory Committee, commission-candidate Selection Committee, and Local Task Force were all peppered with longtime survivor advocates and others with connections to the Justice Fund, the Beloved Community Center, or their allied organizations. Few of these supporters were identified as such in grant-seeking or promotional documents. Survivor influence would prove especially problematic with the Local Task Force, which was, in essence, the guts of the truth and reconciliation effort in Greensboro. From early on, said one insider, the meetings were "generally controlled by a leadership group that met before the LTF." That group included the Johnsons, Ed Whitfield, and Lewis Brandon, plus project cochairs Carolyn Allen (former mayor and Kmart campaign supporter), Beloved Community cofounder Rev. Zeb Holler, and Rev. Gregory Headen of the Pulpit Forum and the Kmart campaign.

In June 2002 a Transitional Justice Center memo outlined the steps the project would need to take to create a written mandate for setting up a truth commission in Greensboro. One of the first questions in the memo was "What effect does the identity of those who issue the mandate have on the potential success of the commission?"

This was a hugely important question given the local distrust of Johnson and the Justice Fund. Setting up sufficient separation between the project, the task force, and the commission was essential to ensuring the complete independence of the investigative body. There was also the not-inconsequential matter of community-wide confusion between the different entities. The project leadership seemed content to allow that situation to fester, giving little more than lip service to the notion of independence while in fact exacerbating the confusion.

In January 2003 project cochairs Carolyn Allen and Zeb Holler held a news conference to issue a declaration of the commission's intent, which stated that "a full accounting of the relevant factors connected to [the 1979] tragedy has yet to be entered into the public record and the public consciousness." A commission would be established, they said, to seek

> the truth amidst all the data and perspectives surrounding this complex situation. . . .
> We believe that by helping to clear up lingering confusion, division and ill feelings and by promoting reconciliation among individuals, sectors and institutions within our community, the project will transcend the hurtful legacy of the events of November 3, 1979.

Both the declaration and the advisory committee document that accompanied it expressed noble concepts and lofty goals, although neither did much to avoid compounding the organizational identity question. But that issue paled in light of what was left out of the many documents laying out the commission's responsibilities: there was no mechanism for establishing, no strategy for developing, and no method of ensuring an active reconciliation component in the plans. And there never would be.

Even without that knowledge, many in Greensboro were skeptical: the survivors and their allies were too deeply entwined in the process for anything resembling fairness to come out of a commission organized by them, no matter how many big name "moderates" were attached to it. Others in Greensboro saw no need to reopen a case that had been legally settled—by written agreement of all parties—in 1985. And significant resistance, including outright opposition, came from those who had been on the receiving end of the survivors' wrath. To paraphrase Signe Waller, the Truth and Reconciliation Project reaped what its initiators had sown with their hostility and their never-ending accusations of city involvement in conspiracy, political assassination, and elaborate cover-up.

Concern grew within the Local Task Force as well. A major challenge for the task force was recruiting organizations and individuals to support the truth and reconciliation process publicly and to make credible the project's claims of broad-based community support. Once again, a survivors' advocacy video became a primary education and organizing tool. For more than a few viewers, though, the one-sided nature of the video was enough to cause them to abandon any plans to participate in the process. As task force members began to question the validity of the story they were presenting, and getting short shrift from leaders for their concerns, there was a steady exodus of people who might have provided balance to the effort, leaving the outreach in the hands of what many began to call the "true believers."

In 2003 Sally Bermanzohn published *Through Survivors' Eyes*, which included interviews and recollections that showcased a humanity the survivors had rarely displayed to any but their closest allies. Marty Nathan confessed to Bermanzohn that after the 1985 anniversary events she went home and had a small breakdown: "I just started screaming: 'I never want to be responsible for a fucking thing ever again! I want to have my own personal grief without some reporter there to write down my responses, to twist them in print. I want to grieve without having the responsibility of teaching someone about the massacre.'"

Nathan had scoffed at her husband's fears about challenging the Klan after what he had experienced in China Grove. After he was killed, she said, "I felt suicidal. I felt responsible for Mike's death. . . . Those arguments we had just before his death pierced my heart."

Bermanzohn deeply regretted her own role in the lead-up to November 3. She wrote that after China Grove "a feeling of dread crept over me and stayed there." But when she expressed her concerns directly to Jerry Tung and the CWP leadership,

> There was no discussion of tactics, of dangers—just my inadequacies. Jerry said that I was timid, that I had lost my bearings and failed to assume leadership. . . .
>
> Once I had discussed it with the top leadership, the rules were that I could not discuss my differences with the (local membership), because that would be "intriguing and conspiring."
>
> After the massacre, I felt terrible that I had not argued against the anti-Klan campaign. I wish I had "intrigued and conspired" and derailed the whole thing.

Some political revelations were equally dramatic. In the federal criminal trial, Paul Bermanzohn had testified that he and Sally wrote the 1980 book *The True Story of the Greensboro Massacre*. Nearly twenty years later Sally Bermanzohn wrote that she began working on the book at the instruction of the CWP. But with a new baby and a partially paralyzed husband to care for she simply could not meet the party's demands, especially when it insisted that the book be completed in time for release during the 1980 state murder trial. Jerry Tung, she wrote, "took it out of my hands and gave it to a committee." Both Bermanzohns were listed as authors, "but Paul was too sick to do any of it. . . . Mainly it was the CWP national leadership's view of things."

Another revelation, one that the civil trial jurors had feared, was that Jerry Tung demanded that the settlement money be turned over to the party. The widows objected. Tung accused Nathan of being "disloyal and selfish." Standing her ground, Nathan said, "was heartbreaking. But the bottom line was that the money belonged to the victims. They could donate it to CWP . . . if they chose, but it was their choice."

Such openness and poignant personal reflections, had they been aired early on, would have gone a long way to defuse hostility toward and skepticism of the demonstrators, if not the CWP itself. Instead, the party line held sway, and the cadre clung to the impenetrable dogma of the Greensboro "massacre." That legacy increasingly manifested itself in the Local Task Force. As a result, what could have held promise as a broadly based grassroots effort morphed into a political version of musical chairs. Those who didn't sing the "massacre" tune were relegated to the sidelines, leaving survivor advocates in control of the process with less and less input from those who could have provided balance and perspective. As many as one hundred people participated in the task force at one point or another. Many left after six months, leaving the inner circle led by the Johnsons to make crucial decisions on such items as the makeup of the commission Selection Committee and the criteria for those selections.

The Greensboro Truth and Reconciliation Commission was sworn in at a public ceremony on June 12, 2004. A bit over a year earlier a Selection Panel, consisting of representatives of fourteen mostly mainstream organizations (out of thirty the task force had solicited), made a call for the public to nominate candidates for the commission, including a full-page ad in the *Greensboro News and Record*. Although a widely respected district court judge, Lawrence McSwain, chaired the Selection Panel, its cochair was none other than survivor advocate Ed Whitfield. All told, six of the fourteen panelists had ties to the Beloved Community, the Kmart campaign, or the Pulpit Forum.

Seven commissioners were eventually chosen: Cynthia Brown, a leadership development consultant and activist from Durham and member of the project's advisory committee; Patricia Clark of the Fellowship of Reconciliation in New York, a Greensboro Justice Fund grant recipient; Muktha Jost, a professor in the School of Education at North Carolina A&T; Angela Lawrence, a community activist and former member of a public housing residents' council; Robert Peters, a retired corporate attorney; Rev. Mark Sills, director of FaithAction, an interfaith center for fostering diversity, and a member of the TRC Selection Panel; and Barbara Walker, a retired corporate manager and longtime women's rights activist.

Not only did Brown, Clark, Lawrence, and Sills have links with project organizers, Clark and Jost had been directly involved in anti-Klan activities. The commissioners repeatedly insisted that they made every effort to maintain their independence and neutrality, and had these connections been disclosed at the outset, the commissioners might have been able to explain them. As it stands, the nondisclosure raises serious questions about conflicts of interest and partisan maneuvering to achieve a predetermined outcome.

The commission's initial work was mundane: opening and equipping an office, meeting the obligations of the mandate, setting up a fiscal agent to handle donations and other financial aspects of the work. Six months would pass before a permanent staff was hired. Until then, two project staff members ran the office and served as spokespersons, confirming the suspicions of those who feared the project's undue influence over the commission. The hiring of Jill Williams as executive director seemed a wise choice, with her master's degree in conflict resolution and experience in family and group mediation. Research Director Emily Harwell had recently returned from East Timor where she was research coordinator for that country's Commission for Reception, Truth, and Reconciliation. Their high energy and dedication combined with impressive listening and mediation skills persuaded a number of skeptics to participate who might not otherwise have agreed to. Yet the two project staff persons stayed on—one serving as media coordinator.

Harwell and a few interns and assistants did the lion's share of research over the next year. They became the filter through which the commission received much of the information on which it based its findings. Although the commissioners may have maintained their distance from the survivor faction, the staff and researchers could not. Survivors and their advocates not only constituted a hefty portion of the people interviewed by the researchers, they also served as organizers and hosts for community meetings, fund-raisers, and "meet the commission" events, which included staff. Influence peddling did not need to be part of the agenda; positive social interaction with the survivors, with no comparable contact with other protagonists, served the purpose just as well. Although the staff was consistently polite, respectful, and even solicitous to supporters, critics, and opponents alike, the effect of their relationships with advocates began to show.

Public hearings for the commission began on July 15, 2005, with a pageantry that left no doubt as to who occupied the center of the truth and reconciliation universe. Through six days of hearings, the commissioners sat at a long table facing the audience. The five center front-row seats were occupied by poster-sized photographs of each of the slain demonstrators and a long-stemmed white rose.

Behind the commissioners' table was a massive screen on which was shown yet another carefully edited collage of November 3 news videos. This version was distinguished by its ghastly focus on Mike Nathan, his face nearly obliterated by buckshot, sprawled unaided in the street. As the seconds passed, viewers began to feel like voyeurs watching Nathan struggle for one small breath, and then another, and another.

Some 150 people gave formal statements to the commission, but a majority were given on condition of anonymity or otherwise restricted from public inspection. Fifty-eight people gave statements at the public hearings. Naturally enough, about 30 percent of those speakers were survivors, other November 3 demonstrators, or their allies who reiterated the now-familiar litany of accusations of conspiracy and cover-up, and excuses for the CWP's actions. Another third were activists and academics, including more than a few CWP apologists, who addressed historical issues. The balance was dominated by local people who linked Greensboro's problems since 1979 to residual racist, anticommunist, antiunion sentiment brought on by the shootings and their aftermath.

There were also two police officers, the judge and several defense attorneys from the state murder trial, and two witnesses (including the author) who addressed the destructiveness and shortsightedness of the CWP's tactics leading up to November 3.

The commission's Final Report is an odd document. At five-hundred-plus pages, it is at once overly comprehensive and woefully lacking in several major aspects. Determined to put the report in context, its authors went to extraordinary lengths to provide historical detail on the major groups involved: the Klan, the Greensboro police, civil rights and union organizing, and the CWP.

The problem is that, particularly in the Klan and union sections, there is more than enough detail about the violent history of the Klan and corporate union-busting but precious little information about the specific organizations involved in (or accused of orchestrating) the Greensboro killings. Except for Klansman/informant Eddie Dawson's arrest for going "armed to the terror of the public" in 1967, there were no proven instances of violent activities prior to November 3 by the Klan and Nazi members who rode in the caravan or took part in the shootings. There were plenty of citations of violent language and braggadocio but no evidence that those words translated into action.

Likewise, in nearly thirty pages of North Carolina textile-union history, the information on Cone Mills, which the CWP blamed for spearheading the assassination of its leadership, could be counted in paragraphs rather than pages. Even then, the most suspicious activity the authors could find concerns the fact that between 1976 and 1979 Cone's security office contacted the Greensboro Police Department about militant organizers within its mills, sometimes asking them to track license plate numbers but more often requesting police presence when rival groups leafleted at the gates or held demonstrations. For the most part, the report's history on Cone is one of a paternalistic and relatively benign corporate entity.

The Greensboro Police Department came in for its own scrutiny, and much of its history in the report is entwined with that of Nelson Johnson and Ed Dawson. But the officers most directly involved in planning for November 3 remain merely names and ranks on a page. Most of them refused to speak with the commission—understandable given their abysmal performance in planning for November 3. Nonetheless, the commission could have looked into pre-1979 records on these officers to determine if their failure to protect the demonstrators and the neighborhood had any precedent.

Members and supporters of the CWP, by contrast, are profiled extensively in the report, both individually as well as collectively. Including descriptions of activists' early childhoods, initiation into liberal activism in college, and interest in Marx and Mao, the report gives a full and sympathetic portrait of the individuals who dared the Klan to confront them in Greensboro. Yet details about the CWP itself are scant—its history, its leadership, its uncritical allegiance to despots like Mao and Pol Pot, its national strategy and militant tactics.

Scattered throughout the report, however, is eye-opening information about the North Carolina group's plans for the textile mills and its anti-Klan activities. A few CWP allies who gave statements to the commission told of the group's plan to destroy ACTWU, the textile workers' union, by orchestrating its decertification and then moving into the vacuum with the group's own "independent" union. A few others admitted that CWP demonstrators at China Grove had carried concealed handguns and that the group had begun armed "military defense" training for the anti-Klan campaign.

Despite its shortcomings the commission's conclusions were strikingly similar to those of the civil trial jury in *Waller v. Butkovich*:

- Key police officers and Klan/Nazi shooters shared legal and moral responsibility for the killings. Beyond that, the commission determined that "negligence alone is not an adequate explanation" for the police failure to protect the march. Compounding that speculation, a majority of commissioners "*believe* there was intentionality among some in the department to fail to provide adequate information or take any steps to adequately protect the marchers" (author's emphasis).
- The CWP bore at least partial responsibility for goading the Klan with its actions during and following the near fiasco at China Grove, and by physically, if not intellectually, preparing for a violent confrontation in Greensboro. Despite the amount of evidence and testimony detailed in the TRC's Final Report regarding the group's self-serving goals for the Death to the Klan campaign, the commissioners' overall conclusion is that the CWP was "naive."
- The commission found no evidence of a conspiracy to assassinate the CWP leadership on November 3, neither by the Klan and the Nazis nor by the police, the city, federal law enforcement, or Cone Mills. Neither did the commission find any evidence that the district attorneys sabotaged the state murder trial. (In his "concurring opinion" in the annex to the TRC's Final Report, Commissioner Robert Peters vigorously defended the district attorney's trial work and reiterated that rather than rejecting black prospective jurors, as the survivors continued to profess, the prosecutors had accepted all thirty-one who were not disqualified for justifiable personal reasons or stated inability to reach a fair verdict.)

Unfortunately, it takes some very determined digging through the TRC's Final Report to uncover that information. There is no index, and the report's structure is often confusing. The report is heavily weighted with historical background that only tangentially relates to the groups involved in Greensboro. Access to the Final Report is difficult as well. Only a relative handful of hard copies were printed; they are not available for purchase; and only a dozen or so copies are housed at the Greensboro Public Library. The commission's archives remained uncataloged until 2008. Still, they lack important documents—the Selection Committee, for example, kept no formal minutes of its meetings.

The full report can be found on the TRC's Web site (www.greensborotrc.org), but its length makes online examination prohibitive. The more accessible Executive Summary can be printed from the Web site, but that document is even more problematic. It glosses over or completely ignores the information on the CWP detailed in the Final Report. There is no discussion of the near-disastrous confrontation led by the CWP against the Klan in China Grove, no mention that CWP members were carrying concealed firearms at that demonstration, or for that matter that more than one demonstrator was armed and shooting on November 3. It fails to acknowledge that the CWP leadership viewed its anti-Klan campaign as a party-building rather than a union- or community-building strategy, nor does it mention the CWP's avowal that "a confrontation with the Klan would be best if we can get it."

This failure to include what must surely be considered primary causes of the horrors of November 3 cannot have been an oversight. For a body that repeatedly trumpeted the phrase "causes and consequences" to ignore substantial evidence from a host of reliable sources, including former CWP members themselves, would be baffling were double standards not so commonplace throughout the Final Report.

Although both the Klan/Nazis and the CWP were criticized for their use of violent rhetoric in the months leading up to the killings, the CWP was essentially given a pass because, the commission found, the CWP's rhetoric was directed at "an institution and ideology rather than individuals." Ignored was the fact that Nelson Johnson and Paul Bermanzohn twice publicly challenged Klan leaders Joe Grady and Gorrell Pierce by name, that they called the Klansmen "scum," and dared them "to come out from under your rocks" to "face the wrath of the people" in Greensboro on November 3.

As vile as the Klan's rhetoric can be, there was not a single instance of the Klan and Nazis who came to Greensboro publicly insulting or inciting the CWP, either collectively or individually, prior to November 3. Yet the commission declared that "the cultural context of the time made the intent and effect of the violent rhetoric inherently unequal." The problem with using "cultural context" as a standard for judging a specific group or individuals is that it is often prejudicial. Viewing Virgil Griffin's Klan through the lens of the night-riding terrorists of the nineteenth and early twentieth centuries, which the commission often did, is or should be no different than holding the CWP accountable for the Cambodian killing fields because it once supported Pol Pot.

An investigative body that promotes itself as "antiracist" should be especially sensitive to all forms of prejudice. Yet time and again the Greensboro Commission based its judgment of the Klan and Nazis involved in the 1979 shootings on the actions of racist groups from other times and other places. We learn next to nothing from the Final Report about the Klan and Nazis (or, for that matter, police officers, city officials, or district attorneys) as individuals and precious little about their specific organizations. There was no indication that the Greensboro Police Department had an established pattern and practice of violating civil rights or looking the other way on illegal Klan activity, yet the commission felt it necessary to speculate on the "intentionality" of "some" key officers to stand aside as the Klan-CWP confrontation occurred.

At least in that case the commission acknowledged that its accusation was based on belief and not evidence. On an equally critical issue it actually substituted "massacre" myth for factual evidence cited in the report itself: "The GTRC also finds that the City's payment of the [*Waller v. Butkovich*] settlement on behalf of not only the police officers but also on behalf of the Klansmen and Nazis created an appearance . . . of tolerance or indifference towards white supremacy."

The settlement agreement says no such thing. Cited in a dozen footnotes in the report and legally agreed to by each of the plaintiffs in 1985, the settlement released only the city of Greensboro and thirty-seven police and city defendants. Not one Klan member, not one Nazi, not even informant Ed Dawson was named in the settlement. Nothing in that document prevented the plaintiffs from pursuing monetary claims against the Klan and Nazis held liable by the jury.

These lapses, errors, and omissions seem to mock the commission's stated "rigorous review and impartial weighing of evidence" on which it based "well-documented" conclusions. In contrast to this stated objective, the commission's founding documents themselves allowed wide latitude in weighing evidence and reaching conclusions. Past truth commissions have focused on widespread abuses by powerful institutions—mostly governments—against thousands, even millions, of mostly powerless citizens. Commissions have therefore viewed their role as one of providing an uncritical forum in which the victims of those abuses could tell their stories while giving perpetrators a chance not only to take responsibility for their actions but also to seek forgiveness where possible.

But in Greensboro, where the "victims" were at least partially responsible for inciting a single instance of deadly violence, models of past commissions were inadequate. Hostility between the various parties involved remains so deeply entrenched that despite the commission staff's sustained and sincere efforts, Klan member and police participation in the hearings was minimal. The staff had more success convincing state trial officers to participate—the trial judge, several defense attorneys, and all three prosecutors gave lengthy statements. Unfortunately these became fodder for public scorn and attack from the CWP survivors, defeating whatever strides might have been made toward reconciliation.

Reconciliation. The term's prominence in the commission's name, and in the founding project's name, gave most observers reason to believe that it would be a key component, an equal partner with "truth," in the focus and goals of the effort. It was not.

"In hindsight," wrote former task force member John Young, "the tension between the two was in play from day one." The TRC's own mandate alludes to the subtle shift to "healing and reconciliation *through discovering and disseminating the truth* of what happened" (author's emphasis).

Although there was no documentation on this issue, Executive Director Jill Williams justified the shift, saying it was based on the notion that "most" African Americans preferred to focus on "truth" while "most" whites sought reconciliation. Ed Whitfield later expressed outright contempt for the concept of reconciliation: "There are two divergent paths for Truth and Reconciliation processes: one toward seeking truth, giving voice to the voiceless, comforting the downtrodden and confronting the powers that be. The other path is toward avoiding confrontation, muting dissent, glossing over differences, appealing to the broadest possible cultural base and ultimately excusing injustice in the name of reconciling the community while supporting the status quo and those powers that depend on it."

Despite these attitudes, the Greensboro Truth and Community Reconciliation Project had committed to the Andrus Fund (whose total funding for the commission, from initiation to follow-up, was almost one million dollars) to holding a series of postcommission "town hall" meetings to foster discussion and healing. Once again, these meetings were dominated by "massacre" proponents and their allies; few critical voices were heard; and after the first few meetings, participation dwindled to the same handful of original organizers and allies.

Five years of work, thousands of volunteer and staff hours, and more than a million dollars later, Andrus-funded researchers found that the effects of the truth and reconciliation process on Greensboro—its people, its government, its institutions—were negligible at best. The only beneficiaries seem to have been the few former CWP members and carefully vetted commission members who have hit the speakers' circuit and who travel to conferences around the world to promote the latest version of *The True Story of the Greensboro Massacre*.

The media—including documentarians and academics—have become complicit, for the most part uncritically accepting the survivors' story. This effect is compounded by such reliable-sounding bodies as the International Center for Transitional Justice, whose May 2008 activity report reads like it was taken straight from the Greensboro Justice Fund's Web site: the Klan and Nazis "opened fire on . . . activists and labor organizers"; the "full story" was "silenced," and a "skewed view" became the "official version."

Still, we have a right to expect the news media, documentary producers, and academic researchers to probe beyond the easily obtainable, to be especially rigorous in questioning those who have a self-interest in promoting a particular version of their story. Sympathy for the victims, their families, and friends does not grant license to play loose with the facts. If these institutions ignore or reject contradictory evidence, they become little more than scribes for a twenty-first-century version of Radical Chic. Mao would have been proud. Truth and reconciliation luminaries such as Archbishop Desmond Tutu, who endorsed the formation of the Greensboro Commission, might have a different perspective. "Without truth," he has said, "no healing."

Notes

Prologue

1. Lillian Smith, *Killers of the Dream* (New York: Doubleday, Anchor Books Edition, 1963), p. 5.

Chapter 1

1. Unless otherwise noted, all direct quotations, personal histories, and descriptions of people and events are taken from the author's interviews with and observations of the principals.
2. Descriptions of wounds to the decedents are from the autopsy reports, Office of the Chief Medical Examiner for the State of North Carolina, Chapel Hill, North Carolina, November 3 and 5, 1979.
3. Ed Boyd, WTVD-TV, Durham, North Carolina; videotapes taken on-scene, November 3, 1979.
4. Ibid.
5. "Blackbeard" was a nickname given Jim Waller. See Paul C. and Sally A. Bermanzohn, *The True Story of the Greensboro Massacre* (New York: Cesar Cauce Publishers, 1980), p. 63.
6. *State v. Dawson*, 272 N.C. 535, 1967.
7. Frank J. Donner, *The Age of Surveillance: The Aims and Method of America's Political Intelligence System* (New York: Random House, Vintage Books, 1981), p. 73. For a thorough examination of COINTELPRO's actions against political groups, see chapter 6, "Aggressive Intelligence," pp. 177–240.
8. Federal Bureau of Investigation files, North Carolina Knights of the Ku Klux Klan (157-7200).
9. David Hamlin, *The Nazi/Skokie Conflict: A Civil Liberties Battle* (Boston: Beacon Press, 1980), p. 6.

Notes to Pages 12–30   311

10. Author's interviews: Paul Bermanzohn (May 18 and November 1, 1983), Sally Avery Bermanzohn (November 1, 1983 and July 15, 1984), Nelson Johnson (October 25 and 28, 1983), Signe Waller (June 7, August 31, and September 19, 1983), Marty Nathan (April 8, June 2, July 22, and October 31, 1983).
11. Ed McConville, "Oliver Harvey: 'Got to Take Some Risks,'" *Southern Exposure* 6, no. 2 (Summer 1978), "Sick for Justice," pp. 24–28.
12. Author's interviews: Sally Bermanzohn, Howard Fuller (November 20, 1983).
13. Author's interviews: Sally and Paul Bermanzohn, Marty Nathan. See also Bermanzohn and Bermanzohn, *True Story*, pp. 169–97.
14. Emil Malizia, Mark Pinsky, Wilbur Hobby, "State-by-State Profiles: North Carolina," *Southern Exposure* 4, nos. 1–2 (Spring-Summer 1976) "Here Come a Wind: Labor on the Move," pp. 189–91.
15. Vera Buch Weisbord, "Gastonia 1929: Strike at Loray Mill," *Southern Exposure* 1, nos. 3–4 (Winter 1974), "No More Moanin': Voices of Southern Struggle," pp. 185–204.
16. Author's interviews: Sidney Waller (April 18, 1983), Signe Waller, Paul Bermanzohn. See also Bermanzohn and Bermanzohn, *True Story*, pp. 53–97.
17. Author's interviews: Paul Bermanzohn, Nelson Johnson, Howard Fuller. See also Bermanzohn and Bermanzohn, *True Story*, p. 12.
18. Author's interviews: Sidney Waller, Signe Waller, P. Bermanzohn.

Chapter 2

1. Author's interviews: P. and S. Bermanzohn, N. Johnson, Marty Nathan.
2. William H. Chafe, *Civilities and Civil Rights: Greensboro, North Carolina, and the Black Struggle for Freedom* (New York: Oxford University Press, 1981), p. 175.
3. Ibid., p. 201.
4. Ibid., p. 174.
5. Ibid., p. 193n. Chafe's detailed and well-documented account of the events surrounding the A&T violence in 1968 and 1969 appears in chapter 7, "Black Power," pp. 172–202.
6. Ibid., p. 184.
7. Author's interviews: P. Bermanzohn, N. Johnson. See also Bermanzohn and Bermanzohn, *True Story*, pp. 97–133.
8. FBI files, Planned Takeover of Black Colleges by Students for Black Unity (sic) (157-7492), and COINTELPRO: Black Nationalist—Hate Groups, Malcolm X Liberation University (157-6109) (hereinafter cited as COINTELPRO: MXLU).
9. FBI files, COINTELPRO: MXLU. In a memo to FBI headquarters dated December 10, 1969, the FBI Charlotte office noted that the Columbia, South Carolina, FBI office had sought authority "to advise [deleted] of the nature of the MXLU." Columbia was denied authority to make direct contact, but Charlotte requested authority to furnish the person with copies of transcripts from Senate hearings by

the "Subcommittee on Investigations of the Committee on Governmental Operations Concerning Riots, Civil and Criminal Disorders, Part 22." Charlotte said that "although there is little reference to Malcolm X Liberation University, there is a great deal of information concerning [deleted] . . . the Foundation for Community Development. The testimony of [deleted] and [deleted] shows participation by [deleted] and other representatives of the Foundation in racial disorders and violence."

The memo concluded that the information about the foundation, now known to be false, "might preclude further furnishing of funds to Malcolm X Liberation University by the Episcopal Church."

In a memo dated May 30, 1970, Charlotte advised FBI headquarters that a copy of the Senate hearings was furnished to someone, apparently an Episcopal Church leader in South Carolina, who was "appreciative." The person told the FBI that he planned to "appear before the National Headquarters of the Episcopal Church to bring to their attention the 'naivety' [sic] that many officials in the Episcopal Church seem to have in furnishing militants money to operate schools such as Malcolm X Liberation University."

Apparently the church's deliberations on the issue of funding the school were extensive. A July 4, 1972, article in the *Charlotte Observer* reported that Sadaukai withdrew a $75,000 grant request just prior to the church board's vote on it. A July 7, 1976, memo in the FBI's Revolutionary Workers League files (157-10051) noted that the school closed its doors on June 23, 1973.

10. The FBI's "public source" files on SOBU (157-6758) are filled with articles which illustrate Johnson's and Sadaukai's transition from Pan-Africanism to Marxism. Although neither SOBU nor the ALSC (157-8638) investigative files are titled COINTELPRO, the pattern of the ALSC's disintegration seems more than coincidental. It may be significant that the author's COINTELPRO files on Malcolm X University came from an independent source who obtained them prior to 1979. The FBI denied approximately 90 percent of the author's 1983 Freedom of Information Act requests on the various groups involved in the development of the CWP. Statutory exemptions most often cited were that the information was "classified . . . in the interest of national defense or foreign policy, . . . information involving intelligence sources or methods," or "investigatory records compiled for law enforcement purposes, the disclosure of which would . . . reveal the identity of a confidential source" (Elizabeth E. Wheaton, FOI/PA file 243, 266.).
11. *Workers Viewpoint Journal*, May 1975, p. 12.
12. Ibid., December 1975, p. 39; quoted from Mao Tse Tung, "The Correct Handling of Contradictions among People."
13. Ibid., May 1975, p. 39.

Chapter 3

1. Author's interviews: P. Bermanzohn, Jim Wrenn (December 16, 1983). See also Bermanzohn and Bermanzohn, *True Story*, pp. 197–218.

2. Author's interviews: P. and S. Bermanzohn.
3. Jerry Tung, *The Socialist Road* (New York: Cesar Cauce Publishers, 1981), p. 235.
4. Bermanzohn and Bermanzohn, *True Story*, p. 11.
5. FBI files, North Carolina Knights of the KKK (CE 157-7200), Edward W. Dawson (Informant CE 2362 EI). The "CE" prefix indicates that the files are located in the Charlotte, North Carolina FBI field office. Unless otherwise noted, all FBI file numbers cited hereafter are the Charlotte file numbers.
6. Donner, *Age of Surveillance*, p. 227.
7. FBI files, Dawson.
8. It was not the end of Virgil Griffin, though. He prowled the foothills east of Charlotte—Hickory, Gastonia, Lincolnton—and slowly pulled together enough people to form another Klan. Griffin denies being affiliated with, but took the name of, one of the most militant Klans in the country: the Invisible Empire, Knights of the Ku Klux Klan.
9. FBI files, NCKKKK, undated memo, probably from late summer, listing marches and demonstrations involving NCKKKK, Nazis, and other white supremist groups.
10. The Labor Party has proved itself to be the opposite: an ultra-right, nearly fascist sect of ideologues who follow the conspiratorial ramblings of Lyndon LaRouche. See "NCLC: Brownshirts of the Seventies," a special report by Citizens in Defense of Civil Liberties, 343 S. Dearborn St., Chicago, Ill. 60604.
11. FBI files, NCKKKK, undated memo cited above.
12. *Raleigh Times*, August 23, 1977. See also Bill Belleville, "An American Fuhrer," *Cavalier*, February 1981, p. 21.
13. Author's interview: Orville Campbell, publisher, *Chapel Hill Newspaper*.
14. Belleville, *Cavalier*, p. 22.
15. Ibid.
16. FBI files, Harold A. Covington (100-12233), undated memo from apparently official Rhodesian source.
17. Donner, *Age of Surveillance*, pp. 208–9n. See also Hamlin, *Nazi/Skokie*, pp. 5–6.
18. The description is based on the author's observations at the attempted Klan rally.

Chapter 4

1. Mimi Conway, "Cotton Dust Kills and It's Killing Me," *Southern Exposure* 6, no. 2 (Summer 1978) "Sick for Justice: Health Care and Unhealthy Conditions," p. 30.
2. Ibid.
3. Author's interview: Thad Moore (December 11, 1983).
4. FBI files, Workers Viewpoint Organization/Communist Workers Committee (100-12202), *Tell It Like It Is*, August 10, 17, 24, and 31, 1976.
5. FBI files, Revolutionary Workers League (157-10051), "The Union Organizer," August 19, 1976, and WVO/CWC, *Tell It Like It Is*, August 24, 1976.

6. Signe Waller papers, Greensboro, North Carolina, *Tell It Like It Is*, November 16, 1976.
7. Ibid.
8. Bermanzohn and Bermanzohn, *True Story*, p. 120.
9. Ibid.
10. The source for historical information on ACTWU's organizing efforts is a former high-ranking ACTWU official who asked not to be identified. Author's interview (June 1, 1983).
11. Bermanzohn and Bermanzohn, *True Story*, p. 65.
12. Ibid., pp. 137–68.
13. Signe Waller papers.
14. Ibid., "Partners in Class Struggle," December 1980.
15. Ibid., "Reminiscences of Jim," November 1979.
16. Ibid., memo to "comrades," November 22, 1977.
17. Tung, *Socialist Road*, pp. 237–38.
18. Ibid., p. 239.
19. Bermanzohn and Bermanzohn, *True Story*, p. 155.
20. Author's interviews: Julius Fry (June 7, 1983) and unnamed ACTWU official.
21. Author's interview: Fry.
22. Bermanzohn and Bermanzohn, *True Story*, p. 93.
23. Author's interview: Fry.
24. Ibid.
25. Signe Waller papers, "Granite Workers Update," February 1979.
26. Bermanzohn and Bermanzohn, *True Story*, p. 90.
27. Ibid., pp. 91–92.
28. Author's interview: Fry.
29. Tung, *Socialist Road*, p. 233.
30. Hannah Arendt, *The Origins of Totalitarianism* (New York: Harcourt, Brace and Co., 1958), p. 367.
31. Tung, *Socialist Road*, p. 232.
32. Arendt, *Origins*, p. 366.
33. Richard Hofstadter, *American Violence: A Documentary History* (New York: Alfred A. Knopf, 1970), p. 30.

Chapter 5

1. Hamlin, *Nazi/Skokie*, pp. 17–18.
2. Ibid., p. 23.
3. Ibid., pp. 38–39.
4. *Raleigh News and Observer*, August 23 and 25; September 6, 26, and 27; October 3, 5, and 12; November 16; December 18, 1977. *Raleigh Times*, August 23 and 25; September 27, 1977.
5. *Raleigh Times*, April 27, 1978.

6. Lee Weisbecker, *Charlotte Observer*, unpublished notes from the reporter's interview given to the author.
7. *Raleigh Times*, August 23, 1977.
8. Hamlin, *Nazi/Skokie*, p. 135.
9. *Raleigh Times*, April 22, 1978.
10. *Raleigh News and Observer*, May 14, 1978.
11. Ibid., June 16, 1978.
12. Hamlin, *Nazi/Skokie*, p. 171.
13. Ibid., p. 174.
14. U.S. Treasury Department, Bureau of Alcohol, Tobacco and Firearms files, Bernard Butkovich statement to ATF Internal Affairs, November 30, 1979.
15. Bermanzohn and Bermanzohn, *True Story*, pp. 248–54.
16. *Winston-Salem Journal*, February 23, 1979.
17. Ibid., February 24, 1979.
18. Kurt Loggins, Susan Thomas, "The Menace Returns," *Southern Exposure* 8, no. 2 (Summer 1980), "Mark of the Beast," p. 52.
19. Bernard Butkovich testimony, *United States* v. *Virgil Griffin et al.*, U.S. District Court, Middle District—North Carolina (February 8–9, 1984). Butkovich testimony, *James Waller et al.* v. *Bernard Butkovich et al.*, Middle District—North Carolina (May 9–10, 1985). Because there have been no appeals from the litigation resulting from the Greensboro killings, no complete trial transcripts exist. All court testimony cited hereafter is from the author's daily trial notes in *Griffin* and *Waller*. Portions of the transcripts from *State* v. *Jack Fowler* and other 1980 defendants in Superior Court, Guilford County, North Carolina, and *Griffin* were obtained by the Greensboro Civil Rights Fund and are now in the custody of the Christic Institute—South, Winston-Salem, North Carolina.
20. Robert Fulton Dukes testimony, *Griffin* (March 13, 1984) and *Waller* (May 8, 1985).
21. Ibid., *Waller*.
22. Ibid., *Griffin* and *Waller*.
23. Ibid. Dukes acknowledged in testimony that Grady had supplied him with information on the Klan and Nazis prior to November 3, but said that he considered Grady "a concerned citizen" rather than an informant. Dukes denied that he ever paid Grady for his information, and that may be the distinction between the two types of information suppliers. Grady acknowledged in a November 7, 1979, statement to the FBI that he had supplied the ATF with numerous tips in order to "set up" the Nazis because he considered them dangerous.
24. Butkovich testimony, *Griffin* grand jury (CR-83-53-01-09-G), May 3–4, 1982.
25. Butkovich testimony, *Griffin*.
26. Ibid.
27. Ibid.
28. *Greensboro Record*, July 14, 1980.
29. Paul Lucky testimony, *Griffin* (March 19, 1984).
30. Ibid.

31. Author's interview: Lyn Wells, SCEF (May 27, 1984).
32. Ibid.
33. Author's interview: Cleve Sellers (November 22, 1983).
34. Author's interview: Wells.
35. Lucky testimony, *Griffin*.
36. Lt. Edward Klutz, China Grove Police Department, testimony, *Griffin* (March 19, 1984).
37. Signe Waller papers, "Reminiscences."
38. Lucky testimony, *Griffin*.
39. Klutz testimony, *Griffin*.
40. Gorrell Pierce testimony, *Waller* (May 6, 1985).
41. Klutz testimony, *Griffin*.
42. Robert Keefer, WBTV-TV, Charlotte, North Carolina, videotape taken on scene July 8, 1979, evidence in *Griffin* and *Waller*.
43. Lucky testimony, *Griffin*.
44. Raeford Milano Caudle testimony, *Waller* (May 2, 1985).
45. Keefer videotapes.
46. Ibid.
47. Ibid.
48. Lucky testimony, *Griffin*.
49. Caudle, Roland Wayne Wood testimony, *Waller* (Wood, May 3 and 6, 1985).
50. Pierce testimony, *Waller*.
51. *Kannapolis Independent*, July 13, 1979.
52. Gabriel A. Almond, *The Appeals of Communism* (Princeton: Princeton University Press, 1954), p. 30.
53. Bermanzohn and Bermanzohn, *True Story*, pp. 155–56.
54. Ibid., p. 11.
55. Tung, *Socialist Road*, p. 225.

Chapter 6

1. Although there is no documentary evidence to prove this, Covington's pattern of behavior strongly suggests that he was an egotistical, power-hungry despot in search of followers. And like many Third Reich Nazi leaders, when his power base evaporated in 1981, he went into exile.
2. Harold Covington, "Myron Silverstein" letters to the RCP, July 9 and 31, 1979, author's files.
3. Covington letter to RCP, September 11, 1979, author's files.
4. Chief William E. Swing, Greensboro Police Department, "An Administrative Report of the Anti-Klan Rally, Greensboro, North Carolina, November 3, 1979," "A Letter From the Workers Viewpoint Organization," October 18, 1979, Appendix C, p. 43.
5. Capt. Larry Gibson testimony, *Griffin* (February 9, 1984).

Notes to Pages 97–107

6. Butkovich testimony, *Griffin*.
7. Wood statement to Greensboro police and FBI investigators, November 3, 1979.
8. Butkovich ATF Internal Affairs statement.
9. Butkovich testimony, *Griffin* grand jury.
10. Caudle testimony, *Waller*.
11. Ibid.
12. Joe Grady testimony, *Waller* (May 7, 1985).
13. Alma Blount photographs, September 22, 1979, *Southern Exposure* files, Durham, North Carolina.
14. *Greensboro Record*, July 14, 1980.
15. Butkovich testimony, *Griffin* and *Waller*.
16. ATF transcripts of transmissions from body mike worn by Butkovich, September 22, 1979.
17. *Waller* amended complaint, Civil Action 80-605-G, May 3, 1982, p. 17.
18. Caudle testimony, *Waller*.
19. Will Campbell, "Clean Up the Botulism," speech delivered April 10, 1980, printed in *Southern Exposure*, "Mark of the Beast," p. 99.
20. Swing, "Administrative Report," pp. 1–2.
21. Detective Jerry Cooper testimony, *Griffin* (February 10, 1984).
22. Gibson testimony, *Griffin*.
23. "Directive from the SB [Standing Body]: Immediately Take Up the Anti-Klan Campaign and Use It to Build for the Party Fanfare as we Build for a RED HOT Demonstration and Conference on Nov. 3rd," undated, City pretrial defense Exhibit A, *Waller*.
24. Gibson testimony, *Griffin*.
25. Workers Viewpoint Organization news release, "WVO Calls for Demonstration and Conference Against the Klan," October 11, 1979.
26. *Salisbury Evening Post*, October 11, 1979.
27. *Charlotte Observer*, October 12, 1979.
28. Cooper testimony, *Griffin*.
29. Ibid.
30. *Revolutionary Worker* (RCP), October 30, 1981.
31. *Greensboro Daily News*, October 12, 1979.
32. Gibson testimony, *Griffin*.
33. Chris Benson testimony, *Griffin* (February 7, 1984).
34. Lisford Carl Nappier testimony, *Griffin* (February 1, 1984).
35. Benson, Nappier testimony, *Griffin*.
36. Ibid.
37. Virgil Griffin testimony, *Griffin* (March 26, 1984).
38. Nappier testimony, *Griffin*.
39. Cooper testimony, *Griffin*.
40. Ibid.
41. Ibid.
42. *Greensboro Daily News*, October 17, 1979.

43. Swing, "Administrative Report," Appendix C, p. 43.
44. Gibson testimony, *Griffin*.
45. Swing, "Administrative Report," "Application for Parade Permit" (Workers Viewpoint Organization, October 19, 1979), Appendix E, p. 45.
46. Gibson testimony, *Griffin*.
47. Paul Bermanzohn testimony, *Waller* (May 2–3, 1985).
48. Ibid.
49. Bermanzohn and Bermanzohn, *True Story*, p. 13.
50. Ibid., p. 12.

Chapter 7

1. Jerry Paul Smith testimony, *Griffin* (March 30, 1984).
2. Nappier testimony, *Griffin*.
3. Ibid.
4. Ibid.
5. Institute for Southern Studies Special Report, "The Third of November," Durham, North Carolina, 1981, p. 28.
6. Ibid., p. 27.
7. Griffin testimony, *Griffin*.
8. Swing, "Administrative Report," Appendix D, p. 44.
9. Cooper testimony, *Griffin*.
10. Ibid.
11. Brent Fletcher testimony, *Griffin* (February 9, 1984).
12. Ibid.
13. Bermanzohn and Bermanzohn, *True Story*, p. 133.
14. Author's interview: Nelson Johnson.
15. Author's interview: Wells.
16. Andrew Pelczar (resident agent in charge, Greensboro FBI office) testimony, *Waller* (May 14, 1985).
17. Ibid.
18. Author's interviews: Wells, Nelson Johnson.
19. Griffin testimony, *Griffin*.
20. Nappier police-FBI statement, November 3, 1979.
21. Nappier testimony, *Griffin*.
22. Ibid.
23. Sgt. W. D. "Dave" Comer testimony, *Waller* (April 29, 1985).
24. Ibid.
25. Len Bogaty (special agent, Greensboro FBI office) testimony, *Waller* (May 12, 1985).
26. Author's interviews: Nelson Johnson, P. Bermanzohn. WVO news release,

Notes to Pages 116–122 319

"WVO's 'Death to the Klan' March and Conference Calls Out Klan's Secret Supporters," November 1, 1979, City pretrial Exhibit G, *Waller*.
27. Swing, "Administrative Report," p. 4.
28. Institute, "Third of November," p. 28.
29. WVO news release, November 3, 1979.
30. Institute, "Third of November," p. 27.
31. Gibson testimony, *Waller* (April 17, 1985).
32. Cooper testimony, *Waller* (April 15, 1985).
33. Maj. Sylvester Daughtry testimony, *Waller* (April 27, 1985).
34. Swing, "Administrative Report," pp. 7–9, and Appendix N, p. 92.
35. Comer testimony, *Waller*.
36. Butkovich testimony, *Griffin* (February 8–9, 1984).
37. Butkovich testimony, *Waller* (May 9–10, 1985). Wood, Fowler, and Caudle denied in testimony that they asked Butkovich to assist them in getting illegal weapons. They insist it was the other way around. Butkovich acknowledged that as one of his investigatory tactics he "encouraged" the Nazis to procure illegal weapons but did not initiate such discussions.
38. Butkovich testimony, *Griffin* and *Waller*. Smith has consistently denied that he talked with Butkovich about pipe bombs, although he acknowledged in *Griffin* testimony that he and Mark Sherer had exploded one on October 1, 1979. None of the Klan or Nazis present at the November 1 meeting recalled Smith making such a statement. Although Butkovich's supervisor, Fulton Dukes, did not mention pipe bombs in his November 9, 1979, statement to ATF Internal Affairs, he later testified in both *Griffin* and *Waller* that Butkovich reported Smith's statement to him following the meeting at Wood's. Butkovich, in Internal Affairs statements on November 30 and December 7, 1979, mentioned the conversation with Smith, but did not use the clause "of niggers" to describe "a crowd."
39. Butkovich testimony, *Waller*.
40. John C. Westra (special agent in charge, ATF-North Carolina), ATF Internal Affairs statement, November 26, 1979.
41. Butkovich testimony, *Waller*.
42. Ibid. See also Dukes testimony, *Waller* (May 8, 1985).
43. Jerry Smith testimony, *Griffin*.
44. Benson testimony, *Griffin*.
45. Four "K"s stand for Knights of the Ku Klux Klan.
46. Edward W. Dawson, *Griffin* grand jury testimony (July 15, 1982), read into *Griffin* trial record (March 14, 1984).
47. Nelson Johnson interview.
48. Dori Blitz testimony, *Griffin* (February 29, 1984).
49. P. Bermanzohn testimony, *Griffin* (March 1, 1984).
50. Coleman B. "Johnny" Pridmore testimony, *Griffin* (April 2, 1984).
51. WVO leaflet, undated, "*Death* to the Klan!!! Promote Armed Self-Defense of the Community," City pretrial Exhibit F, *Waller*.

Chapter 8

1. Unless otherwise noted, the descriptions of events and movements of people leading up to the shootings are taken from the principals' testimony in *Griffin*.
2. Wood police-FBI statement, November 4, 1979.
3. Ibid.
4. Swing, "Administrative Report," Appendix G, pp. 50–59.
5. Ibid., p. 11; also Appendix L, pp. 87–88.
6. Author's interview: P. Bermanzohn.
7. Institute, "Third of November," p. 29.
8. Swing, "Administrative Report," "Radio Traffic on Frequency 3," Appendix I, p. 66. Unless otherwise noted, all time sequences and quotes from police officers hereafter were taken from Appendix I, pp. 66–81, which is the official transcript of radio transmissions on frequencies 1, 3, and 4 from 11:02.27 to 11:31.56 a.m. on November 3.
9. Boyd videotapes.
10. Ibid.
11. Sgt. James Hightower testimony, *Waller* (April 25, 1985).
12. George Vaughn, WGHP-TV, High Point, North Carolina, filmed interview between Nelson Johnson and reporter Charles Travis, November 3, 1979.
13. Laura Blumenthal, WXII-TV, Winston-Salem, North Carolina. During the 1980 murder trial, Blumenthal submitted to questioning under hypnosis at the request of the Guilford County District Attorney's office. The session was videotaped and a copy was obtained by WUNC-TV in Chapel Hill for the PBS special "88 Seconds in Greensboro." In 1983, the author was allowed to view and take notes from the hypnosis tapes, the source of this quote.

Chapter 9

1. Sherer testified in *Griffin* that his gun jammed when he attempted to fire his second shot. However, in his first statement to the FBI in January 1980, as well as in his grand jury testimony, he said he was positive he fired a shot into the ground, a shot into the air, and a later shot into the side of a car—three shots. Sherer accounted for his precise recollection of three shots, he said, because he fired the gun once again after leaving Greensboro and when he checked the chamber there were two rounds remaining in the six-shooter.

   Sherer changed his testimony in *Griffin*, saying he found three rounds in the chamber and therefore could have only fired twice in Greensboro and once after he left. Between the time of his FBI statement and his testimony in *Griffin*, controversy arose as to whether shots three (Sherer's into the air), four, and five were fired by caravan members or demonstrators. Thus, it was clearly in Sherer's (and the *Griffin* defendants') self-interest to disclaim the one shot that could not be conclusively linked to his gun. Because Sherer's overall testimony raised serious

Notes to Pages 137–159

questions about his credibility, the author has chosen to use his initial admission of three shots, which is backed by the prosecution evidence in *Griffin*.
2. Unless otherwise noted, the descriptions of wounds to the decedents are based on the state medical examiner's autopsy reports.
3. Flowers did not positively identify Sampson in his *Griffin* testimony, but Sampson was the only demonstrator matching that description who was positively identified as having a pistol in the area of the intersection.
4. Toney testified in *Griffin* that he fired twice from the street after he got away from the fight near the pickup, but a spent shell casing from Clark's shotgun was found near the pickup, and Waller and Wrenn were running from the area when the fifth shot was fired. Although Toney's testimony was more credible than Sherer's, the author accepts the prosecution evidence on the sequence of the third, fourth, and fifth shots.

Chapter 10

1. Author's interview: Charles Porter, director, Guilford County Emergency Medical Services (December 1, 1983).
2. Swing, "Administrative Report," Appendix L, p. 88.
3. Bruce Koenig, FBI Technical Services Division, evidence and testimony in *Fowler*, *Griffin* and *Waller*.
4. William E. Sampson, autopsy photograph.
5. Author's interviews: P. and S. Bermanzohn.
6. Boyd videotapes.
7. Ibid.
8. Author's interview: Porter.
9. Author's interview: Sidney Waller.
10. Author's interview: Signe Waller.
11. Boyd videotapes.
12. Author's interview: H. M. "Mickey" Michaux (June 2, 1983).
13. The author has been interrogated by Brereton; the description "formidable" is based on that meeting, as well as on informal discussions with others who have been questioned by him.
14. Author's interview: Jim Coman (June 20, 1983).
15. Swing, "Administrative Report," Appendix K, pp. 84–86.
16. Coy Jarret, Guilford County deputy sheriff, statement to Greensboro police (May 21, 1980).
17. Lawrence Morgan, transcripts of police-FBI statement, November 3, 1979. Unless otherwise noted, all statements attributed to Klan-Nazi suspects and investigators during police-FBI interrogations are taken from the official transcripts of those sessions.
18. Author's interview: Porter.
19. Cesar Cauce autopsy photograph.

Notes to Pages 161–175

20. Author's interview: Jim Wrenn (December 16, 1983).
21. Griffin insisted in *Griffin* testimony that if he used the phrase "remember your Klan oath," it meant only that the others should cooperate with the police if they were questioned. But Max Hayes, Chris Benson, and Barbara Ledford (in a November 5, 1979, statement to the FBI) testified that the statement was made in a menacing way. Ledford told the FBI that Griffin threatened her when she told him she wanted to leave the group; she said that she told him she was leaving anyway, that if he wanted to stop her he would have to shoot her in the back as she walked away. She and Hayes left the group, unharmed, on November 4. But when the FBI attempted to find Ledford for a follow-up interrogation, she could not be found.

Chapter 11

1. *Greensboro Daily News*, November 4, 1979.
2. Ibid.
3. Butkovich grand jury testimony.
4. Ibid.
5. Butkovich's supervisor, Fulton Dukes, said in a November 9, 1979, ATF Internal Affairs statement, "I was contacted by an informant who stated that he was in contact with Melano [sic] Caudle and Caudle wanted to turn himself in to me." Caudle identified the "informant" who arranged his surrender in his *Waller* testimony: Joe Grady.
6. CWP news release, November 4, 1979.
7. CWP news release, November 5, 1979.
8. *Daily News*, November 7, 1979.
9. Ibid.
10. Ibid.
11. *Daily News*, November 7, 1979.
12. *Daily News*, November 9, 1979.
13. Author's interview: Nelson Johnson.
14. *Daily News*, November 9, 1979.
15. *Daily News*, November 10, 1979.
16. *Greensboro Record*, November 9, 1979.
17. FBI files, GREENKIL (44-3527), Brereton memo dated November 10, 1979.
18. *Record*, November 10, 1979.
19. Butkovich deposition, *Waller* (July 17–18, 1984).
20. *Record*, November 10, 1979.
21. Harold Covington FBI statement (November 7, 1979); Joe Grady FBI statements (November 4 and 14, 1979).
22. Unless otherwise noted, descriptions of people and events during the funeral march are based on the author's observations, November 11, 1979.

23. Letter to FBI Director William H. Webster, November 14, 1979.
24. Author's interview: Nelson Johnson.

Chapter 12

1. Unless otherwise noted, all information on the district attorneys and their strategy for prosecuting *Fowler* are based on the author's interviews with Rick Greeson and Jim Coman, conducted together on June 26, September 18, October 27, and November 23, 1983.
2. Donald Havekost testimony, *Griffin* (March 8, 12, and 13, 1984).
3. Author's interviews: Marty Nathan, Signe Waller, Nelson Johnson.
4. A comparison of headlines related to the two groups in the week following the shootings is instructive. (Use of caps and lower case follows differing headline styles in the two newspapers.)

    Klan-Nazis: "Wife says couple joined Klan group in ignorance" (*Record*, November 6, 1979); "Nephew's radical bent surprises Lincolnton deputy" (ibid.); "Jail head reports no disruptions" (ibid.); "The Klan: Communists, not blacks, now target" (*Record*, November 8, 1979); "It was just 'something to do' . . . And 16 year old ended up in jail" (*Record*, November 10, 1979).

    CWP: "A&T Riots: Violence Not New To Leader Of Rally" (*Daily News*, November 4, 1979); "'They All Hate Each Other,' Professor Says Of Leftists" (*Daily News*, November 6, 1979); "WVO 'Targeted' Cone, Other Mills For Infiltration" (ibid.); "CWP Members Refusing To Cooperate With Agents" (*Daily News*, November 7, 1979); "Slain Man 'Was Firing' Gun At Klan Group, Witness Says" (*Daily News*, November 10, 1979); Police Suspect WVO Fired First Shot" (*Daily News*, November 11, 1979); "State Of Emergency Set For CWP Funeral March" (ibid.).
5. *Record*, November 9, 1979.
6. Author's interview: Katherine Fulton (October 23, 1983).
7. Chris Benson FBI statement, November 20, 1979.
8. Benson testimony, *Griffin*.
9. Dukes ATF statement.
10. *Record*, November 8, 1979.
11. Covington FBI statement.
12. Swing, "Administrative Report," title page.
13. Sgt. Dave Comer FBI statement, November 29, 1979.
14. Memo to North Carolina Department of Administration, November 19, 1979.
15. Institute, "Third of November," p. 16.
16. Mark K. Schott, Chairperson, "Report of the Citizens Review Committee," May 22, 1980.
17. Ibid., p. 5.
18. Ibid., p. 10.

19. Ibid., p. 12.
20. Signe Waller papers, "Reminiscences."
21. *Raleigh News and Observer*, January 12, 1980.
22. ATF files, Covington (2610 0979 5006 H [01]).
23. *News and Observer*, January 2, 1980.
24. *Record*, November 8, 1979.
25. *Daily News*, December 9, 1979.
26. Bruce Koenig testimony, *Griffin* (January 27, 1984) and *Waller* (April 1, 1985).
27. Robert S. Cahoon, letter to William H. Webster, November 6, 1980.
28. Transcripts of statements given to the Greensboro Police Department, Tom Clark, Signe Waller, Marty Nathan, Frankie Powell (January 1, 1980); Paul Bermanzohn (February 1, 1980); Floris Cauce, Nelson Johnson (March 6, 1980).
29. *Daily News*, January 16, 1980.
30. *Record*, January 21, 1980.
31. *Daily News*, January 22, 1980.
32. *Record*, January 26, 1980.
33. FBI files, "Greensboro Demonstration," January 30–31, 1980 (157-10168).
34. *Record*, February 4, 1980.
35. FBI files, "Demonstration," January 31, 1980.
36. *Daily News*, February 3, 1980.
37. Porter interview.
38. FBI files, "Demonstration," February 2, 1980.
39. *Daily News*, February 3, 1980.

Chapter 13

1. Author's interviews: Jeff Farran (May 5, 1984) and Percy Wall (August 14, 1984).
2. Author's interviews: Greeson, Coman.
3. Ibid.
4. *Daily News*, July 20, 1980.
5. Ibid.
6. *Record*, July 14, 1980.
7. CWP news release, July 15, 1980.
8. Harold Covington, "The New Order," March 1980.
9. *Raleigh Times*, April 9, 1980.
10. ATF files, Covington, memo submitted by the St. Louis, Missouri, field office dated April 8, 1980.
11. ATF files, Covington, undated letter from Covington inviting party leaders to a "*strictly*" internal" conference on March 22–23, 1980. Covington listed eighteen people who were "officially invited" to the conference, with Allen as the only representative from St. Louis. An ATF memo notes that the day after the conference informant CI/203 met with agent John Bobb and gave him the Covington letter.

Notes to Pages 209–224

12. ATF file, Covington, confidential memo to party leaders dated March 9, 1980.
13. Cook County, Illinois, property records on "Rockwell Hall," 2519 W. 71st St., Chicago. The only circumstance under which the identity of an owner of property in blind trust can be revealed is when a lien is taken against the property for nonpayment of property-related debts. A $3,800 lien was filed against Covington in February 1982, thus making his ownership public record. Covington sold the building in July 1982.
14. *News and Observer*, May 8, 1980.
15. *Raleigh Times*, March 28, 1980.
16. *News and Observer*, May 10–11, 1980.
17. Ibid., May 8, 1980.
18. Ibid., May 11, 1980.
19. Ibid., May 8, 1980.
20. FBI files, North Carolina Knights of the KKK.
21. *Record*, March 3, 1981.
22. *Daily News*, March 4, 1981.

Chapter 14

1. Author's interviews: Greeson, Coman.
2. *Daily News*, August 5, 1980.
3. Ibid.
4. Author's interviews: Greeson, Coman.
5. *Daily News*, August 5, 1980.
6. Koenig report, August 21, 1980.
7. *Daily News*, August 29, 1980.
8. Ibid.
9. Author's interview: anonymous juror (August 2, 1983). The juror quoted in this chapter asked not to be identified.
10. Koenig amended report, September 3, 1980.
11. Author's interviews: Greeson, Coman.
12. Koenig report, August 21, 1980.
13. Ibid.
14. The description of Koenig's demeanor and testimony is based on the Greeson and Coman interviews as well as on the author's observations and trial notes from *Griffin* and *Waller*.
15. *Daily News*, September 25, 1980.
16. Author's interview: Farran.
17. Author's interview: Ed Dawson (January 24, 1981).
18. *Daily News*, October 14, 1980.
19. Author's observations, November 2, 1980.
20. Signe Waller papers.
21. *Waller* civil complaint, November 3, 1980.

Notes to Pages 224–236

22. Author's interview: Greeson, Coman.
23. CWP news release, November 7, 1980.
24. *U.S.* v. *Frank Lee Braswell* indictments, U.S. District Court—Western District, North Carolina (March 3, 1981).
25. Ibid.
26. *News and Observer*, November 23, 1980.
27. Author's interview: anonymous juror.
28. *Daily News*, November 18, 1980.
29. CWP news release, November 17, 1980.

Chapter 15

1. *Daily News*, November 19, 1980.
2. Ibid.
3. Author's interviews: Charles Davis, Beth Kaiser, Sol Jacobs (CJU) (August 13, 1983).
4. Ibid.
5. Ibid.
6. Nelson Johnson letter, December 12, 1980.
7. Author's interview: N. Johnson.
8. Author's interview: Marty Nathan; *Record*, August 20, 1980.
9. Author's interview: Lewis Pitts (July 11, 1983).
10. *Waller* complaint.
11. *Waller*, U.S. Department of Justice motion to dismiss, ruling to deny, 584 FSupp 909 (1984).
12. Author's interview: Michael Johnson (August 28 and October 15, 1984).
13. Michaux letter to Dan Rinzel, May 5, 1981.
14. Title 18, U.S. Code, Section 241.
15. Michaux letter.
16. Section 241.
17. Title 18, U.S. Code, Section 245 (b)(4)(A) and (b)(2)(B).
18. *Daily News*, March 2, 1981.
19. Author's recollection of her conversation with Dawson and her observation of subsequent events, March 1, 1981.
20. Bermanzohn and Bermanzohn, *True Story*.
21. P. Bermanzohn testimony, *Waller*.
22. *Daily News*, July 13, 1981.
23. *News and Observer*, February 15, 1981.
24. *Raleigh Times*, March 31, 1981; *News and Observer*, April 1, 1981.
25. On June 29, 1981, Covington applied for a job as assistant manager at Waldenbooks in Charleston, South Carolina. On his application he said that he had been self-employed as a writer from 1977 to the date of his application. From 1974 to 1976, he wrote, he was an "ordnance NCO" and "bomb disposal trainee" in the

Notes to Pages 236–249

  Rhodesian Army. In the column marked "reason for leaving," he wrote, "We lost." Covington was not hired.
26. *Daily News*, July 15, 1981.
27. Ibid., July 16, 1981.
28. Ibid.
29. *Daily News*, September 12, 1983.
30. *Daily News*, July 17–19, 1981.
31. Ibid.
32. Ibid.
33. Author's interview: Larry King, *Daily News* reporter on the Asheville trials (June 5, 1984).
34. *Daily News*, July 19, 1981.
35. Ibid., September 17, 1981.
36. FBI file, Covington, passport no. B2593026, issued September 24, 1981.
37. Ibid., memo dated July 21, 1982, to FBI Civil Rights Section seeking authority to extradite Covington to testify before the *Griffin* grand jury.

Chapter 16

1. Author's interview: Michael Curtis (January 1981).
2. Institute, "Third of November," pp. 24–31.
3. Ibid., p. 2.
4. Ibid.
5. Ibid.
6. Ibid., p. 18.
7. Ibid.
8. Ibid., p. 32.
9. Charles Davis interview.
10. Author's interview: Bob Hall (June 2, 1983).
11. Author's interviews: Davis, Kaiser, Jacobs.
12. *Daily News*, May 7 and June 2, 1982.
13. Author's interviews: Greeson, Coman.
14. *Waller* amended complaint, May 3, 1982.
15. Ibid., p. 18.
16. Ibid., p. 23.
17. Ibid.
18. Ibid., p. 24.
19. Willena Cannon testimony, *Waller* (May 9, 1984).
20. *Waller* amended, p. 34.
21. Butkovich grand jury testimony.
22. Memo to FBI Civil Rights Section, July 21, 1982.
23. Ibid., attachment.
24. Michael Johnson memo to U.S. Department of Justice, August 20, 1982.

25. Ibid.
26. Ibid.
27. FBI file, GREENKIL, undated memo to FBI legal attache, Ottawa, Canada.
28. Brent Staples, "A Night with the Nazis," *Chicago Reader*, April 1, 1983, p. 16. Chicago Nazis interviewed for this article agreed that during his tenure as party leader, Allen "continued the job of wrecking Nazi credibility that Collin had begun."
29. "88 Seconds in Greensboro," Public Broadcasting System, January 24, 1983.
30. Author's interview: Sol Jacobs.
31. Colman McCarthy, *Washington Post*, August 15, 1982.
32. Benson, Hayes testimony, *Griffin* (February 7, 1984).
33. *U.S.* v. *Mark Sherer*, U.S. District Court—Middle District, North Carolina (March 24, 1983).
34. In *Waller* testimony, both ATF and FBI officials denied that they had ever seen the document and that it was not written on a form used by either agency.
35. *Charlotte Observer*, May 21, 1983.
36. Ibid.
37. *U.S.* v. *Griffin* indictments, Middle District—North Carolina (April 21, 1983).
38. *Daily News*, April 22, 1983.
39. *Griffin*, Judge Edward H. Devitt, "Order In Re Extrajudicial Statements by Counsel and Witnesses," May 13, 1983.
40. Ibid., amended June 18, 1983.
41. Chief Justice Warren E. Burger, letter to clerk of court, Middle District—North Carolina, July 8, 1983.
42. *Griffin*, Judge Thomas Flannery, "Order In Re Extrajudicial Statements," January 5, 1984.
43. *Daily News*, September 16, 1983.
44. Author's observations.
45. Author's interview: Michael Johnson.

Chapter 17

1. Unless otherwise noted, all quotations and descriptions of events in chapters 17 and 18 are based on the author's daily trial notes from *Griffin*. See also *Daily News* and *Winston-Salem Journal* from January 9 through April 16, 1984.
2. *Griffin* jury selection transcripts filed with clerk of court, Middle District—North Carolina, February 24, 1984.
3. Author's interview: Coman.

Chapter 18

1. FBI file, GREENKIL. The polygraph examiner's reports of July 7 and 13, 1982, concerning the shootings and Wood's allegations about Fulton Dukes attempting

to influence his grand jury testimony were included with Michael Johnson's letter of August 20, 1982.
2. *News and Observer*, April 23, 1984.

Chapter 19

1. *Daily News*, November 7, 1985.
2. Unless otherwise noted, all quotations and descriptions of events in this chapter are based on the author's observations and daily trial notes from *Waller*. See also *Daily News* and *Journal*, March 26 through June 9, 1985.
3. The plaintiffs' attorneys argued, apparently successfully, that Paul Bermanzohn's wounds were caused by rifle rather than shotgun fire, and that they were caused by Fowler rather than Roy Toney. Toney was not in court for the 1985 trial; he was in prison on a parole violation. He certainly would not have contradicted the plaintiffs' contention that someone else shot Bermanzohn, but medical and ballistics evidence showed that although Bermanzohn's wounds were atypical of shotgun wounds, the fragments removed from his brain were buckshot.
4. The reasoning behind the jury's decision is speculative. *Waller* jurors contacted by the author declined to be interviewed.

Epilogue

1. Unless otherwise noted, all quotations about and descriptions of the New Democratic Movement are taken from the *New Democratic Movement National Bulletin* 1, no. 1 (July 1985).

    The author attempted to conduct follow-up interviews with the principals and in all cases was denied permission. The Klan and Nazis believed that anyone writing a book on the subject was destined to make a great deal of money from *their* stories, and they refused to be interviewed without financial compensation.

    An attorney for the City defendants threatened libel action when the author sought permission to quote Captain David Williams about the police preparations for the February 2, 1980, march, clearly indicating that permission for any interviews with those directly involved in the November 3 event would be denied.

    Most perplexing, however, was the refusal of the widows and survivors to be interviewed following the conclusion of the 1985 civil suit. Although they had previously been most cooperative and accommodating, the author was "blacklisted," according to their attorney Lewis Pitts, because of two articles she wrote about the trial for the *North Carolina Independent*. Apparently the account of the events presented there was unpalatable to the widows and survivors. They had become so accustomed to having their version of the story accepted that they felt compelled to disassociate themselves from any publication that attempted to present the differing perspectives which underlie the tragedy's entire history.

Therefore, with the exception of the material from the NDM, the information in this epilogue is taken from casual conversations and observations of the parties during the 1985 trial or from third-party sources.
2. Gene Welles, "NDM and New Identity," *Intercom*, August 1985, p. 27 (attachment to *New Democratic Movement National Bulletin*).

Index

African Liberation Support Committee, 30, 31, 44
Allen, Michael, 209, 236, 250, 324
Alvarez, Sally, 234, 235
Amalgamated Clothing and Textile Workers Union (ACTWU), 49, 67, 83, 305; administratorship at Cone Mills, 68, 69, 70; as Textile Workers Union of America, 50, 51, 60, 61, 64
American Civil Liberties Union, 75, 77, 78, 182; and Greensboro Civil Rights Fund, 245, 252, 292
American Federation of State, County and Municipal Employees (AFSCME) Local 77, 23, 36, 38, 49, 58, 59
American Friends Service Committee, 12, 65
American Nazi Party, 232. *See also* National Socialist Party of America; National Socialist White People's Party
anti-communism in North Carolina, 15, 39
anti-Klan: confrontations, 79, 80; demonstrators, 3, 9, 10, 188, 244, 295
anti-unionism in North Carolina, 15, 39

Apple Cellar: sit-ins, 25, 26
"armed to the terror of the public," 11, 128, 155, 247
Arthur, Martha. *See* Nathan, Martha
Asheville, North Carolina: bombing conspiracy, 210, 236, 237, 247, 255
Asian Study Group, 21. *See also* Workers Viewpoint Organization
assassination: of Communist Workers Party leaders, 3, 4, 243; of Martin Luther King, 14, 27
Avery, Sally. *See* Bermanzohn, Sally

Barnes, Claude, 28
Beaver, Geraldine, 115
Bell, Dan, 255, 259–61, 264, 265, 273, 274, 280
Belvin, Detective Herb, 166, 167, 245
Bennett College, 27, 28, 65, 66
Benson, Chris, 99, 106, 186, 252; getaway of, 160, 167, 174, 175; in Greensboro, 130, 136, 138, 153; in Klan planning, 112, 114, 118–20, 123, 126
Benson, Melanie, 106
Bermanzohn, Leola, 191, 292

331

Index

Bermanzohn, Paul, 9–11, 13, 52, 54, 55, 191, 292, 306; and AFSCME Local 77, 56, 58, 59; anti-Klan activities, 80, 85, 93, 104–6, 116; and brown lung, 50, 51, 53; co-author of *The True Story of the Greensboro Massacre*, 235–36, 301; in Communist Workers Committee, 39, 40; in Communist Workers Party, 108–9; at Duke University, 17–24; in "88 Seconds in Greensboro," 250–51; in investigations of killings, 192, 195; on November 3, 1979, 129, 132, 141, 152, 155, 170; radicalization of, 32–34; in *U.S. v. Griffin*, 267–70; in *Waller v. Butkovich*, 246, 281–84; in Workers Viewpoint Organization, 60, 66

Bermanzohn, Sally Avery: in aftermath of shootings, 152, 191, 192; author of *Through Survivors' Eyes*, 300; co-author of *The True Story of the Greensboro Massacre*, 235, 236, 301; at Duke University, 15, 16, 19, 20, 21, 24; in Communist Workers Committee, 32, 34, 36, 58–60; in Workers Viewpoint Organization/Communist Workers Party, 68, 80, 85, 108

Bermanzohn, Sandi, 292

Birth of a Nation: Klan showing of, 80, 82, 83, 88

"Blackbeard": as nickname of Jim Waller, 310n5; the pirate, 11

Black Panthers, 12, 28, 40, 41, 183

"Black Power," 25, 26

Blitz, Allen: on November 3, 1979, 120, 132, 147, 152; riot charges against, 182, 204

Blitz, Dori, 120, 122, 166; in *N.C. v. Fowler*, 219, 221; on November 3, 1979, 129, 132, 139–41; riot charges against, 182, 193; in *U.S. v. Griffin*, 267, 269, 275

Bogaty, Len, 116
Bolshevik Organizing Committee, 38, 39
Bond, Julian, 243
Bost, Fraley, 268, 269, 275
Boyd, Ed: on November 3, 1979, 133–36, 140–41, 146–47; videotapes of, 194, 218, 259, 260
Brandon, Lewis, 295, 298
Braswell, Frank, 97, 210–11; in Asheville bombing conspiracy, 225, 236–38; in Bernard Butkovich grand jury testimony, 247
Braswell, Patsy, 225, 236, 238
Brereton, Thomas: defendant in *Waller v. Butkovich*, 245; and FBI GREENKIL investigation, 156, 159, 166–69, 172–73, 231, 234; in *U.S. v. Griffin*, 248, 253, 255, 262, 264
Briggs, Bruce, 237
Browning, William A., 207, 221–22, 225
brown lung disease (byssinosis), 50–53. See also Carolina Brown Lung Association
Bryant, Sergeant Sam, 133, 140, 147
Buck, Jim, 10, 11; on November 3, 1979, 127, 130–31, 136, 153–54
Burger, U.S. Supreme Court Chief Justice Warren E., 254
Burke, Sergeant Tracy, 127–28, 131–34, 139–40, 151, 155
Butkovich, Bernard, 80, 235, 242; ATF internal affairs investigation, 173, 253; ATF undercover investigation of Nazis, 80–84, 97–99, 118–19, 208, 210–11; in *N.C. v. Fowler*, 219–20; on November 3, 1979, 168–69; pipe bombs, 220, 319; in *U.S. v. Griffin*, 232, 247–48, 250, 265, 275; in *Waller v. Butkovich*, 224, 245–46, 284
Butler, Claire, 146, 152, 277

Cahoon, Robert, 42, 193, 205–6, 218
Campbell, Reverend Will, 100
Cannon, Willena, 182, 246–47, 295

Index

Cannon Mills, 28, 83, 84, 90, 104, 113
Carolina Brown Lung Association, 49, 50, 52, 54–57, 65, 250. *See also* brown lung disease
Carter, President Jimmy, 175, 214, 231, 246
Carter, Rosalyn, 214
Cauce, Cesar, 10, 35, 36, 221, 235, 293; at China Grove, 85; at Duke University, 58, 59; funeral of, 177; in *N.C. v. Fowler*, 213, 219, 226; on November 3, 1979, 133, 138–41, 146, 154; in *U.S. v. Griffin*, 274; in *Waller v. Butkovich*, 230
Cauce, Floris Caton, 35, 85, 162, 213, 216, 277; on November 3, 1979, 137, 152, 159
Caudle, Raeford Milano, 78, 81, 82, 168, 289; blue Ford Fairlane of, 127, 131, 132, 136–40, 146–47, 155, 274; charges dismissed, 203; at China Grove, 87, 90; flight from Greensboro, 156; at Louisburg Klan/Nazi rally, 89, 98, 100; at November 1, 1979, Klan/Nazi meeting, 118–19; on November 3, 1979, 127, 135; semi-automatic AR-180 of, 127, 130, 138, 141, 146, 156, 192, 203, 221; surrender, 169, 186; in *U.S. v. Braswell*, 211, 225, 234, 236–38; in *U.S. v. Griffin*, 253, 273–74, 279
Cavin, Winston, 130
China Grove, North Carolina, 9, 83, 84, 167, 175, 186, 222, 233–34, 241, 248, 259, 300, 305, 306; Community Center, 83, 85, 86, 90, 91; Covington letter to RCP, 96; influence on escalation of WVO anti-Klan work, 91–93, 104, 120, 125, 127; Klan/Nazi discussions of, 111, 113, 119; on November 3, 1979, 126; police in, 85, 86, 96; suspected FBI probe of, 114; in *U.S. v. Griffin*, 268; Westside community, 83–85, 88, 90; WVO anti-Klan march, 85–90

China Grove Committee to Smash the Klan, 91
Christic Institute, 229–30, 252
Citizens for Justice and Unity (CJU), 228, 243, 251
civil rights investigations, criminal. *See* GREENKIL; *United States v. Virgil Griffin*
Clark, Tom, 132, 220, 235; in *N.C. v. Fowler*, 216; on November 3, 1979, 151, 155; pickup truck of, 133, 136, 139, 193, 214; shotgun of, 136–37, 154, 159, 181; in *U.S. v. Griffin*, 267, 269, 273; in *Waller v. Butkovich*, 281–82
Clinton, Michael, 126, 157
COINTELPRO (FBI Counterintelligence Program), 12, 25, 40, 42, 312n10; and NSPA, 12, 46, 98, 99, 209
Collin, Frank, 46, 75–78, 82, 185, 190–91, 209, 236. *See also* National Socialist Party of America
Coman, Jim, 156–57, 162, 168–69, 180, 182, 194; and Bernard Butkovich, 219–20; and Bruce Koenig, 259–60; and CWP witnesses, 195, 204, 213, 216; and Ed Dawson, 205, 220–21; jury selection, 206–8; in *N.C. v. Fowler*, 181, 193, 202, 212, 214, 219, 221–22. See also *North Carolina v. Jack Fowler*
Comer, Sergeant W. D. "Dave": FBI statement of, 188; on November 3, 1979, 132–33, 140; as officer in charge of march, 115–18, 266
Committee to Avenge the CWP Five, 170–71. *See also* Communist Workers Party; Greensboro Civil Rights Fund; Greensboro Justice Fund
Communist, 3, 9; 1974 Klan/Nazi confrontation, 43, 44; study, 20, 22, 24, 32, 34. *See also* Communist Workers Party; Workers Viewpoint Organization

Index   334

Communist Party USA, 20
Communist Workers Committee, 35, 37–39. *See also* Workers Viewpoint Organization
Communist Workers Party (CWP), 3, 4, 9, 21, 46, 190, 230, 243, 245, 295, 297, 301, 303, 304, 305, 306, 308; anti-Klan work, 93, 108, 175; assassination allegations, 161, 165, 169–72, 182–84, 195, 208–9, 214, 224, 228, 235; becomes New Democratic Movement, 289; CWP Five, 170, 173, 177, 183, 208–9, 222, 234–35, 229, 243, 251; conspiracy/coverup allegations, 203–4, 207–9, 216, 224–25, 227, 242; and "Death to the Klan" march, 112, 115, 117, 120, 122, 182, 198; FBI surveillance of, 199; Founding Congress, 35, 93, 100, 108–9; and funeral, 172–75, 177, 203, 222; and Greensboro Civil Rights Fund, 251; labor organizing in North Carolina, 49, 62; in *N.C. v. Fowler*, 182, 193, 195, 212, 226; in 1980 protest, 185, 197, 199, 200–201; party structure, 108, 202; "Red November, Black November," 234–35; regrouping, 166, 202, 229; in *U.S. v. Griffin*, 232–33, 244, 272, 267. *See also* Workers Viewpoint Organization
Cone Mills, 31, 68–70, 84, 224, 246, 294; and ACTWU, 68, 70; WVO in, 31, 34, 38, 39, 49, 61–66, 90; WVO in Haw River plant, 34, 61, 55, 68–69; WVO in Revolution plant, 61, 68; WVO in White Oak plant, 62, 63, 66, 68–70, 96; and WVO/RCP confrontation, 107
Confederate Knights of the KKK, 41
Congressional Black Caucus, 292
conspiracy, 3, 4, 159, 245; to violate civil rights, 4, 228, 231–32, 245. *See also* United States Code, Title 18;

United States v. Virgil Griffin; *Waller v. Butkovich*
Cooley, Jim, 263–64, 274, 276
Cooper, Detective Jerry, 101, 104, 116, 171, 188, 205; and Ed Dawson, 105, 107, 112–13, 117, 126, 241; in march planning, 115, 118; on November 3, 1979, 127–28, 131–34, 136, 138, 140, 147, 151; in *U.S. v. Griffin*, 265–66; in *Waller v. Butkovich*, 281
"the correct line," 21, 31–34, 38, 57, 60, 66, 190
cover-up: CWP allegations, 3, 4, 243, 245
Covington, Harold A., 75–78, 81, 95–98, 199, 209–11; in Africa, 45, 46, 76, 96; and AFT, 82, 173, 208, 247; attorney general campaign, 191, 209, 210; conspiracy allegations about, 45, 46, 171, 249; in exile, 236, 238, 316n1; and FBI, 175, 187, 248, 249, 250; at Louisburg Klan/Nazi meeting, 99, 114; as "Myron Silverstein," 45, 95, 99, 171; at November 1, 1979, Klan/Nazi meeting, 118–19; takeover of NSPA, 190–91, 209; and United Racist Front, 99–100. *See also* National Socialist Part of America
Crawford, Daisy, 113–14

Daughtry, Lieutenant Sylvester, 117, 131, 133–34, 136, 139–40, 151
Davis, Don, 130, 140
Dawson, Edward W., 9, 10, 26, 27, 41–44, 46, 48, 104, 125, 161, 166, 235, 245, 286, 307; "armed to the terror of the public," 41, 155, 304; CWP allegations of conspiracy, 171, 182; on "88 Seconds," 250; exposed as informant, 171; and the FBI, 12, 40, 41, 104, 116, 186; and the Greensboro Police Department, 105, 107, 112, 113, 115, 128, 171, 205; at Lincolnton

Index 335

Klan rally, 107, 110–12, 233; in *N.C. v. Fowler*, 204–5, 219–21; on November 1, 1979, 116–17, 120; on November 3, 1979, 125–27, 130–31, 136, 153–55; Swan Quarter riot, 11; in "The Third of November," 241–42; in *U.S. v. Griffin*, 232, 253–54, 258–59, 265–66, 273–74, 278–79; in *Waller v. Butkovich*, 224, 245–46, 281
"Death to the Klan," 9, 120, 125, 233–34, 295
Decatur, Alabama, anti-Klan march, 80, 84, 108
Doctor, Bobby, 189
Dorsett, George, 26, 41–43. *See also* Confederate Knights of the KKK; United Klans of America
Douglas, Robert, 206
Dudley High School, 27
Duke, James B., 13
Duke University, 13, 15, 16, 24, 35, 36; School of Medicine, 11, 19, 32; union organizing at, 13–16, 18, 31, 59. *See also* AFSCME Local 77
Dukes, Robert "Fulton," 81, 173, 119–20; in *U.S. v. Griffin*, 247, 249, 250, 265, 315n23; in *Waller v. Butkovich*, 315n23
Durham County General Hospital, 19, 21, 24
Durham County Health Department, 19
Durham Organizing Committee, 32, 34. *See also* Communist Workers Committee; Workers Viewpoint Organization

Edgemont community: Durham, North Carolina, 15
Edmisten, Rufus, 248
"88 Seconds in Greensboro," 250–51
Ellis, C.P., 59, 60, 184
Evars, Medgar, 197
extremists, 5

Farran, Jeff, 192, 206, 265, 275–77
February 2, 1980, march, 195–201, 203
Federal Bureau of Investigation (FBI), 3, 4, 20, 40–46, 97, 168, 170, 199, 235; and ATF, 208, 253; COINTELPRO, 11–12, 27, 29–30, 183; and Ed Dawson, 44, 112, 186, 241; GREENKIL investigation, 172, 175, 181, 186–88, 191–92, 231, 238, 248–50, 259, 261; hunt for fugitives, 175, 238, 248–50; surveillance of WVO/CWP, 114, 175, 199; Technical Service Division, 181, 194; in *Waller v. Butkovich*, 245, 247, 282, 284. *See also* Brereton, Thomas; GREENKIL
Federated Knights of the Ku Klux Klan, 79–80, 83–84, 86, 90, 95, 99. *See also* Grady, Joe; Pierce, Gorrell
Findley, Charles, 127
Flanagan, Norajean, 255, 264, 268–69, 275. *See also United States v. Virgil Griffin*
Flannery, Judge Thomas A., 254–58, 260–62, 267, 269–79, 277–79, 282. *See also United States v. Virgil Griffin*
Fletcher, Brent, 113, 127, 160, 241, 259; on November 3, 1979, 130, 136, 153–54; police surveillance of house, 128, 131; rendezvous at his house, 123, 125, 127; and shot number two, 136, 219; suicide of, 286
Flowers, Harold, 126, 137, 146–47, 155, 157, 203
Foundation for Community Development, 25, 27, 29
Fowler, Jack, 78, 81, 99, 118, 236; in epilogue, 287; FBI hunt for, 168–69, 175, 186–87; in *N.C. v. Fowler*, 192, 205–6, 221; on November 3, 1979, 127, 131, 137, 140–41, 146, 155–56, 167; in *U.S. v. Griffin*, 253–54, 258, 275
Fowler, Rick, 167

Index

Franklin, Billy Joe, 126, 157, 163, 203
Fratkin, Elliot, 292
Fry, Julius, 62, 68–70. *See also*
  Amalgamated Clothing and Textile
  Workers Union
Fuller, Howard (Owusu Sadaukai),
  24–31, 58–59, 70; as Sadaukai, 28–31,
  34, 38–40; in WVO/RWL polemics,
  39–40. *See also* Malcolm X Liberation
  University; Revolutionary Workers
  League

Gastonia, North Carolina, 15–16
Gibson, Captain Larry, 101, 104, 107–8.
  See also parade permit
Goldstein, Signe Burke. *See* Waller,
  Signe
Grady, Joe, 79–83, 95, 100, 104, 249,
  306; at China Grove, 87–88, 90; as an
  informant, 175, 186–87, 250, 315n23,
  322n5; Nazi hostility toward, 98, 118
GREENKIL, 3–4, 156. *See also*
  Brereton, Thomas; *United States v.
  Virgil Griffin*
Greensboro, North Carolina, 3, 5, 15, 25,
  31, 38; Ed Dawson in, 41; image of
  civility, 78–79, 203; last public Klan
  rally, 48; 1979 killings in, 4, 12, 21,
  25, 45, 99; reactions to killings, 165,
  189, 243; reactions to *N.C. v. Fowler*
  acquittals, 227–28; state of emergency
  for funerals, 170, 172, 174; in *Waller
  v. Butkovich*, 281–82. *See also*
  Greensboro Police Department
Greensboro Association of Poor People,
  27–29. *See also* Johnson, Nelson
Greensboro Chamber of Commerce, 245
Greensboro Citizens Review Committee,
  189–90
Greensboro City Council, 243
Greensboro Civil Rights Fund, 183,
  252, 254, 281–82, 292. *See also*
  Greensboro Justice Fund; *Waller v.
  Butkovich*

Greensboro Coliseum, 198, 235
Greensboro Daily News: names Ed
  Dawson as informant, 204, 219
"Greensboro Five." *See* Communist
  Workers Party: CWP Five
Greensboro Human Relations
  Commission, 243
Greensboro Justice Fund, 229, 230, 234,
  243, 245–46, 251, 293, 295, 296, 297,
  298, 299, 309. *See also* Committee to
  Avenge the CWP Five; Greensboro
  Civil Rights Fund
Greensboro Police Department, 3–4,
  9, 26–27, 183, 185, 205, 208, 222,
  225, 235, 307; administrative report,
  187–88; and Ed Dawson, 44, 112, 171,
  205, 242; and February 2 march, 198,
  200–201; and funeral march, 170, 172,
  174–75, 177; investigation of killings,
  172, 181, 194; as part of assassination
  theory, 171, 183; planning for "Death
  to the Klan" march, 101, 105, 107–8,
  116–17; Police-Fire Emergency,
  147–48; surveillance of WVO at Cone,
  101, 304; in *Waller v. Butkovich*, 224,
  245–47, 284. *See also* Greensboro
  Citizens Review Committee
Greensboro Police, Tactical Squad,
  115, 127, 165, 171, 188, 220, 266;
  on November 3, 1979, 128, 131, 133,
  140; planning for "Death to the Klan"
  march, 117–18
Greensboro Record: Butkovich story,
  208, 236. *See also* Woodall, Martha
Greensboro Truth and Reconciliation
  Commission, 294, 300; final
  report of, 304, 305, 306; hearings
  of, 303; members of, 299, 302;
  postcommission hearings of, 308
Greeson, Hal, 206, 278
Greeson, Rick, 180, 193–94, 212, 214,
  222; and Bernard Butkovich, 219; and
  Bruce Koenig sound analysis, 218–19,
  259–60; and CWP witnesses, 195,

Index

204, 213, 216; and Ed Dawson, 205; first degree murder charge, 180–81; jury selection, 206–8. See also *North Carolina v. Jack Fowler*
Griffin, Linda, 123, 153, 160
Griffin, Virgil, 42–46, 48, 76, 126, 186, 214, 307, 313n8; escape from Greensboro, 155, 160–62, 166–67, 171, 174–75, 241; in epilogue, 286; and Klan oath, 163, 167, 260, 273, 322n21 (chap. 10); 1976 FBI/ATF investigation of, 210; on November 3, 1979, 124–25, 127, 130, 138, 153; planning for "Death to the Klan" march, 99–100, 106–7, 110, 112, 114, 119–20, 122–23; in *U.S. v. Griffin*, 252–54, 258–61, 264, 266, 272–73, 278–80. See also Invisible Empire, Knights of the KKK; North Carolina Knights of the Ku Klux Klan; *United States v. Virgil Griffin*
Grimes, Willie, 28
Guilford County Emergency Medical Service (EMS), 151, 154, 159–60, 200

Hall, Cindy, 125, 130, 153, 155
Hall, Roy, 265
Hampton, Fred, 12, 29, 41. See also Black Panthers
Hampton, Captain Trevor, 115–16, 122
Hanes, Arthur, 42
Hartsoe, Rene, 115, 126, 160, 174
Hartsoe, Terry, 115, 126, 136, 157, 159, 203
Harwell, Fred, 261, 263–64, 267, 269–70
Hatcher, Jerry, 99
Havekost, Donald, 182, 214–15, 270–71, 276. See also neutron activation analysis
Hayes, Max, 153, 167, 252
Hinckley, John, 236
"Hitlerfest," 209
Holocaust, 191
Hughes, Chip, 251
Hunt, Governor James B., 249

Identity Ministry, 289
Imbus, Dr. H. "Bud," 50
informants, 27, 41, 43; FBI, 12, 26, 27, 30; Greensboro Police Department, 4, 241. See also Dawson, Edward W.; Dorsett, George
Institute for Southern Studies, 51, 196, 245; "The Third of November," 241–43, 250–51
Interreligious Foundation for Community Organization (IFCO), 186
Invisible Empire, Knights of the KKK, 99, 100, 106–7, 112. See also Griffin, Virgil

Jackson, Jesse, 263
Jennings, Neill, 206, 221, 265
Jewish Defense League, 79, 82
Johnson, Bill, 64, 65, 70
Johnson, Butch, 16, 175
Johnson, Joyce, 28, 31, 38, 60, 85, 91, 296
Johnson, Michael, 231–34, 244–45, 249, 255
Johnson, Nelson, 25–30, 34, 38, 40, 60–61, 64, 93, 101, 113, 166, 193, 234, 292, 295, 296, 298, 304, 306; call for federal intervention, 228, 231; charged with riot, 182, 204, 247; at China Grove, 84–86, 90–92, 96; at Cone Mills, 49; at Decatur, Alabama, 80; and February 2, 1980, march, 196–97, 199; and funeral march, 172, 174, 177–78; Klan/Nazi discussions of, 119, 167; on November 3, 1979, 132, 134, 155; planning the "Death to the Klan" march, 104, 107–8, 116–17, 120; response to killings, 185; in *U.S. v. Griffin*, 253; in *Waller v. Butkovich*, 246. See also Bolshevik Organizing Committee; Communist Workers Party; Workers Viewpoint Organization
Jones, Bob, 41, 42

Index

juror: *N.C. v. Fowler*, 216–17, 219, 221–22, 225

Kannapolis, North Carolina, 28
Kelley-Springfield Tire Company, 56. See also United Rubber Workers of America
Kernersville, North Carolina, 249
King, Martin Luther, 11, 13–15, 229
"Klan/Nazi" trial. See *North Carolina v. Jack Fowler*
Knight, Douglas, 16
Koenig, Bruce: in *N.C. v. Fowler*, 214, 217–19, 242; in *U.S. v. Griffin*, 259–60; in *Waller v. Butkovich*, 276
Korotkin, Gayle, 183, 194–95, 224, 229; in Greensboro Civil Rights Fund, 251–52; in *N.C. v. Fowler*, 203, 207, 212–13; in *U.S. v. Griffin*, 277, 280
Ku Klux Klan, 3, 4, 9–12, 16, 27, 41, 42, 48; image of growth in 1979, 79; as "pathology of the white ghetto," 100, 101. See also Invisible Empire, Knights of the KKK; North Carolina Knights of the Ku Klux Klan
Kunstier, William, 203

labor organizers, militant, 15, 21. See also Communist Workers Party; *Waller v. Butkovich*; Workers Viewpoint Organization
League, Sergeant Art, 133, 140, 147
Ledford, Barbara, 116, 126, 167, 174
Lee, Robert, 56–58
Lemons, Larry, 276–77
Lenin, Nikolai, 13, 21, 31. See also Communist Workers Party; Workers Viewpoint Organization
Levin, Elliot, 292
Lincoln Community Health Center, 213
Lincoln County Fairgrounds, 123, 126
Lincoln Hospital, 19
Lincolnton Klan rally, 107–10, 233, 241

Linsin, Greg, 255, 259, 267, 270–71
Liuzzo, Viola, 12
Long, Judge James, 206, 213, 216, 221, 224, 226
Louisburg Klan/Nazi rally, 95, 98, 100, 114, 167
Lucky, Paul, 83, 85, 86, 88

McBride, Claude "Junior," 127, 131, 156, 168–69, 186, 203
McCarthy, Colman, 251
McGloin, Tim, 21, 33, 184
McHargue's Gun Shop, 99
McLain, Lee, 126, 136, 138, 157, 203
McLean Trucking Company, 81–82, 248
Malcolm X Liberation University (MXLU), 28–31, 311–12n9. See also Fuller, Howard
Manduley, Octavio, 207, 226
Manzella, Rand, 63–65, 193, 204, 246–47; charged with being "armed to the terror of the public," 155, 182, 247; on November 3, 1979, 146–47, 155, 182. See also "armed to the terror of the public"
Mao Tse Tung, 13, 21, 31–32; Maoist philosophy, 65
Maplewood Cemetery, 170, 172
Marx, Karl, 13, 31; Marxist philosophy, 20–24, 30–32, 55, 65
Matthews, David Wayne, 99, 106, 115, 126, 153; in *N.C. v. Fowler*, 182, 193, 203, 218, 221; on November 3, 1979, 125–26, 137–39, 146–47, 157, 159, 162–63; in *U.S. v. Griffin*, 253–54, 256, 258, 263, 274, 279; in *Waller v. Butkovich*, 281
Matthews, John, 131–32, 136, 140, 266
Matthews, Linda, 115
Medical Committee for Human Rights, 18–19, 21
Mehrige, Judge Robert R., 282, 284
Melvin, Mayor Jim, 165, 227

Michaux, H. M. "Mickey," 156, 162, 168–69, 208, 230–32, 234, 258
Miller, Ruby Sweet. *See* Sweet, Ruby
Moore, Thad, 51–55. *See also* Carolina Brown Lung Association
Morgan, Lawrence, 126, 146, 181; in *N.C. v. Fowler*, 23, 205–6, 221; on November 3, 1979, 126, 131, 136–38, 140, 146–47, 157
Morningside Homes, 3, 116, 122, 130, 160, 195, 210, 227, 247, 296; concerns of residents, 163–64, 170, 172, 189; on November 3, 1979, 129, 132, 134, 140, 151
Morningside Homes Community Center, 137, 171
Morningside Homes Residents Council, 171

Nappier, Lisford Carl, 106–7, 111, 114–15, 203; on November 3, 1979, 126, 136, 138, 146–47, 157, 163; in *U.S. v. Griffin*, 262–63
Nathan, Esther, 15, 161
Nathan, Martha "Marty" Arthur, 14, 35–37, 56, 85, 90–100, 170, 184, 216, 295, 300; and "88 Seconds in Greensboro," 250; and Greensboro Civil Rights Fund, 251–52, 229, 292; in *N.C. v. Fowler*, 213–14, 193–94; on November 3, 1979, 132, 161; and United Rubber Workers, 56–57
Nathan, Dr. Michael Ronald, 10, 14–19, 35–37, 60, 90, 125, 154, 221, 229, 235; at China Grove, 85; deathbed induction into CWP, 170; funeral, 177; legacy of, 293; in *N.C. v. Fowler*, 213, 226; on November 3, 1979, 132, 141, 146, 152, 155, 161; in *Waller v. Butkovich*, 230, 246, 281
Nathan, Leah, 14, 85, 125, 161, 293
National Anti-Klan Network, 186, 196
National Labor Relations Board (NLRB), 58–59. *See also* American Federation of State, County and Municipal Employees Local 77
National Socialist Party of America (NSPA), 3, 12, 100, 250; and Jack Fowler escape, 175; in North Carolina, 45–46, 78, 95, 97–99, 153; and Parma, Ohio, rally, 81–82; and Skokie, Illinois, march, 75–78; takeover and purges, 191, 236. *See also* Collin, Frank; Covington, Harold A.
National Socialist White People's Party, 12, 43, 45, 76
Neely, Sandra. *See* Smith, Sandra Neely
Neely, Mr. and Mrs. Smith, 28
neutron activation analysis, 181–82. *See also* Havekost, Donald
"New Communists," 13, 21–22, 31–32, 37, 95. *See also* Communist Workers Party; Revolutionary Workers League; Workers Viewpoint Organization
New Democratic Movement, 289–92
Nixon, President Richard M., 20, 23, 25, 51, 245
North Carolina: "progressive" image of, 4
North Carolina Agricultural and Technical State University (A&T): 1969 disturbances at, 25–29, 296; student responses to killings, 185, 197, 200, 243
North Carolina Human Relations Commission, 188–89
North Carolina Knights of the Ku Klux Klan (NCKKKK), 12, 42–44, 46. *See also* Dawson, Edward W.; Griffin, Virgil
North Carolina National Guard, 27–28, 172, 177, 200
North Carolina Occupational Safety and Health Project (NCOSH), 56
North Carolina Public Interest Research Group (NC-PIRG), 51

Index

North Carolina v. Jack Fowler ("Klan/Nazi" trial), 42, 229, 237, 244; conspiracy charges dropped, 202; CWP refusal to testify, 203; first degree murder charge, 206; jury deliberations in, 224–26; jury selection, 206–8; self-defense claims, 214, 217, 224–25; videotapes as evidence in, 192–93. *See also* Coman, Jim; Greeson, Rick; Koenig, Bruce
November 3, 1979: killings in Greensboro, 123–164

occupational health activists, 51, 53. *See also* Carolina Brown Lung Association; United Rubber Workers of America
October League, 21, 63
O'Neal, William, 40–41
Operating Engineers: Local 465, 24
Operation Breakthrough, 19, 24–25
Orangeburg, South Carolina: shootings in, 26
Overcash, Richard, 85–86

Pan-Africanism: black revolutionary split over, 28–31
parade permit: confusion about, 128, 188; and Ed Dawson, 130, 171, 241; for funeral march, 170, 172, 174; for November 3, 1979, march, 104, 108, 116–17, 130, 233
Parma, Ohio: Nazi rally, 247
Pelles, Don, 269
Pelles, Roz, 269
Pierce, Gorrell, 86, 90, 95, 186, 306; at Louisburg Klan/Nazi rally, 99, 100, 104; on November 3, 1979, 127, 131; and *U.S. v. Braswell*, 208, 211, 225, 236–38; and WVO "open letter," 112, 118–19
Pierce, Roger, 99, 118, 225, 238
Pittman, Detective Jerry, 167, 187
Pitts, Lewis, 229–30, 246, 293; in Greensboro Civil Rights Fund, 251–52; and *U.S. v. Griffin*, 244, 253–54, 280
polemics, 21, 31, 37, 93, 197; between Revolutionary Workers League and Workers Viewpoint Organization, 39, 59, 66, 93
Porter, Charles, 154, 159–60
Porter, Leon, 274
Powell, Frankie: on November 3, 1979, 137, 139, 155; in *U.S. v. Griffin*, 266–67, 269
Pridmore, Coleman Blair "Johnny," 106, 118; 122–23; in epilogue, 289; in *N.C. v. Fowler*, 203, 205–6, 221; on November 3, 1979, 124–25, 137–38, 140, 157; in *U.S. v. Griffin*, 253, 275
Prose, Dr. Neil, 228–29
provocateurs, FBI, 12. *See also* COINTELPRO
purges: Pan-Africanists versus Marxists, 31

Ray, James Earl, 42, 125, 234
Reagan, President Ronald, 231–32, 236
Red November, Black November, 234, 236
Reston, James, Jr., 250
revolutionaries, 4, 5, 12, 13, 31; black, 24, 25, 30; in brown lung organizing, 52, 54; national socialist, 45, 76–78; studies of, 20–22, 32, 37–39
Revolutionary Communist Party, 79, 82, 105, 209; and Ed Dawson, 105, 107, 110; and Harold Covington, 95, 171, 248; WVO confrontations with, 97, 107
Revolutionary Workers League, 21, 23, 31, 34, 37–39, 40, 49, 59. *See also* Fuller, Howard
Revolutionary Youth League, 120, 133
Revolution Organizing Committee, 64
Roberson, Eugene, 115, 126, 262–63
Robinson, Dr. Steven, 161

Index   341

Rowe, Gary Thomas, 12
Russell, Lacy, 182, 204

Sadaukai, Owusu. *See* Fuller, Howard
Sampson, Dale Deering, 62–63, 162, 216; and Greensboro Civil Rights Fund, 292; on November 3, 1979, 132, 137, 159; in *U.S. v. Griffin*, 269, 270, 280
Sampson, William Evan, 10, 62–64, 68–70, 177, 235; legacy of, 293; in *N.C. v. Fowler*, 182, 213, 226, 229; on November 3, 1979, 132, 137, 141, 146–47, 152, 154; in *Waller v. Butkovich* and *U.S. v. Griffin*, 276–77, 268–69
Schlosser, Michael, 157, 180, 194, 203–5, 236, 242–43, 249
self-defense, 3, 193. *See also North Carolina v. Jack Fowler*
Sellars, Cleve, 30, 31, 184–85; and February 2, 1980, march, 185, 196–97, 200–201
Shannon, Roger, 99, 118–19, 249–50. *See also* Thompson submachine gun
Sherer, Mark, 106, 123–24, 136, 186, 214, 218, 281; on November 3, 1979, 153, 160, 166, 174–75; shots fired by, 136, 138, 219; in *U.S. v. Griffin*, 252, 259–61, 275. *See also* Koenig, Bruce; shots fired
shots fired: shot one, 135, 136, 183, 219; shot two, 136, 219; shot three, 136; shot four, 138; shot five, 138, 321n4 (chap. 9); shots three, four, and five, 216–18, 259, 278, 320n1 (chap. 9); shot twelve, 139. *See also* Koenig, Bruce
Sims, Percy, 182, 204
Skokie, Illinois, 75, 77–78, 185. *See also* Collin, Frank
Smith, Jerry Paul, 99, 106, 110, 114, 163, 234; in epilogue, 289; "James Earl Ray is My Hero" sign, 125, 234; in *N.C. v.*

Fowler, 203, 205–6, 218–19, 221; on November 3, 1979, 125, 130, 139–41, 146–47, 157, 166, 245; and pipe bomb, 119, 173, 220, 265, 274–75, 319n38; planning for counterdemonstration, 118, 120, 122–23; in *U.S. v. Griffin*, 248, 253–54, 258, 279
Smith, Mark, 31, 34, 38, 60–61, 173, 196
Smith, Paul, 160, 260
Smith, Sandra Neely, 10, 28–29, 31, 34, 38, 182, 235; funeral, 173, 177; investigation of, 113–14; legacy of, 293; on November 3, 1979, 137, 146, 152, 154, 170; in *U.S. v. Griffin*, 213, 274, 277; in *Waller v. Butkovich*, 226, 230, 246, 281; and Workers Viewpoint Organization, 50, 60–61, 64, 68, 85, 93
Smith, Paul, 160, 260
Snyder, Keith, 210–11
South Africa: Harold Covington in, 46, 249–50
Southern Christian Leadership Conference (SCLC), 12, 80, 185–86, 196
Southern Conference Educational Fund (SCEF), 83, 84, 93, 113–14, 184, 196. *See also* Wells, Lyn
Spoon, Lieutenant Paul, 115, 118, 188, 281; on November 3, 1979, 131–34, 136, 138, 140
Stanley, Len, 54–58, 250–51
Stephenson, Rexford, 220, 270, 276
Stone, Mark Andrew, 270
Students Organized for Black Unity (SOBU), 28–31, 312n10
Swain, Mike. *See* Sweat, Michael
Swan Quarter, North Carolina, 11, 12, 42
Sweat, Michael (Mike Swain), 210; and ATF Asheville bombing conspiracy, 225, 236–37. *See also* Asheville, North Carolina: bombing conspiracy
Sweet, Ruby, 115, 126, 161, 174, 263–64
Swing, Chief William E., 165, 171, 187, 198

Index

Talbert, Shorty, 99, 118, 225, 236
"Tell It Like It Is," 58–59
Thomas, Abla, 40
Thomas, Captain Byron L., 168–69, 220–21, 242
Thompson sub-machine guns: Butkovich investigation of, 97, 118, 219, 248–50
Toney, Roy, 126, 329; in *N.C. v. Fowler*, 193, 203; on November 3, 1979, 137, 141, 146, 157, 159; in *U.S. v. Griffin*, 253–54, 258, 268, 275
Trade Union Education League (TUEL), 67–68, 70, 93. *See also* Waller, Dr. James Michael; Workers Viewpoint Organization
True Story of the Greensboro Massacre, 235–36, 268, 308, 309
Tung, Jerry, 39–40, 60, 63, 66–67, 70–71, 301; and CWP Founding Congress, 108–9; and New Democratic Movement, 290–91. *See also* Communist Workers Party; New Democratic Movement; Workers Viewpoint Organization

union organizing, 16, 20, 24; Marxist strategy for, 31. *See also* Amalgamated Clothing and Textile Workers Union; American Federation of State, County and Municipal Employees; Trade Union Education League; United Rubber Workers of America
United Klans of America, 12, 41–42
United Mine Workers: Black Lung Association, 51
United Racist Front, 99–100, 258
United Rubber Workers of America, 57–58, 65. *See also* Lee, Robert
United States Code, Title 18: Section 241, 231–33; Section 245 (b) (2) (B), 233, 253; Section 245 (b) (4) (A), 231–33, 253; Section 371, 253. *See also* Johnson, Michael; *United States v. Virgil Griffin*

United States Commission on Civil Rights: Southern office, 189. *See also* Doctor, Bobby
United States Department of Justice, 77, 185, 243–44; Community Relations Service, 185; in *U.S. v. Braswell*, 255; in *U.S. v. Griffin*, 231, 249, 254–55; in *Waller v. Butkovich*, 230, 245
United States Department of Treasury: and Asheville bombing conspiracy, 97, 209–11, 225, 236; Bureau of Alcohol, Tobacco and Firearms (ATF), 4, 80, 82, 208, 235, 243; internal affairs investigation of Bernard Butkovich, 173, 253; investigation of Wayne Wood, 80–81, 97–100; and Joe Grady, 186–87; St. Louis informant in NSPA, 209, 236; undercover policies, 119, 169, 208; in *U.S. v. Braswell*, 236–38, 255; in *U.S. v. Griffin* grand jury testimony, 247, 250, 254; in *Waller v. Butkovich*, 245–47, 249, 268, 282, 284. *See also* Allen, Michael; Asheville, North Carolina: bombing conspiracy; Butkovich, Bernard; Grady, Joe; *United States v. Virgil Griffin*; Wood, Roland Wayne
United States Labor Party, 44, 124–25
United States v. Virgil Griffin: gag order, 254–55; grand jury investigation, 4, 46, 244, 245, 249–54; trial of, 256–59, 274, 278–79. *See also* Griffin, Virgil

videotapes: evidence in *N.C. v. Fowler*, 212, 214, 216, 217, 221. *See also* Boyd, Ed

Wall, Percy, 192, 205–6
Waller, Dr. James Michael, 10, 16–18, 21, 163, 166; and Carolina Brown Lung Association, 53–55; at China Grove, 85; in Communist Workers Committee, 32, 34; and Communist Workers Party, 93, 108–9, 113; at

Cone Haw River plant, 61, 65, 68–70; and "correct line," 190; at Duke University Hospital, 22–24; funeral march for, 177; legacy of, 293; and *N.C. v. Fowler*, 181–82, 183, 213, 216, 226; on November 3, 1979, 129, 132, 136–39, 141, 152, 154–55; and Revolutionary Communist Party, 105–6; and *U.S. v. Griffin*, 269, 273, 275; and *Waller v. Butkovich*, 230, 235. *See also* Communist Workers Committee; Communist Workers Party; Trade Union Education League; Workers Viewpoint Organization
Waller, Jane, 154–55
Waller, Sidney, 154–55, 190
Waller, Signe, 16, 96, 154, 214, 216, 222, 277, 296, 300; "About Jim," 190; in the aftermath, 162, 166, 202, 224; at China Grove, 85; and CWP "martyr" story, 183; in epilogue, 292; at funeral march, 177; and Workers Viewpoint Organization, 65–68; and *N.C. v. Fowler*, 203–4, 212; on November 3, 1979, 129, 132, 134, 152, 159
Waller v. Butkovich, 4, 167, 251, 270, 289, 294, 305, 306, 307; amended complaint, 245–47; conspiracy charges in, 224, 229–30, 246–47; in "The Third of November," 241–42; trial of, 281–84
Waters, Jim, 129, 140, 146–47, 218, 259
Weatherman, 12
Wells, Lyn, 114, 184–85, 195–96, 198–99
Westra, John, 247
White, Kate, 137, 161
"White Carolina," 184
Whitfield, Ed, 295, 298, 302, 308
Williams, Captain David C., 199
Windsor Community Center, 112, 117, 188, 210, 269; on November 3, 1979, 129–30, 132, 134
Wood, Paula, 168

Wood, Roland Wayne, 78, 155–56, 186, 225, 236; ATF investigation of, 81–82, 98, 173, 210, 247–48, 253; at China Grove, 87, 90; at Louisburg Klan/Nazi rally, 95, 97–99; at Nazi "roast," 118–20; in *N.C. v. Fowler*, 203, 205, 208, 221; on November 3, 1979, 127, 130, 137–40, 157, 167–69; in *U.S. v. Griffin*, 218, 249–50, 253–54, 258, 265, 273; in *Waller v. Butkovich*, 281, 283; and "White Carolina," 184. *See also* United States Department of Treasury: Bureau of Alcohol, Tobacco and Firearms
Woodall, Martha, 208, 211, 236
Workers Viewpoint Journal, 31–32, 66
Workers Viewpoint Organization, 21, 32, 34, 37, 39–40, 100, 183, 233, 266; and ACTWU, 68, 70; at China Grove, 84–86, 88, 90–92; at Cone Haw River plant, 34, 55, 61, 69; at Cone Mills, 31, 34, 38–39, 49, 64–65, 90; at Cone Revolution plant, 61; at Cone White Oak plant, 62, 63, 66, 96; and "Death to the Klan" march, 101, 104, 112, 116, 119–20, 129, 132, 134; and FBI, 114, 186; intensification of politics, 60–69, 78–79, 83, 93–95; mergers of, 38, 60; and Revolutionary Communist Party, 96–97, 107; and Revolutionary Workers League, 59–60; trade union strategy of, 67–71; union organizing attempts, 56, 113. *See also* Communist Workers Committee; Communist Workers Party; Trade Union Education League
Wrenn, Jim, 138, 146, 155, 161, 170, 182
Wright, Lacey, 51–55, 64–65, 250. *See also* Carolina Brown Lung Association

Youth Educational Services, 25

"Zigzag": and Jack Fowler, 156, 167, 175
Zwerling, Reverend Philip, 229

www.ingramcontent.com/pod-product-compliance
Lightning Source LLC
Chambersburg PA
CBHW032000220426
43664CB00005B/86